An Introduction to Formal Languages and Automata

Third Edition

Peter Linz
University of California at Davis

JONES AND BARTLETT PUBLISHERS
Sudbury, Massachusetts
BOSTON   TORONTO   LONDON   SINGAPORE

World Headquarters
Jones and Bartlett Publishers
40 Tall Pine Drive
Sudbury, MA 01776
978-443-5000
info@jbpub.com
www.jbpub.com

Jones and Bartlett Publishers
  Canada
2406 Nikanna Road
Mississauga, ON L5C 2W6
CANADA

Jones and Bartlett Publishers
  International
Barb House, Barb Mews
London W6 7PA
UK

Library of Congress Cataloging-in-Publication Data

Linz, Peter.
    An introduction to formal languages and automata / Peter Linz.--3rd ed.
        p. cm.
    Includes bibliographical references and index.
    ISBN 0-7637-1422-4
    1. Formal languages.   2. Machine theory.   I. Title.

QA267.3 .L56 2000
511.3--dc21   00-062546

Chief Executive Officer: Clayton Jones
Chief Operating Officer: Don W. Jones, Jr.
Executive Vice President and Publisher: Tom Manning
V.P., Managing Editor: Judith H. Hauck
V.P., College Editorial Director: Brian L. McKean
V.P., Design and Production: Anne Spencer
V.P., Sales and Marketing: Paul Shepardson
V.P., Manufacturing and Inventory Control: Therese Bräuer
Senior Acquisitions Editor: Michael Stranz
Development and Product Manager: Amy Rose
Marketing Director: Jennifer Jacobson
Production Coordination: Trillium Project Management
Cover Design: Night & Day Design
Composition: Northeast Compositors
Printing and Binding: Courier Westford
Cover printing: John Pow Company, Inc.

Cover Image © Jim Wehtje

This book was typeset in Textures 2.1 on a Macintosh G4. The font families used were Computer Modern, Optima, and Futura. The first printing was printed on 50 lb. Decision 94 Opaque.

Printed in the United States of America

04 03 02 01   10 9 8 7 6 5 4 3 2

Preface

This book is designed for an introductory course on formal languages, automata, computability, and related matters. These topics form a major part of what is known as the theory of computation. A course on this subject matter is now standard in the computer science curriculum and is often taught fairly early in the program. Hence, the prospective audience for this book consists primarily of sophomores and juniors majoring in computer science or computer engineering.

Prerequisites for the material in this book are a knowledge of some higher-level programming language (commonly C, C++, or Java) and familiarity with the fundamentals of data structures and algorithms. A course in discrete mathematics that includes set theory, functions, relations, logic, and elements of mathematical reasoning is essential. Such a course is part of the standard introductory computer science curriculum.

The study of the theory of computation has several purposes, most importantly (1) to familiarize students with the foundations and principles of computer science, (2) to teach material that is useful in subsequent courses, and (3) to strengthen students' ability to carry out formal and rigorous mathematical arguments. The presentation I have chosen for this text favors the first two purposes, although I would argue that it also serves the third. To present ideas clearly and to give students insight into the material, the text stresses intuitive motivation and illustration of ideas through examples. When there is a choice, I prefer arguments that are easily grasped to those that are concise and elegant but difficult in concept. I state definitions and theorems precisely and give the motivation for proofs, but often leave out the routine and tedious details. I believe that this is desirable for pedagogical reasons. Many proofs are unexciting applications of induction or contradiction, with differences that are specific to particular problems. Presenting such arguments in full detail is not only unnecessary, but interferes with the flow of the story. Therefore, quite a few of the proofs are sketchy and someone who insists on completeness may consider them lacking in detail. I do not see this as a drawback. Mathematical skills are not the byproduct of reading someone else's arguments, but come from thinking about the essence of a problem, discovering ideas suitable to make the point, then carrying them out in precise detail. The latter skill certainly has to be learned, and I think that the proof sketches in this text provide very appropriate starting points for such a practice.

Students in computer science sometimes view a course in the theory of computation as unnecessarily abstract and of little practical consequence. To convince them otherwise, one needs to appeal to their specific interests and strengths, such as tenacity and inventiveness in dealing with hard-to-solve problems. Because of this, my approach emphasizes learning through problem solving.

By a problem-solving approach, I mean that students learn the material primarily through problem-type illustrative examples that show the motivation behind the concepts, as well as their connection to the theorems and definitions. At the same time, the examples may involve a nontrivial aspect, for which students must discover a solution. In such an approach, homework exercises contribute to a major part of the learning process. The exercises at the end of each section are designed to illuminate and illustrate the material and call on students' problem-solving ability at various levels. Some of the exercises are fairly simple, picking up where the discussion in the text leaves off and asking students to carry on for another step or two. Other exercises are very difficult, challenging even the best minds. A good mix of such exercises can be a very effective teaching tool. To help instructors, I have provided separately an instructor's guide that outlines the solutions of the exercises and suggests their pedagogical value. Students need not be asked to solve all problems but should be assigned those which support the goals of the course and the viewpoint of the instructor. Computer science curricula differ from institution to institution; while a few emphasize the theoretical side, others are almost entirely oriented toward practical application. I believe that this text can serve either of these extremes, provided that the exercises are selected carefully with the students' background and interests in mind. At the same time, the instructor needs to inform the students about the level of abstraction that is expected of them. This is particularly true of the proof oriented exercises. When I say "prove that" or "show that," I have in mind that the student should think about how a proof might be constructed and then produce a clear argument. How formal such a proof should be needs to be determined by the instructor, and students should be given guidelines on this early in the course.

The content of the text is appropriate for a one-semester course. Most of the material can be covered, although some choice of emphasis will have to be made. In my classes, I generally gloss over proofs, skimpy as they are in the text. I usually give just enough coverage to make the result plausible, asking students to read the rest on their own. Overall, though, little can be skipped entirely without potential difficulties later on. A few sections, which are marked with an asterisk, can be omitted without loss to later material. Most of the material, however, is essential and must be covered.

The first edition of this book was published in 1990, the second appeared in 1996. The need for yet another edition is gratifying and indicates that my approach, via languages rather than computations, is still viable. The changes for the second edition were evolutionary rather than revolutionary and addressed the inevitable inaccuracies and obscurities of the first edition. It seems, however, that the second edition had reached a point of stability that requires few changes, so the bulk of the third edition is identical to the previous one. The major new feature of the third edition is the inclusion of a set of solved exercises.

Initially, I felt that giving solutions to exercises was undesirable because it limited the number of problems that can be assigned for homework. However, over the years I have received so many requests for assistance from students everywhere that I concluded that it is time to relent. In this edition I have included solutions to a small number of exercises. I have also added some new exercises to keep from reducing the unsolved problems too much. In selecting exercises for solution, I have favored those that have significant instructional values. For this reason, I give not only the answers, but show the reasoning that is the basis for the final result. Many exercises have the same theme; often I choose a representative case to solve, hoping that a student who can follow the reasoning will be able to transfer it to a set of similar instances. I believe that solutions to a carefully selected set of exercises can help students increase their problem-solving skills and still leave instructors a good set of unsolved exercises. In the text, exercises for which a solution or a hint is given are identified with **S**.

Also in response to suggestions, I have identified some of the harder exercises. This is not always easy, since the exercises span a spectrum of difficulty and because a problem that seems easy to one student may give considerable trouble to another. But there are some exercises that have posed a challenge for a majority of my students. These are marked with a single star ($\star$). There are also a few exercises that are different from most in that they have no clear-cut answer. They may call for speculation, suggest additional reading, or require some computer programming. While they are not suitable for routine homework assignment, they can serve as entry points for further study. Such exercises are marked with a double star ($\star\star$).

Over the last ten years I have received helpful suggestions from numerous reviewers, instructors, and students. While there are too many individuals to mention by name, I am grateful to all of them. Their feedback has been invaluable in my attempts to improve the text.

Peter Linz

Contents

Chapter 1

INTRODUCTION TO THE THEORY OF COMPUTATION

Computer science is a practical discipline. Those who work in it often have a marked preference for useful and tangible problems over theoretical speculation. This is certainly true of computer science students who are interested mainly in working on difficult applications from the real world. Theoretical questions are interesting to them only if they help in finding good solutions. This attitude is appropriate, since without applications there would be little interest in computers. But given this practical orientation, one might well ask "why study theory?"

The first answer is that theory provides concepts and principles that help us understand the general nature of the discipline. The field of computer science includes a wide range of special topics, from machine design to programming. The use of computers in the real world involves a wealth of specific detail that must be learned for a successful application. This makes computer science a very diverse and broad discipline. But in spite of this diversity, there are some common underlying principles. To study these basic principles, we construct abstract models of computers and computation. These models embody the important features that are common to both hardware and software, and that are essential to many of the special and complex constructs we encounter while working with computers. Even when such models are too simple to be applicable immediately to real-world situations, the insights we gain from studying them provide the foundations on which specific development is based. This approach is of course not unique to computer science. The construction of models is one of the essentials of any scientific discipline, and the usefulness of a discipline is often dependent on the existence of simple, yet powerful, theories and laws.

A second, and perhaps not so obvious answer, is that the ideas we will discuss have some immediate and important applications. The fields of digital design, programming languages, and compilers are the most obvious examples, but there are many others. The concepts we study here run like a thread through much of computer science, from operating systems to pattern recognition.

The third answer is one of which we hope to convince the reader. The subject matter is intellectually stimulating and fun. It provides many challenging, puzzle-like problems that can lead to some sleepless nights. This is problem-solving in its pure essence.

In this book, we will look at models that represent features at the core of all computers and their applications. To model the hardware of a computer, we introduce the notion of an **automaton** (plural, **automata**). An automaton is a construct that possesses all the indispensable features of a digital computer. It accepts input, produces output, may have some temporary storage, and can make decisions in transforming the input into the output. A **formal language** is an abstraction of the general characteristics of programming languages. A formal language consists of a set of symbols and some rules of formation by which these symbols can be combined into entities called sentences. A formal language is the set of all strings permitted by the rules of formation. Although some of the formal languages we study here are simpler than programming languages, they have many of the same essential features. We can learn a great deal about programming languages from formal languages. Finally, we will formalize the concept of a mechanical computation by giving a precise definition of the term **algorithm** and study the kinds of problems that are (and are not) suitable for solution by such mechanical means. In the course of our study, we will show the close connection between these abstractions and investigate the conclusions we can derive from them.

In the first chapter, we look at these basic ideas in a very broad way to set the stage for later work. In Section 1.1, we review the main ideas from mathematics that will be required. While intuition will frequently be our guide in exploring ideas, the conclusions we draw will be based on rigorous arguments. This will involve some mathematical machinery, although these requirements are not extensive. The reader will need a reasonably good grasp of the terminology and of the elementary results of set theory, functions, and relations. Trees and graph structures will be used frequently, although little is needed beyond the definition of a labeled, directed graph. Perhaps the most stringent requirement is the ability to follow proofs and an understanding of what constitutes proper mathematical reasoning. This includes familiarity with the basic proof techniques of deduction, induction, and proof by contradiction. We will assume that the reader has this necessary background. Section 1.1 is included to review some of the main results that will be used and to establish a notational common ground for subsequent discussion.

In Section 1.2, we take a first look at the central concepts of languages, grammars, and automata. These concepts occur in many specific forms throughout the book. In Section 1.3, we give some simple applications of these general ideas to illustrate that these concepts have widespread uses in computer science. The discussion in these two sections will be intuitive rather than rigorous. Later, we will make all of this much more precise; but for the moment, the goal is to get a clear picture of the concepts with which we are dealing.

1.1 Mathematical Preliminaries and Notation

Sets

A **set** is a collection of elements, without any structure other than membership. To indicate that x is an element of the set S, we write $x \in S$. The statement that x is not in S is written $x \notin S$. A set is specified by enclosing some description of its elements in curly braces; for example, the set of integers 0, 1, 2 is shown as

$$S = \{0, 1, 2\}.$$

Ellipses are used whenever the meaning is clear. Thus, $\{a, b, ..., z\}$ stands for all the lower-case letters of the English alphabet, while $\{2, 4, 6, ...\}$ denotes the set of all positive even integers. When the need arises, we use more explicit notation, in which we write

$$S = \{i : i > 0, i \text{ is even}\} \tag{1.1}$$

for the last example. We read this as "S is set of all i, such that i is greater than zero, and i is even," implying of course that i is an integer.

The usual set operations are **union** ($\cup$), **intersection** ($\cap$), and **difference** ($-$), defined as

$$S_1 \cup S_2 = \{x : x \in S_1 \text{ or } x \in S_2\},$$
$$S_1 \cap S_2 = \{x : x \in S_1 \text{ and } x \in S_2\},$$
$$S_1 - S_2 = \{x : x \in S_1 \text{ and } x \notin S_2\}.$$

Another basic operation is **complementation.** The complement of a set S, denoted by $\overline{S}$, consists of all elements not in S. To make this meaningful, we need to know what the **universal set** U of all possible elements is. If U is specified, then

$$\overline{S} = \{x : x \in U, x \notin S\}.$$

The set with no elements, called the **empty set** or the **null set** is denoted by $\varnothing$. From the definition of a set, it is obvious that

$$S \cup \varnothing = S - \varnothing = S,$$
$$S \cap \varnothing = \varnothing,$$
$$\overline{\varnothing} = U,$$
$$\overline{\overline{S}} = S.$$

The following useful identities, known as the **DeMorgan's laws,**

$$\overline{S_1 \cup S_2} = \overline{S}_1 \cap \overline{S}_2, \tag{1.2}$$

$$\overline{S_1 \cap S_2} = \overline{S}_1 \cup \overline{S}_2, \tag{1.3}$$

are needed on several occasions.

A set S_1 is said to be a **subset of** S if every element of S_1 is also an element of S. We write this as

$$S_1 \subseteq S.$$

If $S_1 \subseteq S$, but S contains an element not in S_1 we say that S_1 is a **proper subset** of S; we write this as

$$S_1 \subset S.$$

If S_1 and S_2 have no common element, that is, $S_1 \cap S_2 = \varnothing$, then the sets are said to be **disjoint.**

A set is said to be finite if it contains a finite number of elements; otherwise it is infinite. The size of a finite set is the number of elements in it; this is denoted by $|S|$.

A given set normally has many subsets. The set of all subsets of a set S is called the **powerset** of S and is denoted by 2^S. Observe that 2^S is a set of sets.

Example 1.1   If S is the set $\{a, b, c\}$, then its powerset is

$$2^S = \{\varnothing, \{a\}, \{b\}, \{c\}, \{a, b\}, \{a, c\}, \{b, c\}, \{a, b, c\}\}.$$

Here $|S| = 3$ and $|2^S| = 8$. This is an instance of a general result; if S is finite, then

$$|2^S| = 2^{|S|}.$$

In many of our examples, the elements of a set are ordered sequences of elements from other sets. Such sets are said to be the **Cartesian product** of other sets. For the Cartesian product of two sets, which itself is a set of ordered pairs, we write

$$S = S_1 \times S_2 = \{(x, y) : x \in S_1, y \in S_2\}.$$

Example 1.2   Let $S_1 = \{2, 4\}$ and $S_2 = \{2, 3, 5, 6\}$. Then

$$S_1 \times S_2 = \{(2, 2), (2, 3), (2, 5), (2, 6), (4, 2), (4, 3), (4, 5), (4, 6)\}.$$

Note that the order in which the elements of a pair are written matters. The pair $(4, 2)$ is in $S_1 \times S_2$, but $(2, 4)$ is not.

The notation is extended in an obvious fashion to the Cartesian product of more than two sets; generally

$$S_1 \times S_2 \times \cdots \times S_n = \{(x_1, x_2, ..., x_n) : x_i \in S_i\}.$$

Functions and Relations

A **function** is a rule that assigns to elements of one set a unique element of another set. If f denotes a function, then the first set is called the **domain** of f, and the second set is its **range.** We write

$$f : S_1 \to S_2$$

to indicate that the domain of f is a subset of S_1 and that the range of f is a subset of S_2. If the domain of f is all of S_1, we say that f is a **total function** on S_1; otherwise f is said to be a **partial function.**

In many applications, the domain and range of the functions involved are in the set of positive integers. Furthermore, we are often interested only in the behavior of these functions as their arguments become very large. In such cases an understanding of the growth rates is often sufficient and a common order of magnitude notation can be used. Let $f(n)$ and $g(n)$ be functions whose domain is a subset of the positive integers. If there exists a positive constant c such that for all n

$$f(n) \leq cg(n),$$

we say that f has **order at most** g. We write this as

$$f(n) = O(g(n)).$$

If

$$|f(n)| \geq c|g(n)|,$$

then f has **order at least** g, for which we use

$$f(n) = \Omega(g(n)).$$

Finally, if there exist constants c_1 and c_2 such that

$$c_1|g(n)| \leq |f(n)| \leq c_2|g(n)|,$$

f and g have the **same order of magnitude**, expressed as

$$f(n) = \Theta(g(n)).$$

In this order of magnitude notation, we ignore multiplicative constants and lower order terms that become negligible as n increases.

Example 1.3   Let

$$f(n) = 2n^2 + 3n,$$
$$g(n) = n^3,$$
$$h(n) = 10n^2 + 100.$$

Then

$$f(n) = O(g(n)),$$
$$g(n) = \Omega(h(n)),$$
$$f(n) = \Theta(h(n)).$$

In order of magnitude notation, the symbol $=$ should not be interpreted as equality and order of magnitude expressions cannot be treated like ordinary expressions. Manipulations such as

$$O(n) + O(n) = 2O(n)$$

are not sensible and can lead to incorrect conclusions. Still, if used properly, the order of magnitude arguments can be effective, as we will see in later chapters on the analysis of algorithms. ∎

Some functions can be represented by a set of pairs

$$\{(x_1, y_1), (x_2, y_2), ...\},$$

where x_i is an element in the domain of the function, and y_i is the corresponding value in its range. For such a set to define a function, each x_i can occur at most once as the first element of a pair. If this is not satisfied, the set is called a **relation.** Relations are more general than functions: in a function each element of the domain has exactly one associated element in the range; in a relation there may be several such elements in the range.

One kind of relation is that of **equivalence,** a generalization of the concept of equality (identity). To indicate that a pair (x, y) is an equivalence relation, we write

$$x \equiv y.$$

A relation denoted by $\equiv$ is considered an equivalence if it satisfies three rules: the reflexivity rule

$$x \equiv x \text{ for all } x,$$

the symmetry rule

$$\text{if } x \equiv y \text{ then } y \equiv x,$$

and the transitivity rule

$$\text{if } x \equiv y \text{ and } y \equiv z, \text{ then } x \equiv z.$$

Example 1.4 Consider the relation on the set of nonnegative integers defined by

$$x \equiv y,$$

if and only if

$$x \bmod 3 = y \bmod 3.$$

Then $2 \equiv 5$, $12 \equiv 0$, and $0 = 36$. Clearly this is an equivalence relation, as it satisfies reflexivity, symmetry, and transitivity.

Graphs and Trees

A graph is a construct consisting of two finite sets, the set $V = \{v_1, v_2, ..., v_n\}$ of **vertices** and the set $E = \{e_1, e_2, ..., e_m\}$ of **edges.** Each edge is a pair of vertices from V, for instance

$$e_i = (v_j, v_k)$$

is an edge from v_j to v_k. We say that the edge e_i is an outgoing edge for v_j and an incoming edge for v_k. Such a construct is actually a directed graph (digraph), since we associate a direction (from v_j to v_k) with each edge. Graphs may be labeled, a label being a name or other information associated with parts of the graph. Both vertices and edges may be labeled.

Figure 1.1

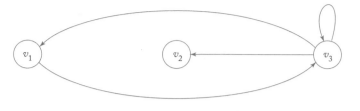

Graphs are conveniently visualized by diagrams in which the vertices are represented as circles and the edges as lines with arrows connecting the vertices. The graph with vertices $\{v_1, v_2, v_3\}$ and edges $\{(v_1, v_3), (v_3, v_1),$ $(v_3, v_2), (v_3, v_3)\}$ is depicted in Figure 1.1.

A sequence of edges $(v_i, v_j), (v_j, v_k), \ldots, (v_m, v_n)$ is said to be a **walk** from v_i to v_n. The length of a walk is the total number of edges traversed in going from the initial vertex to the final one. A walk in which no edge is repeated is said to be a **path;** a path is **simple** if no vertex is repeated. A walk from v_i to itself with no repeated edges is called a **cycle** with **base** v_i. If no vertices other than the base are repeated in a cycle, then it is said to be simple. In Figure 1.1, $(v_1, v_3), (v_3, v_2)$ is a simple path from v_1 to v_2. The sequence of edges $(v_1, v_3), (v_3, v_3), (v_3, v_1)$ is a cycle, but not a simple one. If the edges of a graph are labeled, we can talk about the label of a walk. This label is the sequence of edge labels encountered when the path is traversed. Finally, an edge from a vertex to itself is called a **loop.** In Figure 1.1 there is a loop on vertex v_3.

On several occasions, we will refer to an algorithm for finding all simple paths between two given vertices (or all simple cycles based on a vertex). If we do not concern ourselves with efficiency, we can use the following obvious method. Starting from the given vertex, say v_i, list all outgoing edges $(v_i, v_k), (v_i, v_l), \ldots$. At this point, we have all paths of length one starting at v_i. For all vertices $v_k, v_l, \ldots$ so reached, we list all outgoing edges as long as they do not lead to any vertex already used in the path we are constructing. After we do this, we will have all simple paths of length two originating at v_i. We continue this until all possibilities are accounted for. Since there are only a finite number of vertices, we will eventually list all simple paths beginning at v_i. From these we select those ending at the desired vertex.

Trees are a particular type of graph. A tree is a directed graph that has no cycles, and that has one distinct vertex, called the **root,** such that there is exactly one path from the root to every other vertex. This definition implies that the root has no incoming edges and that there are some vertices without outgoing edges. These are called the **leaves** of the tree. If there is an edge from v_i to v_j, then v_i is said to be the **parent** of v_j, and v_j the **child** of v_i. The **level** associated with each vertex is the number of edges in the path from the root to the vertex. The **height** of the tree is the largest level number of any vertex. These terms are illustrated in Figure 1.2.

Figure 1.2

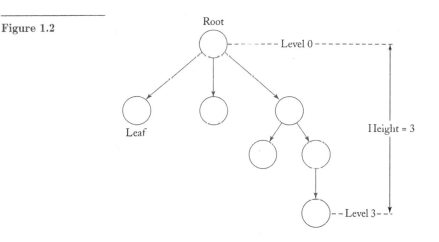

At times, we want to associate an ordering with the nodes at each level; in such cases we talk about **ordered trees.**

More details on graphs and trees can be found in most books on discrete mathematics.

Proof Techniques

An important requirement for reading this text is the ability to follow proofs. In mathematical arguments, we employ the accepted rules of deductive reasoning, and many proofs are simply a sequence of such steps. Two special proof techniques are used so frequently that it is appropriate to review them briefly. These are **proof by induction** and **proof by contradiction.**

Induction is a technique by which the truth of a number of statements can be inferred from the truth of a few specific instances. Suppose we have a sequence of statements $P_1, P_2, \ldots$ we want to prove to be true. Furthermore, suppose also that the following holds:

1. For some $k \geq 1$, we know that $P_1, P_2, \ldots, P_k$ are true.

2. The problem is such that for any $n \geq k$, the truths of $P_1, P_2, \ldots, P_n$ imply the truth of P_{n+1}.

We can then use induction to show that every statement in this sequence is true.

In a proof by induction, we argue as follows: From Condition 1 we know that the first k statements are true. Then Condition 2 tells us that P_{k+1} also must be true. But now that we know that the first $k+1$ statements are true, we can apply Condition 2 again to claim that P_{k+2} must be true, and so on. We need not explicitly continue this argument because the pattern is clear. The chain of reasoning can be extended to any statement. Therefore, every statement is true.

The starting statements $P_1, P_2, \ldots P_k$ are called the **basis** of the induction. The step connecting P_n with P_{n+1} is called the **inductive step.** The inductive step is generally made easier by the **inductive assumption** that $P_1, P_2, \ldots, P_n$ are true. In a formal inductive argument, we show all three parts explicitly.

Example 1.5

A binary tree is a tree in which no parent can have more than two children. Prove that a binary tree of height n has at most 2^n leaves.

Proof: If we denote the maximum number of leaves of a binary tree of height n by $l(n)$, then we want to show that

$$l(n) \leq 2^n.$$

Basis: Clearly $l(0) = 1 = 2^0$ since a tree of height 0 can have no nodes other than the root, that is, it has at most one leaf.

Inductive Assumption: $l(i) \leq 2^i$, for $i = 0, 1, \ldots, n$.

Inductive Step: To get a binary tree of height $n + 1$ from one of height n, we can create, at most, two leaves in place of each previous one. Therefore

$$l(n + 1) = 2l(n).$$

Now, using the inductive assumption, we get

$$l(n + 1) \leq 2 \times 2^n = 2^{n+1}.$$

Thus, our claim is also true for $n + 1$. Since n can be any number, the statement must be true for all n. ■

Here we introduce the symbol ■ that is used in this book to denote the end of a proof.

Example 1.6

Show that

$$S_n = \sum_{i=0}^{n} i = \frac{n(n + 1)}{2}. \tag{1.4}$$

First we note that

$$S_{n+1} = S_n + n + 1.$$

We then make the inductive assumption that (1.4) holds for S_n; if this is so, then

$$S_{n+1} = \frac{n(n+1)}{2} + n + 1$$
$$= \frac{(n+2)(n+1)}{2}.$$

Thus (1.4) holds for S_{n+1} and we have justified the inductive step. Since (1.4) is obviously true for $n = 1$, we have a basis and have proved (1.4) by induction for all n.

In this last example we have been a little less formal in identifying the basis, inductive assumption, and inductive step, but they are there and are essential. To keep our subsequent discussions from becoming too formal, we will generally prefer the style of the second example. However, if you have difficulty in following or constructing a proof, go back to the more explicit form of Example 1.5.

Inductive reasoning can be difficult to grasp. It helps to notice the close connection between induction and recursion in programming. For example, the recursive definition of a function $f(n)$, where n is any positive integer, often has two parts. One involves the definition of $f(n+1)$ in terms of $f(n), f(n-1), ..., f(1)$. This corresponds to the inductive step. The second part is the "escape" from the recursion, which is accomplished by defining $f(1), f(2), ...f(k)$ nonrecursively. This corresponds to the basis of induction. As in induction, recursion allows us to draw conclusions about all instances of the problem, given only a few starting values and using the recursive nature of the problem.

Proof by contradiction is another powerful technique that often works when everything else fails. Suppose we want to prove that some statement P is true. We then assume, for the moment, that P is false and see where that assumption leads us. If we arrive at a conclusion that we know is incorrect, we can lay the blame on the starting assumption and conclude that P must be true. The following is a classic and elegant example.

Example 1.7   A rational number is a number that can be expressed as the ration of two integers n and m so that n and m have no common factor. A real number that is not rational is said to be irrational. Show that $\sqrt{2}$ is irrational.

As in all proofs by contradiction, we assume the contrary of what we want to show. Here we assume that $\sqrt{2}$ is a rational number so that it can be written as

$$\sqrt{2} = \frac{n}{m}, \tag{1.5}$$

where n and m are integers without a common factor. Rearranging (1.5), we have

$$2m^2 = n^2.$$

Therefore n^2 must be even. This implies that n is even, so that we can write $n = 2k$ or

$$2m^2 = 4k^2,$$

and

$$m^2 = 2k^2.$$

Therefore m is even. But this contradicts our assumption that n and m have no common factors. Thus, m and n in (1.5) cannot exist and $\sqrt{2}$ is not a rational number.

This example exhibits the essence of a proof by contradiction. By making a certain assumption we are led to a contradiction of the assumption or some known fact. If all steps in our argument are logically sound, we must conclude that our initial assumption was false.

EXERCISES

1. Use induction on the size of S to show that if S is a finite set then $\left|2^S\right| = 2^{|S|}$.

2. Show that if S_1 and S_2 are finite sets with $|S_1| = n$ and $|S_2| = m$, then

$$|S_1 \cup S_2| \le n + m.$$

3. If S_1 and S_2 are finite sets, show that $|S_1 \times S_2| = |S_1||S_2|$.

4. Consider the relation between two sets defined by $S_1 \equiv S_2$ if and only if $|S_1| = |S_2|$. Show that this is an equivalence relation.

5. Prove DeMorgan's laws, Equations (1.2) and (1.3). **5**

6. Occasionally, we need to use the union and intersection symbols in a manner analogous to the summation sign Σ. We define

$$\bigcup_{p \in \{i,j,k,\ldots\}} S_p = S_i \cup S_j \cup S_k \cdots$$

with an analogous notation for the intersection of several sets.
With this notation, the general DeMorgan's laws are written as

$$\overline{\bigcup_{p \in P} S_p} = \bigcap_{p \in P} \overline{S_p}$$

and

$$\overline{\bigcap_{p \in P} S_p} = \bigcup_{p \in P} \overline{S_p}.$$

Prove these identities when P is a finite set. ⓢ

7. Show that

$$S_1 \cup S_2 = \overline{\overline{S_1} \cap \overline{S_2}}.$$

8. Show that $S_1 = S_2$ if and only if

$$\left(S_1 \cap \overline{S_2} \right) \cup \left(\overline{S_1} \cap S_2 \right) = \varnothing.$$

9. Show that

$$S_1 \cup S_2 - \left(S_1 \cap \overline{S_2} \right) = S_2. \quad ⓢ$$

10. Show that

$$S_1 \times (S_2 \cup S_3) = (S_1 \times S_2) \cup (S_1 \times S_3).$$

11. Show that if $S_1 \subseteq S_2$, then $\overline{S_2} \subseteq \overline{S_1}$.

12. Give conditions on S_1 and S_2 necessary and sufficient to ensure that

$$S_1 = (S_1 \cup S_2) - S_2. \quad ⓢ$$

13. Show that if $f(n) = O(g(n))$ and $g(n) = O(f(n))$, then $f(n) = \Theta(g(n))$.

14. Show that $2^n = O(3^n)$ but $2^n \neq \Theta(3^n)$.

15. Show that the following order-of-magnitude results hold.

   (a) $n^2 + 5 \log n = O\left(n^2\right)$

   (b) $3^n = O(n!)$

   (c) $n! = O(n^n)$ ⓢ

16. Prove that if $f(n) = O(g(n))$ and $g(n) = O(h(n))$, then $f(n) = O(h(n))$.

17. Show that if $f(n) = O\left(n^2\right)$ and $g(n) = O\left(n^3\right)$, then

$$f(n) + g(n) = O\left(n^3\right)$$

and

$$f(n)\, g(n) = O\left(n^6\right).$$

18. In Exercise 17, is it true that $g(n)/f(n) = O(n)$?

19. Assume that $f(n) = 2n^2 + n$ and $g(n) = O(n^2)$. What is wrong with the following argument?

$$f(n) = O(n^2) + O(n),$$

so that

$$f(n) - g(n) = O(n^2) + O(n) - O(n^2).$$

Therefore,

$$f(n) - g(n) = O(n).$$

20. Draw a picture of the graph with vertices $\{v_1, v_2, v_3\}$ and edges $\{(v_1, v_1), (v_1, v_2), (v_2, v_3), (v_2, v_1), (v_3, v_1)\}$. Enumerate all cycles with base v_1.

21. Let $G = (V, E)$ be any graph. Prove the following claim: If there is any walk between $v_i \in V$ and $v_j \in V$, then there must be a path of length no larger than $|V| - 1$ between these two vertices.

22. Consider graphs in which there is at most one edge between any two vertices. Show that under this condition a graph with n vertices has at most n^2 edges.

23. Show that

$$\sum_{i=1}^{n} i^2 = \frac{n(n+1)(2n+1)}{6}.$$

24. Show that

$$\sum_{i=1}^{n} \frac{1}{i^2} \leq 2 - \frac{1}{n}.$$

25. Prove that for all $n \geq 4$ the inequality $2^n < n!$ holds.

26. Show that $\sqrt{8}$ is not a rational number.

27. Show that $2 - \sqrt{2}$ is irrational. Ⓢ

28. Prove or disprove the following statements.

    (a) The sum of a rational and an irrational number must be irrational.

    (b) The sum of two positive irrational numbers must be irrational.

    (c) The product of a rational and an irrational number must be irrational.

29. Show that every positive integer can be expressed as the product of prime numbers. Ⓢ

★ 30. Prove that the set of all prime numbers is infinite.

31. A prime pair consists of two primes that differ by two. There are many prime pairs, for example, 11 and 13, 17 and 19, etc. Prime triplets are three numbers $n, n+2, n+4$ that are all prime. Show that the only prime triplets are $(1, 3, 5)$ and $(3, 5, 7)$.

1.2 Three Basic Concepts

Three fundamental ideas are the major themes of this book: **languages, grammars,** and **automata.** In the course of our study we will explore many results about these concepts and about their relationship to each other. First, we must understand the meaning of the terms.

Languages

We are all familiar with the notion of natural languages, such as English and French. Still, most of us would probably find it difficult to say exactly what the word "language" means. Dictionaries define the term informally as a system suitable for the expression of certain ideas, facts, or concepts, including a set of symbols and rules for their manipulation. While this gives us an intuitive idea of what a language is, it is not sufficient as a definition for the study of formal languages. We need a precise definition for the term.

We start with a finite, nonempty set Σ of symbols, called the **alphabet.** From the individual symbols we construct **strings,** which are finite sequences of symbols from the alphabet. For example, if the alphabet $\Sigma = \{a, b\}$, then $abab$ and $aaabbba$ are strings on Σ. With few exceptions, we will use lower case letters $a, b, c, \ldots$ for elements of Σ and $u, v, w, \ldots$ for string names. We will write, for example,

$$w = abaaa$$

to indicate that the string named w has the specific value $abaaa$.

The **concatenation** of two strings w and v is the string obtained by appending the symbols of v to the right end of w, that is, if

$$w = a_1 a_2 \cdots a_n$$

and

$$v = b_1 b_2 \cdots b_m,$$

then the concatenation of w and v, denoted by wv, is

$$wv = a_1 a_2 \cdots a_n b_1 b_2 \cdots b_m.$$

The **reverse** of a string is obtained by writing the symbols in reverse order; if w is a string as shown above, then its reverse w^R is

$$w^R = a_n \cdots a_2 a_1.$$

The **length** of a string w, denoted by $|w|$, is the number of symbols in the string. We will frequently need to refer to the **empty string,** which is a string with no symbols at all. It will be denoted by λ. The following simple relations

$$|\lambda| = 0,$$
$$\lambda w = w\lambda = w,$$

hold for all w.

Any string of consecutive characters in some w is said to be a **substring** of w. If

$$w = vu,$$

then the substrings v and u are said to be a **prefix** and a **suffix** of w, respectively. For example, if $w = abbab$, then $\{\lambda, a, ab, abb, abba, abbab\}$ is the set of all prefixes of w, while bab, ab, b are some of its suffixes.

Simple properties of strings, such as their length, are very intuitive and probably need little elaboration. For example, if u and v are strings, then the length of their concatenation is the sum of the individual lengths, that is,

$$|uv| = |u| + |v|. \tag{1.6}$$

But although this relationship is obvious, it is useful to be able to make it precise and prove it. The techniques for doing so are important in more complicated situation.

√ **Example 1.8**   Show that (1.6) holds for any u and v. To prove this, we first need a definition of the length of a string. We make such a definition in a recursive fashion by

$$|a| = 1,$$
$$|wa| = |w| + 1,$$

for all $a \in \Sigma$ and w any string on Σ. This definition is a formal statement of our intuitive understanding of the length of a string: the length of a single symbol is one, and the length of any string is increased by one if we add another symbol to it. With this formal definition, we are ready to prove (1.6) by induction.

By definition, (1.6) holds for all u of any length and all v of length 1, so we have a basis. As an inductive assumption, we take that (1.6) holds for all u of any length and all v of length $1, 2, ..., n$. Now take any v of length $n + 1$ and write it as $v = wa$. Then,

$$|v| = |w| + 1,$$
$$|uv| = |uwa| = |uw| + 1.$$

But by the inductive hypothesis (which is applicable since w is of length n),

$$|uw| = |u| + |w|,$$

so that

$$|uv| = |u| + |w| + 1 = |u| + |v|.$$

Therefore, (1.6) holds for all u and all v of length up to $n + 1$, completing the inductive step and the argument.

If w is a string, then w^n stands for the string obtained by repeating w n times. As a special case, we define

$$w^0 = \lambda,$$

for all w.

If Σ is an alphabet, then we use Σ^* to denote the set of strings obtained by concatenating zero or more symbols from Σ. The set Σ^* always contains λ. To exclude the empty string, we define

$$\Sigma^+ = \Sigma^* - \{\lambda\}.$$

While Σ is finite by assumption, Σ^* and Σ^+ are always infinite since there is no limit on the length of the strings in these sets.

A language is defined very generally as a subset of Σ^*. A string in a language L will be called a **sentence of** L. This definition is quite broad; any set of strings on an alphabet Σ can be considered a language. Later we will study methods by which specific languages can be defined and described; this will enable us to give some structure to this rather broad concept. For the moment, though, we will just look at a few specific examples.

Example 1.9 Let $\Sigma = \{a, b\}$. Then

$$\Sigma^* = \{\lambda, a, b, aa, ab, ba, bb, aaa, aab, ...\}.$$

The set

$$\{a, aa, aab\}$$

is a language on Σ. Because it has a finite number of sentences, we call it a finite language. The set

$$L = \{a^n b^n : n \geq 0\}$$

is also a language on Σ. The strings $aabb$ and $aaaabbbb$ are in the language L, but the string abb is not in L. This language is infinite. Most interesting languages are infinite.

Since languages are sets, the union, intersection, and difference of two languages are immediately defined. The complement of a language is defined with respect to Σ^*; that is, the complement of L is

$$\overline{L} = \Sigma^* - L.$$

The reverse of a language is the set of all string reversals, that is,

$$L^R = \left\{ w^R : w \in L \right\}.$$

The concatenation of two languages L_1 and L_2 is the set of all strings obtained by concatenating any element of L_1 with any element of L_2; specifically,

$$L_1 L_2 = \left\{ xy : x \in L_1, y \in L_2 \right\}.$$

We define L^n as L concatenated with itself n times, with the special cases

$$L^0 = \{\lambda\}$$

and

$$L^1 = L$$

for every language L.

Finally, we define the **star-closure** of a language as

$$L^* = L^0 \cup L^1 \cup L^2 \cdots$$

and the **positive closure** as

$$L^+ = L^1 \cup L^2 \cdots.$$

Example 1.10   If

$$L = \left\{ a^n b^n : n \geq 0 \right\},$$

then

$$L^2 = \left\{ a^n b^n a^m b^m : n \geq 0, m \geq 0 \right\}.$$

Note that n and m in the above are unrelated; the string $aabbaaabbb$ is in L^2.

The reverse of L is easily described in set notations as

$$L^R = \left\{ b^n a^n : n \geq 0 \right\},$$

but it is considerably harder to describe $\overline{L}$ or L^* this way. A few tries will quickly convince you of the limitation of set notation for the specification of complicated languages.

Grammars

To study languages mathematically, we need a mechanism to describe them. Everyday language is imprecise and ambiguous, so informal descriptions in English are often inadequate. The set notation used in Examples 1.9 and 1.10 is more suitable, but limited. As we proceed we will learn about several language-definition mechanisms that are useful in different circumstances. Here we introduce a common and powerful one, the notion of a **grammar.**

A grammar for the English language tells us whether a particular sentence is well-formed or not. A typical rule of English grammar is "a sentence can consist of a noun phrase followed by a predicate." More concisely we write this as

$$\langle sentence \rangle \rightarrow \langle noun\_phrase \rangle \langle predicate \rangle ,$$

with the obvious interpretation. This is of course not enough to deal with actual sentences. We must now provide definitions for the newly introduced constructs $\langle noun\_phrase \rangle$ and $\langle predicate \rangle$. If we do so by

$$\langle noun\_phrase \rangle \rightarrow \langle article \rangle \langle noun \rangle ,$$
$$\langle predicate \rangle \rightarrow \langle verb \rangle ,$$

and if we associate the actual words "a" and "the" with $\langle article \rangle$, "boy" and "dog" with $\langle noun \rangle$, and "runs" and "walks" with $\langle verb \rangle$, then the grammar tells us that the sentences "a boy runs" and "the dog walks" are properly formed. If we were to give a complete grammar, then in theory, every proper sentence could be explained this way.

This example illustrates the definition of a general concept in terms of simple ones. We start with the top level concept, here $\langle sentence \rangle$, and successively reduce it to the irreducible building blocks of the language. The generalization of these ideas leads us to formal grammars.

Definition 1.1

A grammar G is defined as a quadruple

$$G = (V, T, S, P) ,$$

where V is a finite set of objects called **variables,**
T is a finite set of objects called **terminal symbols,**
$S \in V$ is a special symbol called the **start** variable,
P is a finite set of **productions.**

It will be assumed without further mention that the sets V and T are non-empty and disjoint.

The production rules are the heart of a grammar; they specify how the grammar transforms one string into another, and through this they define a language associated with the grammar. In our discussion we will assume that all production rules are of the form

$$x \rightarrow y,$$

where x is an element of $(V \cup T)^+$ and y is in $(V \cup T)^*$. The productions are applied in the following manner: given a string w of the form

$$w = uxv,$$

we say the production $x \rightarrow y$ is applicable to this string, and we may use it to replace x with y, thereby obtaining a new string

$$z = uyv.$$

This is written as

$$w \Rightarrow z.$$

We say that w **derives** z or that z is derived from w. Successive strings are derived by applying the productions of the grammar in arbitrary order. A production can be used whenever it is applicable, and it can be applied as often as desired. If

$$w_1 \Rightarrow w_2 \Rightarrow \cdots \Rightarrow w_n,$$

we say that w_1 derives w_n and write

$$w_1 \stackrel{*}{\Rightarrow} w_n.$$

The $*$ indicates that an unspecified number of steps (including zero) can be taken to derive w_n from w_1. Thus

$$w \stackrel{*}{\Rightarrow} w$$

is always the case.

By applying the production rules in a different order, a given grammar can normally generate many strings. The set of all such terminal strings is the language defined or generated by the grammar.

Definition 1.2

Let $G = (V, T, S, P)$ be a grammar. Then the set

$$L(G) = \left\{ w \in T^* : S \stackrel{*}{\Rightarrow} w \right\}$$

is the language generated by G.

If $w \in L(G)$, then the sequence

$$S \Rightarrow w_1 \Rightarrow w_2 \Rightarrow \cdots \Rightarrow w_n \Rightarrow w$$

is a **derivation** of the sentence w. The strings $S, w_1, w_2, ..., w_n$, which contain variables as well as terminals, are called **sentential forms** of the derivation.

Example 1.11   Consider the grammar

$$G = (\{S\}, \{a, b\}, S, P),$$

with P given by

$$S \rightarrow aSb,$$
$$S \rightarrow \lambda.$$

Then

$$S \Rightarrow aSb \Rightarrow aaSbb \Rightarrow aabb,$$

so we can write

$$S \stackrel{*}{\Rightarrow} aabb.$$

The string $aabb$ is a sentence in the language generated by G, while $aaSbb$ is a sentential form.

A grammar G completely defines $L(G)$, but it may not be easy to get a very explicit description of the language from the grammar. Here, however, the answer is fairly clear. It is not hard to conjecture that

$$L(G) = \{a^n b^n : n \geq 0\},$$

and it is easy to prove it. If we notice that the rule $S \rightarrow aSb$ is recursive, a proof by induction readily suggests itself. We first show that all sentential forms must have the form

$$w_i = a^i S b^i. \tag{1.7}$$

Suppose that (1.7) holds for all sentential forms w_i of length $2i + 1$ or less. To get another sentential form (which is not a sentence), we can only apply the production $S \rightarrow aSb$. This gets us

$$a^i Sb^i \Rightarrow a^{i+1} Sb^{i+1},$$

so that every sentential form of length $2i + 3$ is also of the form (1.7). Since (1.7) is obviously true for $i = 1$, it holds by induction for all i. Finally, to get a sentence, we must apply the production $S \rightarrow \lambda$, and we see that

$$S \overset{*}{\Rightarrow} a^n Sb^n \Rightarrow a^n b^n$$

represents all possible derivations. Thus, G can derive only strings of the form $a^n b^n$.

We also have to show that all strings of this form can be derived. This is easy; we simply apply $S \rightarrow aSb$ as many times as needed, followed by $S \rightarrow \lambda$.

Example 1.12   Find a grammar that generates

$$L = \left\{ a^n b^{n+1} : n \geq 0 \right\}.$$

The idea behind the previous example can be extended to this case. All we need to do is generate an extra b. This can be done with a production $S \rightarrow Ab$, with other productions chosen so that A can derive the language in the previous example. Reasoning in this fashion, we get the grammar $G = (\{S, A\}, \{a, b\}, S, P)$, with productions

$$S \rightarrow Ab,$$
$$A \rightarrow aAb,$$
$$A \rightarrow \lambda.$$

Derive a few specific sentences to convince yourself that this works.

The above examples are fairly easy ones, so rigorous arguments may seem superfluous. But often it is not so easy to find a grammar for a language described in an informal way or to give an intuitive characterization of the language defined by a grammar. To show that a given language is indeed generated by a certain grammar G, we must be able to show (a) that every $w \in L$ can be derived from S using G, and (b) that every string so derived is in L.

Example 1.13   Take $\Sigma = \{a, b\}$, and let $n_a(w)$ and $n_b(w)$ denote the number of a's and b's in the string w, respectively. Then the grammar G with productions

$$S \to SS,$$
$$S \to \lambda,$$
$$S \to aSb,$$
$$S \to bSa,$$

generates the language

$$L = \{w : n_a(w) = n_b(w)\}.$$

This claim is not so obvious, and we need to provide convincing arguments.

First, it is clear that every sentential form of G has an equal number of a's and b's, since the only productions that generate an a, namely $S \to aSb$ and $S \to bSa$ simultaneously generate a b. Therefore every element of $L(G)$ is in L. It is a little harder to see that every string in L can be derived with G.

Let us begin by looking at the problem in outline, considering the various forms $w \in L$ can have. Suppose w starts with an a and ends with a b. Then it has the form

$$w = aw_1b,$$

where w_1 is also in L. We can think of this case as being derived starting with

$$S \Rightarrow aSb,$$

if S does indeed derive any string in L. A similar argument can be made if w starts with a b and ends with an a. But this does not take care of all cases, since a string in L can begin and end with the same symbol. If we write down a string of this type, say, $aabbba$, we see that it can be considered as the concatenation of two shorter strings $aabb$ and ba, both of which are in L. Is this true in general? To show that this is indeed so, we can use the following argument: Suppose that, starting at the left end of the string, we count $+1$ for an a and -1 for a b. If a string w starts and ends with a, then the count will be $+1$ after the leftmost symbol and -1 immediately before the rightmost one. Therefore, the count has to go through zero somewhere in the middle of the string, indicating that such a string must have the form

$$w = w_1w_2,$$

where both w_1 and w_2 are in L. This case can be taken care of by the production $S \to SS$.

Once we see the argument intuitively, we are ready to proceed more rigorously. Again we use induction. Assume that all $w \in L$ with $|w| \leq 2n$

can be derived with G. Take any $w \in L$ of length $2n + 2$. If $w = aw_1b$, then w_1 is in L, and $|w_1| = 2n$. Therefore, by assumption,

$$S \overset{*}{\Rightarrow} w_1.$$

Then

$$S \Rightarrow aSb \overset{*}{\Rightarrow} aw_1b = w$$

is possible, and w can be derived with G. Obviously, similar arguments can be made if $w = bw_1a$.

If w is not of this form, that is, if it starts and ends with the same symbol, then the counting argument tells us that it must have the form $w = w_1w_2$, with w_1 and w_2 both in L and of length less than or equal to $2n$. Hence again we see that

$$S \Rightarrow SS \overset{*}{\Rightarrow} w_1S \overset{*}{\Rightarrow} w_1w_2 = w$$

is possible.

Since the inductive assumption is clearly satisfied for $n = 1$, we have a basis, and the claim is true for all n, completing our argument.

■

Normally, a given language has many grammars that generate it. Even though these grammars are different, they are equivalent in some sense. We say that two grammars G_1 and G_2 are **equivalent** if they generate the same language, that is, if

$$L(G_1) = L(G_2).$$

As we will see later, it is not always easy to see if two grammars are equivalent.

✓ Example 1.14   Consider the grammar $G_1 = (\{A, S\}, \{a, b\}, S, P_1)$, with P_1 consisting of the productions

$$S \rightarrow aAb | \lambda,$$
$$A \rightarrow aAb | \lambda.$$

Here we introduce a convenient shorthand notation in which several production rules with the same left-hand side are written on a single line, with alternative right-hand sides separated by |. In this notation, $S \rightarrow aAb | \lambda$ stands for the two productions $S \rightarrow aAb$ and $S \rightarrow \lambda$.

This grammar is equivalent to the grammar G in Example 1.11. The equivalence is easy to prove by showing that

$$L(G_1) = \{a^n b^n : n \geq 0\}.$$

We leave this as an exercise.

■

Automata

An automaton is an abstract model of a digital computer. As such, every automaton includes some essential features. It has a mechanism for reading input. It will be assumed that the input is a string over a given alphabet, written on an **input file,** which the automaton can read but not change. The input file is divided into cells, each of which can hold one symbol. The input mechanism can read the input file from left to right, one symbol at a time. The input mechanism can also detect the end of the input string (by sensing an end of file condition). The automaton can produce output of some form. It may have a temporary **storage** device, consisting of an unlimited number of cells, each capable of holding a single symbol from an alphabet (not necessarily the same one as the input alphabet). The automaton can read and change the contents of the storage cells. Finally, the automaton has a **control unit,** which can be in any one of a finite number of **internal states,** and which can change state in some defined manner. Figure 1.3 shows a schematic representation of a general automation.

An automaton is assumed to operate in a discrete time frame. At any given time, the control unit is in some internal state, and the input mechanism is scanning a particular symbol on the input file. The internal state of the control unit at the next time step is determined by the **next-state** or **transition function.** This transition function gives the next state in terms of the current state, the current input symbol, and the information currently in the temporary storage. During the transition from one time interval to the next, output may be produced or the information in the temporary storage changed. The term **configuration** will be used to refer to a particular state of the control unit, input file, and temporary storage. The transition of the automaton from one configuration to the next will be called a **move.**

This general model covers all the automata we will discuss in this book. A finite-state control will be common to all specific cases, but differences

Figure 1.3

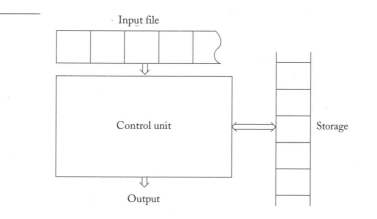

Input file

Control unit

Storage

Output

will arise from the way in which the output can be produced and the nature of the temporary storage. The nature of the temporary storage has the stronger effect on particular types of automata.

For subsequent discussions, it will be necessary to distinguish between **deterministic automata** and **nondeterministic automata.** A deterministic automaton is one in which each move is uniquely determined by the current configuration. If we know the internal state, the input, and the contents of the temporary storage, we can predict the future behavior of the automaton exactly. In a nondeterministic automaton, this is not so. At each point, a nondeterministic automaton may have several possible moves, so we can only predict a set of possible actions. The relation between deterministic and nondeterministic automata of various types will play a significant role in our study.

An automaton whose output response is limited to a simple "yes" or "no" is called an **accepter.** Presented with an input string, an accepter either accepts the string or rejects it. A more general automaton, capable of producing strings of symbols as output, is called a **transducer.** Although we will give some simple examples of transducers in the next section, our primary interest in this book is in accepters.

EXERCISES

1. Use induction on n to show that $|u^n| = n |u|$ for all strings u and all n.

2. The reverse of a string, introduced informally above, can be defined more precisely by the recursive roles

$$a^R = a,$$
$$(wa)^R = aw^R,$$

for all $a \in \Sigma$, $w \in \Sigma^*$. Use this to prove that

$$(uv)^R = v^R u^R,$$

for all $u, v \in \Sigma^+$. Ⓢ

3. Prove that $\left(w^R\right)^R = w$ for all $w \in \Sigma^*$.

4. Let $L = \{ab, aa, baa\}$. Which of the following strings are in L^*: $abaabaaabaa$, $aaaabaaaa$, $baaaaabaaaab$, $baaaaabaa$? Ⓢ

5. Consider the languages in Examples 1.12 and 1.13. For which is it true that $L = L^*$?

6. Are there languages for which $\overline{L^*} = \overline{L}^*$?

7. Prove that

$$(L_1 L_2)^R = L_2^R L_1^R$$

for all languages L_1 and L_2.

8. Show that $(L^*)^* = L^*$ for all languages.

9. Prove or disprove the following claims.

   (a) $(L_1 \cup L_2)^R = L_1^R \cup L_2^R$ for all languages L_1 and L_2.

   (b) $(L^R)^* = (L^*)^R$ for all languages L.

10. Find grammars for $\Sigma = \{a, b\}$ that generate the sets of

    (a) all strings with exactly one a,

    (b) all strings with at least one a,

    (c) all strings with no more than three a's.

    (d) all strings with at least three a's. **S**

    In each case, give convincing arguments that the grammar you give does indeed generate the indicated language.

11. Give a simple description of the language generated by the grammar with productions

    $$S \rightarrow aA,$$
    $$A \rightarrow bS,$$
    $$S \rightarrow \lambda. \quad \text{\textbf{S}}$$

12. What language does the grammar with these productions generate?

    $$S \rightarrow Aa,$$
    $$A \rightarrow B,$$
    $$B \rightarrow Aa. \quad \text{\textbf{S}}$$

13. For each of the following languages, find a grammar that generates it.

    (a) $L_1 = \{a^n b^m : n \geq 0, m > n\}$ **S**

    (b) $L_2 = \{a^n b^{2n} : n \geq 0\}$

    (c) $L_3 = \{a^{n+2} b^n : n \geq 1\}$

    (d) $L_4 = \{a^n b^{n-3} : n \geq 3\}$ **S**

    (e) $L_1 L_2$

    (f) $L_1 \cup L_2$

    (g) L_1^3

    (h) L_1^*

    (i) $L_1 - \overline{L_4}$

★14. Find grammars for the following languages on $\Sigma = \{a\}$.

    (a) $L = \{w : |w| \bmod 3 = 0\}$

    (b) $L = \{w : |w| \bmod 3 > 0\}$ **S**

    (c) $L = \{w : |w| \bmod 3 \neq |w| \bmod 2\}$

    (d) $L = \{w : |w| \bmod 3 \geq |w| \bmod 2\}$

15. Find a grammar that generates the language

$$L = \left\{ ww^R : w \in \{a, b\}^+ \right\}.$$

Give a complete justification for your answer.

16. Using the notation of Example 1.13, find grammars for the languages below. Assume $\Sigma = \{a, b\}$.

    (a) $L = \{w : n_a(w) = n_b(w) + 1\}$ **S**

    (b) $L = \{w : n_a(w) > n_b(w)\}$

★ (c) $L = \{w : n_a(w) = 2n_b(w)\}$

    (d) $L = \{w \in \{a, b\}^* : |n_a(w) - n_b(w)| = 1\}$

17. Repeat Exercises 16(a) and 16(d) with $\Sigma = \{a, b, c\}$

18. Complete the arguments in Example 1.14, showing that $L(G_1)$ does in fact generate the given language.

19. Are the two grammars with respective productions

$$S \rightarrow aSb\,|ab|\,\lambda,$$

and

$$S \rightarrow aAb|ab,$$
$$A \rightarrow aAb|\lambda,$$

equivalent? Assume that S is the start symbol in both cases.

20. Show that the grammar $G = (\{S\}, \{a, b\}, S, P)$, with productions

$$S \rightarrow SS\,|SSS|\,aSb\,|bSa|\,\lambda,$$

is equivalent to the grammar in Example 1.13.

★ 21. So far, we have given examples of only relatively simple grammars; every production had a single variable on the left side. As we will see, such grammars are very important, but Definition 1.1 allows more general forms. Consider the grammar $G = (\{A, B, C, D, E, S\}, \{a\}, S, P)$, with productions

$$S \rightarrow ABaC,$$
$$Ba \rightarrow aaB,$$
$$BC \rightarrow DC|E,$$
$$aD \rightarrow Da,$$
$$AD \rightarrow AB,$$
$$aE \rightarrow Ea,$$
$$AE \rightarrow \lambda.$$

Derive three different sentences in $L(G)$. From these, make a conjecture about $L(G)$.

1.3 Some Applications*

Although we stress the abstract and mathematical nature of formal languages and automata, it turns out that these concepts have widespread applications in computer science and are, in fact, a common theme that connects many specialty areas. In this section, we present some simple examples to give the reader some assurance that what we study here is not just a collection of abstractions, but is something that helps us understand many important, real problems.

Formal languages and grammars are used widely in connection with programming languages. In most of our programming, we work with a more or less intuitive understanding of the language in which we write. Occasionally though, when using an unfamiliar feature, we may need to refer to precise descriptions such as the syntax diagrams found in most programming texts. If we write a compiler, or if we wish to reason about the correctness of a program, a precise description of the language is needed at almost every step. Among the ways in which programming languages can be defined precisely, grammars are perhaps the most widely used.

The grammars that describe a typical language like Pascal or C are very extensive. For an example, let us take a smaller language that is part of this larger one.

Example 1.15   The set of all legal identifiers in Pascal is a language. Informally, it is the set of all strings starting with a letter and followed by an arbitrary number of letters or digits. The grammar below makes this informal definition precise.

$$\langle id \rangle \rightarrow \langle letter \rangle \langle rest \rangle,$$
$$\langle rest \rangle \rightarrow \langle letter \rangle \langle rest \rangle \,|\, \langle digit \rangle \langle rest \rangle \,|\, \lambda,$$
$$\langle letter \rangle \rightarrow a \,|\, b \,|\, \cdots \,|\, z$$
$$\langle digit \rangle \rightarrow 0 \,|\, 1 \,|\, \cdots \,|\, 9$$

In this grammar, the variables are $\langle id \rangle$, $\langle letter \rangle$, $\langle digit \rangle$, and $\langle rest \rangle$, and $a, b, ..., z, 0, 1, ..., 9$ the terminals. A derivation of the identifier $a0$ is

$$\langle id \rangle \Rightarrow \langle letter \rangle \langle rest \rangle$$
$$\Rightarrow a \langle rest \rangle$$
$$\Rightarrow a \langle digit \rangle \langle rest \rangle$$
$$\Rightarrow a0 \langle rest \rangle$$
$$\Rightarrow a0.$$

---

*As explained in the Preface, an asterisk following a heading indicates optional material.

Figure 1.4

$$\text{1} \xrightarrow{\quad\quad\quad\quad a \quad\quad\quad\quad} \text{2}$$

The definition of programming languages through grammars is common and very useful. But there are alternatives that are often convenient. For example, we can describe a language by an accepter, taking every string that is accepted as part of the language. To talk about this in a precise way, we will need to give a more formal definition of an automaton. We will do this shortly; for the moment, let us proceed in a more intuitive way.

An automaton can be represented by a graph in which the vertices give the internal states and the edges transitions. The labels on the edges show what happens (in terms of input and output) during the transition. For example, Figure 1.4 represents a transition from State 1 to State 2, which is taken when the input symbol is a. With this intuitive picture in mind, let us look at another way of describing Pascal identifiers.

Example 1.16   Figure 1.5 is an automaton that accepts all legal Pascal identifiers. Some interpretation is necessary. We assume that initially the automaton is in State 1; we indicate this by drawing an arrow (not originating in any vertex) to this state. As always, the string to be examined is read left to right, one character at each step. When the first symbol is a letter, the automaton goes into State 2, after which the rest of the string is immaterial. State 2 therefore represents the "yes" state of the accepter. Conversely, if the first symbol is a digit, the automaton will go into State 3, the "no" state, and remain there. In our solution, we assume that no input other than letters or digits is possible.

Figure 1.5

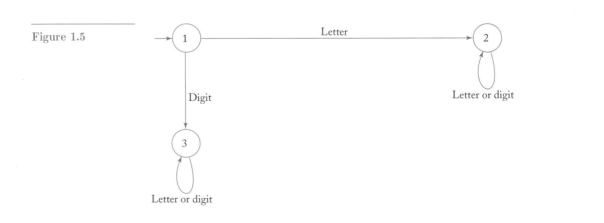

Compilers and other translators that convert a program from one language to another make extensive use of the ideas touched on in these examples. Programming languages can be defined precisely through grammars, as in Example 1.15, and both grammars and automata play a fundamental role in the decision processes by which a specific piece of code is accepted as satisfying the conditions of a programming language. The above example gives a first hint of how this is done; subsequent examples will expand on this observation.

Another important application area is digital design, where transducer concepts are prevalent. Although this is a subject that we will not treat extensively here, we will give a simple example. In principle, any digital computer can be viewed as an automaton, but such a view is not necessarily appropriate. Suppose we consider the internal registers and main memory of a computer as the automaton's control unit. Then the automaton has a total of 2^n internal states, where n is the total number of bits in the registers and memory. Even for small n, this is such a large number that the result is impossible to work with. But if we look at a much smaller unit, then automata theory becomes a useful design tool.

Example 1.17 A binary adder is an integral part of any general purpose computer. Such an adder takes two bit strings representing numbers, and produces their sum as output. For simplicity, let us assume that we are dealing only with positive integers and that we use a representation in which

$$x = a_0 a_1 \cdots a_n$$

stands for the integer

$$v(x) = \sum_{i=0}^{n} a_i 2^i.$$

This is the usual binary representation in reverse.

A serial adder processes two such numbers $x = a_0 a_1 \cdots a_n$, and $y = b_0 b_1 \cdots b_n$, bit by bit, starting at the left end. Each bit addition creates a digit for the sum as well as a carry digit for the next higher position. A binary addition table (Figure 1.6) summarizes the process.

A block diagram of the kind we saw when we first studied computers is given in Figure 1.7. It tells us that an adder is a box that accepts two bits and produces their sum bit and a possible carry. It describes what an adder does, but explains little about its internal workings. An automaton (now a transducer) can make this much more explicit.

The input to the transducer are the bit pairs (a_i, b_i), the output will be the sum bit d_i. Again, we represent the automaton by a graph now labeling

Figure 1.6

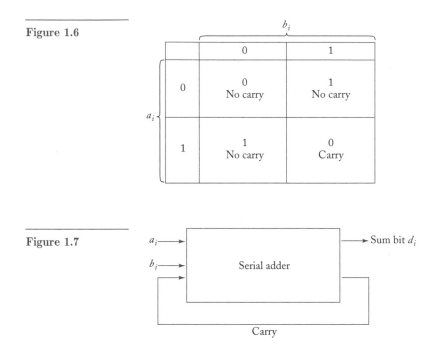

Figure 1.7

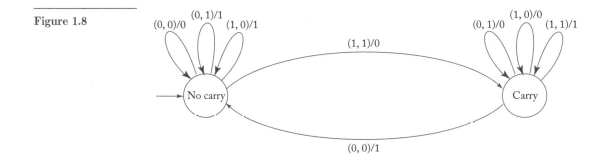

the edges $(a_i, b_i) / d_i$. The carry from one step to the next is remembered by the automaton via two internal states labeled "carry" and "no carry." Initially, the transducer will be in state "no carry." It will remain in this state until a bit pair $(1, 1)$ is encountered; this will generate a carry that takes the automaton into the "carry" state. The presence of a carry is then taken into account when the next bit pair is read. A complete picture of a serial adder is given in Figure 1.8. Follow this through with a few examples to convince yourself that it works correctly.

As this example indicates, the automaton serves as a bridge between the very high-level, functional description of a circuit and its logical implementation through transistors, gates, and flip-flops. The automaton clearly shows the decision logic, yet it is formal enough to lend itself to precise

Figure 1.8

mathematical manipulation. For this reason, digital design methods rely heavily on concepts from automata theory. The interested reader should look at a typical text on this topic, for example Kovahi 1978.

Exercises

1. Give a grammar for the set integer numbers in C. Ⓢ

2. Design an accepter for integers in C.

3. Give a grammar that generates all reals in C.

4. Suppose that a certain programming language permits only identifiers that begin with a letter, contain at least one but no more than three digits, and can have any number of letters. Give a grammar and an accepter for such a set of identifiers.

5. Give a grammar for the **var** declaration in Pascal.

6. In the roman number system, numbers are represented by strings on the alphabet $\{M, D, C, L, X, V, I\}$. Design an accepter that accepts such strings only if they are properly formed roman numbers. For simplicity, replace the "subtraction" convention in which the number nine is represented by IX with an addition equivalent that uses VIIII instead.

7. We assumed that an automaton works in a framework of discrete time steps, but this aspect has little influence on our subsequent discussion. In digital design, however, the time element assumes considerable significance.

   In order to synchronize signals arriving from different parts of the computer, delay circuitry is needed. A unit-delay transducer is one that simply reproduces the input (viewed as a continual stream of symbols) one time unit later. Specifically, if the transducer reads as input a symbol a at time t, it will reproduce that symbol as output at time $t + 1$. At time $t = 0$, the transducer outputs nothing. We indicate this by saying that the transducer translates input $a_1 a_2 \cdots$ into output $\lambda a_1 a_2 \cdots$.

   Draw a graph showing how such a unit-delay transducer might be designed for $\Sigma = \{a, b\}$. Ⓢ

8. An n-unit delay transducer is one that reproduces the input n time units later; that is, the input $a_1 a_2 \cdots$ is translated into $\lambda^n a_1 a_2 \cdots$, meaning again that the transducer produces no output for the first n time slots.

   (a) Construct a two-unit delay transducer on $\Sigma = \{a, b\}$.

   (b) Show that an n-unit delay transducer must have at least $|\Sigma|^n$ states.

9. The two's complement of a binary string, representing a positive integer, is formed by first complementing each bit, then adding one to the lowest-order bit. Design a transducer for translating bit strings into their two's complement, assuming that the binary number is represented as in Example 1.17, with lower-order bits at the left of the string.

10. Design a transducer to convert a binary string into octal. For example, the bit string 001101110 should produce the output 156.   **S**

11. Let $a_1 a_2 \cdots$ be an input bit string. Design a transducer that computes the parity of every substring of three bits. Specifically, the transducer should produce output

$$\pi_1 = \pi_2 = 0,$$
$$\pi_i = (a_{i-2} + a_{i-1} + a_i) \bmod 2, i = 3, 4, \ldots$$

For example, the input 110111 should produce 000001.   **S**

12. Design a transducer that accepts bit strings $a_1 a_2 a_3 \ldots$ and computes the binary value of each set of three consecutive bits modulo five. More specifically, the transducer should produce $m_1, m_2, m_3, \ldots$, where

$$m_1 = m_2 = 0,$$
$$m_i = (4a_i + 2a_{i-1} + a_{i-2}) \bmod 5, \quad i = 3, 4, \ldots$$

13. Digital computers normally represent all information by bit strings, using some type of encoding. For example, character information can be encoded using the well-known ASCII system.

    For this exercise, consider the two alphabets $\{a, b, c, d\}$ and $\{0, 1\}$, respectively, and an encoding from the first to the second, defined by $a \rightarrow 00$, $b \rightarrow 01$, $c \rightarrow 10$, $d \rightarrow 11$. Construct a transducer for decoding strings on $\{0, 1\}$ into the original message. For example, the input 010011 should generate as output *bad*.

14. Let x and y be two positive binary numbers. Design a transducer whose output is $max(x, y)$.

Chapter 2

FINITE
AUTOMATA

ur introduction in the first chapter to the basic concepts of computation, particularly the discussion of automata, was brief and informal. At this point, we have only a general understanding of what an automaton is and how it can be represented by a graph. To progress, we must be more precise, provide formal definitions, and start to develop rigorous results. We begin with finite accepters, which are a simple, special case of the general scheme introduced in the last chapter. This type of automaton is characterized by having no temporary storage. Since an input file cannot be rewritten, a finite automaton is severely limited in its capacity to "remember" things during the computation. A finite amount of information can be retained in the control unit by placing the unit into a specific state. But since the number of such states is finite, a finite automaton can only deal with situations in which the information to be stored at any time is strictly bounded. The automaton in Example 1.16 is an instance of a finite accepter.

_____

2.1 Deterministic Finite Accepters

The first type of automaton we study in detail are finite accepters that are deterministic in their operation. We start with a precise formal definition of deterministic accepters.

Deterministic Accepters and Transition Graphs

Definition 2.1

A **deterministic finite accepter** or **dfa** is defined by the quintuple

$$M = (Q, \Sigma, \delta, q_0, F),$$

where

> Q is a finite set of **internal states,**
> Σ is a finite set of symbols called the **input alphabet,**
> $\delta : Q \times \Sigma \to Q$ is a total function called the **transition function,**
> $q_0 \in Q$ is the **initial state,**
> $F \subseteq Q$ is a set of **final states.**

A deterministic finite accepter operates in the following manner. At the initial time, it is assumed to be in the initial state q_0, with its input mechanism on the leftmost symbol of the input string. During each move of the automaton, the input mechanism advances one position to the right, so each move consumes one input symbol. When the end of the string is reached, the string is accepted if the automaton is in one of its final states. Otherwise the string is rejected. The input mechanism can move only from left to right and reads exactly one symbol on each step. The transitions from one internal state to another are governed by the transition function δ. For example, if

$$\delta (q_0, a) = q_1,$$

then if the dfa is in state q_0 and the current input symbol is a, the dfa will go into state q_1.

In discussing automata, it is essential to have a clear and intuitive picture to work with. To visualize and represent finite automata, we use **transition graphs,** in which the vertices represent states and the edges represent transitions. The labels on the vertices are the names of the states, while the labels on the edges are the current values of the input symbol. For example, if q_0 and q_1 are internal states of some dfa M, then the graph associated with M will have one vertex labeled q_0 and another labeled q_1. An edge (q_0, q_1) labeled a represents the transition $\delta (q_0, a) = q_1$. The initial

Figure 2.1

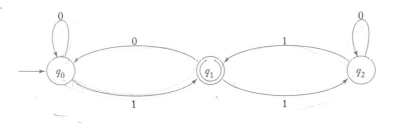

state will be identified by an incoming unlabeled arrow not originating at any vertex. Final states are drawn with a double circle.

More formally, if $M = (Q, \Sigma, \delta, q_0, F)$ is a deterministic finite accepter, then its associated transition graph G_M has exactly $|Q|$ vertices, each one labeled with a different $q_i \in Q$. For every transition rule $\delta(q_i, a) = q_j$, the graph has an edge (q_i, q_j) labeled a. The vertex associated with q_0 is called the **initial vertex**, while those labeled with $q_f \in F$ are the **final vertices.** It is a trivial matter to convert from the $(Q, \Sigma, \delta, q_0, F)$ definition of a dfa to its transition graph representation and vice versa.

Example 2.1

The graph in Figure 2.1 represents the dfa

$$M = (\{q_0, q_1, q_2\}, \{0, 1\}, \delta, q_0, \{q_1\}),$$

where δ is given by

$$\delta(q_0, 0) = q_0, \qquad \delta(q_0, 1) = q_1,$$
$$\delta(q_1, 0) = q_0, \qquad \delta(q_1, 1) = q_2,$$
$$\delta(q_2, 0) = q_2, \qquad \delta(q_2, 1) = q_1.$$

This dfa accepts the string 01. Starting in state q_0, the symbol 0 is read first. Looking at the edges of the graph, we see that the automaton remains in state q_0. Next, the 1 is read and the automaton goes into state q_1. We are now at the end of the string and, at the same time, in a final state q_1. Therefore, the string 01 is accepted. The dfa does not accept the string 00, since after reading two consecutive 0's, it will be in state q_0. By similar reasoning, we see that the automaton will accept the strings 101, 0111, and 11001, but not 100 or 1100.

It is convenient to introduce the extended transition function $\delta^* : Q \times \Sigma^* \to Q$. The second argument of δ^* is a string, rather than a single symbol, and its value gives the state the automaton will be in after reading that string. For example, if

$$\delta(q_0, a) = q_1$$

and

$$\delta\left(q_1, b\right) = q_2,$$

then

$$\delta^*\left(q_0, ab\right) = q_2.$$

Formally, we can define δ^* recursively by

$$\left\{ \begin{array}{ll} \delta^*\left(q, \lambda\right) = q, & (2.1) \\ \delta^*\left(q, wa\right) = \delta\left(\delta^*\left(q, w\right), a\right), & (2.2) \end{array} \right.$$

for all $q \in Q$, $w \in \Sigma^*$, $a \in \Sigma$. To see why this is appropriate, let us apply these definitions to the simple case above. First, we use (2.2) to get

$$\delta^*\left(q_0, ab\right) = \delta\left(\delta^*\left(q_0, a\right), b\right). \qquad (2.3)$$

But

$$\begin{aligned} \delta^*\left(q_0, a\right) &= \delta\left(\delta^*\left(q_0, \lambda\right), a\right) \\ &= \delta\left(q_0, a\right) \\ &= q_1. \end{aligned}$$

Substituting this into (2.3), we get

$$\delta^*\left(q_0, ab\right) = \delta\left(q_1, b\right) = q_2,$$

as expected.

Languages and Dfa's

Having made a precise definition of an accepter, we are now ready to define formally what we mean by an associated language. The association is obvious: the language is the set of all the strings accepted by the automaton.

Definition 2.2

The language accepted by a dfa $M = (Q, \Sigma, \delta, q_0, F)$ is the set of all strings on Σ accepted by M. In formal notation,

$$L\left(M\right) = \left\{w \in \Sigma^* : \delta^*\left(q_0, w\right) \in F\right\}.$$

Note that we require that δ, and consequently δ^*, be total functions. At each step, a unique move is defined, so that we are justified in calling such an automaton deterministic. A dfa will process every string in Σ^* and either accept it or not accept it. Nonacceptance means that the dfa stops in a nonfinal state, so that

$$\overline{L(M)} = \{w \in \Sigma^* : \delta^*(q_0, w) \notin F\}.$$

Example 2.2   Consider the dfa in Figure 2.2

In drawing Figure 2.2 we allowed the use of two labels on a single edge. Such multiply labeled edges are shorthand for two or more distinct transitions: the transition is taken whenever the input symbol matches any of the edge labels.

The automaton in Figure 2.2 remains in its initial state q_0 until the first b is encountered. If this is also the last symbol of the input, then the string is accepted. If not, the dfa goes into state q_2, from which it can never escape. The state q_2 is a **trap state.** We see clearly from the graph that the automaton accepts all strings consisting of an arbitrary number of a's, followed by a single b. All other input strings are rejected. In set notation, the language accepted by the automaton is

$$L = \{a^n b : n \geq 0\}.$$

These examples show how convenient transition graphs are for working with finite automata. While it is possible to base all arguments strictly on the properties of the transition function and its extension through (2.1) and (2.2), the results are hard to follow. In our discussion, we use graphs, which are more intuitive, as far as possible. To do so, we must of course have some assurance that we are not misled by the representation and that arguments based on graphs are as valid as those that use the formal properties of δ. The following preliminary result gives us this assurance.

Figure 2.2

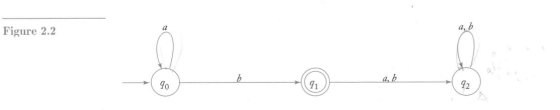

Theorem 2.1

Let $M = (Q, \Sigma, \delta, q_0, F)$ be a deterministic finite accepter, and let G_M be its associated transition graph. Then for every q_i, $q_j \in Q$, and $w \in \Sigma^+$, $\delta^* (q_i, w) = q_j$ if and only if there is in G_M a walk with label w from q_i to q_j.

Proof: This claim is fairly obvious from an examination of such simple cases as Example 2.1. It can be proved rigorously using an induction on the length of w. Assume that the claim is true for all strings v with $|v| \leq n$. Consider then any w of length $n + 1$ and write it as

$$w = va.$$

Suppose now that $\delta^* (q_i, v) = q_k$. Since $|v| = n$, there must be a walk in G_M labeled v from q_i to q_k. But if $\delta^* (q_i, w) = q_j$, then M must have a transition $\delta (q_k, a) = q_j$, so that by construction G_M has an edge (q_k, q_j) with label a. Thus there is a walk in G_M labeled $va = w$ between q_i and q_j. Since the result is obviously true for $n = 1$, we can claim by induction that, for every $w \in \Sigma^+$,

$$\delta^* (q_i, w) = q_j \tag{2.4}$$

implies that there is a walk in G_M from q_i to q_j labeled w.

The argument can be turned around in a straightforward way to show that the existence of such a path implies (2.4), thus completing the proof. ■

Again, the result of the theorem is so intuitively obvious that a formal proof seems unnecessary. We went through the details for two reasons. The first is that it is a simple, yet typical example of an inductive proof in connection with automata. The second is that the result will be used over and over, so stating and proving it as a theorem lets us argue quite confidently using graphs. This makes our examples and proofs more transparent than they would be if we used the properties of δ^*.

While graphs are convenient for visualizing automata, other representations are also useful. For example, we can represent the function δ as a table. The table in Figure 2.3 is equivalent to Figure 2.2. Here the row label is the current state, while the column label represents the current input symbol. The entry in the table defines the next state.

It is apparent from this example that a dfa can easily be implemented as a computer program; for example, as a simple table-lookup or as a sequence of "if" statements. The best implementation or representation depends on the specific application. Transition graphs are very convenient for the kinds of arguments we want to make here, so we use them in most of our discussions.

In constructing automata for languages defined informally, we employ reasoning similar to that for programming in higher-level languages. But the

Figure 2.3

	a	b
q_0	q_0	q_1
q_1	q_2	q_2
q_2	q_2	q_2

programming of a dfa is tedious and sometimes conceptually complicated by the fact that such an automaton has few powerful features.

Example 2.3   Find a deterministic finite accepter that recognizes the set of all strings on $\Sigma = \{a, b\}$ starting with the prefix ab.

The only issue here is the first two symbols in the string; after they have been read, no further decisions need to be made. We can therefore solve the problem with an automaton that has four states; an initial state, two states for recognizing ab ending in a final trap state, and one nonfinal trap state. If the first symbol is an a and the second is a b, the automaton goes to the final trap state, where it will stay since the rest of the input does not matter. On the other hand, if the first symbol is not an a or the second one is not a b, the automaton enters the nonfinal trap state. The simple solution is shown in Figure 2.4.

Figure 2.4

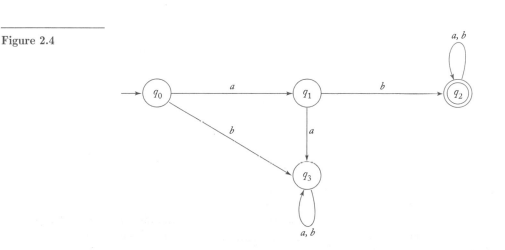

Figure 2.5

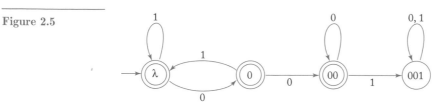

Example 2.4   Find a dfa that accepts all the strings on $\{0, 1\}$, except those containing the substring 001.

In deciding whether the substring 001 has occurred, we need to know not only the current input symbol, but we also need to remember whether or not it has been preceded by one or two 0s. We can keep track of this by putting the automaton into specific states and labeling them accordingly. Like variable names in a programming language, state names are arbitrary and can be chosen for mnemonic reasons. For example, the state in which two 0s were the immediately preceding symbols can be labeled simply 00.

If the string starts with 001, then it must be rejected. This implies that there must be a path labeled 001 from the initial state to a nonfinal state. For convenience, this nonfinal state is labeled 001. This state must be a trap state, because later symbols do not matter. All other states are accepting states.

This gives us the basic structure of the solution, but we still must add provisions for the substring 001 occurring in the middle of the input. We must define Q and δ so that whatever we need to make the correct decision is remembered by the automaton. In this case, when a symbol is read, we need to know some part of string to the left, for example, whether or not the two previous symbols were 00. If we label the states with the relevant symbols, it is very easy to see what the transitions must be. For example,

$$\delta(00, 0) = 00,$$

because this situation arises only if there are three consecutive 0s. We are only interested in the last two, a fact we remember by keeping the dfa in the state 00. A complete solution is shown in Figure 2.5. We see from this example how useful mnemonic labels on the states are for keeping track of things. Trace a few strings, such as 100100 and 1010100, to see that the solution is indeed correct.

Regular Languages

Every finite automaton accepts some language. If we consider all possible finite automata, we get a set of languages associated with them. We will call such a set of languages a **family.** The family of languages that is accepted by deterministic finite accepters is quite limited. The structure and properties of the languages in this family will become clearer as our study proceeds; for the moment we will simply attach a name to this family.

Definition 2.3

A language L is called **regular** if and only if there exists some deterministic finite accepter M such that

$$L = L(M).$$

Example 2.5   Show that the language

$$L = \{awa : w \in \{a, b\}^*\}$$

is regular. To show that this or any other language is regular, all we have to do is find a dfa for it. The construction of a dfa for this language is similar to Example 2.3, but a little more complicated. What this dfa must do is check whether a string begins and ends with an a; what is between is immaterial. The solution is complicated by the fact that there is no explicit way of testing the end of the string. This difficulty is overcome by simply putting the dfa into a final state whenever the second a is encountered. If this is not the end of the string, and another b is found, it will take the dfa out of the final state. Scanning continues in this way, each a taking the automaton back to its final state. The complete solution is shown in Figure 2.6. Again, trace a few examples to see why this works. After one or two tests, it will be obvious that the dfa accepts a string if and only if it begins and ends with an a. Since we have constructed a dfa for the language, we can claim that, by definition, the language is regular.

Example 2.6   Let L be the language in Example 2.5. Show that L^2 is regular. Again we show that the language is regular by constructing a dfa for it. We can write an explicit expression for L^2, namely,

$$L^2 = \{aw_1aaw_2a : w_1, w_2 \in \{a, b\}^*\}.$$

Therefore, we need a dfa that recognizes two consecutive strings of essentially the same form (but not necessarily identical in value). The diagram

Figure 2.6

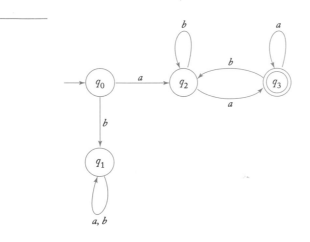

in Figure 2.6 can be used as a starting point, but the vertex q_3 has to be modified. This state can no longer be final since, at this point, we must start to look for a second substring of the form awa. To recognize the second substring, we replicate the states of the first part (with new names), with q_3 as the beginning of the second part. Since the complete string can be broken into its constituent parts wherever aa occurs, we let the first occurrence of two consecutive a's be the trigger that gets the automaton into its second part. We can do this by making $\delta(q_3, a) = q_4$. The complete solution is in Figure 2.7. This dfa accepts L^2, which is therefore regular.

Figure 2.7

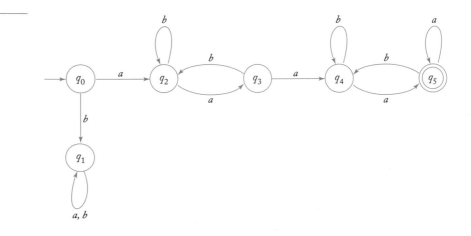

The last example suggests the conjecture that if a language L is regular, so are $L^2, L^3, ...$ We will see later that this is indeed correct.

EXERCISES

1. Which of the strings 0001, 01001, 0000110 are accepted by the dfa in Figure 2.1?

2. For $\Sigma = \{a, b\}$, construct dfa's that accept the sets consisting of

   (a) all strings with exactly one a,

   (b) all strings with at least one a,

   (c) all strings with no more than three a's, **S**

   (d) all strings with at least one a and exactly two b's.

   (e) all the strings with exactly two a's and more than two b's.

3. Show that if we change Figure 2.6, making q_3 a nonfinal state and making q_0, q_1, q_2 final states, the resulting dfa accepts $\overline{L}$.

4. Generalize the observation in the previous exercise. Specifically, show that if $M = (Q, \Sigma, \delta, q_0, F)$ and $\widehat{M} = (Q, \Sigma, \delta, q_0, Q - F)$ are two dfa's then $\overline{L(M)} = L\left(\widehat{M}\right)$.

5. Give dfa's for the languages

   (a) $L = \left\{ ab^5 w b^4 : w \in \{a, b\}^* \right\}$ **S**

   (b) $L = \{w_1 ab w_2 : w_1 \in \{a, b\}^*, w_2 \in \{a, b\}^*\}$

6. Give a set notation description of the language accepted by the automaton depicted in the following diagram. Can you think of a simple verbal characterization of the language?

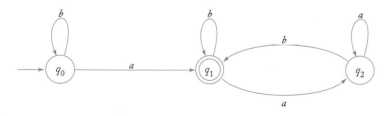

7. Find dfa's for the following languages on $\Sigma = \{a, b\}$.

   (a) $L = \{w : |w| \bmod 3 = 0\}$ **S**

   (b) $L = \{w : |w| \bmod 5 \neq 0\}$

   (c) $L = \{w : n_a(w) \bmod 3 > 1\}$

   (d) $L = \{w : n_a(w) \bmod 3 > n_b(w) \bmod 3\}$ **S**

(e) $L = \{w : (n_a(w) - n_b(w)) \bmod 3 > 0\}$

(f) $L = \{w : |n_a(w) - n_b(w)| \bmod 3 < 2\}$

★ 8. A run in a string is a substring of length at least two, as long as possible and consisting entirely of the same symbol. For instance, the string *abbbaab* contains a run of *b*'s of length three and a run of *a*'s of length two. Find dfa's for the following languages on $\{a, b\}$.

(a) $L = \{w : w \text{ contains no runs of length less than four}\}$

(b) $L = \{w : \text{ every run of } a\text{'s has length either two or three}\}$

(c) $L = \{w : \text{ there are at most two runs of } a\text{'s of length three}\}$

(d) $L = \{w : \text{ there are exactly two runs of } a\text{'s of length 3}\}$

9. Consider the set of strings on $\{0, 1\}$ defined by the requirements below. For each construct an accepting dfa.

(a) Every 00 is followed immediately by a 1. For example, the strings 101, 0010, 0010011001 are in the language, but 0001 and 00100 are not. **S**

(b) all strings containing 00 but not 000.

(c) The leftmost symbol differs from the rightmost one.

(d) Every substring of four symbols has at most two 0's. For example, 001110 and 011001 are in the language, but 10010 is not since one of its substrings, 0010, contains three zeros. **S**

(e) All strings of length five or more in which the fourth symbol from the right end is different from the leftmost symbol.

(f) All strings in which the leftmost two symbols and the rightmost two symbols are identical.

★ 10. Construct a dfa that accepts strings on $\{0, 1\}$ if and only if the value of the string, interpreted as a binary representation of an integer, is zero modulo five. For example, 0101 and 1111, representing the integers 5 and 15, respectively, are to be accepted.

11. Show that the language $L = \{vwv : v, w \in \{a, b\}^*, |v| = 2\}$ is regular.

12. Show that $L = \{a^n : n \geq 4\}$ is regular.

13. Show that the language $L = \{a^n : n \geq 0, n \neq 4\}$ is regular. **S**

14. Show that the language $L = \{a^n : n = i + jk, i, k \text{ fixed}, j = 0, 1, 2, ...\}$ is regular.

15. Show that the set of all real numbers in C is a regular language.

16. Show that if L is regular, so is $L - \{\lambda\}$.

17. Use (2.1) and (2.2) to show that

$$\delta^*(q, wv) = \delta^*(\delta^*(q, w), v)$$

for all $w, v \in \Sigma^*$.

18. Let L be the language accepted by the automaton in Figure 2.2. Find a dfa that accepts L^2.

19. Let L be the language accepted by the automaton in Figure 2.2. Find a dfa for the language $L^2 - L$.

20. Let L be the language in Example 2.5. Show that L^* is regular.

21. Let G_M be the transition graph for some dfa M. Prove the following.

    (a) If $L(M)$ is infinite, then G_M must have at least one cycle for which there is a path from the initial vertex to some vertex in the cycle and a path from some vertex in the cycle to some final vertex.

    (b) If $L(M)$ is finite, then no such cycle exists. **S**

22. Let us define an operation *truncate*, which removes the rightmost symbol from any string. For example, *truncate* $(aaaba)$ is $aaab$. The operation can be extended to languages by

    $$truncate\,(L) = \{truncate\,(w) : w \in L\}.$$

    Show how, given a dfa for any regular language L, one can construct a dfa for *truncate* (L). From this, prove that if L is a regular language not containing λ, then *truncate* (L) is also regular.

23. Let $x = a_0 a_1 \cdots a_n, y = b_0 b_1 \cdots b_n, z = c_0 c_1 \cdots c_n$ be binary numbers as defined in Example 1.17. Show that the set of strings of triplets

    $$\begin{pmatrix} a_0 \\ b_0 \\ c_0 \end{pmatrix} \begin{pmatrix} a_1 \\ b_1 \\ c_1 \end{pmatrix} \cdots \begin{pmatrix} a_n \\ b_n \\ c_n \end{pmatrix},$$

    where the a_i, b_i, c_i are such that $x + y = z$ is a regular language.

24. While the language accepted by a given dfa is unique, there are normally many dfa's that accept a language. Find a dfa with exactly six states that accepts the same language as the dfa in Figure 2.4. **S**

2.2 Nondeterministic Finite Accepters

Finite accepters are more complicated if we allow them to act nondeterministically. Nondeterminism is a powerful, but at first sigh, unusual idea. We normally think of computers as completely deterministic, and the element of choice seems out of place. Nevertheless, nondeterminism is a useful notion, as we shall see as we proceed.

Definition of a Nondeterministic Accepter

Nondeterminism means a choice of moves for an automaton. Rather than prescribing a unique move in each situation, we allow a set of possible moves. Formally, we achieve this by defining the transition function so that its range is a set of possible states.

Definition 2.4

A **nondeterministic finite accepter** or **nfa** is defined by the quintuple

$$M = (Q, \Sigma, \delta, q_0, F),$$

where Q, Σ, q_0, F are defined as for deterministic finite accepters, but

$$\delta : Q \times (\Sigma \cup \{\lambda\}) \rightarrow 2^Q.$$

Note that there are three major differences between this definition and the definition of a dfa. In a nondeterministic accepter, the range of δ is in the powerset 2^Q, so that its value is not a single element of Q, but a subset of it. This subset defines the set of all possible states that can be reached by the transition. If, for instance, the current state is q_1, the symbol a is read, and

$$\delta(q_1, a) = \{q_0, q_2\},$$

then either q_0 or q_2 could be the next state of the nfa. Also, we allow λ as the second argument of δ. This means that the nfa can make a transition without consuming an input symbol. Although we still assume that the input mechanism can only travel to the right, it is possible that it is stationary on some moves. Finally, in an nfa, the set $\delta(q_i, a)$ may be empty, meaning that there is no transition defined for this specific situation.

Like dfa's, nondeterministic accepters can be represented by transition graphs. The vertices are determined by Q, while an edge (q_i, q_j) with label a is in the graph if and only if $\delta(q_i, a)$ contains q_j. Note that since a may be the empty string, there can be some edges labeled λ.

A string is accepted by an nfa if there is some sequence of possible moves that will put the machine in a final state at the end of the string. A string is rejected (that is, not accepted) only if there is no possible sequence of moves by which a final state can be reached. Nondeterminism can therefore be viewed as involving "intuitive" insight by which the best move can be chosen at every state (assuming that the nfa wants to accept every string).

Figure 2.8

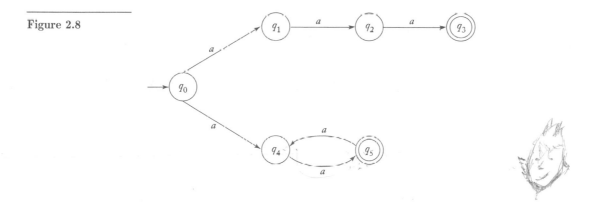

Example 2.7   Consider the transition graph in Figure 2.8. It describes a nondeterministic accepter since there are two transitions labeled a out of q_0.

Example 2.8   A nondeterministic automaton is shown in Figure 2.9. It is nondeterministic not only because several edges with the same label originate from one vertex, but also because it has a λ-transition. Some transition, such as $\delta(q_2, 0)$ are unspecified in the graph. This is to be interpreted as a transition to the empty set, that is, $\delta(q_2, 0) = \varnothing$. The automaton accepts strings λ, 1010, and 101010, but not 110 and 10100. Note that for 10 there are two alternative walks, one leading to q_0, the other to q_2. Even though q_2 is not a final state, the string is accepted because one walk leads to a final state.

Again, the transition function can be extended so its second argument is a string. We require of the extended transition function δ^* that if

$$\delta^*(q_i, w) = Q_j,$$

then Q_j is the set of all possible states the automaton may be in, having started in state q_i and having read w. A recursive definition of δ^*, analogous to (2.1) and (2.2), is possible, but not particularly enlightening. A more easily appreciated definition can be made through transition graphs.

Figure 2.9

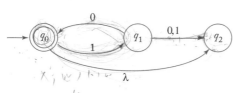

Definition 2.5

For an nfa, the extended transition function is defined so that $\delta^* (q_i, w)$ contains q_j if and only if there is a walk in the transition graph from q_i to q_j labeled w. This holds for all $q_i, q_j \in Q$ and $w \in \Sigma^*$.

Example 2.9   Figure 2.10 represents an nfa. It has several λ-transitions and some undefined transitions such as $\delta (q_2, a)$.

Suppose we want to find $\delta^* (q_1, a)$ and $\delta^* (q_2, \lambda)$. There is a walk labeled a involving two λ-transitions from q_1 to itself. By using some of the λ-edges twice, we see that there are also walks involving λ-transitions to q_0 and q_2. Thus

$$\delta^* (q_1, a) = \{q_0, q_1, q_2\} .$$

Since there is a λ-edge between q_2 and q_0, we have immediately that $\delta^* (q_2, \lambda)$ contains q_0. Also, since any state can be reached from itself by making no move, and consequently using no input symbol, $\delta^* (q_2, \lambda)$ also contains q_2. Therefore

$$\delta^* (q_2, \lambda) = \{q_0, q_2\} .$$

Using as many λ-transitions as needed, you can also check that

$$\delta^* (q_2, aa) = \{q_0, q_1, q_2\} .$$

The definition of δ^* through labeled walks is somewhat informal, so it is useful to look at it a little more closely. Definition 2.5 is proper, since between any vertices v_i and v_j there is either a walk labeled w or there is not, indicating that δ^* is completely defined. What is perhaps a little harder to see is that this definition can always be used to find $\delta^* (q_i, w)$.

In Section 1.1, we described an algorithm for finding all simple paths between two vertices. We cannot use this algorithm directly since, as Example 2.9 shows, a labeled walk is not always a simple path. We can modify the simple path algorithm, removing the restriction that no vertex or edge

Figure 2.10

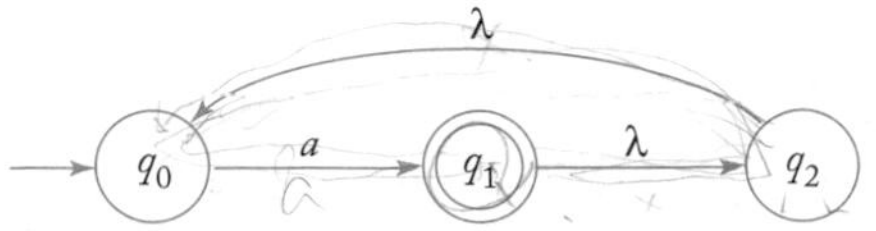

can be repeated. The new algorithm will now generate successively all walks of length one, length two, length three, and so on.

There is still a difficulty. Given a w, how long can a walk labeled w be? This is not immediately obvious. In Example 2.9, the walk labeled a between q_1 and q_2 has length four. The problem is caused by the λ-transitions, which lengthen the walk but do not contribute to the label. The situation is saved by this observation: If between two vertices v_i and v_j there is any walk labeled w, then there must be some walk labeled w of length no more than $\Lambda + (1 + \Lambda) |w|$, where Λ is the number of λ-edges in the graph. The argument for this is: While λ-edges may be repeated, there is always a walk in which every repeated λ-edge is separated by an edge labeled with a nonempty symbol. Otherwise, the walk contains a cycle labeled λ, which can be replaced by a simple path without changing the label of the walk. We leave a formal proof of this claim as an exercise.

With this observation, we have a method for computing $\delta^* (q_i, w)$. We evaluate all walks of length at most $\Lambda + (1 + \Lambda) |w|$ originating at v_i. We select from them those that are labeled w. The terminating vertices of the selected walks are the elements of the set $\delta^* (q_i, w)$.

As we have remarked, it is possible to define δ^* in a recursive fashion as was done for the deterministic case. The result is unfortunately not very transparent, and arguments with the extended transition function defined this way are hard to follow. We prefer to use the more intuitive and more manageable alternative in Definition 2.5.

As for dfa's, the language accepted by an nfa is defined formally by the extended transition function.

Definition 2.6

The language L accepted by an nfa $M = (Q, \Sigma, \delta, q_0, F)$ is defined as the set of all strings accepted in the above sense. Formally,

$$L(M) = \{w \in \Sigma^* : \delta^* (q_0, w) \cap F \neq \varnothing\}.$$

In words, the language consists of all strings w for which there is a walk labeled w from the initial vertex of the transition graph to some final vertex.

Example 2.10 What is the language accepted by the automaton in Figure 2.9? It is easy to see from the graph that the only way the nfa can stop in a final state is if the input is either a repetition of the string 10 or the empty string. Therefore the automaton accepts the language $L = \{(10)^n : n \geq 0\}$.

What happens when this automaton is presented with the string $w = 110$? After reading the prefix 11, the automaton finds itself in state q_2, with the transition $\delta(q_2, 0)$ undefined. We call such a situation a **dead configuration,** and we can visualize it as the automaton simply stopping without further action. But we must always keep in mind that such visualizations are imprecise and carry with them some danger of misinterpretation. What we can say precisely is that

$$\delta^*(q_0, 110) = \varnothing.$$

Thus, no final state can be reached by processing $w = 110$, and hence the string is not accepted.

Why Nondeterminism?

In reasoning about nondeterministic machines, we should be quite cautious in using intuitive notions. Intuition can easily lead us astray, and we must be able to give precise arguments to substantiate our conclusions. Nondeterminism is a difficult concept. Digital computers are completely deterministic; their state at any time is uniquely predictable from the input and the initial state. Thus it is natural to ask why we study nondeterministic machines at all. We are trying to model real systems, so why include such nonmechanical features as choice? We can answer this question in various ways.

Many deterministic algorithms require that one make a choice at some stage. A typical example is a game-playing program. Frequently, the best move is not known, but can be found using an exhaustive search with backtracking. When several alternatives are possible, we choose one and follow it until it becomes clear whether or not it was best. If not, we retreat to the last decision point and explore the other choices. A nondeterministic algorithm that can make the best choice would be able to solve the problem without backtracking, but a deterministic one can simulate nondeterminism with some extra work. For this reason, nondeterministic machines can serve as models of search-and-backtrack algorithms.

Nondeterminism is sometimes helpful in solving problems easily. Look at the nfa in Figure 2.8. It is clear that there is a choice to be made. The first alternative leads to the acceptance of the string a^3, while the second accepts all strings with an even number of a's. The language accepted by the nfa is $\left\{a^3\right\} \cup \left\{a^{2n} : n \geq 1\right\}$. While it is possible to find a dfa for this language, the nondeterminism is quite natural. The language is the union of two quite different sets, and the nondeterminism lets us decide at the outset which case we want. The deterministic solution is not as obviously related to the definition. As we go on, we will see other and more convincing examples of the usefulness of nondeterminism.

In the same vein, nondeterminism is an effective mechanism for describing some complicated languages concisely. Notice that the definition of a grammar involves a nondeterministic element. In

$$S \rightarrow aSb | \lambda$$

we can at any point choose either the first or the second production. This lets us specify many different strings using only two rules.

Finally, there is a technical reason for introducing nondeterminism. As we will see, certain results are more easily established for nfa's than for dfa's. Our next major result indicates that there is no essential difference between these two types of automata. Consequently, allowing nondeterminism often simplifies formal arguments without affecting the generality of the conclusion.

EXERCISES

1. Prove in detail the claim made in the previous section that if in a transition graph there is a walk labeled w, there must be some walk labeled w of length no more than $\Lambda + (1 + \Lambda) |w|$.

2. Find a dfa that accepts the language defined by the nfa in Figure 2.8.

3. In Figure 2.9, find $\delta^* (q_0, 1011)$ and $\delta^* (q_1, 01)$.

4. In Figure 2.10, find $\delta^* (q_0, a)$ and $\delta^* (q_1, \lambda)$. Ⓢ

5. For the nfa in Figure 2.9, find $\delta^* (q_0, 1010)$ and $\delta^* (q_1, 00)$.

6. Design an nfa with no more than five states for the set $\{abab^n : n \geq 0\} \cup \{aba^n : n \geq 0\}$.

7. Construct an nfa with three states that accepts the language $\{ab, abc\}^*$. Ⓢ

8. Do you think Exercise 7 can be solved with fewer than three states? Ⓢ

9. (a) Find an nfa with three states that accepts the language

$$L = \{a^n : n \geq 1\} \cup \left\{ b^m a^k : m \geq 0, k \geq 0 \right\}.$$

(b) Do you think the language in part (a) can be accepted by an nfa with fewer than three states?

10. Find an nfa with four states for $L = \{a^n : n \geq 0\} \cup \{b^n a : n \geq 1\}$.

11. Which of the strings 00, 01001, 10010, 000, 0000 are accepted by the following nfa?

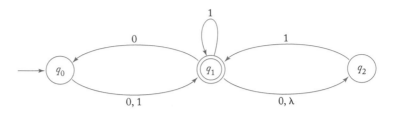

12. What is the complement of the language accepted by the nfa in Figure 2.10?

13. Let L be the language accepted by the nfa in Figure 2.8. Find an nfa that accepts $L \cup \{a^5\}$.

14. Give a simple description of the language in Exercise 12.

15. Find an nfa that accepts $\{a\}^*$ and is such that if in its transition graph a single edge is removed (without any other changes), the resulting automaton accepts $\{a\}$. **Ⓢ**

16. Can Exercise 15 be solved using a dfa? If so, give the solution; if not, give convincing arguments for your conclusion.

17. Consider the following modification of Definition 2.6. An nfa with multiple initial states is defined by the quintuple

$$M = (Q, \Sigma, \delta, Q_0, F),$$

where $Q_0 \subseteq Q$ is a set of possible initial states. The language accepted by such an automaton is defined as

$$L(M) = \{w : \delta^*(q_0, w) \text{ contains } q_f, \text{ for any } q_0 \in Q_0, q_f \in F\}.$$

Show that for every nfa with multiple initial states there exists an nfa with a single initial state that accepts the same language. **Ⓢ**

18. Suppose that in Exercise 17 we made the restriction $Q_0 \cap F = \varnothing$. Would this affect the conclusion?

19. Use Definition 2.5 to show that for any nfa

$$\delta^*(q, wv) = \bigcup_{p \in \delta^*(q,w)} \delta^*(p, v),$$

for all $q \in Q$ and all $w, v \in \Sigma^*$.

20. An nfa in which (a) there are no λ-transitions, and (b) for all $q \in Q$ and all $a \in \Sigma$, $\delta(q, a)$ contains at most one element, is sometimes called an **incomplete dfa**. This is reasonable since the conditions make it such that there is never any choice of moves.

For $\Sigma = \{a, b\}$, convert the incomplete dfa below into a standard dfa.

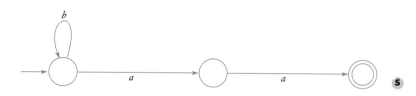

2.3 Equivalence of Deterministic and Nondeterministic Finite Accepters

We now come to a fundamental question. In what sense are dfa's and nfa's different? Obviously, there is a difference in their definition, but this does not imply that there is any essential distinction between them. To explore this question, we introduce the notion of equivalence between automata.

Definition 2.7

Two finite accepters M_1 and M_2 are said to be equivalent if

$$L(M_1) = L(M_2),$$

that is, if they both accept the same language.

As mentioned, there are generally many accepters for a given language, so any dfa or nfa has many equivalent accepters.

Example 2.11   The dfa shown in Figure 2.11 is equivalent to the nfa in Figure 2.9 since they both accept the language $\{(10)^n : n \geq 0\}$.

Figure 2.11

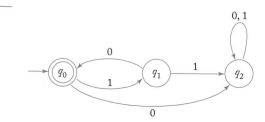

When we compare different classes of automata, the question invariably arises whether one class is more powerful than the other. By more powerful we mean that an automaton of one kind can achieve something that cannot be done by any automaton of the other kind. Let us look at this question for finite accepters. Since a dfa is in essence a restricted kind of nfa, it is clear that any language that is accepted by a dfa is also accepted by some nfa. But the converse is not so obvious. We have added nondeterminism, so it is at least conceivable that there is a language accepted by some nfa for which we cannot find a dfa. But it turns out that this is not so. The classes of dfa's and nfa's are equally powerful: For every language accepted by some nfa there is a dfa that accepts the same language.

This result is not obvious and certainly has to be demonstrated. The argument, like most arguments in this book, will be constructive. This means that we can actually give a way of converting any nfa into an equivalent dfa. The construction is not hard to understand; once the principle is clear it becomes the starting point for a rigorous argument. The rationale for the construction is the following. After an nfa has read a string w, we may not know exactly what state it will be in, but we can say that it must be in one state of a set of possible states, say $\{q_i, q_j, ..., q_k\}$. An equivalent dfa after reading the same string must be in some definite state. How can we make these two situations correspond? The answer is a nice trick: label the states of the dfa with a set of states in such a way that, after reading w, the equivalent dfa will be in a single state labeled $\{q_i, q_j, ..., q_k\}$. Since for a set of $|Q|$ states there are exactly $2^{|Q|}$ subsets, the corresponding dfa will have a finite number of states.

Most of the work in this suggested construction lies in the analysis of the nfa to get the correspondence between possible states and inputs. Before getting to the formal description of this, let us illustrate it with a simple example.

Example 2.12   Convert the nfa in Figure 2.12 to an equivalent dfa. The nfa starts in state q_0, so the initial state of the dfa will be labeled $\{q_0\}$. After reading an a, the nfa can be in state q_1 or, by making a λ-transition, in state q_2. Therefore the corresponding dfa must have a state labeled $\{q_1, q_2\}$ and a transition

$$\delta\left(\{q_0\}, a\right) = \{q_1, q_2\}.$$

In state q_0, the nfa has no specified transition when the input is b, therefore

$$\delta\left(\{q_0\}, b\right) = \varnothing.$$

A state labeled $\varnothing$ represents an impossible move for the nfa and, therefore, means nonacceptance of the string. Consequently, this state in the dfa must be a nonfinal trap state.

Figure 2.12

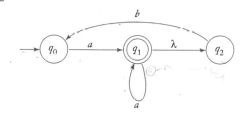

We have now introduced into the dfa the state $\{q_1, q_2\}$, so we need to find the transitions out of this state. Remember that this state of the dfa corresponds to two possible states of the nfa, so we must refer back to the nfa. If the nfa is in state q_1 and reads an a, it can go to q_1. Furthermore, from q_1 the nfa can make a λ-transition to q_2. If, for the same input, the nfa is in state q_2, then there is no specified transition. Therefore

$$\delta(\{q_1, q_2\}, a) = \{q_1, q_2\}.$$

Similarly,

$$\delta(\{q_1, q_2\}, b) = \{q_0\}.$$

At this point, every state has all transitions defined. The result, shown in Figure 2.13, is a dfa, equivalent to the nfa with which we started. The nfa in Figure 2.12 accepts any string for which $\delta^*(q_0, w)$ contains q_1. For the corresponding dfa to accept every such w, any state whose label includes q_1 must be made a final state.

Figure 2.13

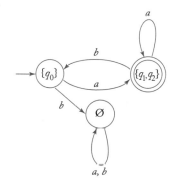

Theorem 2.2   Let L be the language accepted by a nondeterministic finite accepter $M_N = (Q_N, \Sigma, \delta_N, q_0, F_N)$. Then there exists a deterministic finite accepter $M_D = (Q_D, \Sigma, \delta_D, \{q_0\}, F_D)$ such that

$$L = L(M_D).$$

Proof: Given M_N, we use the procedure nfa_to_dfa below to construct the transition graph G_D for M_D. To understand the construction, remember that G_D has to have certain properties. Every vertex must have exactly $|\Sigma|$ outgoing edges, each labeled with a different element of Σ. During the construction, some of the edges may be missing, but the procedure continues until they are all there.

procedure: nfa_to_dfa

1. Create a graph G_D with vertex $\{q_0\}$. Identify this vertex as the initial vertex.

2. Repeat the following steps until no more edges are missing.

   Take any vertex $\{q_i, q_j, ..., q_k\}$ of G_D that has no outgoing edge for some $a \in \Sigma$.

   Compute $\delta^*(q_i, a), \delta^*(q_j, a) ..., \delta^*(q_k, a)$.

   Then form the union of all these δ^*, yielding the set $\{q_l, q_m, ..., q_n\}$.

   Create a vertex for G_D labeled $\{q_l, q_m, ..., q_n\}$ if it does not already exist.

   Add to G_D an edge from $\{q_i, q_j, ..., q_k\}$ to $\{q_l, q_m, ..., q_n\}$ and label it with a.

3. Every state of G_D whose label contains any $q_f \in F_N$ is identified as a final vertex.

4. If M_N accepts λ, the vertex $\{q_0\}$ in G_D is also made a final vertex.

It is clear that this procedure always terminates. Each pass through the loop in Step 2 adds an edge to G_D. But G_D has at most $2^{|Q_N|}|\Sigma|$ edges, so that the loop eventually stops. To show that the construction also gives the correct answer, we argue by induction on the length of the input string.

Assume that for every v of length less than or equal to n, the presence in G_N of a walk labeled v from q_0 to q_i implies that in G_D there is a walk labeled v from $\{q_0\}$ to a state $Q_i = \{..., q_i, ...\}$. Consider now any $w = va$ and look at a walk in G_N labeled w from q_0 to q_l. There must then be a walk labeled v from q_0 to q_i and an edge (or a sequence of edges) labeled a from q_i to q_l. By the inductive assumption, in G_D there will be a walk labeled v from $\{q_0\}$ to Q_i. But by construction, there will be an edge from Q_i to some state whose label contains q_l. Thus the inductive assumption holds for all strings of length $n + 1$. As it is obviously true for $n = 1$, it is true for all n. The result then is that whenever $\delta_N^*(q_0, w)$ contains a final state q_f, so does the label of $\delta_D^*(q_0, w)$. To complete the proof, we reverse the argument to show that if the label of $\delta_D^*(q_0, w)$ contains q_f, so must $\delta_N^*(q_0, w)$. ∎

The arguments in this proof, although correct, are admittedly somewhat terse, showing only the major steps. We will follow this practice in the rest of the book, emphasizing the basic ideas in a proof and omitting minor details, which you may want to fill in yourself.

The construction in the above proof is tedious but important. Let us do another example to make sure we understand all the steps.

Example 2.13   Convert the nfa in Figure 2.14 into an equivalent deterministic machine. Since $\delta_N(q_0, 0) = \{q_0, q_1\}$, we introduce the state $\{q_0, q_1\}$ in G_D and add an edge labeled 0 between $\{q_0\}$ and $\{q_0, q_1\}$. In the same way, considering $\delta_N(q_0, 1) = \{q_1\}$ gives us the new state $\{q_1\}$ and an edge labeled 1 between it and $\{q_0\}$.

There are now a number of missing edges, so we continue, using the construction of Theorem 2.2. With $a = 0$, $i = 0$, $j = 1$, we compute

$$\delta_N^*(q_0, 0) \cup \delta_N^*(q_1, 0) = \{q_0, q_1, q_2\}.$$

This gives us the new state $\{q_0, q_1, q_2\}$ and the transition

$$\delta_D(\{q_0, q_1\}, 0) = \{q_0, q_1, q_2\}.$$

Then, using $a = 1$, $i = 0$, $j = 1$, $k = 2$,

$$\delta_N^*(q_0, 1) \cup \delta_N^*(q_1, 1) \cup \delta_N^*(q_2, 1) = \{q_1, q_2\}$$

makes it necessary to introduce yet another state $\{q_1, q_2\}$. At this point, we have the partially constructed automaton shown in Figure 2.15. Since there are still some missing edges, we continue until we obtain the complete solution in Figure 2.16.

Figure 2.14

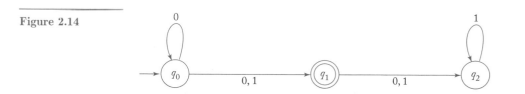

Figure 2.15

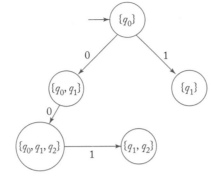

Figure 2.16

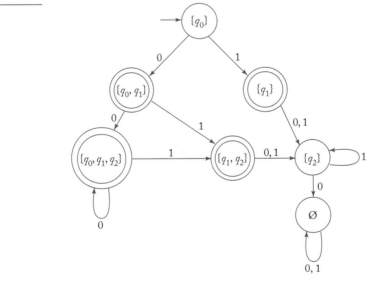

One important conclusion we can draw from Theorem 2.2 is that every language accepted by an nfa is regular.

EXERCISES

1. Use the construction of Theorem 2.2 to convert the nfa in Figure 2.10 to a dfa. Can you see a simpler answer more directly?

2. Convert the nfa in Exercise 11, Section 2.2 into an equivalent dfa. **S**

3. Convert the following nfa into an equivalent dfa.

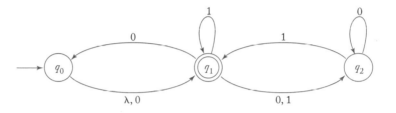

4. Carefully complete the arguments in the proof of Theorem 2.2. Show in detail that if the label of $\delta_D^*(q_0, w)$ contains q_f, then $\delta_N^*(q_0, w)$ also contains q_f.

5. Is it true that for any nfa $M = (Q, \Sigma, \delta, q_0, F)$ the complement of $L(M)$ is equal to the set $\{w \in \Sigma^* : \delta^*(q_0, w) \cap F = \varnothing\}$? If so, prove it. If not, give a counterexample.

6. Is it true that for every nfa $M = (Q, \Sigma, \delta, q_0, F)$ the complement of $L(M)$ is equal to the set $\{w \in \Sigma^* : \delta^*(q_0, w) \cap (Q - F) \neq \varnothing\}$? If so, prove it; if not, give a counterexample.

7. Prove that for every nfa with an arbitrary number of final states there is an equivalent nfa with only one final state. Can we make a similar claim for dfa's? **S**

8. Find an nfa without λ-transitions and with a single final state that accepts the set $\{a\} \cup \{b^n : n \geq 1\}$. **S**

★ 9. Let L be a regular language that does not contain λ. Show that there exists an nfa without λ-transitions and with a single final state that accepts L.

10. Define a dfa with multiple initial states in an analogous way to the corresponding nfa in Exercise 17, Section 2.2. Does there always exist an equivalent dfa with a single initial state?

11. Prove that all finite languages are regular. **S**

12. Show that if L is regular, so is L^R.

13. Give a simple verbal description of the language accepted by the dfa in Figure 2.16. Use this to find another dfa, equivalent to the given one, but with fewer states.

★14. Let L be any language. Define $even(w)$ as the string obtained by extracting from w the letters in even-numbered positions; that is, if

$$w = a_1 a_2 a_3 a_4 ...,$$

then

$$even(w) = a_2 a_4 ....$$

Corresponding to this, we can define a language

$$even(L) = \{even(w) : w \in L\}.$$

Prove that if L is regular, so is $even(L)$. **Ⓢ**

15. From a language L we create a new language $chop2(L)$ by removing the two leftmost symbols of every string in L. Specifically,

$$chop2(L) = \{w : vw \in L, \text{ with } |v| = 2\}.$$

Show that if L is regular then $chop2(L)$ is also regular. **Ⓢ**

2.4 Reduction of the Number of States in Finite Automata*

Any dfa defines a unique language, but the converse is not true. For a given language, there are many dfa's that accept it. There may be a considerable difference in the number of states of such equivalent automata. In terms of the questions we have considered so far, all solutions are equally satisfactory, but if the results are to be applied in a practical setting, there may be reasons for preferring one over another.

Example 2.14   The two dfa's depicted in Figure 2.17(a) and 2.17(b) are equivalent, as a few test strings will quickly reveal. We notice some obviously unnecessary features of Figure 2.17(a). The state q_5 plays absolutely no role in the automaton since it can never be reached from the initial state q_0. Such a state is inaccessible, and it can be removed (along with all transitions relating to it) without affecting the language accepted by the automaton. But even after the removal of q_5, the first automaton has some redundant parts. The states reachable subsequent to the first move $\delta(q_0, 0)$ mirror those reachable from a first move $\delta(q_0, 1)$. The second automaton combines these two options.   ∎

Figure 2.17

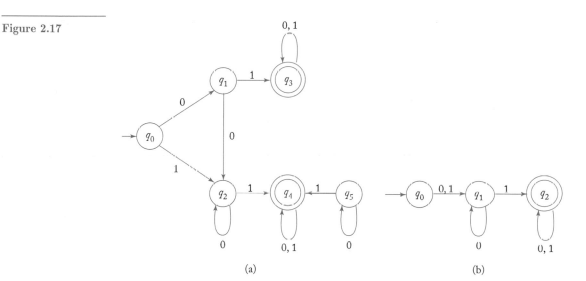

(a)   (b)

From a strictly theoretical point of view, there is little reason for preferring the automaton in Figure 2.17(b) over that in Figure 2.17(a). However, in terms of simplicity, the second alternative is clearly preferable. Representation of an automaton for the purpose of computation requires space proportional to the number of states. For storage efficiency, it is desirable to reduce the number of states as far as possible. We now describe an algorithm that accomplishes this.

Definition 2.8

Two states p and q of a dfa are called **indistinguishable** if

$$\delta^* (p, w) \in F \text{ implies } \delta^* (q, w) \in F,$$

and

$$\delta^* (p, w) \notin F \text{ implies } \delta^* (q, w) \notin F,$$

for all $w \in \Sigma^*$. If, on the other hand, there exists some string $w \in \Sigma^*$ such that

$$\delta^* (p, w) \in F \text{ and } \delta^* (q, w) \notin F,$$

or vice versa, then the states p and q are said to be **distinguishable** by a string w.

Clearly, two states are either indistinguishable or distinguishable. Indistinguishability has the properties of an equivalence relations: if p and q are indistinguishable and if q and r are also indistinguishable, then so are p and r, and all three states are indistinguishable.

One method for reducing the states of a dfa is based on finding and combining indistinguishable states. We first describe a method for finding pairs of distinguishable states.

procedure: mark

1. Remove all inaccessible states. This can be done by enumerating all simple paths of the graph of the dfa starting at the initial state. Any state not part of some path is inaccessible.

2. Consider all pairs of states (p, q). If $p \in F$ and $q \notin F$ or vice versa, mark the pair (p, q) as distinguishable.

3. Repeat the following step until no previously unmarked pairs are marked.

   For all pairs (p, q) and all $a \in \Sigma$, compute $\delta(p, a) = p_a$ and $\delta(q, a) = q_a$. If the pair (p_a, q_a) is marked as distinguishable, mark (p, q) as distinguishable.

We claim that this procedure constitutes an algorithm for marking all distinguishable pairs.

Theorem 2.3

The procedure *mark*, applied to any dfa $M = (Q, \Sigma, \delta, q_0, F)$, terminates and determines all pairs of distinguishable states.

Proof: Obviously, the procedure terminates, since there are only a finite number of pairs that can be marked. It is also easy to see that the states of any pair so marked are distinguishable. The only claim that requires elaboration is that the procedure finds all distinguishable pairs.

Note first that states q_i and q_j are distinguishable with a string of length n, if and only if there are transitions

$$\delta(q_i, a) = q_k \tag{2.5}$$

and

$$\delta(q_j, a) = q_l, \tag{2.6}$$

for some $a \in \Sigma$, with q_k and q_l distinguishable by a string of length $n - 1$. We use this first to show that at the completion of the nth pass through the loop in step 3, all states distinguishable by strings of length n or less have been marked. In step 2, we mark all pairs indistinguishable by λ, so we have a basis with $n = 0$ for an induction. We now assume that the claim is true for all $i = 0, 1, ..., n - 1$. By this inductive assumption, at the beginning of the nth pass through the loop, all states distinguishable by strings of length up to $n - 1$ have been marked. Because of (2.5) and (2.6) above, at the end of this pass, all states distinguishable by strings of length up to n will be marked. By induction then, we can claim that, for any n, at the completion of the nth pass, all pairs distinguishable by strings of length n or less have been marked.

To show that this procedure marks all distinguishable states, assume that the loop terminates after n passes. This means that during the nth pass no new states were marked. From (2.5) and (2.6), it then follows that there cannot be any states distinguishable by a string of length n, but not distinguishable by any shorter string. But if there are no states distinguishable only by strings of length n, there cannot be any states distinguishable only by strings of length $n + 1$, and so on. As a consequence, when the loop terminates, all distinguishable pairs have been marked. ∎

After the marking algorithm has been executed, we use the results to partition the state set Q of the dfa into disjoint subsets $\{q_i, q_j, ..., q_k\}$, $\{q_l, q_m, ..., q_n\}, ...$, such that any $q \in Q$ occurs in exactly one of these subsets, that elements in each subset are indistinguishable, and that any two elements from different subsets are distinguishable. Using the results sketched in Exercise 11 at the end of this section, it can be shown that such a partitioning can always be found. From these subsets we construct the minimal automaton by the next procedure.

procedure: reduce

Given a dfa $M = (Q, \Sigma, \delta, q_0, F)$, we construct a reduced dfa $\widehat{M} = \left(\widehat{Q}, \Sigma, \widehat{\delta}, \widehat{q}_0, \widehat{F} \right)$ as follows.

1. Use procedure *mark* to find all pairs of distinguishable states. Then from this, find the sets of all indistinguishable states, say $\{q_i, q_j, ..., q_k\}$, $\{q_l, q_m, ..., q_n\}$, etc., as described above.

2. For each set $\{q_i, q_j, ..., q_k\}$ of such indistinguishable states, create a state labeled $ij \cdots k$ for M.

3. For each transition rule of M of the form

$$\delta (q_r, a) = q_p,$$

find the sets to which q_r and q_p belong. If $q_r \in \{q_i, q_j, ..., q_k\}$ and $q_p \in \{q_l, q_m, ..., q_n\}$, add to $\widehat{\delta}$ a rule

$$\widehat{\delta} (ij \cdots k, a) = lm \cdots n.$$

4. The initial state $\widehat{q_0}$ is that state of $\widehat{M}$ whose label includes the 0.

5. $\widehat{F}$ is the set of all the states whose label contains i such that $q_i \in F$.

Example 2.15   Consider the automaton depicted in Figure 2.18.

In step 2, the procedure *mark* will identify distinguishable pairs (q_0, q_4), (q_1, q_4), (q_2, q_4), and (q_3, q_4). In some pass through the step 3 loop, the procedure computes

$$\delta(q_1, 1) = q_4$$

and

$$\delta(q_0, 1) = q_3.$$

Since (q_3, q_4) is a distinguishable pair, the pair (q_0, q_1) is also marked. Continuing this way, the marking algorithm eventually marks the pairs (q_0, q_1), (q_0, q_2), (q_0, q_3), (q_0, q_4), (q_1, q_4), (q_2, q_4) and (q_3, q_4) as distinguishable, leaving the indistinguishable pairs (q_1, q_2), (q_1, q_3) and (q_2, q_3). Therefore, the states q_1, q_2, q_3 are all indistinguishable, and all of the states have been partitioned into the sets $\{q_0\}$, $\{q_1, q_2, q_3\}$ and $\{q_4\}$. Applying steps 2 and 3 of the procedure *reduce* then yields the dfa in Figure 2.19.

Figure 2.18

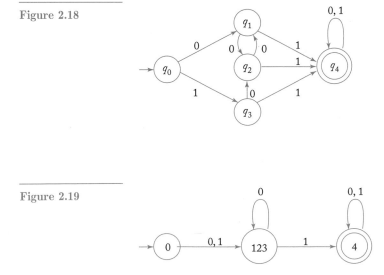

Figure 2.19

Theorem 2.4   Given any dfa M, application of the procedure *reduce* yields another dfa $\widehat{M}$ such that

$$L(M) = L\left(\widehat{M}\right).$$

Furthermore, $\widehat{M}$ is minimal in the sense that there is no other dfa with a smaller number of states which also accepts $L(M)$.

Proof: There are two parts. The first is to show that the dfa created by *reduce* is equivalent to the original dfa. This is relatively easy and we can use inductive arguments similar to those used in establishing the equivalence of dfa's and nfa's. All we have to do is to show that $\delta^*(q_i, w) = q_j$ if and only if the label of $\widehat{\delta}^*(q_i, w)$ is of the form $...j....$ We will leave this as an exercise.

The second part, to show that $\widehat{M}$ is minimal, is harder. Suppose $\widehat{M}$ has states $\{p_0, p_1, p_2, ..., p_m\}$, with p_0 the initial state. Assume that there is an equivalent dfa M_1, with transition function δ_1 and initial state q_0, equivalent to $\widehat{M}$, but with fewer states. Since there are no inaccessible states in $\widehat{M}$, there must be distinct strings $w_1, w_2, ..., w_m$ such that

$$\widehat{\delta}^*(p_0, w_i) = p_i, i = 1, 2, ..., m.$$

But since M_1 has fewer states than $\widehat{M}$, there must be at least two of these strings, say w_k and w_l, such that

$$\delta_1^*(q_0, w_k) = \delta_1^*(q_0, w_l).$$

Since p_k and p_l are distinguishable, there must be some string x such that $\widehat{\delta}^*(p_0, w_k x) = \widehat{\delta}^*(p_k, x)$ is a final state, and $\widehat{\delta}^*(q_0, w_l x) = \widehat{\delta}^*(p_l, x)$ is a nonfinal state (or vice versa). In other words, $w_k x$ is accepted by $\widehat{M}$ and $w_l x$ is not. But note that

$$\begin{aligned}
\delta_1^*(q_0, w_k x) &= \delta_1^*(\delta_1^*(q_0, w_k), x) \\
&= \delta_1^*(\delta_1^*(q_0, w_l), x) \\
&= \delta_1^*(q_0, w_l x).
\end{aligned}$$

Thus, M_1 either accepts both $w_k x$ and $w_l x$ or rejects both, contradicting the assumption that $\widehat{M}$ and M_1 are equivalent. This contradiction proves that M_1 cannot exist. ∎

EXERCISES

1. Minimize the number of states in the dfa in Figure 2.16.

2. Find minimal dfa's for the languages below. In each case prove that the result is minimal.

   (a) $L = \{a^n b^m : n \geq 2, m \geq 1\}$

   (b) $L = \{a^n b : n \geq 0\} \cup \{b^n a : n \geq 1\}$

   (c) $L = \{a^n : n \geq 0, n \neq 3\}$ **S**

   (d) $L = \{a^n : n \neq 2 \text{ and } n \neq 4\}$.

3. Show that the automaton generated by procedure *reduce* is deterministic.

4. Minimize the states in the dfa depicted in the following diagram.

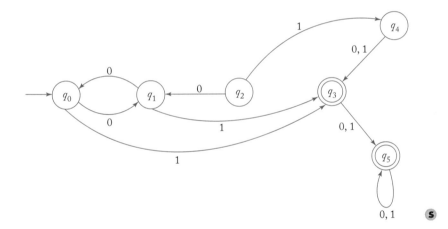

5. Show that if L is a nonempty language such that any w in L has length at least n, then any dfa accepting L must have at least $n + 1$ states.

6. Prove or disprove the following conjecture. If $M = (Q, \Sigma, \delta, q_0, F)$ is a minimal dfa for a regular language L, then $\widehat{M} = (Q, \Sigma, \delta, q_0, Q - F)$ is a minimal dfa for $\overline{L}$. **S**

7. Show that indistinguishability is an equivalence relation but that distinguishability is not.

8. Show the explicit steps of the suggested proof of the first part of Theorem 2.4, namely, that $\widehat{M}$ is equivalent to the original dfa.

★★ 9. Write a computer program that produces a minimal dfa for any given dfa.

10. Prove the following: If the states q_a and q_b are indistinguishable, and if q_a and q_c are distinguishable, then q_b and q_c must be distinguishable. **S**

11. Consider the following process, to be done after the completion of the procedure *mark*. Start with some state, say, q_0. Put all states not marked distinguishable from q_0 into an equivalence set with q_0. Then take another state, not in the preceding equivalence set, and do the same thing. Repeat until there are no more states available. Then formalize this suggestion to make it an algorithm, and prove that this algorithm does indeed partition the original state set into equivalence sets.

Chapter 3

Regular Languages and Regular Grammars

ccording to our definition, a language is regular if there exists a finite accepter for it. Therefore, every regular language can be described by some dfa or some nfa. Such a description can be very useful, for example, if we want to show the logic by which we decide if a given string is in a certain language. But in many instances, we need more concise ways of describing regular languages. In this chapter, we look at other ways of representing regular languages. These representations have important practical applications, a matter that is touched on in some of the examples and exercises.

3.1 Regular Expressions

One way of describing regular languages is via the notation of **regular expressions.** This notation involves a combination of strings of symbols from some alphabet Σ, parentheses, and the operators $+$, $\cdot$, and $*$. The simplest case is the language $\{a\}$, which will be denoted by the regular expression a. Slightly more complicated is the language $\{a, b, c\}$, for which, using the $+$ to denote union, we have the regular expression $a+b+c$. We use $\cdot$ for concatenation and $*$ for star-closure in a similar way. The expression $(a + b \cdot c)^*$ stands for the star-closure of $\{a\} \cup \{bc\}$, that is, the language $\{\lambda, a, bc, aa, abc, bca, bcbc, aaa, aabc, ...\}$.

Formal Definition of a Regular Expression

We construct regular expressions from primitive constituents by repeatedly applying certain recursive rules. This is similar to the way we construct familiar arithmetic expressions.

Definition 3.1

Let Σ be a given alphabet. Then

1. $\varnothing, \lambda$, and $a \in \Sigma$ are all regular expressions. These are called **primitive regular expressions.**

2. If r_1 and r_2 are regular expressions, so are $r_1 + r_2$, $r_1 \cdot r_2$, r_1^*, and (r_1).

3. A string is a regular expression if and only if it can be derived from the primitive regular expressions by a finite number of applications of the rules in (2).

Example 3.1   For $\Sigma = \{a, b, c\}$, the string

$$(a + b \cdot c)^* \cdot (c + \varnothing)$$

is a regular expression, since it is constructed by application of the above rules. For example, if we take $r_1 = c$ and $r_2 = \varnothing$, we find that $c + \varnothing$ and $(c + \varnothing)$ are also regular expressions. Repeating this, we eventually generate the whole string. On the other hand, $(a + b+)$ is not a regular expression, since there is no way it can be constructed from the primitive regular expressions.

Languages Associated with Regular Expressions

Regular expressions can be used to describe some simple languages. If r is a regular expression, we will let $L(r)$ denote the language associated with r. This language is defined as follows:

Definition 3.2

The language $L(r)$ denoted by any regular expression r is defined by the following rules.

1. $\varnothing$ is a regular expression denoting the empty set,

2. λ is a regular expression denoting $\{\lambda\}$,

3. for every $a \in \Sigma$, a is a regular expression denoting $\{a\}$.

If r_1 and r_2 are regular expressions, then

4. $L(r_1 + r_2) = L(r_1) \cup L(r_2)$,

5. $L(r_1 \cdot r_2) = L(r_1)L(r_2)$,

6. $L((r_1)) = L(r_1)$,

7. $L(r_1^*) = (L(r_1))^*$.

The last four rules of this definition are used to reduce $L(r)$ to simpler components recursively; the first three are the termination conditions for this recursion. To see what language a given expression denotes, we apply these rules repeatedly.

Example 3.2   Exhibit the language $L(a^* \cdot (a + b))$ in set notation.

$$
\begin{aligned}
L(a^* \cdot (a + b)) &= L(a^*)L(a + b) \\
&= (L(a))^* (L(a) \cup L(b)) \\
&= \{\lambda, a, aa, aaa, ...\} \{a, b\} \\
&= \{a, aa, aaa, ..., b, ab, aab, ...\}
\end{aligned}
$$

There is one problem with rules (4) to (7) in Definition 3.2. They define a language precisely if r_1 and r_2 are given, but there may be some ambiguity in breaking a complicated expression into parts. Consider, for example, the regular expression $a \cdot b + c$. We can consider this as being made up of $r_1 = a \cdot b$ and $r_2 = c$. In this case, we find $L(a \cdot b + c) = \{ab, c\}$. But there is nothing in Definition 3.2 to stop us from taking $r_1 = a$ and $r_2 = b + c$. We now get a different result, $L(a \cdot b + c) = \{ab, ac\}$. To overcome this, we could require that all expressions be fully parenthesized, but this gives cumbersome results. Instead, we use a convention familiar from mathematics and programming languages. We establish a set of precedence rules for evaluation in which star-closure precedes concatenation and concatenation precedes union. Also, the symbol for concatenation may be omitted, so we can write $r_1 r_2$ for $r_1 \cdot r_2$.

With a little practice, we can see quickly what language a particular regular expression denotes.

Example 3.3   For $\Sigma = \{a, b\}$, the expression

$$r = (a + b)^* (a + bb)$$

is regular. It denotes the language

$$L(r) = \{a, bb, aa, abb, ba, bbb, ...\}.$$

We can see this by considering the various parts of r. The first part, $(a + b)^*$, stands for any string of a's and b's. The second part, $(a + bb)$ represents either an a or a double b. Consequently, $L(r)$ is the set of all strings on $\{a, b\}$, terminated by either an a or a bb.

Example 3.4   The expression

$$r = (aa)^* (bb)^* b$$

denotes the set of all strings with an even number of a's followed by an odd number of b's; that is

$$L(r) = \{a^{2n} b^{2m+1} : n \geq 0, \ m \geq 0\}.$$

Going from an informal description or set notation to a regular expression tends to be a little harder.

Example 3.5   For $\Sigma = \{0, 1\}$, give a regular expression r such that

$$L(r) = \{w \in \Sigma^* : w \text{ has at least one pair of consequtive zeros}\}.$$

One can arrive at an answer by reasoning something like this: Every string in $L(r)$ must contain 00 somewhere, but what comes before and what goes after is completely arbitrary. An arbitrary string on $\{0, 1\}$ can be denoted by $(0 + 1)^*$. Putting these observations together, we arrive at the solution

$$r = (0 + 1)^* 00 (0 + 1)^*.$$

Example 3.6   Find a regular expression for the language

$$L = \{w \in \{0, 1\}^* : w \text{ has no pair of consecutive zeros}\}.$$

Even though this looks similar to Example 3.5, the answer is harder to construct. One helpful observation is that whenever a 0 occurs, it must be followed immediately by a 1. Such a substring may be preceded and followed by an arbitrary number of 1's. This suggests that the answer involves the repetition of strings of the form $1 \cdots 101 \cdots 1$, that is, the language denoted by the regular expression $(1^*011^*)^*$. However, the answer is still incomplete, since the strings ending in 0 or consisting of all 1's are unaccounted for. After taking care of these special cases we arrive at the answer

$$r = (1^*011^*)^* (0 + \lambda) + 1^* (0 + \lambda).$$

If we reason slightly differently, we might come up with another answer. If we see L as the repetition of the strings 1 and 01, the shorter expression

$$r = (1 + 01)^* (0 + \lambda)$$

might be reached. Although the two expressions look different, both answers are correct, as they denote the same language. Generally, there are an unlimited number of regular expressions for any given language.

Note that this language is the complement of the language in Example 3.5. However, the regular expressions are not very similar and do not suggest clearly the close relationship between the languages.

The last example introduces the notion of equivalence of regular expressions. We say the two regular expressions are equivalent if they denote the same language. One can derive a variety of rules for simplifying regular expressions (see Exercise 18 in the following exercise section), but since we have little need for such manipulations we will not pursue this.

EXERCISES

1. Find all strings in $L\left((a+b)^* b (a+ab)^*\right)$ of length less than four.

2. Does the expression $((0+1)(0+1)^*)^* 00 (0+1)^*$ denote the language in Example 3.5? Ⓢ

3. Show that $r = (1 + 01)^* (0 + 1^*)$ also denotes the language in Example 3.6. Find two other equivalent expressions.

4. Find a regular expression for the set $\{a^n b^m : (n+m) \text{ is even}\}$.

5. Give regular expressions for the following languages.

    (a) $L_1 = \{a^n b^m, n \geq 4, m \leq 3\}$, Ⓢ

    (b) $L_2 = \{a^n b^m : n < 4, m \leq 3\}$,

    (c) The complement of L_1, Ⓢ

    (d) The complement of L_2.

6. What languages do the expressions $(\varnothing^*)^*$ and $a\varnothing$ denote?

7. Give a simple verbal description of the language $L\left((aa)^* b (aa)^* + a (aa)^* ba (aa)^*\right)$.

8. Give a regular expression for L^R, where L is the language in Exercise 1.

9. Give a regular expression for $L = \{a^n b^m : n \geq 1, m \geq 1, nm \geq 3\}$. Ⓢ

10. Find a regular expression for $L = \{ab^n w : n \geq 3, w \in \{a, b\}^+\}$.

11. Find a regular expression for the complement of the language in Example 3.4.

12. Find a regular expression for $L = \{vwv : v, w \in \{a, b\}^*, |v| = 2\}$. Ⓢ

13. Find a regular expression for

    $$L = \{w \in \{0,1\}^* : w \text{ has exactly one pair of consecutive zeros}\}.$$

14. Give regular expressions for the following languages on $\Sigma = \{a, b, c\}$.

    (a) all strings containing exactly one a,

    (b) all strings containing no more than three a's,

    (c) all strings that contain at least one occurrence of each symbol in Σ, Ⓢ

    (d) all strings that contain no run of a's of length greater than two,

    ★ (e) all strings in which all runs of a's have lengths that are multiples of three.

15. Write regular expressions for the following languages on $\{0, 1\}$.

    (a) all strings ending in 01,

    (b) all strings not ending in 01,

    (c) all strings containing an even number of 0's, ⓢ

    (d) all strings having at least two occurrences of the substring 00 (Note that with the usual interpretation of a substring, 000 contains two such occurrences),

    (e) all strings with at most two occurrences of the substring 00,

    ★ (f) all strings not containing the substring 101.

16. Find regular expressions for the following languages on $\{a, b\}$.

    (a) $L = \{w : |w| \bmod 3 = 0\}$ ⓢ

    (b) $L = \{w : n_a(w) \bmod 3 = 0\}$

    (c) $L = \{w : n_a(w) \bmod 5 > 0\}$

17. Repeat parts (a), (b), and (c) of Exercise 16, with $\Sigma = \{a, b, c\}$.

18. Determine whether or not the following claims are true for all regular expressions r_1 and r_2. The symbol $\equiv$ stands for equivalence of regular expressions in the sense that both expressions denote the same language.

    (a) $(r_1^*)^* \equiv r_1^*$,

    (b) $r_1^* (r_1 + r_2)^* \equiv (r_1 + r_2)^*$,

    (c) $(r_1 + r_2)^* \equiv (r_1^* r_2^*)^*$, ⓢ

    (d) $(r_1 r_2)^* \equiv r_1^* r_2^*$.

19. Give a general method by which any regular expression r can be changed into $\widehat{r}$ such that $(L(r))^R = L(\widehat{r})$.

20. Prove rigorously that the expressions in Example 3.6 do indeed denote the specified language.

21. For the case of a regular expression r that does not involve λ or $\varnothing$, give a set of necessary and sufficient conditions that r must satisfy if $L(r)$ is to be infinite. ⓢ

22. Formal languages can be used to describe a variety of two-dimensional figures. Chain-code languages are defined on the alphabet $\Sigma = \{u, d, r, l\}$, where these symbols stand for unit-length straight lines in the directions up, down, right, and left, respectively. An example of this notation is $urdl$, which stands for the square with sides of unit length. Draw pictures of the figures denoted by the expressions $(rd)^*$, $(urddru)^*$, and $(ruldr)^*$.

23. In Exercise 22, what are sufficient conditions on the expression so that the picture is a closed contour in the sense that the beginning and ending point are the same? Are these conditions also necessary? ⓢ

24. Find an nfa that accepts the language $L\left(aa^*\left(a+b\right)\right)$.

25. Find a regular expression that denotes all bit strings whose value, when interpreted as a binary integer, is greater than or equal to 40. **S**

26. Find a regular expression for all bit strings, with leading bit 1, interpreted as a binary integer, with values not between 10 and 30.

3.2 Connection Between Regular Expressions and Regular Languages

As the terminology suggests, the connection between regular languages and regular expressions is a close one. The two concepts are essentially the same; for every regular language there is a regular expression, and for every regular expression there is a regular language. We will show this in two parts.

Regular Expressions Denote Regular Languages

We first show that if r is a regular expression, then $L(r)$ is a regular language. Our definition says that a language is regular if it is accepted by some dfa. Because of the equivalence of nfa's and dfa's, a language is also regular if it is accepted by some nfa. We now show that if we have any regular expression r, we can construct an nfa that accepts $L(r)$. The construction for this relies on the recursive definition for $L(r)$. We first construct simple automata for parts (1), (2), and (3) of Definition 3.2 on page 73, then show how they can be combined to implement the more complicated parts (4), (5), and (7).

Theorem 3.1

Let r be a regular expression. Then there exists some nondeterministic finite accepter that accepts $L(r)$. Consequently, $L(r)$ is a regular language.

Proof: We begin with automata that accept the languages for the simple regular expressions $\varnothing$, λ, and $a \in \Sigma$. These are shown in Figure 3.1(a), (b), and (c), respectively. Assume now that we have automata $M(r_1)$ and $M(r_2)$ that accept languages denoted by regular expressions r_1 and r_2, respectively. We need not explicitly construct these automata, but may represent them schematically, as in Figure 3.2. In this schema, the graph vertex at the left represents the initial state, the one on the right the final state. In Exercise 7, Section 2.3 we claimed that for every nfa there is an equivalent one with a single final state, so we lose nothing in assuming that there is only one final state. With $M(r_1)$ and $M(r_2)$ represented in this way, we then construct automata for the regular expressions $r_1 + r_2$, $r_1 r_2$, and r_1^*. The constructions are shown in Figures 3.3 to 3.5. As indicated

Figure 3.1
(a) nfa accepts ∅.
(b) nfa accepts {λ}.
(c) nfa accepts {a}.

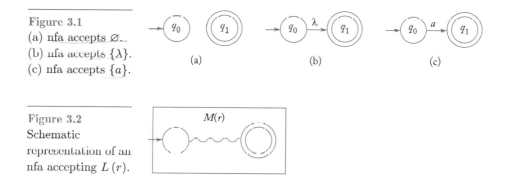

(a)   (b)   (c)

Figure 3.2
Schematic
representation of an
nfa accepting $L(r)$.

$M(r)$

in the drawings, the initial and final states of the constituent machines lose their status and are replaced by new initial and final states. By stringing together several such steps, we can build automata for arbitrary complex regular expressions.

It should be clear from the interpretation of the graphs in Figures 3.3 to 3.5 that this construction works. To argue more rigorously, we can give a formal method for constructing the states and transitions of the combined machine from the states and transitions of the parts, then prove by induction on the number of operators that the construction yields an automaton that accepts the language denoted by any particular regular expression. We will not belabor this point, as it is reasonably obvious that the results are always correct.   ∎

Example 3.7   Find an nfa which accepts $L(r)$, where

$$r = (a + bb)^* (ba^* + \lambda).$$

Figure 3.3
Automaton for
$L(r_1 + r_2)$.

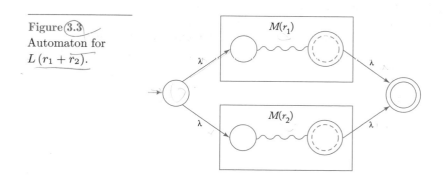

$M(r_1)$

$M(r_2)$

Figure 3.4
Automaton for
$L(r_1 r_2)$.

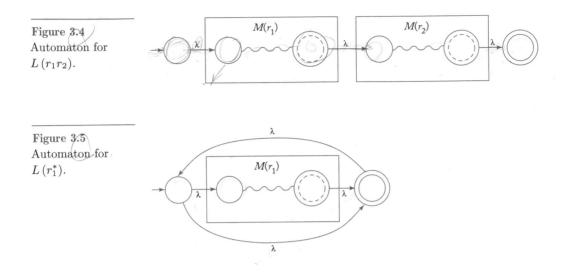

Figure 3.5
Automaton for
$L(r_1^*)$.

Automata for $(a + bb)$ and $(ba^* + \lambda)$, constructed directly from first principles, are given in Figure 3.6. Putting these together using the construction in Theorem 3.1, we get the solution in Figure 3.7

Figure 3.6
(a) M_1 accepts
$L(a + bb)$.
(b) M_2 accepts
$L(ba^* + \lambda)$.

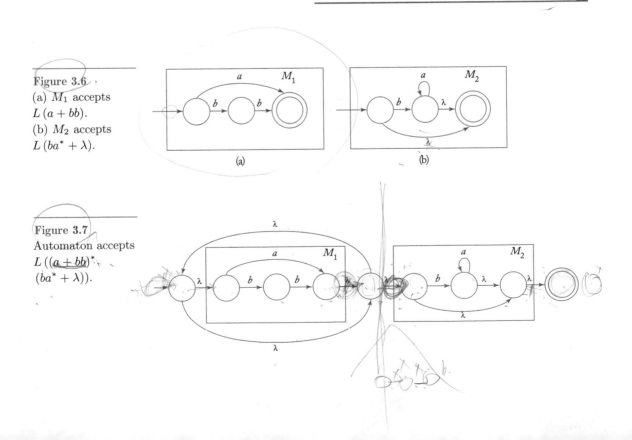

Figure 3.7
Automaton accepts
$L((a + bb)^*$
$(ba^* + \lambda))$.

Regular Expressions for Regular Languages

It is intuitively reasonable that the converse of Theorem 3.1 should hold, and that for every regular language, there should exist a corresponding regular expression. Since any regular language has an associated nfa and hence a transition graph, all we need to do is to find a regular expression capable of generating the labels of all the walks from q_0 to any final state. This does not look too difficult but it is complicated by the existence of cycles that can often be traversed arbitrarily, in any order. This creates a bookkeeping problem that must be handled carefully. There are several ways to do this; one of the more intuitive approaches requires a side trip into what are called **generalized transition graphs.** Since this idea is used here in a limited way and plays no role in our further discussion, we will deal with it informally.

A generalized transition graph is a transition graph whose edges are labeled with regular expressions; otherwise it is the same as the usual transition graph. The label of any walk from the initial state to a final state is the concatenation of several regular expressions, and hence itself a regular expression. The strings denoted by such regular expressions are a subset of the language accepted by the generalized transition graph, with the full language being the union of all such generated subsets.

Example 3.8	Figure 3.8 represents a generalized transition graph. The language accepted by it is $L(a^* + a^* (a + b) c^*)$, as should be clear from an inspection of the graph. The edge (q_0, q_0) labeled a is a cycle that can generate any number of a's, that is, it represents $L(a^*)$. We could have labeled this edge a^* without changing the language accepted by the graph. ■

The graph of any nondeterministic finite accepter can be considered a generalized transition graph if the edge labels are interpreted properly. An edge labeled with a single symbol a is interpreted as an edge labeled with the expression a, while an edge labeled with multiple symbols $a, b, \ldots$ is interpreted as an edge labeled with the expression $a + b + \ldots$. From this observation, it follows that for every regular language, there exists a

Figure 3.8

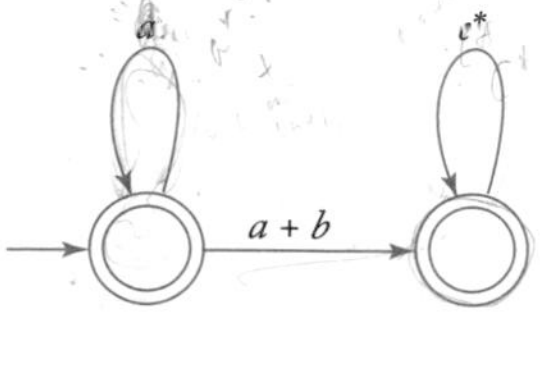

Figure 3.9

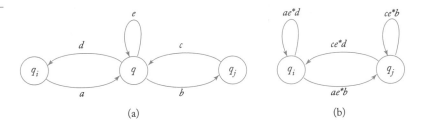

(a)　　　　　　　(b)

generalized transition graph that accepts it. Conversely, every language accepted by a generalized transition graph is regular. Since the label of every walk in a generalized transition graph is a regular expression, this appears to be an immediate consequence of Theorem 3.1. However, there are some subtleties in the argument; we will not pursue them here, but refer the reader instead to Exercise 16, Section 4.3 for details.

Equivalence for generalized transition graphs is defined in terms of the language accepted. Consider a generalized transition graph with states $\{q, q_i, q_j, ...\}$, where q is neither a final nor an initial state, and for which we want to create an equivalent generalized transition graph with one less state by removing q. We can do this if we do not change the language denoted by the set of labels that can be generated as we go from q_0 to q_f. The construction that achieves this is illustrated in Figure 3.9, where the state q is to be removed and the edge labels $a, b, ...$ stand for general expressions. The case depicted is the most general in the sense that q has outgoing edges to all three vertices q_i, q_j, q. In cases where an edge is missing in (a), we omit the corresponding edge in (b).

The construction in Figure 3.9 shows which edges have to be introduced so that the language of the generalized transition graph does not change when we remove q and all its incoming and outgoing edges. The complete process requires that this be done for all pairs (q_i, q_j) in $Q - \{q\}$ before removing q. Although we will not formally prove this, it can be shown that the construction yields an equivalent generalized transition graph. Accepting this, we are ready to show how any nfa can be associated with a regular expression.

Theorem 3.2　Let L be a regular language. Then there exists a regular expression r such that $L = L(r)$.

Proof: Let M be an nfa that accepts L. We can assume without any loss of generality that M has only one final state and that $q_0 \notin F$. We interpret the graph of M as a generalized transition graph and apply the above construction to it. To remove a vertex labeled q, we use the scheme in Figure 3.9 for all pairs (q_i, q_j). After all the new edges have been added,

Figure 3.10

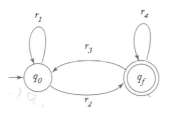

q with all its incident edges can be removed. We continue this process, removing one vertex after the other, until we reach the situation shown in Figure 3.10. A regular expression that denotes the language accepted by this graph is

$$r = r_1^* r_2 \left(r_4 + r_3 r_1^* r_2 \right)^* . \tag{3.1}$$

Since the sequence of generalized transition graphs are all equivalent to the initial one, we can prove by an induction on the number of states in the generalized transition graph that the regular expression in (3.1) denotes L. ∎

Example 3.9   Consider the nfa in Figure 3.11(a). The corresponding generalized transition graph after removal of state q_1 is shown in Figure 3.11(b). Making the identification $r_1 - b + ab^*a$, $r_2 = ab^*b$, $r_3 = \varnothing$, $r_4 - a + b$, we arrive at the regular expression

$$r = \left(b + ab^*a\right)^* ab^*b \left(a + b\right)^*$$

for the original automaton. The construction involved in Theorem 3.2 is tedious and tends to give very lengthy answers, but it is completely routine and always works.

Figure 3.11

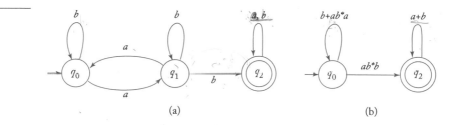

(a)   (b)

Example 3.10	Find a regular expression for the language

$$L = \left\{ w \in \{a,b\}^* : n_a(w) \text{ is even and } n_b(w) \text{ is odd} \right\}.$$

An attempt to construct a regular expression directly from this description leads to all kinds of difficulties. On the other hand, finding a nfa for it is easy as long as we use vertex labeling effectively. We label the vertices with EE to denote an even number of a's and b's, with OE to denote an odd number of a's and an even number of b's, and so on. With this we easily get the solution in Figure 3.12.

We can now apply the conversion to a regular expression in a mechanical way. First, we remove the state labeled OE, giving the generalized transition graph in Figure 3.13.

Next, we remove the vertex labeled OO. This gives Figure 3.14. Finally, we apply (3.1) with

$$r_1 = aa + ab\,(bb)^*\,ba,$$
$$r_2 = b + ab\,(bb)^*\,a,$$
$$r_3 = b + a\,(bb)^*\,ba,$$
$$r_4 = a\,(bb)^*\,a.$$

Figure 3.12

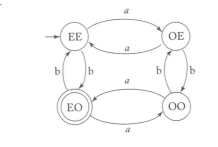

Figure 3.13

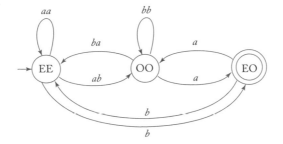

Figure 3.14

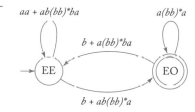

The final expression is long and complicated, but the way to get it is relatively straightforward.

Regular Expressions for Describing Simple Patterns

In Example 1.15 and in Exercise 15, Section 2.1, we explored the connection between finite accepters and some of the simpler constituents of programming languages, such as identifiers, or integers and real numbers. The relation between finite automata and regular expressions means that we can also use regular expressions as a way of describing these features. This is easy to see; for example, the set of all acceptable Pascal integers is defined by the regular expression

$$sdd^*,$$

where s stands for the sign, with possible values from $\{+, -, \lambda\}$, and d stands for the digits 0 to 9.

Pascal integers are a simple case of what is sometimes called a "pattern," a term that refers to a set of objects having some common properties. Pattern matching refers to assigning a given object to one of several categories. Often, the key to successful pattern matching is finding an effective way to describe the patterns. This is a complicated and extensive area of computer science to which we can only briefly allude. The example below is a simplified, but nevertheless instructive, demonstration of how the ideas we have talked about so far have been found useful in pattern matching.

Example 3.11   An application of pattern matching occurs in text editing. All text editors allow files to be scanned for the occurrence of a given string; most editors extend this to permit searching for patterns. For example, the editor *ed* in the UNIX operating system recognizes the command

$$/aba^*c/$$

as an instruction to search the file for the first occurrence of the string ab, followed by an arbitrary number of a's, followed by a c. We see from this example that the UNIX editor can recognize regular expressions (although it uses a somewhat different convention for specifying regular expressions than the one used here).

A challenging task in such an application is to write an efficient program for recognizing string patterns. Searching a file for occurrences of a given string is a very simple programming exercise, but here the situation is more complicated. We have to deal with an unlimited number of arbitrarily complicated patterns; furthermore, the patterns are not fixed beforehand, but created at run time. The pattern description is part of the input, so the recognition process must be flexible. To solve this problem, ideas from automata theory are often used.

If the pattern is specified by a regular expression, the pattern recognition program can take this description and convert it into an equivalent nfa using the construction in Theorem 3.1. Theorem 2.2 may then be used to reduce this to a dfa. This dfa, in the form of a transition table, is effectively the pattern-matching algorithm. All the programmer has to do is to provide a driver that gives the general framework for using the table. In this way we can automatically handle a large number of patterns that are defined at run time.

The efficiency of the program must be considered also. The construction of finite automata from regular expressions using Theorems 2.1 and 3.1 tends to yield automata with many states. If memory space is a problem, the state reduction method described in Section 2.4 is helpful.

EXERCISES

1. Use the construction in Theorem 3.1 to find an nfa that accepts the language $L\left(ab^{*}aa + bba^{*}ab\right)$.

2. Find an nfa that accepts the complement of the language in Exercise 1.

3. Give an nfa that accepts the language $L\left((a+b)^{*}b\left(a+bb\right)^{*}\right)$. **S**

4. Find dfa's that accept the following languages.

   (a) $L\left(aa^{*} + aba^{*}b^{*}\right)$ **S**

   (b) $L\left(ab\left(a+ab\right)^{*}\left(a+aa\right)\right)$

   (c) $L\left(\left(abab\right)^{*} + \left(aaa^{*} + b\right)^{*}\right)$

   (d) $L\left(\left(\left(aa^{*}\right)^{*}b\right)^{*}\right)$

5. Find dfa's that accept the following languages.

  (a) $L = L\left(ab^*a^*\right) \cup L\left((ab)^*\,ba\right)$,

  (b) $L = L\left(ab^*a^*\right) \cap L\left((ab)^*\,ba\right)$.

6. Find an nfa for Exercise 15(f), Section 3.1. Use this to derive a regular expression for that language.

7. Give explicit rules for the construction suggested in Figure 3.9 when various edges in 3.9(a) are missing. **S**

8. Consider the following generalized transition graph.

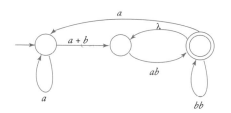

  (a) Find an equivalent generalized transition graph with only two states. **S**

  (b) What is the language accepted by this graph? **S**

9. What language is accepted by the following generalized transition graph?

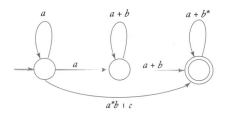

10. Find regular expressions for the languages accepted by the following automata.

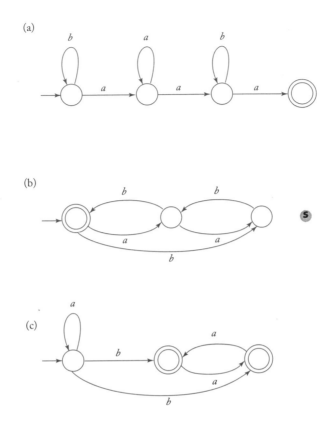

11. Rework Example 3.10, this time eliminating the state OO first.

12. Find a regular expression for the following languages on $\{a, b\}$.

(a) $L = \{w : n_a(w) \text{ and } n_b(w) \text{ are both even}\}$

(b) $L = \{w : (n_a(w) - n_b(w)) \bmod 3 = 1\}$

(c) $L = \{w : (n_a(w) - n_b(w)) \bmod 3 \neq 0\}$

(d) $L = \{w : 2n_a(w) + 3n_b(w) \text{ is even}\}$

13. Find a regular expression that generates the set of all strings of triplets defining correct binary addition as in Exercise 23, Section 2.1.

14. Prove that the constructions suggested by Figure 3.9 generate equivalent generalized transition graphs.

15. Write a regular expression for the set of all Pascal real numbers.

16. Find a regular expression for Pascal sets whose elements are integer numbers.

17. In some applications, such as programs that check spelling, we may not need an exact match of the pattern, only an approximate one. Once the notion

of an approximate match has been made precise, automata theory can be applied to construct approximate pattern matchers. As an illustration of this, consider patterns derived from the original ones by insertion of one symbol. Let L be a regular language on Σ and define

$$insert\,(L) = \{uav : a \in \Sigma, uv \in L\}.$$

In effect, $insert\,(L)$ contains all the words created from L by inserting a spurious symbol anywhere in a word.

★ (a) Given an nfa for L, show how one can construct an nfa for $insert\,(L)$. ⑤

★★ (b) Discuss how you might use this to write a pattern recognition program for $insert\,(L)$, using as input a regular expression for L.

★ 18. Analogous to the previous exercise, consider all words that can be formed from L by dropping a single symbol of the string. Formally define this operation $drop$ for languages. Construct an nfa for $drop\,(L)$, given an nfa for L.

19. Use the construction in Theorem 3.1 to find nfa's for $L\,(a\varnothing)$ and $L\,(\varnothing^*)$. Is the result consistent with the definition of these languages?

3.3 Regular Grammars

A third way of describing regular languages is by means of certain simple grammars. Grammars are often an alternative way of specifying languages. Whenever we define a language family through an automaton or in some other way, we are interested in knowing what kind of grammar we can associate with the family. First, we look at grammars that generate regular languages.

Right- and Left-Linear Grammars

Definition 3.3

A grammar $G = (V, T, S, P)$ is said to be **right-linear** if all productions are of the form

$$A \rightarrow xB,$$
$$A \rightarrow x,$$

where $A,\ B \in V$, and $x \in T^*$. A grammar is said to be **left-linear** if all productions are of the form

$$A \rightarrow Bx,$$

or

$$A \rightarrow x.$$

A **regular grammar** is one that is either right-linear or left-linear.

Note that in a regular grammar, at most one variable appears on the right side of any production. Furthermore, that variable must consistently be either the rightmost or leftmost symbol of the right side of any production.

Example 3.12   The grammar $G_1 = (\{S\}, \{a, b\}, S, P_1)$, with P_1 given as

$$S \rightarrow abS|a$$

is right-linear. The grammar $G_2 = (\{S, S_1, S_2\}, \{a, b\}, S, P_2)$, with productions

$$S \rightarrow S_1ab,$$
$$S_1 \rightarrow S_1ab|S_2,$$
$$S_2 \rightarrow a,$$

is left-linear. Both G_1 and G_2 are regular grammars.

The sequence

$$S \Rightarrow abS \Rightarrow ababS \Rightarrow ababa$$

is a derivation with G_1. From this single instance it is easy to conjecture that $L(G_1)$ is the language denoted by the regular expression $r = (ab)^* a$. In a similar way, we can see that $L(G_2)$ is the regular language $L\left(aab(ab)^*\right)$.

Example 3.13   The grammar $G = (\{S, A, B\}, \{a, b\}, S, P)$ with productions

$$S \rightarrow A,$$
$$A \rightarrow aB|\lambda,$$
$$B \rightarrow Ab,$$

is not regular. Although every production is either in right-linear or left-linear form, the grammar itself is neither right-linear nor left-linear, and

therefore is not regular. The grammar is an example of a **linear grammar.**
A linear grammar is a grammar in which at most one variable can occur
on the right side of any production, without restriction on the position of
this variable. Clearly, a regular grammar is always linear, but not all linear
grammars are regular.

Our next goal will be to show that regular grammars are associated
with regular languages and that for every regular language there is a regular
grammar. Thus, regular grammars are another way of talking about regular
languages.

Right-Linear Grammars Generate Regular Languages

First, we show that a language generated by a right-linear grammar is always
regular. To do so, we construct an nfa that mimics the derivations of a right-
linear grammar. Note that the sentential forms of a right-linear grammar
have the special form in which there is exactly one variable and it occurs as
the rightmost symbol. Suppose now that we have a step in a derivation

$$ab \cdots cD \Rightarrow ab \cdots cdE,$$

arrived at by using a production $D \rightarrow dE$. The corresponding nfa can
imitate this step by going from state D to state E when a symbol d is
encountered. In this scheme, the state of the automaton corresponds to the
variable in the sentential form, while the part of the string already processed
is identical to the terminal prefix of the sentential form. This simple idea is
the basis for the following theorem.

Theorem 3.3

Let $G = (V, T, S, P)$ be a right-linear grammar. Then $L(G)$ is a regular
language.

Proof: We assume that $V = \{V_0, V_1, ...\}$, that $S = V_0$, and that we have
productions of the form $V_0 \rightarrow v_1 V_i, V_i \rightarrow v_2 V_j, ...$ or $V_n \rightarrow v_l, ...$ If w is
a string in $L(G)$, then because of the form of the productions in G, the
derivation must have the form

$$\begin{aligned}
V_0 &\Rightarrow v_1 V_i \\
&\Rightarrow v_1 v_2 V_j \\
&\overset{*}{\Rightarrow} v_1 v_2 \cdots v_k V_n \\
&\Rightarrow v_1 v_2 \cdots v_k v_l = w.
\end{aligned} \tag{3.2}$$

The automaton to be constructed will reproduce the derivation by "consuming" each of these v's in turn. The initial state of the automaton will

be labeled V_0, and for each variable V_i there will be a nonfinal state labeled V_i. For each production

$$V_i \rightarrow a_1 a_2 \cdots a_m V_j,$$

the automaton will have transitions to connect V_i and V_j that is, δ will be defined so that

$$\delta^* (V_i, a_1 a_2 \cdots a_m) = V_j.$$

For each production

$$V_i \rightarrow a_1 a_2 \cdots a_m,$$

the corresponding transition of the automaton will be

$$\delta^* (V_i, a_1 a_2 \cdots a_m) = V_f,$$

where V_f is a final state. The intermediate states that are needed to do this are of no concern and can be given arbitrary labels. The general scheme is shown in Figure 3.15. The complete automaton is assembled from such individual parts.

Suppose now that $w \in L(G)$ so that (3.2) is satisfied. In the nfa there is, by construction, a path from V_0 to V_i labeled v_1, a path from V_i to V_j labeled v_2, and so on, so that clearly

$$V_f \in \delta^* (V_0, w),$$

and w is accepted by M.

Conversely, assume that w is accepted by M. Because of the way in which M was constructed, to accept w the automaton has to pass through a sequence of states $V_0, V_i, \ldots$ to V_f, using paths labeled $v_1, v_2, \ldots$. Therefore, w must have the form

$$w = v_1 v_2 \cdots v_k v_l$$

Figure 3.15

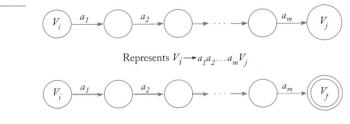

Represents $V_i \rightarrow a_1 a_2 \ldots a_m V_j$

Represents $V_i \rightarrow a_1 a_2 \ldots a_m$

Figure 3.16

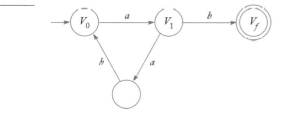

and the derivation

$$V_o \Rightarrow v_1 V_i \Rightarrow v_1 v_2 V_j \overset{*}{\Rightarrow} v_1 v_2 \cdots v_k V_k \Rightarrow v_1 v_2 \cdots v_k v_l$$

is possible. Hence w is in $L(G)$, and the theorem is proved. ∎

Example 3.14   Construct a finite automaton that accepts the language generated by the grammar

$$V_0 \rightarrow aV_1,$$
$$V_1 \rightarrow abV_0 | b.$$

We start the transition graph with vertices V_0, V_1, and V_f. The first production rule creates an edge labeled a between V_0 and V_1. For the second rule, we need to introduce an additional vertex so that there is a path labeled ab between V_1 and V_0. Finally, we need to add an edge labeled b between V_1 and V_f, giving the automaton shown in Figure 3.16. The language generated by the grammar and accepted by the automaton is the regular language $L\left((aab)^* ab\right)$.

Right-Linear Grammars for Regular Languages

To show that every regular language can be generated by some right-linear grammar, we start from the dfa for the language and reverse the construction shown in Theorem 3.3. The states of the dfa now become the variables of the grammar, and the symbols causing the transitions become the terminals in the productions.

Theorem 3.4   If L is a regular language on the alphabet Σ, then there exists a right-linear grammar $G = (V, \Sigma, S, P)$ such that $L = L(G)$.

Proof: Let $M = (Q, \Sigma, \delta, q_0, F)$ be a dfa that accepts L. We assume that $Q = \{q_0, q_1, ..., q_n\}$ and $\Sigma = \{a_1, a_2, ..., a_m\}$. Construct the right-linear grammar $G = (V, \Sigma, S, P)$ with

$$V = \{q_0, q_1, ..., q_n\}$$

and $S = q_0$. For each transition

$$\delta(q_i, a_j) = q_k$$

of M, we put in P the production

$$q_i \to a_j q_k. \tag{3.3}$$

In addition, if q_k is in F, we add to P the production

$$q_k \to \lambda. \tag{3.4}$$

We first show that G defined in this way can generate every string in L. Consider $w \in L$ of the form

$$w = a_i a_j \cdots a_k a_l.$$

For M to accept this string it must make moves via

$$\delta(q_0, a_i) = q_p,$$
$$\delta(q_p, a_j) = q_r,$$

$$\vdots$$

$$\delta(q_s, a_k) = q_t,$$
$$\delta(q_t, a_l) = q_f \in F.$$

By construction, the grammar will have one production for each of these δ's. Therefore we can make the derivation

$$q_0 \Rightarrow a_i q_p \Rightarrow a_i a_j q_r \overset{*}{\Rightarrow} a_i a_j \cdots a_k q_t$$
$$\Rightarrow a_i a_j \cdots a_k a_l q_f \Rightarrow a_i a_j \cdots a_k a_l, \tag{3.5}$$

with the grammar G, and $w \in L(G)$.

Conversely, if $w \in L(G)$, then its derivation must have the form (3.5). But this implies that

$$\delta^*(q_0, a_i a_j \cdots a_k a_l) = q_f,$$

completing the proof. ∎

Figure 3.17

$\delta(q_0, a) = \{q_1\}$	$q_0 \longrightarrow aq_1$
$\delta(q_1, a) = \{q_2\}$	$q_1 \longrightarrow aq_2$
$\delta(q_2, b) = \{q_2\}$	$q_2 \longrightarrow bq_2$
$\delta(q_2, a) = \{q_f\}$	$q_2 \longrightarrow aq_f$
$q_f \in F$	$q_f \longrightarrow \lambda$

For the purpose of constructing a grammar, it is useful to note that the restriction that M be a dfa is not essential to the proof of Theorem 3.4. With minor modification, the same construction can be used if M is an nfa.

Example 3.15 Construct a right-linear grammar for $L(aab^*a)$. The transition function for an nfa, together with the corresponding grammar productions, is given in Figure 3.17. The result was obtained by simply following the construction in Theorem 3.4. The string $aaba$ can be derived with the constructed grammar by

$$q_0 \Rightarrow aq_1 \Rightarrow aaq_2 \Rightarrow aabq_2 \Rightarrow aabaq_f \Rightarrow aaba.$$

Equivalence Between Regular Languages and Regular Grammars

The previous two theorems establish the connection between regular languages and right-linear grammars. One can make a similar connection between regular languages and left-linear grammars, thereby showing the complete equivalence of regular grammars and regular languages.

Theorem 3.5 A language L is regular if and only if there exists a left-linear grammar G such that $L = L(G)$.

Proof: We only outline the main idea. Given any left-linear grammar with productions of the form

$$A \rightarrow Bv,$$

or

$$A \rightarrow v,$$

we construct from it a right-linear grammar $\widehat{G}$ by replacing every such production of G with

$$A \to v^R B,$$

or

$$A \to v^R,$$

respectively. A few examples will make it clear quickly that $L(G) = \left(L\left(\widehat{G} \right) \right)^R$. Next, we use Exercise 12, Section 2.3, which tells us that the reverse of any regular language is also regular. Since $\widehat{G}$ is right-linear, $L\left(\widehat{G} \right)$ is regular. But then so are $L\left(\left(\widehat{G} \right) \right)^R$ and $L(G)$. ∎

Putting Theorems 3.4 and 3.5 together, we arrive at the equivalence of regular languages and regular grammars.

Theorem 3.6   A language L is regular if and only if there exists a regular grammar G such that $L = L(G)$.

We now have several ways of describing regular languages: dfa's, nfa's, regular expressions, and regular grammars. While in some instance one or the other of these may be most suitable, they are all equally powerful. They all give a complete and unambiguous definition of a regular language. The connection between all these concepts is established by the four theorems in this chapter, as shown in Figure 3.18.

Figure 3.18

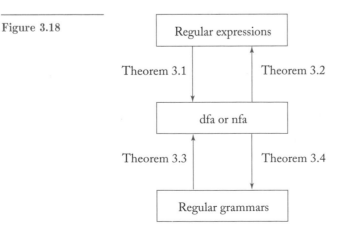

EXERCISES

1. Construct a dfa that accepts the language generated by the grammar

$$S \rightarrow abA,$$
$$A \rightarrow baB,$$
$$B \rightarrow aA|bb.$$

2. Find a regular grammar that generates the language $L(aa^*(ab+a)^*)$.

3. Construct a left linear grammar for the language in Exercise 1.

4. Construct right- and left-linear grammars for the language

$$L = \{a^n b^m : n \geq 2, m \geq 3\}. \;\; \text{\textcircled{s}}$$

5. Construct a right-linear grammar for the language $L((aab^*ab)^*)$.

6. Find a regular grammar that generates the language on $\Sigma = \{a, b\}$ consisting of all strings with no more than three a's.

7. In Theorem 3.5, prove that $L\left(\widehat{G}\right) = (L(G))^R$. \;\; \text{\textcircled{s}}

8. Suggest a construction by which a left-linear grammar can be obtained from an nfa directly.

9. Find a left-linear grammar for the language in Exercise 5.

10. Find a regular grammar for the language $L = \{a^n b^m : n+m \text{ is even}\}$. \;\; \text{\textcircled{s}}

11. Find a regular grammar that generates the language

$$L = \{w \in \{a, b\}^* : n_a(w) + 3n_b(w) \text{ is even}\}.$$

12. Find regular grammars for the following languages on $\{a, b\}$.

    (a) $L = \{w : n_a(w) \text{ and } n_b(w) \text{ are both even}\}$ \;\; \text{\textcircled{s}}

    (b) $L = \{w : (n_a(w) - n_b(w)) \bmod 3 = 1\}$

    (c) $L = \{w : (n_a(w) - n_b(w)) \bmod 3 \neq 0\}$

    (d) $L = \{w : |n_a(w) - n_b(w)| \text{ is odd}\}.$

13. Show that for every regular language not containing λ there exists a right-linear grammar whose productions are restricted to the forms

$$A \rightarrow aB$$

or

$$A \rightarrow a,$$

where $A, B \in V$ and $a \in T$.

14. Show that any regular grammar G for which $L(G) \neq \varnothing$ must have at least one production of the form

$$A \to x,$$

    where $A \in V$ and $x \in T^*$.

15. Find a regular grammar that generates the set of all Pascal real numbers.

16. Let $G_1 = (V_1, \Sigma, S_1, P_1)$ be right-linear and $G_2 = (V_2, \Sigma, S_2, P_2)$ be a left linear grammar, and assume that V_1 and V_2 are disjoint. Consider the linear grammar $G = (\{S\} \cup V_1 \cup V_2, \Sigma, S, P)$, where S is not in $V_1 \cup V_2$ and $P = \{S \to S_1 | S_2\} \cup P_1 \cup P_2$. Show that $L(G)$ is regular. **S**

Chapter 4

Properties of
Regular Languages

e have defined regular languages, studied some ways in which they can be represented, and have seen a few examples of their usefulness. We now raise the question of how general regular languages are. Could it be that every formal language is regular? Perhaps any set we can specify can be accepted by some, albeit very complex, finite automaton. As we will see shortly, the answer to this conjecture is definitely no. But to understand why this is so, we must inquire more deeply into the nature of regular languages and see what properties the whole family has.

The first question we raise is what happens when we perform operations on regular languages. The operations we consider are simple set operations, such as concatenation, as well as operations in which each string of a language is changed, as for instance in Exercise 22, Section 2.1. Is the resulting language still regular? We refer to this as a **closure** question. Closure properties, although mostly of theoretical interest, help us in discriminating between the various language families we will encounter.

A second set of questions about language families deals with our ability to decide on certain properties. For example, can we tell whether a language is finite or not? As we will see, such questions are easily answered for regular languages, but are not as easily answered for other language families.

Finally we consider the important question: How can we tell whether a given language is regular or not? If the language is in fact regular, we can always show it by giving some dfa, regular expression, or regular grammar for it. But if it is not, we need another line of attack. One way to show a language is not regular is to study the general properties of regular languages, that is, characteristics that are shared by all regular languages. If we know of some such property, and if we can show that the candidate language does not have it, then we can tell that the language is not regular.

In this chapter, we look at a variety of properties of regular languages. These properties tell us a great deal about what regular languages can and cannot do. Later, when we look at the same questions for other language families, similarities and differences in these properties will allow us to contrast the various language families.

4.1 Closure Properties of Regular Languages

Consider the following question: Given two regular languages L_1 and L_2, is their union also regular? In specific instances, the answer may be obvious, but here we want to address the problem in general. Is it true for all regular L_1 and L_2? It turns out that the answer is yes, a fact we express by saying that the family of regular languages is **closed under union**. We can ask similar questions about other types of operations on languages; this leads us to the study of the closure properties of languages in general.

Closure properties of various language families under different operations are of considerable theoretical interest. At first sight, it may not be clear what practical significance these properties have. Admittedly, some of them have very little, but many results are useful. By giving us insight into the general nature of language families, closure properties help us answer other, more practical questions. We will see instances of this (Theorem 4.7 and Example 4.13) later in this chapter.

Closure under Simple Set Operations

We begin by looking at the closure of regular languages under the common set operations, such as union and intersection.

Theorem 4.1

If L_1 and L_2 are regular languages, then so are $L_1 \cup L_2$, $L_1 \cap L_2$, $L_1 L_2$, $\overline{L_1}$ and L_1^*. We say that the family of regular languages is closed under union, intersection, concatenation, complementation, and star-closure.

Proof: If L_1 and L_2 are regular, then there exist regular expressions r_1 and r_2 such that $L_1 = L(r_1)$ and $L_2 = L(r_2)$. By definition, $r_1 + r_2$, $r_1 r_2$, and

r_1^* are regular expressions denoting the languages $L_1 \cup L_2$, $L_1 L_2$, and L_1^*, respectively. Thus, closure under union, concatenation, and star-closure is immediate.

To show closure under complementation, let $M - (Q, \Sigma, \delta, q_0, F)$ be a dfa that accepts L_1. Then the dfa

$$\widehat{M} = (Q, \Sigma, \delta, q_0, Q - F)$$

accepts $\overline{L_1}$. This is rather straightforward; we have already suggested the result in Exercise 4 in Section 2.1. Note that in the definition of a dfa, we assumed δ^* to be a total function, so that $\delta^*(q_0, w)$ is defined for all $w \in \Sigma^*$. Consequently either $\delta^*(q_0, w)$ is a final state, in which case $w \in L$, or $\delta^*(q_0, w) \in Q - F$ and $w \subset \overline{L}$.

Demonstrating closure under intersection takes a little more work. Let $L_1 = L(M_1)$ and $L_2 = L(M_2)$, where $M_1 = (Q, \Sigma, \delta_1, q_0, F_1)$ and $M_2 = (P, \Sigma, \delta_2, p_0, F_2)$ are dfa's. We construct from M_1 and M_2 a combined automaton $\widehat{M} = \left(\widehat{Q}, \Sigma, \widehat{\delta}, (q_0, p_0), \widehat{F}\right)$, whose state set $\widehat{Q} = Q \times P$ consists of pairs (q_i, p_j), and whose transition function $\widehat{\delta}$ is such that $\widehat{M}$ is in state (q_i, p_j) whenever M_1 is in state q_i and M_2 is in state p_j. This is achieved by taking

$$\widehat{\delta}\left((q_i, p_j), a\right) = (q_k, p_l),$$

whenever

$$\delta_1(q_i, a) = q_k$$

and

$$\delta_2(p_j, a) = p_l.$$

$\widehat{F}$ is defined as the set of all (q_i, p_j), such that $q_i \in F_1$ and $p_j \in F_2$. Then it is a simple matter to show that $w \in L_1 \cap L_2$ if and only if it is accepted by $\widehat{M}$. Consequently, $L_1 \cap L_2$ is regular. ∎

The proof of closure under intersection is a good example of a constructive proof. Not only does it establish the desired result, but it also shows explicitly how to construct a finite accepter for the intersection of two regular languages. Constructive proofs occur throughout this book; they are important because they give us insight into the results and often serve as the starting point for practical algorithms. Here, as in many cases, there are shorter but nonconstructive (or at least not so obviously constructive) arguments. For closure under intersection, we start with DeMorgan's law, Equation (1.3), taking the complement of both sides. Then

$$L_1 \cap L_2 = \overline{\overline{L_1} \cup \overline{L_2}}$$

for any languages L_1 and L_2. Now, if L_1 and L_2 are regular, then by closure under complementation, so are $\overline{L}_1$ and $\overline{L}_2$. Using closure under union, we next get that $\overline{L}_1 \cup \overline{L}_2$ is regular. Using closure under complementation once more, we see that

$$\overline{\overline{L}_1 \cup \overline{L}_2} = L_1 \cap L_2$$

is regular.

The following example is a variation on the same idea.

Example 4.1   Show that the family of regular languages is closed under difference. In other words, we want to show that if L_1 and L_2 are regular, then $L_1 - L_2$ is necessarily regular also.

The needed set identity is immediately obvious from the definition of a set difference, namely

$$L_1 - L_2 = L_1 \cap \overline{L}_2.$$

The fact that L_2 is regular implies that $\overline{L}_2$ is also regular. Then, because of the closure of regular languages under intersection, we know that $L_1 \cap \overline{L}_2$ is regular, and the argument is complete.

■

A variety of other closure properties can be derived directly by elementary arguments.

Theorem 4.2   The family of regular languages is closed under reversal.

Proof: The proof of this theorem was suggested as an exercise in Section 2.3. Here are the details. Suppose that L is a regular language. We then construct an nfa with a single final state for it. By Exercise 7, Section 2.3, this is always possible. In the transition graph for this nfa we make the initial vertex a final vertex, the final vertex the initial vertex, and reverse the direction on all the edges. It is a fairly straightforward matter to show that the modified nfa accepts w^R if and only if the original nfa accepts w. Therefore, the modified nfa accepts L^R, proving closure under reversal.   ■

Closure under Other Operations

In addition to the standard operations on languages, one can define other operations and investigate closure properties for them. There are many such results; we select only two typical ones. Others are explored in the exercises at the end of this section.

Definition 4.1

Suppose Σ and Γ are alphabets. Then a function

$$h : \Sigma \rightarrow \Gamma^*$$

is called a **homomorphism.** In words, a homomorphism is a substitution in which a single letter is replaced with a string. The domain of the function h is extended to strings in an obvious fashion; if

$$w = a_1 a_2 \cdots a_n,$$

then

$$h(w) = h(a_1) h(a_2) \cdots h(a_n).$$

If L is a language on Σ, then its **homomorphic image** is defined as

$$h(L) = \{ h(w) : w \in L \}.$$

Example 4.2   Let $\Sigma = \{a, b\}$ and $\Gamma = \{a, b, c\}$ and define h by

$$h(a) = ab,$$
$$h(b) = bbc.$$

Then $h(aba) = abbbcab$. The homomorphic image of $L = \{aa, aba\}$ is the language $h(L) = \{abab, abbbcab\}$.

If we have a regular expression r for a language L, then a regular expression for $h(L)$ can be obtained by simply applying the homomorphism to each Σ symbol of r.

Example 4.3   Take $\Sigma = \{a, b\}$ and $\Gamma = \{b, c, d\}$. Define h by

$$h(a) = dbcc,$$
$$h(b) = bdc.$$

If L is the regular language denoted by

$$r = (a + b^*)(aa)^*,$$

then

$$r_1 = \left(dbcc + (bdc)^*\right)(dbccdbcc)^*$$

denotes the regular language $h(L)$.

The general result on the closure of regular languages under any homomorphism follows from this example in an obvious manner.

Theorem 4.3   Let h be a homomorphism. If L is a regular language, then its homomorphic image $h(L)$ is also regular. The family of regular languages is therefore closed under arbitrary homomorphisms.

Proof: Let L be a regular language denoted by some regular expression r. We find $h(r)$ by substituting $h(a)$ for each symbol $a \in \Sigma$ of r. It can be shown directly by an appeal to the definition of a regular expression that the result is a regular expression. It is equally easy to see that the resulting expression denotes $h(L)$. All we need to do is to show that for every $w \in L(r)$, the corresponding $h(w)$ is in $L(h(r))$ and conversely that for every v in $L(h(r))$ there is a w in L, such that $v = h(w)$. Leaving the details as an exercise, we claim that $h(L)$ is regular. ∎

Definition 4.2

Let L_1 and L_2 be languages on the same alphabet. Then the **right quotient** of L_1 with L_2 is defined as

$$L_1/L_2 = \{x : xy \in L_1 \text{ for some } y \in L_2\}. \tag{4.1}$$

To form the right quotient of L_1 with L_2, we take all the strings in L_1 that have a suffix belonging to L_2. Every such string, after removal of this suffix, belongs to L_1/L_2;

Example 4.4   If

$$L_1 = \{a^n b^m : n \geq 1, m \geq 0\} \cup \{ba\}$$

and

$$L_2 = \{b^m : m \geq 1\},$$

then

$$L_1/L_2 = \{a^n b^m : n \geq 1, m \geq 0\}.$$

The strings in L_2 consist of one or more b's. Therefore, we arrive at the answer by removing one or more b's from those strings in L_1 that terminate with at least one b as a suffix.

Note that here L_1, L_2, and L_1/L_2 are all regular. This suggests that the right quotient of any two regular languages is also regular. We will prove this in the next theorem by a construction that takes the dfa's for L_1 and L_2 and constructs from them a dfa for L_1/L_2. Before we describe the construction in full, let us see how it applies to this example. We start with a dfa for L_1; say the automaton $M_1 = (Q, \Sigma, \delta, q_0, F)$ in Figure 4.1. Since an automaton for L_1/L_2 must accept any prefix of strings in L_1, we will try to modify M_1 so that it accepts x if there is any y satisfying (4.1).

Figure 4.1

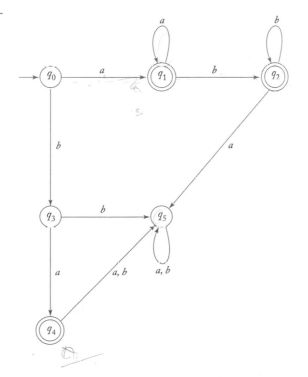

Figure 4.2

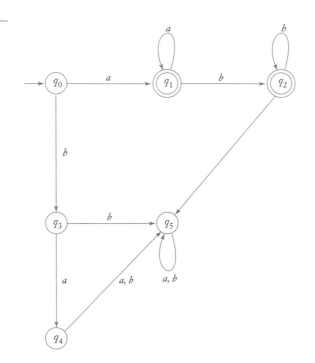

The difficulty comes in finding whether there is some y such that $xy \in L_1$ and $y \in L_2$. To solve it, we determine, for each $q \in Q$, whether there is a walk to a final state labeled v such that $v \in L_2$. If this is so, any x such that $\delta(q_0, x) = q$ will be in L_1/L_2. We modify the automaton accordingly to make q a final state.

To apply this to our present case, we check each state q_0, q_1, q_2, q_3, q_4, q_5 to see whether there is a walk labeled bb^* to any of the q_1, q_2, or q_4. We see that only q_1 and q_2 qualify; q_0, q_3, q_4 do not. The resulting automaton for L_1/L_2 is shown in Figure 4.2. Check it to see that the construction works. The idea is generalized in the next theorem.

Theorem 4.4

If L_1 and L_2 are regular languages, then L_1/L_2 is also regular. We say that the family of regular languages is closed under right quotient with a regular language.

Proof: Let $L_1 = L(M)$, where $M = (Q, \Sigma, \delta, q_0, F)$ is a dfa. We construct another dfa $\widehat{M} = \left(Q, \Sigma, \delta, q_0, \widehat{F}\right)$ as follows. For each $q_i \in Q$, determine if there exists a $y \in L_2$ such that

$$\delta^*(q_i, y) = q_f \in F.$$

This can be done by looking at dfa's $M_i = (Q, \Sigma, \delta, q_i, F)$. The automaton M_i is M with the initial state q_0 replaced by q_i. We now determine whether there exists a y in $L(M_i)$ that is also in L_2. For this, we can use the construction for the intersection of two regular languages given in Theorem 4.1, finding the transition graph for $L_2 \cap L(M_i)$. If there is any path between its initial vertex and any final vertex, then $L_2 \cap L(M_i)$ is not empty. In that case, add q_i to $\widehat{F}$. Repeating this for every $q_i \in Q$, we determine $\widehat{F}$ and thereby construct $\widehat{M}$.

To prove that $L(\widehat{M}) = L_1/L_2$, let x be any element of L_1/L_2. Then there must be a $y \in L_2$ such that $xy \in L_1$. This implies that

$$\delta^*(q_0, xy) \in F,$$

so that there must be some $q \in Q$ such that

$$\delta^*(q_0, x) = q$$

and

$$\delta^*(q, y) \in F.$$

Therefore, by construction, $q \in \widehat{F}$, and $\widehat{M}$ accepts x because $\delta^*(q_0, x)$ is in $\widehat{F}$.

Conversely, for any x accepted by $\widehat{M}$, we have

$$\delta^*(q_0, x) = q \in \hat{F}.$$

But again by construction, this implies that there exists a $y \in L_2$ such that $\delta^*(q, y) \in F$. Therefore xy is in L_1, and x is in L_1/L_2. We therefore conclude that

$$L(\widehat{M}) = L_1/L_2,$$

and from this that L_1/L_2 is regular. ∎

Example 4.5   Find L_1/L_2 for

$$L_1 = L(a^* baa^*),$$
$$L_2 = L(ab^*).$$

We first find a dfa that accepts L_1. This is easy, and a solution is given in Figure 4.3. The example is simple enough so that we can skip the formalities of the construction. From the graph in Figure 4.3 it is quite evident that

$$L(M_0) \cap L_2 = \varnothing,$$
$$L(M_1) \cap L_2 = \{a\} \neq \varnothing,$$
$$L(M_2) \cap L_2 = \{a\} \neq \varnothing,$$
$$L(M_3) \cap L_2 = \varnothing.$$

Figure 4.3

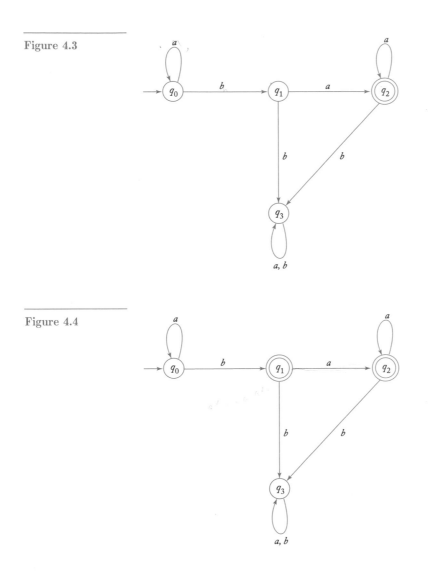

Figure 4.4

Therefore, the automaton accepting L_1/L_2 is determined. The result is shown in Figure 4.4. It accepts the language denoted by the regular expression of $a^*b + a^*baa^*$, which can be simplified to a^*ba^*. Thus $L_1/L_2 = L(a^*ba^*)$.

Exercises

1. Fill in the details of the constructive proof of closure under intersection in Theorem 4.1.

2. Use the construction in Theorem 4.1 to find nfa's that accept

   (a) $L\left((a+b)\,a^*\right) \cap L\left(baa^*\right)$, **s**

   (b) $L\left(ab^*a^*\right) \cap L\left(a^*b^*a\right)$.

3. In Example 4.1 we showed closure under difference for regular languages, but the proof was nonconstructive. Provide a constructive argument for this result.

4. In the proof of Theorem 4.3, show that $h\left(r\right)$ is a regular expression. Then show that $h\left(r\right)$ denotes $h\left(L\right)$.

5. Show that the family of regular languages is closed under finite union and intersection, that is, if $L_1, L_2, ..., L_n$ are regular, then

$$L_U = \bigcup_{i=\{1,2,...,n\}} L_i$$

   and

$$L_I = \bigcap_{i=\{1,2,...,n\}} L_i$$

   are also regular.

6. The **symmetric difference** of two sets S_1 and S_2 is defined as

$$S_1 \ominus S_2 = \{x : x \in S_1 \text{ or } x \in S_2, \text{ but } x \text{ is not in both } S_1 \text{ and } S_2\}.$$

   Show that the family of regular languages is closed under symmetric difference.

7. The *nor* of two languages is

$$nor\left(L_1, L_2\right) = \{w : w \notin L_1 \text{ and } w \notin L_2\}.$$

   Show that the family of regular languages is closed under the *nor* operation. **s**

8. Define the complementary or (*cor*) of two languages by

$$cor\left(L_1, L_2\right) = \left\{w : w \in \overline{L}_1 \quad \text{or} \quad w \in \overline{L}_2\right\}.$$

   Show that the family of regular languages is closed under the *cor* operation.

9. Which of the following are true for all regular languages and all homomorphisms?

   (a) $h\left(L_1 \cup L_2\right) = h\left(L_1\right) \cup h\left(L_2\right)$

   (b) $h\left(L_1 \cap L_2\right) = h\left(L_1\right) \cap h\left(L_2\right)$

   (c) $h\left(L_1 L_2\right) = h\left(L_1\right) h\left(L_2\right)$

10. Let $L_1 = L(a^*baa^*)$ and $L_2 = L(aba^*)$. Find L_1/L_2.

11. Show that $L_1 = L_1L_2/L_2$ is not true for all languages L_1 and L_2.

★ 12. Suppose we know that $L_1 \cup L_2$ is regular and that L_1 is finite. Can we conclude from this that L_2 is regular? **S**

13. If L is a regular language, prove that $L_1 = \{uv : u \in L, |v| = 2\}$ is also regular.

14. If L is a regular language, prove that the language $\{uv : u \in L, v \in L^R\}$ is also regular. **S**

15. The left quotient of a language L_1 with respect to L_2 is defined as

$$L_2/L_1 = \{y : x \in L_2, xy \in L_1\}.$$

Show that the family of regular languages is closed under the left quotient with a regular language.

16. Show that, if the statement "If L_1 is regular and $L_1 \cup L_2$ is also regular, then L_2 must be regular" were true for all L_1 and L_2, then all languages would be regular. **S**

17. The *tail* of a language is defined as the set of all suffixes of its strings, that is

$$tail(L) = \{y : xy \in L \text{ for some } x \in \Sigma^*\}.$$

Show that if L is regular, so is $tail(L)$.

18. The *head* of a language is the set of all prefixes of its strings, that is,

$$head(L) = \{x : xy \in L \text{ for some } y \in \Sigma^*\}.$$

Show that the family of regular languages is closed under this operation. **S**

19. Define an operation *third* on strings and languages as

$$third(a_1a_2a_3a_4a_5a_6\cdots) = a_3a_6\cdots$$

with the appropriate extension of this definition to languages. Prove the closure of the family of regular languages under this operation.

20. For a string $a_1a_2\cdots a_n$ define the operation *shift* as

$$shift(a_1a_2\cdots a_n) = a_2\cdots a_na_1.$$

From this, we can define the operation on a language as

$$shift(L) = \{v : v = shift(w) \text{ for some } w \in L\}.$$

Show that regularity is preserved under the *shift* operation.

21. Define

$$exchange(a_1a_2\cdots a_{n-1}a_n) = a_na_2\cdots a_{n-1}a_1,$$

and

$$exchange(L) = \{v : v = exchange(w) \text{ for some } w \in L\}.$$

Show that the family of regular languages is closed under *exchange*.

★ 22. The shuffle of two languages L_1 and L_2 is defined as

$$shuffle\,(L_1, L_2) = \{w_1 v_1 w_2 v_2 \cdots w_m v_m : w_1 w_2 ... w_m \in L_1,$$
$$v_1 v_2 ... v_m \in L_2, \text{ for all } w_i, v_i \in \Sigma^*\}$$

Show that the family of regular languages is closed under the shuffle operation.

★ 23. Define an operation *minus5* on a language L as the set of all strings of L with the fifth symbol from the left removed (strings of length less than five are left unchanged). Show that the family of regular languages is closed under the *minus5* operation.

★ 24. Define the operation *leftside* on L by

$$leftside\,(L) = \left\{w : ww^R \in L\right\}.$$

Is the family of regular languages closed under this operation?

25. The *min* of a language L is defined as

$$min\,(L) = \left\{w \in L : \text{ there is no } u \in L, v \in \Sigma^+, \text{ such that } w = uv\right\}.$$

Show that the family of regular languages is closed under the *min* operation.

26. Let G_1 and G_2 be two regular grammars. Show how one can derive regular grammars for the languages

(a) $L\,(G_1) \cup L\,(G_2)$ **S**

(b) $L\,(G_1)\,L\,(G_2)$ **S**

(c) $L\,(G_1)^*$ **S**

4.2 Elementary Questions about Regular Languages

We now come to a very fundamental issue: Given a language L and a string w, can we determine whether or not w is an element of L? This is the **membership** question and a method for answering it is called a membership algorithm. Very little can be done with languages for which we cannot find efficient membership algorithms. The question of the existence and nature of membership algorithms will be of great concern in later discussions; it is an issue that is often difficult. For regular languages, though, it is an easy matter.

We first consider what exactly we mean when we say "given a language...." In many arguments, it is important that this be unambiguous. We have used several ways of describing regular languages: informal verbal descriptions, set notation, finite automata, regular expressions, and regular grammars. Only the last three are sufficiently well defined for use in theorems. We therefore say that a regular language is given in a **standard representation** if and only if it is described by a finite automaton, a regular expression, or a regular grammar.

Theorem 4.5

Given a standard representation of any regular language L on Σ and any $w \in \Sigma^*$, there exists an algorithm for determining whether or not w is in L.

Proof: We represent the language by some dfa, then test w to see if it is accepted by this automaton. ■

Other important questions are whether a language is finite or infinite, whether two languages are the same, and whether one language is a subset of another. For regular languages at least, these questions are easily answered.

Theorem 4.6

There exists an algorithm for determining whether a regular language, given in standard representation, is empty, finite, or infinite.

Proof: The answer is apparent if we represent the language as a transition graph of a dfa. If there is a simple path from the initial vertex to any final vertex, then the language is not empty.

To determine whether or not a language is infinite, find all the vertices that are the base of some cycle. If any of these are on a path from an initial to a final vertex, the language is infinite. Otherwise, it is finite. ■

The question of the equality of two languages is also an important practical issue. Often several definitions of a programming language exist, and we need to know whether, in spite of their different appearances, they specify the same language. This is generally a difficult problem; even for regular languages the argument is not obvious. It is not possible to argue on a sentence-by-sentence comparison, since this works only for finite languages. Nor is it easy to see the answer by looking at the regular expressions, grammars, or dfa's. An elegant solution uses the already established closure properties.

Theorem 4.7

Given standard representations of two regular languages L_1 and L_2, there exists an algorithm to determine whether or not $L_1 = L_2$.

Proof: Using L_1 and L_2 we define the language

$$L_3 = \left(L_1 \cap \overline{L_2}\right) \cup \left(\overline{L_1} \cap L_2\right).$$

By closure, L_3 is regular, and we can find a dfa M that accepts L_3. Once we have M we can then use the algorithm in Theorem 4.6 to determine if L_3 is empty. But from Exercise 8, Section 1.1 we see that $L_3 = \varnothing$ if and only if $L_1 = L_2$. ∎

These results are fundamental, in spite of being obvious and unsurprising. For regular languages, the questions raised by Theorems 4.5 to 4.7 can be answered easily, but this is not always the case when we deal with larger families of languages. We will encounter questions like these on several occasions later on. Anticipating a little, we will see that the answers become increasingly more difficult, and eventually impossible to find.

EXERCISES

For all the exercises in this section, assume that regular languages are given in standard representation.

1. Show that there exists an algorithm to determine whether or not $w \in L_1 - L_2$, for any given w and any regular languages L_1 and L_2. **Ⓢ**

2. Show that there exists an algorithm for determining if $L_1 \subseteq L_2$, for any regular languages L_1 and L_2. **Ⓢ**

3. Show that there exists an algorithm for determining if $\lambda \in L$, for any regular language L.

4. Show that for any regular L_1 and L_2, there is an algorithm to determine whether or not $L_1 = L_1/L_2$.

5. A language is said to be a *palindrome* language if $L = L^R$. Find an algorithm for determining if a given regular language is a palindrome language. **Ⓢ**

6. Exhibit an algorithm for determining whether or not a regular language L contains any string w such that $w^R \in L$.

7. Exhibit an algorithm that, given any three regular languages, L, L_1, L_2, determines whether or not $L = L_1 L_2$.

8. Exhibit an algorithm that, given any regular language L, determines whether or not $L = L^*$.

9. Let L be a regular language on Σ and $\widehat{w}$ be any string in Σ^*. Find an algorithm to determine if L contains any w such that $\widehat{w}$ is a substring of it, that is, such that $w = u\widehat{w}v$, with $u, v \in \Sigma^*$.

10. Show that there is an algorithm to determine if $L = shuffle(L, L)$ for any regular L.

11. The operation $tail(L)$ is defined as

$$tail(L) = \{v : uv \in L, u, v \in \Sigma^*\}.$$

Show that there is an algorithm for determining whether or not $L = tail\,(L)$ for any regular L.

12. Let L be any regular language on $\Sigma = \{a, b\}$. Show that an algorithm exists for determining if L contains any strings of even length. **S**

13. Find an algorithm for determining whether a regular language L contains an infinite number of even-length strings.

14. Describe an algorithm which, when given a regular grammar G, can tell us whether or not $L\,(G) = \Sigma^*$.

4.3 Identifying Nonregular Languages

Regular languages can be infinite, as most of our examples have demonstrated. The fact that regular languages are associated with automata that have finite memory, however, imposes some limits on the structure of a regular language. Some narrow restrictions must be obeyed if regularity is to hold. Intuition tells us that a language is regular only if, in processing any string, the information that has to be remembered at any stage is strictly limited. This is true, but has to be shown precisely to be used in any meaningful way. There are several ways in which this precision can be achieved.

Using the Pigeonhole Principle

The term "pigeonhole principle" is used by mathematicians to refer to the following simple observation. If we put n objects into m boxes (pigeonholes), and if $n > m$, then at least one box must have more than one item in it. This is such an obvious fact that it is surprising how many deep results can be obtained from it.

Example 4.6   Is the language $L = \{a^n b^n : n \geq 0\}$ regular? The answer is no, as we show using a proof by contradiction.

Suppose L is regular. Then some dfa $M = (Q, \{a, b\}, \delta, q_0, F)$ exists for it. Now look at $\delta^*\left(q_0, a^i\right)$ for $i = 1, 2, 3, \dots$. Since there are an unlimited number of i's, but only a finite number of states in M, the pigeonhole principle tells us that there must be some state, say q, such that

$$\delta^*\left(q_0, a^n\right) = q$$

and

$$\delta^*\left(q_0, a^m\right) = q,$$

with $n \neq m$. But since M accepts $a^n b^n$ we must have

$$\delta^* (q, b^n) = q_f \in F.$$

From this we can conclude that

$$\delta^* (q_0, a^m b^n) = \delta^* (\delta^* (q_0, a^m), b^n)$$
$$= \delta^* (q, b^n)$$
$$= q_f.$$

This contradicts the original assumption that M accepts $a^m b^n$ only if $n = m$, and leads us to conclude that L cannot be regular. ∎

In this argument, the pigeonhole principle is just a way of stating precisely what we mean when we say that a finite automaton has a limited memory. To accept all $a^n b^n$, an automaton would have to differentiate between all prefixes a^n and a^m. But since there are only a finite number of internal states with which to do this, there are some n and m for which the distinction cannot be made.

In order to use this type of argument in a variety of situations, it is convenient to codify it as a general theorem. There are several ways to do this; the one we give here is perhaps the most famous one.

A Pumping Lemma

The following result, known as the **pumping lemma** for regular languages, uses the pigeonhole principle in another form. The proof is based on the observation that in a transition graph with n vertices, any walk of length n or longer must repeat some vertex, that is, contain a cycle.

Theorem 4.8   Let L be an infinite regular language. Then there exists some positive integer m such that any $w \in L$ with $|w| \geq m$ can be decomposed as

$$w = xyz,$$

with

$$|xy| \leq m,$$

and

$$|y| \geq 1,$$

such that

$$w_i = xy^i z, \tag{4.2}$$

is also in L for all $i = 0, 1, 2, \ldots.$

To paraphrase this, every sufficiently long string in L can be broken into three parts in such a way that an arbitrary number of repetitions of the middle part yields another string in L. We say that the middle string is "pumped," hence the term pumping lemma for this result.

Proof: If L is regular, there exists a dfa that recognizes it. Let such a dfa have states labeled $q_0, q_1, q_2, ..., q_n$. Now take a string w in L such that $|w| \geq m = n + 1$. Since L is assumed to be infinite, this can always be done. Consider the set of states the automaton goes through as it processes w, say

$$q_0, q_i, q_j, ..., q_f.$$

Since this sequence has exactly $|w| + 1$ entries, at least one state must be repeated, and such a repetition must start no later than the nth move. Thus the sequence must look like

$$q_0, q_i, q_j, ..., q_r, ..., q_r, ..., q_f,$$

indicating there must be substrings x, y, z of w such that

$$\delta^* (q_0, x) = q_r,$$
$$\delta^* (q_r, y) = q_r,$$
$$\delta^* (q_r, z) = q_f,$$

with $|xy| \leq n + 1 = m$ and $|y| \geq 1$. From this it immediately follows that

$$\delta^* (q_0, xz) = q_f,$$

as well as

$$\delta^* (q_0, xy^2 z) = q_f,$$
$$\delta^* (q_0, xy^3 z) = q_f,$$

and so on, completing the proof of the theorem. ■

We have given the pumping lemma only for infinite languages. Finite languages, although always regular, cannot be pumped since pumping automatically creates an infinite set. The theorem does hold for finite languages, but it is vacuous. The m in the pumping lemma is to be taken larger than the longest string, so that no string can be pumped.

The pumping lemma, like the pigeonhole argument in Example 4.6, is used to show that certain languages are not regular. The demonstration is always by contradiction. There is nothing in the pumping lemma, as we have stated it here, which can be used for proving that a language is regular.

Even if we could show (and this is normally quite difficult) that any pumped string must be in the original language, there is nothing in the statement of Theorem 4.8 that allows us to conclude from this that the language is regular.

Example 4.7   Using the pumping lemma to show that $L = \{a^n b^n : n \geq 0\}$ is not regular. Assume that L is regular, so that the pumping lemma must hold. We do not know the value of m, but whatever it is, we can always choose $n = m$. Therefore, the substring y must consist entirely of a's. Suppose $|y| = k$. Then the string obtained by using $i = 0$ in Equation (4.2) is

$$w_0 = a^{m-k}b^m$$

and is clearly not in L. This contradicts the pumping lemma and thereby indicates that the assumption that L is regular must be false.

In applying the pumping lemma, we must keep in mind what the theorem says. We are guaranteed the existence of an m as well as the decomposition xyz, but we do not know what they are. We cannot claim that we have reached a contradiction just because the pumping lemma is violated for some specific values of m or xyz. On the other hand, the pumping lemma holds for every $w \in L$ and every i. Therefore, if the pumping lemma is violated even for one w or i, then the language cannot be regular.

The correct argument can be visualized as a game we play against an opponent. Our goal is to win the game by establishing a contradiction of the pumping lemma, while the opponent tries to foil us. There are four moves in the game.

1. The opponent picks m.

2. Given m, we pick a string w in L of length equal or greater than m. We are free to choose any w, subject to $w \in L$ and $|w| \geq m$.

3. The opponent chooses the decomposition xyz, subject to $|xy| \leq m, |y| \geq 1$. We have to assume that the opponent makes the choice that will make it hardest for us to win the game.

4. We try to pick i in such a way that the pumped string w_i, defined in Equation (4.2), is not in L. If we can do so, we win the game.

A strategy that allows us to win whatever the opponent's choices is tantamount to a proof that the language is not regular. In this, Step 2 is crucial. While we cannot force the opponent to pick a particular decomposition of w, we may be able to choose w so that the opponent is very

Figure 4.5

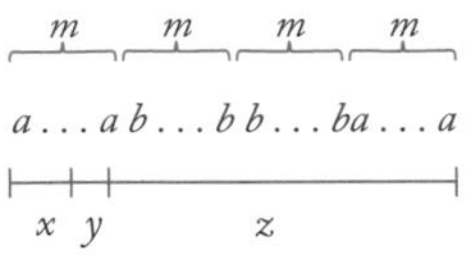

$$\overbrace{a\ldots a}^{m}\overbrace{b\ldots b}^{m}\overbrace{b\ldots b}^{m}\overbrace{a\ldots a}^{m}$$

$$\underset{x \ \ y \qquad z}{\underbrace{\qquad\qquad\qquad\qquad}}$$

restricted in Step 3, forcing a choice of x, y, and z that allows us to produce a violation of pumping lemma on our next move.

Example 4.8   Let $\Sigma = \{a, b\}$. Show that

$$L = \left\{ww^R : w \in \Sigma^*\right\}$$

is not regular.

Whatever m the opponent picks on Step 1, we can always choose a w as shown in Figure 4.5. Because of this choice, and the requirement that $|xy| \le m$, the opponent is restricted in Step 3 to choosing a y that consists entirely of a's. In Step 4, we use $i = 0$. The string obtained in this fashion has fewer a's on the left than on the right and so cannot be of the form ww^R. Therefore L is not regular.

Note that if we had chosen w too short, then the opponent could have chosen a y with an even number of b's. In that case, we could not have reached a violation of the pumping lemma on the last step. We would also fail if we were to choose a string consisting of all a's, say,

$$w = a^{2m},$$

which is in L. To defeat us, the opponent need only pick

$$y = aa.$$

Now w_i is in L for all i, and we lose.

To apply the pumping lemma we cannot assume that the opponent will make a wrong move. If, in the case where we pick $w = a^{2m}$, the opponent were to pick

$$y = a,$$

then w_0 is a string of odd length and therefore not in L. But any argument that assumes that the opponent is so accommodating is automatically incorrect.

Example 4.9 Let $\Sigma = \{a, b\}$. The language

$$L = \{w \in \Sigma^* : n_a(w) < n_b(w)\}$$

is not regular.

Suppose we are given m. Since we have complete freedom in choosing w, we pick $w = a^m b^{m+1}$. Now, because $|xy|$ cannot be greater than m, the opponent cannot do anything but pick a y with all a's, that is

$$y = a^k, \qquad 1 \le k \le m.$$

We now pump up, using $i = 2$. The resulting string

$$w_2 = a^{m+k} b^{m+1}$$

is not in L. Therefore, the pumping lemma is violated, and L is not regular.

Example 4.10 The language

$$L = \left\{ (ab)^n a^k : n > k, k \ge 0 \right\}$$

is not regular.

Given m, we pick as our string

$$w = (ab)^{m+1} a^m$$

which is in L. Because of the constraint $|xy| \le m$, both x and y must be in the part of the string made up of ab's. The choice of x does not affect the argument, so let us see what can be done with y. If our opponent picks $y = a$, we choose $i = 0$ and get a string not in $L\left((ab)^* a^*\right)$. If the opponent picks $y = ab$, we can choose $i = 0$ again. Now we get the string $(ab)^m a^m$, which is not in L. In the same way, we can deal with any possible choice by the opponent, thereby proving our claim.

Example 4.11 Show that

$$L = \left\{ a^{n!} : n \ge 0 \right\}$$

is not regular.

Given the opponent's choice for m, we pick as w the string $a^{m!}$ (unless the opponent picks $m < 3$, in which case we can use $a^{3!}$ as w). The various decompositions of w obviously differ only in the lengths of the substrings. Suppose the opponent picks y such that

$$|y| = k \leq m.$$

We then look at xz which has length $m! - k$. This string is in L only if there exists a j such that

$$m! - k = j!$$

But this is impossible, since for $m > 2$ and $k \leq m$ we have

$$m! - k > (m - 1)!$$

Therefore, the language is not regular.

In some cases, closure properties can be used to relate a given problem to one we have already classified. This may be much simpler than a direct application of the pumping lemma.

Example 4.12   Show that the language

$$L = \left\{ a^n b^k c^{n+k} : n \geq 0, k \geq 0 \right\}$$

is not regular.

It is not difficult to apply the pumping lemma directly, but it is even easier to use closure under homomorphism. Take

$$h(a) = a, h(b) = a, h(c) = c$$

then

$$h(L) = \left\{ a^{n+k} c^{n+k} : n + k \geq 0 \right\}$$
$$= \left\{ a^i c^i : i \geq 0 \right\},$$

but we know this language is not regular; therefore L cannot be regular either.

Example 4.13   Show that the language

$$L = \left\{ a^n b^l : n \neq l \right\}$$

is not regular.

Here we need a bit of ingenuity to apply the pumping lemma directly. Choosing a string with $n = l + 1$ or $n = l + 2$ will not do, since our opponent can always choose a decomposition that will make it impossible to pump the string out of the language (that is, pump it so that it has an equal number of a's and b's). We must be more inventive. Let us take $n = m!$ and $l = (m + 1)!$. If the opponent now chooses a y (by necessity consisting of all a's) of length $k < n$, we pump i times to generate a string with $m! + (i - 1)k$ a's. We can get a contradiction of the pumping lemma if we can pick i such that

$$m! + (i - 1)k = (m + 1)!$$

This is always possible since

$$i = 1 + \frac{m\, m!}{k}$$

and $k \leq m$. The right side is therefore an integer, and we have succeeded in violating the conditions of the pumping lemma.

However, there is a much more elegant way of solving this problem. Suppose L were regular. Then, by Theorem 4.1, $\overline{L}$ and the language

$$L_1 - \overline{L} \cap L\left(a^* b^*\right)$$

would also be regular. But $L_1 = \{a^n b^n : n \geq 0\}$, which we have already classified as nonregular. Consequently, L cannot be regular.

∎

The pumping lemma is difficult for several reasons. Its statement is complicated, and it is easy to go astray in applying it. But even if we master the technique, it may still be hard to see exactly how to use it. The pumping lemma is like a game with complicated rules. Knowledge of the rules is essential, but that alone is not enough to play a good game. You also need a good strategy to win. If you can apply the pumping lemma correctly to some of the more difficult cases in this book, you are to be congratulated.

EXERCISES

1. Prove the following version of the pumping lemma. If L is regular, then there is an m such that, every $w \in L$ of length greater than m can be decomposed as

$$w = xyz,$$

with

$$|yz| \leq m,$$
$$|y| \geq 1,$$

such that $xy^i z$ is in L for all i.

2. Prove the following generalization of the pumping lemma, which includes Theorem 4.8 as well as Exercise 1 as special cases.

   If L is regular, then there exists an m, such that the following holds for every sufficiently long $w \in L$ and every one of its decompositions $w = u_1 v u_2$, with $u_1, u_2 \in \Sigma^*, |v| \geq m$. The middle string v can be written as $v = xyz$, with $|xy| \leq m, |y| \geq 1$, such that $u_1 xy^i zu_2 \in L$ for all $i = 0, 1, 2, ...$ Ⓢ

3. Show that the language $L = \{w : n_a(w) = n_b(w)\}$ is not regular. Is L^* regular?

4. Prove that the following languages are not regular.

   (a) $L = \{a^n b^l a^k : k \geq n + l\}$ Ⓢ

   (b) $L = \{a^n b^l a^k : k \neq n + l\}$

   (c) $L = \{a^n b^l a^k : n = l \text{ or } l \neq k\}$

   (d) $L = \{a^n b^l : n \leq l\}$

   (e) $L = \{w : n_a(w) \neq n_b(w)\}$ Ⓢ

   (f) $L = \{ww : w \in \{a, b\}^*\}$

   (g) $L = \{wwww^R : w \in \{a, b\}^*\}$

5. Determine if the following languages on $\Sigma = \{a\}$ are regular.

   (a) $L = \{a^n : n \geq 2, n \text{ is a prime number}\}$ Ⓢ

   (b) $L = \{a^n : n \text{ is not a prime number}\}$

   (c) $L = \{a^n : n = k^2 \text{ for some } k \geq 0\}$

   (d) $L = \{a^n : n = 2^k \text{ for some } k \geq 0\}$

   (e) $L = \{a^n : n \text{ is the product of two prime numbers}\}$

   (f) $L = \{a^n : n \text{ is either prime or the product of two or more prime numbers}\}$

6. Apply the pumping lemma directly to show the result in Example 4.12.

7. Show that the following language is not regular.

$$L = \{a^n b^k : n > k\} \cup \{a^n b^k : n \neq k - 1\}$$

8. Prove or disprove the following statement. If L_1 and L_2 are nonregular languages, then $L_1 \cup L_2$ is also nonregular. Ⓢ

9. Consider the languages below. For each, make a conjecture whether or not it is regular. Then prove your conjecture.

   (a) $L = \{a^n b^l a^k : n + l + k > 5\}$ Ⓢ

   (b) $L = \{a^n b^l a^k : n > 5, l > 3, k \leq l\}$ Ⓢ

   (c) $L = \{a^n b^l : n/l \text{ is an integer}\}$

   (d) $L = \{a^n b^l : n + l \text{ is a prime number}\}$

   (e) $L = \{a^n b^l : n < l < 2n\}$

   (f) $L = \{a^n b^l : n \geq 100, l \leq 100\}$

   (g) $L = \{a^n b^l : |n - l| = 2\}$.

10. Is the following language regular?
$$L = \{w_1 c w_2 : w_1, w_2 \in \{a, b\}^*, w_1 \neq w_2\}$$

11. Let L_1 and L_2 be regular languages. Is the language $L = \{w : w \in L_1, w^R \in L_2\}$ necessarily regular? Ⓢ

12. Apply the pigeonhole argument directly to the language in Example 4.8.

13. Are the following languages regular?

    (a) $L = \{u w w^R v : u, v, w \in \{a, b\}^+\}$ Ⓢ

    ★ (b) $L = \{u w w^R v : u, v, w \in \{a, b\}^+, |u| \geq |v|\}$ Ⓢ

14. Is the following language regular?
$$L = \{w w^R v : v, w \in \{a, b\}^+\}$$

15. Let P be an infinite but countable set, and associate with each $p \in P$ a language L_p. The smallest set containing every L_p is the union over the infinite set P; it will be denoted by $\cup_{p \in P} L_P$. Show by example that the family of regular languages is not closed under infinite union. Ⓢ

★ 16. Consider the argument in Section 3.2 that the language associated with any generalized transition graph is regular. The language associated with such a graph is
$$L = \bigcup_{p \in P} L(r_p),$$

where P is the set of all walks through the graph and r_p is the expression associated with a walk p. The set of walks is generally infinite, so that in light of Exercise 15, it does not immediately follow that L is regular. Show that in this case, because of the special nature of P, the infinite union is regular.

★ 17. Is the family of regular languages closed under infinite intersection? **5**

18. Suppose that we know that $L_1 \cup L_2$ and L_1 are regular. Can we conclude from this that L_2 is regular?

19. In the chain code language in Exercise 22, Section 3.1, let L be the set of all $w \in \{u, r, l, d\}^*$ that describe rectangles. Show that L is not a regular language.

Chapter 5

Context-Free
Languages

 n the last chapter, we discovered that not all languages are regular. While regular languages are effective in describing certain simple patterns, one does not need to look very far for examples of nonregular languages. The relevance of these limitations to programming languages becomes evident if we reinterpret some of the examples. If in $L = \{a^n b^n : n \geq 0\}$ we substitute a left parenthesis for a and a right parenthesis for b, then parentheses strings such as (()) and ((())) are in L, but (() is not. The language therefore describes a simple kind of nested structure found in programming languages, indicating that some properties of programming languages require something beyond regular languages. In order to cover this and other more complicated features we must enlarge the family of languages. This leads us to consider **context-free** languages and grammars.

We begin this chapter by defining context-free grammars and languages, illustrating the definitions with some simple examples. Next, we consider the important membership problem; in particular we ask how we can tell if a given string is derivable from a given grammar. Explaining a sentence through its grammatical derivation is familiar to most of us from a study of natural languages and is called **parsing.** Parsing is a way of describing sentence structure. It is important whenever we need to understand the meaning of a sentence, as we do for instance in translating from one language to another. In computer science, this is relevant in interpreters, compilers, and other translating programs.

The topic of context-free languages is perhaps the most important aspect of formal language theory as it applies to programming languages. Actual programming languages have many features that can be described elegantly by means of context-free languages. What formal language theory tells us about context-free languages has important applications in the design of programming languages as well as in the construction of efficient compilers. We touch upon this briefly in Section 5.3.

5.1 Context-Free Grammars

The productions in a regular grammar are restricted in two ways: the left side must be a single variable, while the right side has a special form. To create grammars that are more powerful, we must relax some of these restrictions. By retaining the restriction on the left side, but permitting anything on the right, we get context-free grammars.

Definition 5.1

A grammar $G = (V, T, S, P)$ is said to be **context-free** if all productions in P have the form

$$A \rightarrow x,$$

where $A \in V$ and $x \in (V \cup T)^*$.

A language L is said to be context-free if and only if there is a context-free grammar G such that $L = L(G)$.

Every regular grammar is context-free, so a regular language is also a context-free one. But, as we know from simple examples such as $\{a^n b^n\}$, there are nonregular languages. We have already shown in Example 1.11 that this language can be generated by a context-free grammar, so we see that the family of regular languages is a proper subset of the family of context-free languages.

Context-free grammars derive their name from the fact that the substitution of the variable on the left of a production can be made any time such a variable appears in a sentential form. It does not depend on the symbols in the rest of the sentential form (the context). This feature is the consequence of allowing only a single variable on the left side of the production.

Examples of Context-Free Languages

Example 5.1   The grammar $G = (\{S\}, \{a, b\}, S, P)$, with productions

$$S \rightarrow aSa,$$
$$S \rightarrow bSb,$$
$$S \rightarrow \lambda,$$

is context-free. A typical derivation in this grammar is

$$S \Rightarrow aSa \Rightarrow aaSaa \Rightarrow aabSbaa \Rightarrow aabbaa.$$

This makes it clear that

$$L(G) = \{ww^R : w \subset \{a, b\}^*\}.$$

The language is context-free, but as shown in Example 4.8, it is not regular.

Example 5.2   The grammar G, with productions

$$S \rightarrow abB,$$
$$A \rightarrow aaBb,$$
$$B \rightarrow bbAa,$$
$$A \rightarrow \lambda,$$

is context-free. We leave it to the reader to show that

$$L(G) = \{ab(bbaa)^n bba(ba)^n : n \geq 0\}.$$

Both of the above examples involve grammars that are not only context-free, but linear. Regular and linear grammars are clearly context-free, but a context-free grammar is not necessarily linear.

Example 5.3 The language

$$L = \{a^n b^m : n \neq m\}$$

is context-free.

To show this, we need to produce a context-free grammar for the language. The case of $n = m$ was solved in Example 1.11 and we can build on that solution. Take the case $n > m$. We first generate a string with an equal number of a's and b's, then add extra a's on the left. This is done with

$$S \rightarrow AS_1,$$
$$S_1 \rightarrow aS_1b|\lambda,$$
$$A \rightarrow aA|a.$$

We can use similar reasoning for the case $n < m$, and we get the answer

$$S \rightarrow AS_1|S_1B,$$
$$S_1 \rightarrow aS_1b|\lambda,$$
$$A \rightarrow aA|a,$$
$$B \rightarrow bB|b.$$

The resulting grammar is context-free, hence L is a context-free language. However, the grammar is not linear.

The particular form of the grammar given here was chosen for the purpose of illustration; there are many other equivalent context-free grammars. In fact, there are some simple linear ones for this language. In Exercise 25 at the end of this section you are asked to find one of them.

Example 5.4 Consider the grammar with productions

$$S \rightarrow aSb|SS|\lambda.$$

This is another grammar that is context-free, but not linear. Some strings in $L(G)$ are $abaabb$, $aababb$, and $ababab$. It is not difficult to conjecture and prove that

$$L = \{w \in \{a, b\}^* : n_a(w) = n_b(w) \text{ and } n_a(v) \geq n_b(v),$$
$$\text{where } v \text{ is any prefix of } w\}. \tag{5.1}$$

We can see the connection with programming languages clearly if we replace a and b with left and right parentheses, respectively. The language L

includes such strings as (()) and () () () and is in fact the set of all properly nested parenthesis structures for the common programming languages.

Here again there are many other equivalent grammars. But, in contrast to Example 5.3, it is not so easy to see if there are any linear ones. We will have to wait until Chapter 8 before we can answer this question. ∎

Leftmost and Rightmost Derivations

In context-free grammars that are not linear, a derivation may involve sentential forms with more than one variable. In such cases, we have a choice in the order in which variables are replaced. Take for example the grammar $G = (\{A, B, S\}, \{a, b\}, S, P)$ with productions

$$\textbf{1.}\ S \rightarrow AB.$$
$$\textbf{2.}\ A \rightarrow aaA.$$
$$\textbf{3.}\ A \rightarrow \lambda.$$
$$\textbf{4.}\ B \rightarrow Bb.$$
$$\textbf{5.}\ B \rightarrow \lambda.$$

It is easy to see that this grammar generates the language $L(G) = \{a^{2n}b^m : n \geq 0, m \geq 0\}$.

Consider now the two derivations

$$S \overset{1}{\Rightarrow} AB \overset{2}{\Rightarrow} aaAB \overset{3}{\Rightarrow} aaB \overset{4}{\Rightarrow} aaBb \overset{5}{\Rightarrow} aab$$

and

$$S \overset{1}{\Rightarrow} AB \overset{4}{\Rightarrow} ABb \overset{2}{\Rightarrow} aaABb \overset{5}{\Rightarrow} aaAb \overset{3}{\Rightarrow} aab.$$

In order to show which production is applied, we have numbered the productions and written the appropriate number on the $\rightarrow$ symbol. From this we see that the two derivations not only yield the same sentence but use exactly the same productions. The difference is entirely in the order in which the productions are applied. To remove such irrelevant factors, we often require that the variables be replaced in a specific order.

Definition 5.2

A derivation is said to be **leftmost** if in each step the leftmost variable in the sentential form is replaced. If in each step the rightmost variable is replaced, we call the derivation **rightmost**.

Figure 5.1

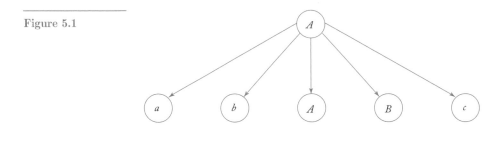

Example 5.5   Consider the grammar with productions

$$S \rightarrow aAB,$$
$$A \rightarrow bBb,$$
$$B \rightarrow A|\lambda.$$

Then

$$S \Rightarrow aAB \Rightarrow abBbB \Rightarrow abAbB \Rightarrow abbBbbB \Rightarrow abbbbB \Rightarrow abbbb$$

is a leftmost derivation of the string $abbbb$. A rightmost derivation of the same string is

$$S \Rightarrow aAB \Rightarrow aA \Rightarrow abBb \Rightarrow abAb \Rightarrow abbBbb \Rightarrow abbbb.$$

Derivation Trees

A second way of showing derivations, independent of the order in which productions are used, is by a **derivation tree**. A derivation tree is an ordered tree in which nodes are labeled with the left sides of productions and in which the children of a node represent its corresponding right sides. For example, Figure 5.1 shows part of a derivation tree representing the production

$$A \rightarrow abABc.$$

In a derivation tree, a node labeled with a variable occurring on the left side of a production has children consisting of the symbols on the right side of that production. Beginning with the root, labeled with the start symbol and ending in leaves that are terminals, a derivation tree shows how each variable is replaced in the derivation. The following definition makes this notion precise.

Definition 5.3

Let $G = (V, T, S, P)$ be a context-free grammar. An ordered tree is a derivation tree for G if and only if it has the following properties.

1. The root is labeled S.

2. Every leaf has a label from $T \cup \{\lambda\}$.

3. Every interior vertex (a vertex which is not a leaf) has a label from V.

4. If a vertex has label $A \in V$, and its children are labeled (from left to right) $a_1, a_2, ..., a_n$, then P must contain a production of the form

$$A \rightarrow a_1 a_2 \cdots a_n.$$

5. A leaf labeled λ has no siblings, that is, a vertex with a child labeled λ can have no other children.

A tree that has properties 3, 4 and 5, but in which 1 does not necessarily hold and in which property 2 is replaced by:

2a. Every leaf has a label from $V \cup T \cup \{\lambda\}$

is said to be a **partial derivation tree.**

The string of symbols, obtained by reading the leaves of the tree from left to right, omitting any λ's encountered, is said to be the **yield** of the tree. The descriptive term *left to right* can be given a precise meaning. The yield is the string of terminals in the order they are encountered when the tree is traversed in a depth-first manner, always taking the leftmost unexplored branch.

Example 5.6   Consider the grammar G, with productions

$$S \rightarrow aAB,$$
$$A \rightarrow bBb,$$
$$B \rightarrow A | \lambda.$$

The tree in Figure 5.2 is a partial derivation tree for G, while the tree in Figure 5.3 is a derivation tree. The string $abBbB$, which is the yield of the first tree, is a sentential form of G. The yield of the second tree, $abbbb$ is a sentence of $L(G)$.

Figure 5.2

Figure 5.3

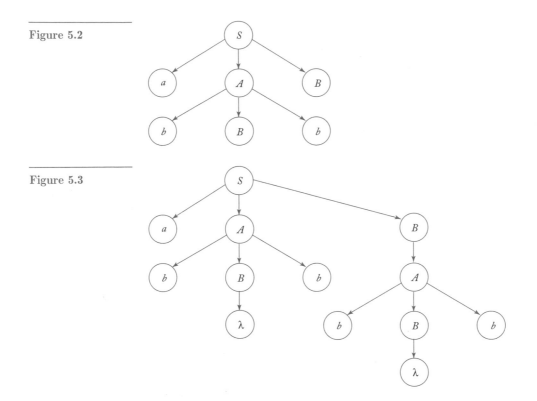

Relation Between Sentential Forms and Derivation Trees

Derivation trees give a very explicit and easily comprehended description of a derivation. Like transition graphs for finite automata, this explicitness is a great help in making arguments. First, though, we must establish the connection between derivations and derivation trees.

Theorem 5.1

Let $G = (V, T, S, P)$ be a context-free grammar. Then for every $w \in L(G)$, there exists a derivation tree of G whose yield is w. Conversely, the yield of any derivation tree is in $L(G)$. Also, if t_G is any partial derivation tree for G whose root is labeled S, then the yield of t_G is a sentential form of G.

Proof: First we show that for every sentential form of $L(G)$ there is a corresponding partial derivation tree. We do this by induction on the number of steps in the derivation. As a basis, we note that the claimed result is true for every sentential form derivable in one step. Since $S \Rightarrow u$ implies that there is a production $S \rightarrow u$, this follows immediately from Definition 5.3.

Assume that for every sentential form derivable in n steps, there is a corresponding partial derivation tree. Now any w derivable in $n + 1$ steps must be such that

$$S \stackrel{*}{\Rightarrow} xAy, \quad x, y \in (V \cup T)^*, \quad A \in V,$$

in n steps, and

$$xAy \Rightarrow xa_1a_2 \cdots a_my = w, a_1 \in V \cup T.$$

Since by the inductive assumption there is a partial derivation tree with yield xAy, and since the grammar must have production $A \to a_1a_2 \cdots a_m$, we see that by expanding the leaf labeled A, we get a partial derivation tree with yield $xa_1a_2 \cdots a_my = w$. By induction, we therefore claim that the result is true for all sentential forms.

In a similar vein, we can show that every partial derivation tree represents some sentential form. We will leave this as an exercise.

Since a derivation tree is also a partial derivation tree whose leaves are terminals, it follows that every sentence in $L(G)$ is the yield of some derivation tree of G and that the yield of every derivation tree is in $L(G)$. ∎

Derivation trees show which productions are used in obtaining a sentence, but do not give the order of their application. Derivation trees are able to represent any derivation, reflecting the fact that this order is irrelevant, an observation which allows us to close a gap in the preceding discussion. By definition, any $w \in L(G)$ has a derivation, but we have not claimed that it also had a leftmost or rightmost derivation. However, once we have a derivation tree, we can always get a leftmost derivation by thinking of the tree as having been built in such a way that the leftmost variable in the tree was always expanded first. Filling in a few details, we are led to the not surprising result that any $w \in L(G)$ has a leftmost and a rightmost derivation (for details, see Exercise 24 at the end of this section).

EXERCISES

1. Complete the arguments in Example 5.2, showing that the language given is generated by the grammar.

2. Draw the derivation tree corresponding to the derivation in Example 5.1.

3. Give a derivation tree for $w = abbbaabbaba$ for the grammar in Example 5.2. Use the derivation tree to find a leftmost derivation.

4. Show that the grammar in Example 5.4 does in fact generate the language described in Equation 5.1.

5. Is the language in Example 5.2 regular?

6. Complete the proof in Theorem 5.1 by showing that the yield of every partial derivation tree with root S is a sentential form of G.

7. Find context-free grammars for the following languages (with $n \geq 0$, $m \geq 0$).

    (a) $L = \{a^n b^m : n \leq m + 3\}$ Ⓢ

    (b) $L = \{a^n b^m : n \neq m - 1\}$

    (c) $L = \{a^n b^m : n \neq 2m\}$

    (d) $L = \{a^n b^m : 2n \leq m \leq 3n\}$ Ⓢ

    (e) $L = \{w \in \{a, b\}^* : n_a(w) \neq n_b(w)\}$

    (f) $L = \{w \in \{a, b\}^* : n_a(v) \geq n_b(v)$, where v is any prefix of $w\}$

    (g) $L = \{w \in \{a, b\}^* : n_a(w) = 2n_b(w) + 1\}$.

8. Find context-free grammars for the following languages (with $n \geq 0$, $m \geq 0$, $k \geq 0$).

    (a) $L = \{a^n b^m c^k : n = m$ or $m \leq k\}$ Ⓢ

    (b) $L = \{a^n b^m c^k : n = m$ or $m \neq k\}$

    (c) $L = \{a^n b^m c^k : k = n + m\}$

    (d) $L = \{a^n b^m c^k : n + 2m = k\}$

    (e) $L = \{a^n b^m c^k : k = |n - m|\}$ Ⓢ

    (f) $L = \{w \in \{a, b, c\}^* : n_a(w) + n_b(w) \neq n_c(w)\}$

    (g) $L = \{a^n b^m c^k, k \neq n + m\}$

    (h) $L = \{a^n b^n c^k : k \geq 3\}$.

9. Find a context-free grammar for $head(L)$, where L is the language in Exercise 7(a) above. For the definition of $head$ see Exercise 18, Section 4.1.

10. Find a context-free grammar for $\Sigma = \{a, b\}$ for the language $L = \{a^n w w^R b^n : w \in \Sigma^*, n \geq 1\}$.

★11. Given a context-free grammar G for a language L, show how one can create from G a grammar $\widehat{G}$ so that $L\left(\widehat{G}\right) = head(L)$.

12. Let $L = \{a^n b^n : n \geq 0\}$.

    (a) Show that L^2 is context-free. Ⓢ

    (b) Show that L^k is context-free for any given $k \geq 1$.

    (c) Show that $\overline{L}$ and L^* are context-free.

13. Let L_1 be the language in Exercise 8(a) and L_2 the language in Exercise 8(d). Show that $L_1 \cup L_2$ is a context-free language.

14. Show that the following language is context-free.

$$L = \left\{uvwv^R : u, v, w \in \{a, b\}^+, |u| = |w| = 2\right\}$$

★15. Show that the complement of the language in Example 5.1 is context-free. Ⓢ

16. Show that the complement of the language in Exercise 8(b) is context-free.

17. Show that the language $L = \{w_1 c w_2 : w_1, w_2 \in \{a, b\}^+, w_1 \neq w_2^R\}$, with $\Sigma = \{a, b, c\}$, is context-free.

18. Show a derivation tree for the string $aabbbb$ with the grammar

$$S \to AB | \lambda,$$
$$A \to aB,$$
$$B \to Sb.$$

Give a verbal description of the language generated by this grammar.

19. Consider the grammar with productions

$$S \to aaB,$$
$$A \to bBb | \lambda,$$
$$B \to Aa.$$

Show that the string $aabbabba$ is not in the language generated by this grammar. **S**

20. Consider the derivation tree below.

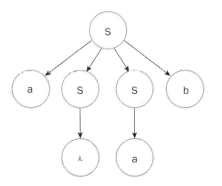

Find a simple grammar G for which this is the derivation tree of the string aab. Then find two more sentences of $L(G)$.

21. Define what one might mean by properly nested parenthesis structures involving two kinds of parentheses, say () and [ ]. Intuitively, properly nested strings in this situation are ([ ]), ([[ ]]) [()], but not ([)] or (([]. Using your definition, give a context-free grammar for generating all properly nested parentheses.

22. Find a context-free grammar for the set of all regular expressions on the alphabet $\{a, b\}$. **S**

23. Find a context-free grammar that can generate all the production rules for context-free grammars with $T = \{a, b\}$ and $V = \{A, B, C\}$.

24. Prove that if G is a context-free grammar, then every $w \in L(G)$ has a leftmost and rightmost derivation. Give an algorithm for finding such derivations from a derivation tree.

25. Find a linear grammar for the language in Example 5.3.

26. Let $G = (V, T, S, P)$ be a context-free grammar such that every one of its productions is of the form $A \rightarrow v$, with $|v| = k > 1$. Show that the derivation tree for any $w \in L(G)$ has a height h such that

$$\log_k |w| \leq h \leq \frac{(|w| - 1)}{k - 1}.$$

5.2 Parsing and Ambiguity

We have so far concentrated on the generative aspects of grammars. Given a grammar G, we studied the set of strings that can be derived using G. In cases of practical applications, we are also concerned with the analytical side of the grammar: given a string w of terminals, we want to know whether or not w is in $L(G)$. If so, we may want to find a derivation of w. An algorithm that can tell us whether w is in $L(G)$ is a membership algorithm. The term **parsing** describes finding a sequence of productions by which a $w \in L(G)$ is derived.

Parsing and Membership

Given a string w in $L(G)$, we can parse it in a rather obvious fashion: we systematically construct all possible (say, leftmost) derivations and see whether any of them match w. Specifically, we start at round one by looking at all productions of the form

$$S \rightarrow x,$$

finding all x that can be derived from S in one step. If none of these result in a match with w, we go to the next round, in which we apply all applicable productions to the leftmost variable of every x. This gives us a set of sentential forms, some of them possibly leading to w. On each subsequent round, we again take all leftmost variables and apply all possible productions. It may be that some of these sentential forms can be rejected on the grounds that w can never be derived from them, but in general, we will have on each round a set of possible sentential forms. After the first round, we have sentential forms that can be derived by applying a single production, after the second round we have the sentential forms that can be derived in two steps, and so on. If $w \in L(G)$, then it must have a leftmost derivation of finite length. Thus, the method will eventually give a leftmost derivation of w.

For reference below, we will call this the **exhaustive search parsing** method. It is a form of **top-down parsing**, which we can view as the construction of a derivation tree from the root down.

Example 5.7   Consider the grammar

$$S \rightarrow SS \,|aSb|\, bSa|\lambda$$

and the string $w = aabb$. Round one gives us

1. $S \Rightarrow SS,$

2. $S \Rightarrow aSb,$

3. $S \Rightarrow bSa,$

4. $S \Rightarrow \lambda.$

The last two of these can be removed from further consideration for obvious reasons. Round two then yields sentential forms

$$S \Rightarrow SS \Rightarrow SSS,$$
$$S \Rightarrow SS \Rightarrow aSbS,$$
$$S \Rightarrow SS \Rightarrow bSaS,$$
$$S \Rightarrow SS \Rightarrow S,$$

which are obtained by replacing the leftmost S in sentential form 1 with all applicable substitutes. Similarly, from sentential form 2 we get the additional sentential forms

$$S \Rightarrow aSb \Rightarrow aSSb,$$
$$S \Rightarrow aSb \Rightarrow aaSbb,$$
$$S \Rightarrow aSb \Rightarrow abSab,$$
$$S \Rightarrow aSb \Rightarrow ab.$$

Again, several of these can be removed from contention. On the next round, we find the actual target string from the sequence

$$S \Rightarrow aSb \Rightarrow aaSbb \Rightarrow aabb.$$

Therefore $aabb$ is in the language generated by the grammar under consideration.

Exhaustive search parsing has serious flaws. The most obvious one is its tediousness; it is not to be used where efficient parsing is required. But even when efficiency is a secondary issue, there is a more pertinent objection. While the method always parses a $w \in L(G)$, it is possible that it never terminates for strings not in $L(G)$. This is certainly the case in the previous example; with $w = abb$, the method will go on producing trial sentential forms indefinitely unless we build into it some way of stopping.

The problem of nontermination of exhaustive search parsing is relatively easy to overcome if we restrict the form that the grammar can have. If we examine Example 5.7, we see that the difficulty comes from the productions $S \rightarrow \lambda$; this production can be used to decrease the length of successive sentential forms, so that we cannot tell easily when to stop. If we do not have any such productions, then we have many fewer difficulties. In fact, there are two types of productions we want to rule out, those of the form $A \rightarrow \lambda$ as well as those of the form $A \rightarrow B$. As we will see in the next chapter, this restriction does not affect the power of the resulting grammars in any significant way.

Example 5.8   The grammar

$$S \rightarrow SS \,|aSb|\, bSa \,|ab|\, ba$$

satisfies the given requirements. It generates the language in Example 5.7 without the empty string.

Given any $w \in \{a, b\}^+$, the exhaustive search parsing method will always terminate in no more than $|w|$ rounds. This is clear because the length of the sentential form grows by at least one symbol in each round. After $|w|$ rounds we have either produced a parsing or we know that $w \notin L(G)$.

The idea in this example can be generalized and made into a theorem for context-free languages in general.

Theorem 5.2   Suppose that $G = (V, T, S, P)$ is a context-free grammar which does not have any rules of the form

$$A \rightarrow \lambda,$$

or

$$A \rightarrow B,$$

where $A, B \in V$. Then the exhaustive search parsing method can be made into an algorithm which, for any $w \in \Sigma^*$, either produces a parsing of w, or tells us that no parsing is possible.

Proof: For each sentential form, consider both its length and the number of terminal symbols. Each step in the derivation increases at least one of these. Since neither the length of a sentential form nor the number of terminal symbols can exceed $|w|$, a derivation cannot involve more than $2|w|$ rounds, at which time we either have a successful parsing or w cannot be generated by the grammar. ∎

While the exhaustive search method gives a theoretical guarantee that parsing can always be done, its practical usefulness is limited because the number of sentential forms generated by it may be excessively large. Exactly how many sentential forms are generated differs from case to case; no precise general result can be established, but we can put some rough upper bounds on it. If we restrict ourselves to leftmost derivations, we can have no more than $|P|$ sentential forms after one round, no more than $|P|^2$ sentential forms after the second round, and so on. In the proof of Theorem 5.2, we observed that parsing cannot involve more than $2|w|$ rounds; therefore, the total number of sentential forms cannot exceed

$$M = |P| + |P|^2 + \cdots + |P|^{2|w|} . \tag{5.2}$$

This indicates that the work for exhaustive search parsing may grow exponentially with the length of the string, making the cost of the method prohibitive. Of course, Equation (5.2) is only a bound, and often the number of sentential forms is much smaller. Nevertheless, practical observation shows that exhaustive search parsing is very inefficient in most cases.

The construction of more efficient parsing methods for context-free grammars is a complicated matter that belongs to a course on compilers. We will not pursue it here except for some isolated results.

Theorem 5.3

For every context-free grammar there exists an algorithm that parses any $w \in L(G)$ in a number of steps proportional to $|w|^3$.

There are several known methods to achieve this, but all of them are sufficiently complicated that we cannot even describe them without developing some additional results. In Section 6.3 we will take this question up again briefly. More details can be found in Harrison 1978 and Hopcroft and Ullman 1979. One reason for not pursuing this in detail is that even these algorithms are unsatisfactory. A method in which the work rises with the third power of the length of the string, while better than an exponential algorithm, is still quite inefficient, and a compiler based on it would need an excessive amount of time to parse even a moderately long program. What we would like to have is a parsing method which takes time proportional to the length of the string. We refer to such a method as a **linear time** parsing algorithm. We do not know any linear time parsing methods for context-free languages in general, but such algorithms can be found for restricted, but important, special cases.

Definition 5.4

A context-free grammar $G = (V, T, S, P)$ is said to be a **simple grammar** or **s-grammar** if all its productions are of the form

$$A \rightarrow ax,$$

where $A \in V$, $a \in T$, $x \in V^*$, and any pair (A, a) occurs at most once in P.

Example 5.9

The grammar

$$S \rightarrow aS \,|bSS|\, c$$

is an s-grammar. The grammar

$$S \rightarrow aS \,|bSS|\, aSS|c$$

is not an s-grammar because the pair (S, a) occurs in the two productions $S \rightarrow aS$ and $S \rightarrow aSS$.

While s-grammars are quite restrictive, they are of some interest. As we will see in the next section, many features of common programming languages can be described by s-grammars.

If G is an s-grammar, then any string w in $L(G)$ can be parsed with an effort proportional to $|w|$. To see this, look at the exhaustive search method and the string $w = a_1 a_2 \cdots a_n$. Since there can be at most one rule with S on the left, and starting with a_1 on the right, the derivation must begin with

$$S \Rightarrow a_1 A_1 A_2 \cdots A_m.$$

Next, we substitute for the variable A_1, but since again there is at most one choice, we must have

$$S \overset{*}{\Rightarrow} a_1 a_2 B_1 B_2 \cdots A_2 \cdots A_m.$$

We see from this that each step produces one terminal symbol and hence the whole process must be completed in no more that $|w|$ steps.

Ambiguity in Grammars and Languages

On the basis of our argument we can claim that given any $w \in L(G)$, exhaustive search parsing will produce a derivation tree for w. We say "a" derivation tree rather than "the" derivation tree because of the possibility that a number of different derivation trees may exist. This situation is referred to as **ambiguity**.

Definition 5.5

A context-free grammar G is said to be **ambiguous** if there exists some $w \in L(G)$ that has at least two distinct derivation trees. Alternatively, ambiguity implies the existence of two or more leftmost or rightmost derivations.

Example 5.10   The grammar in Example 5.4, with productions $S \rightarrow aSb|SS|\lambda$, is ambiguous. The sentence $aabb$ has the two derivation trees shown in Figure 5.4.

Ambiguity is a common feature of natural languages, where it is tolerated and dealt with in a variety of ways. In programming languages, where there should be only one interpretation of each statement, ambiguity must be removed when possible. Often we can achieve this by rewriting the grammar in an equivalent, unambiguous form.

Figure 5.4

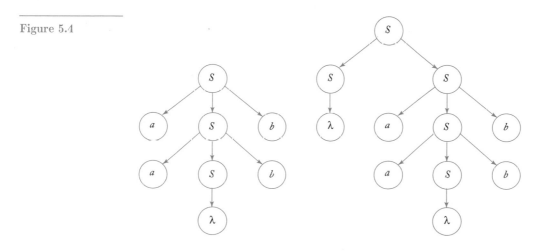

Figure 5.5
Two derivation
trees for $a + b*c$.

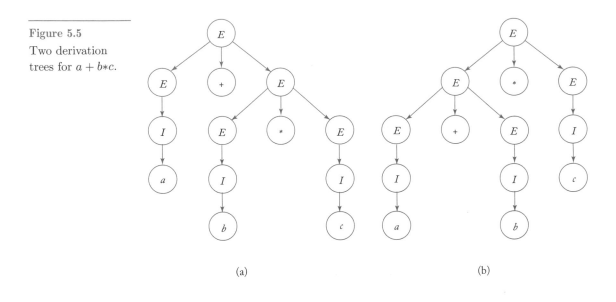

(a)   (b)

Example 5.11   Consider the grammar $G = (V, T, E, P)$ with

$$V = \{E, I\},$$
$$T = \{a, b, c, +, *, (,)\},$$

and productions

$$E \rightarrow I,$$
$$E \rightarrow E + E,$$
$$E \rightarrow E*E,$$
$$E \rightarrow (E),$$
$$I \rightarrow a \,|b| \,c.$$

The strings $(a + b)*c$ and $a*b + c$ are in $L(G)$. It is easy to see that this grammar generates a restricted subset of arithmetic expressions for C and Pascal-like programming languages. The grammar is ambiguous. For instance, the string $a + b*c$ has two different derivation trees, as shown in Figure 5.5.

One way to resolve the ambiguity is, as is done in programming manuals, to associate precedence rules with the operators $+$ and $*$. Since $*$ normally has higher precedence than $+$, we would take Figure 5.5(a) as the correct parsing as it indicates that $b*c$ is a subexpression to be evaluated before performing the addition. However, this resolution is completely outside the grammar. It is better to rewrite the grammar so that only one parsing is possible.

Figure 5.6

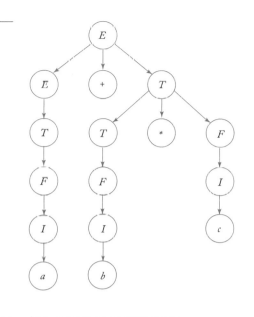

Example 5.12

To rewrite the grammar in Example 5.11 we introduce new variables, taking V as $\{E, T, F, I\}$ and replace the productions with

$$E \rightarrow T,$$
$$T \rightarrow F,$$
$$F \rightarrow I,$$
$$E \rightarrow E + T,$$
$$T \rightarrow T * F,$$
$$F \rightarrow (E),$$
$$I \rightarrow a \mid b \mid c.$$

A derivation tree of the sentence $a + b * c$ is shown in Figure 5.6. No other derivation tree is possible for this string: the grammar is unambiguous. It also is equivalent to the grammar in Example 5.11. It is not too hard to justify these claims in this specific instance, but, in general, the questions of whether a given context-free grammar is ambiguous or whether two given context-free grammars are equivalent are very difficult to answer. In fact, we will later show that there are no general algorithms by which these questions can always be resolved.

In the foregoing example the ambiguity came from the grammar in the sense that it could be removed by finding an equivalent unambiguous grammar. In some instances, however, this is not possible because the ambiguity is in the language.

Definition 5.6

If L is a context-free language for which there exists an unambiguous grammar, then L is said to be unambiguous. If every grammar that generates L is ambiguous, then the language is called **inherently ambiguous.**

It is a somewhat difficult matter even to exhibit an inherently ambiguous language. The best we can do here is give an example with some reasonably plausible claim that it is inherently ambiguous.

Example 5.13   The language

$$L = \{a^n b^n c^m\} \cup \{a^n b^m c^m\},$$

with n and m non-negative, is an inherently ambiguous context-free language.

That L is context-free is easy to show. Notice that

$$L = L_1 \cup L_2,$$

where L_1 is generated by

$$S_1 \rightarrow S_1 c | A,$$
$$A \rightarrow aAb | \lambda,$$

and L_2 is given by an analogous grammar with start symbol S_2 and productions

$$S_2 \rightarrow aS_2 | B,$$
$$B \rightarrow bBc | \lambda.$$

Then L is generated by the combination of these two grammars with the additional production

$$S \rightarrow S_1 | S_2.$$

The grammar is ambiguous since the string $a^n b^n c^n$ has two distinct derivations, one starting with $S \Rightarrow S_1$, the other with $S \Rightarrow S_2$. It does of course not follow from this that L is inherently ambiguous as there might exist some other nonambiguous grammars for it. But in some way L_1 and L_2 have conflicting requirements, the first putting a restriction on the number of a's and b's, while the second does the same for b's and c's. A few tries will quickly convince you of the impossibility of combining these requirements in a single set of rules that cover the case $n = m$ uniquely. A rigorous argument, though, is quite technical. One proof can be found in Harrison 1978.

EXERCISES

1. Find an s-grammar for $L(aaa^*b + b)$.

2. Find an s-grammar for $L = \{a^n b^n : n \geq 1\}$. **S**

3. Find an s-grammar for $L - \{a^n b^{n+1} : n \geq 2\}$.

4. Show that every s-grammar is unambiguous.

5. Let $G = (V, T, S, P)$ be an s-grammar. Give an expression for the maximum size of P in terms of $|V|$ and $|T|$.

6. Show that the following grammar is ambiguous.

$$S \rightarrow AB | aaB,$$
$$A \rightarrow a | Aa,$$
$$B \rightarrow b. \; \textbf{S}$$

7. Construct an unambiguous grammar equivalent to the grammar in Exercise 6.

8. Give the derivation tree for $(((a \mid b) * c)) + a + b$, using the grammar in Example 5.12.

9. Show that a regular language cannot be inherently ambiguous. **S**

10. Give an unambiguous grammar that generates the set of all regular expressions on $\Sigma = \{a, b\}$.

11. Is it possible for a regular grammar to be ambiguous?

12. Show that the language $L = \{ww^R : w \in \{a, b\}^*\}$ is not inherently ambiguous.

13. Show that the following grammar is ambiguous.

$$S \rightarrow aSbS | bSaS | \lambda$$

14. Show that the grammar in Example 5.4 is ambiguous, but that the language denoted by it is not. **S**

15. Show that the grammar in Example 1.13 is ambiguous.

16. Show that the grammar in Example 5.5 is unambiguous.

17. Use the exhaustive search parsing method to parse the string *abbbbbb* with the grammar in Example 5.5. In general, how many rounds will be needed to parse any string w in this language?

18. Show that the grammar in Example 1.14 is unambiguous.

19. Prove the following result. Let $G = (V, T, S, P)$ be a context-free grammar in which every $A \in V$ occurs on the left side of at most one production. Then G is unambiguous.

20. Find a grammar equivalent to that in Example 5.5 which satisfies the conditions of Theorem 5.2. Ⓢ

5.3 Context-Free Grammars and Programming Languages

One of the most important uses of the theory of formal languages is in the definition of programming languages and in the construction of interpreters and compilers for them. The basic problem here is to define a programming language precisely and to use this definition as the starting point for the writing of efficient and reliable translation programs. Both regular and context-free languages are important in achieving this. As we have seen, regular languages are used in the recognition of certain simple patterns which occur in programming languages, but as we argued in the introduction to this chapter, we need context-free languages to model more complicated aspects.

As with most other languages, we can define a programming language by a grammar. It is traditional in writing on programming languages to use a convention for specifying grammars called the *Backus-Naur* form or BNF. This form is in essence the same as the notation we have used here, but the appearance is different. In BNF, variables are enclosed in triangular brackets. Terminal symbols are written without any special marking. BNF also uses subsidiary symbols such as |, much in the way we have done. Thus, the grammar in Example 5.12 might appear in BNF as

$$\langle expression \rangle ::= \langle term \rangle \,|\, \langle expression \rangle + \langle term \rangle \,,$$
$$\langle term \rangle ::= \langle factor \rangle \,|\, \langle term \rangle * \langle factor \rangle \,,$$

and so on. The symbols $+$ and $*$ are terminals. The symbol | is used as an alternator as in our notation, but ::= is used instead of $\rightarrow$. BNF descriptions of programming languages tend to use more explicit variable identifiers to make the intent of the production explicit. But otherwise there are no significant differences between the two notations.

Many parts of a Pascal-like programming language are susceptible to definition by restricted forms of context-free grammars. For example, a Pascal **if-then-else** statement can be defined as

$$\langle if\_statement \rangle ::= if \,\, \langle expression \rangle \,\, \langle then\_clause \rangle \,\, \langle else\_clause \rangle \,.$$

Here the keyword *if* is a terminal symbol. All other terms are variables which still have to be defined. If we check this against Definition 5.4, we see that this looks like an s-grammar production. The variable ⟨*if_statement*⟩ on the left is always associated with the terminal *if* on the right. For this reason such a statement is easily and efficiently parsed. We see here a reason why we use keywords in programming languages. Keywords not only provide some visual structure that can guide the reader of a program, but also make the work of a compiler much easier.

Unfortunately, not all features of a typical programming language can be expressed by an s-grammar. The rules for ⟨*expression*⟩ above are not of this type, so that parsing becomes less obvious. The question then arises for what grammatical rules we can permit and still parse efficiently. In compilers, extensive use has been made of what are called LL and LR grammars, which have the ability to express the less obvious features of a programming language, yet allow us to parse in linear time. This is not a simple matter, and much of it is beyond the scope of our discussion. We will briefly touch on this topic in Chapter 6, but for our purposes it suffices to realize that such grammars exist and have been widely studied.

In connection with this, the issue of ambiguity takes on added significance. The specification of a programming language must be unambiguous, otherwise a program may yield very different results when processed by different compilers or run on different systems. As Example 5.11 shows, a naive approach can easily introduce ambiguity in the grammar. To avoid such mistakes we must be able to recognize and remove ambiguities. A related question is whether a language is or is not inherently ambiguous. What we need for this purpose are algorithms for detecting and removing ambiguities in context-free grammars and for deciding whether or not a context-free language is inherently ambiguous. Unfortunately, these are very difficult tasks, impossible in the most general sense, as we will see later.

Those aspects of a programming language which can be modeled by a context-free grammar are usually referred to as its **syntax.** However, it is normally the case that not all programs which are syntactically correct in this sense are in fact acceptable programs. For Pascal, the usual BNF definition allows constructs such as

$$var\ x, y : real;$$
$$x, z : integer$$

or

$$var\ x : integer;$$
$$x := 3.2.$$

Neither of these two constructs is acceptable to a Pascal compiler, since they violate other constraints, such as "an integer variable cannot be assigned a real value." This kind of rule is part of programming language semantics, since it has to do with how we interpret the meaning of a particular construct.

Programming language semantics are a complicated matter. Nothing as elegant and concise as context-free grammars exists for the specification of programming language semantics, and consequently some semantic features may be poorly defined or ambiguous. It is an ongoing concern both in programming languages and in formal language theory to find effective methods for defining programming language semantics. Several methods have been proposed, but none of them have been as universally accepted and as successful for semantic definition as context-free languages have been for syntax.

EXERCISES

1. Give a complete definition of ⟨*expression*⟩ for Pascal.

2. Give a BNF definition for the Pascal **while** statement (leaving the general concept ⟨*statement*⟩ undefined).

3. Give a BNF grammar that shows the relation between a Pascal program and its subprograms.

4. Give a BNF definition of a FORTRAN **do** statement.

5. Give a definition of the correct form of the **if-else** statement in C.

6. Find examples of features of C that cannot be described by context-free grammars.

Chapter 6

Simplification of Context-Free Grammars and Normal Forms

Before we can study context-free languages in greater depth, we must attend to some technical matters. The definition of a context-free grammar imposes no restriction whatsoever on the right side of a production. However, complete freedom is not necessary, and in fact, is a detriment in some arguments. In Theorem 5.2, we saw the convenience of certain restrictions on grammatical forms; eliminating rules of the form $A \rightarrow \lambda$ and $A \rightarrow B$ made the arguments easier. In many instances, it is desirable to place even more stringent restrictions on the grammar. Because of this, we need to look at methods for transforming an arbitrary context-free grammar into an equivalent one that satisfies certain restrictions on its form. In this chapter we study several transformations and substitutions that will be useful in subsequent discussions.

We also investigate **normal forms** for context-free grammars. A normal form is one that, although restricted, is broad enough so that any grammar has an equivalent normal-form version. We introduce two of the most useful of these, the **Chomsky normal form** and the **Greibach normal form**. Both have many practical and theoretical uses. An immediate application of the Chomsky normal form to parsing is given in Section 6.3.

The somewhat tedious nature of the material in this chapter lies in the fact that many of the arguments are manipulative and give little intuitive insight. For our purposes, this technical aspect is relatively unimportant and can be read casually. The various conclusions are significant; they will be used many times in later discussions.

6.1 Methods for Transforming Grammars

We first raise an issue that is somewhat of a nuisance with grammars and languages in general: the presence of the empty string. The empty string plays a rather singular role in many theorems and proofs, and it is often necessary to give it special attention. We prefer to remove it from consideration altogether, looking only at languages that do not contain λ. In doing so, we do not lose generality, as we see from the following considerations. Let L be any context-free language, and let $G = (V, T, S, P)$ be a context-free grammar for $L - \{\lambda\}$. Then the grammar we obtain by adding to V the new variable S_0, making S_0 the start variable, and adding to P the productions

$$S_0 \rightarrow S | \lambda.$$

generates L. Therefore any nontrivial conclusion we can make for $L - \{\lambda\}$ will almost certainly transfer to L. Also, given any context-free grammar G, there is a method for obtaining $\widehat{G}$ such that $L\left(\widehat{G}\right) = L(G) - \{\lambda\}$ (see Exercise 13 at the end of this section). Consequently, for all practical purposes, there is no difference between context-free languages that include λ and those that do not. For the rest of this chapter, unless otherwise stated, we will restrict our discussion to λ-free languages.

A Useful Substitution Rule

Many rules govern generating equivalent grammars by means of substitutions. Here we give one that is very useful for simplifying grammars in various way. We will not define the term *simplification* precisely, but we will use it nevertheless. What we mean by it is the removal of certain types of undesirable productions; the process does not necessarily result in an actual reduction of the number of rules.

Theorem 6.1   Let $G = (V, T, S, P)$ be a context-free grammar. Suppose that P contains a production of the form

$$A \rightarrow x_1 B x_2.$$

Assume that A and B are different variables and that

$$B \rightarrow y_1 | y_2 | \cdots | y_n$$

is the set of all productions in P which have B as the left side. Let $\widehat{G} = \left(V, T, S, \widehat{P}\right)$ be the grammar in which $\widehat{P}$ is constructed by deleting

$$A \to x_1 B x_2 \tag{6.1}$$

from P, and adding to it

$$A \to x_1 y_1 x_2 \,|\, x_1 y_2 x_2 | \cdots |x_1 y_n x_2.$$

Then

$$L\left(\widehat{G}\right) = L\left(G\right).$$

Proof: Suppose that $w \in L\left(G\right)$, so that

$$S \overset{*}{\Rightarrow}_G w.$$

The subscript on the derivation sign $\Rightarrow$ is used here to distinguish between derivations with different grammars. If this derivation does not involve the production (6.1), then obviously

$$S \overset{*}{\Rightarrow}_{\widehat{G}} w.$$

If it does, then look at the derivation the first time (6.1) is used. The B so introduced eventually has to be replaced; we lose nothing by assuming that this is done immediately (see Exercise 17 at the end of this section). Thus

$$S \overset{*}{\Rightarrow}_G u_1 A u_2 \Rightarrow_G u_1 x_1 B x_2 u_2 \Rightarrow_G u_1 x_1 y_j x_2 u_2.$$

But with grammar $\widehat{G}$ we can get

$$S \overset{*}{\Rightarrow}_{\widehat{G}} u_1 A u_2 \Rightarrow_{\widehat{G}} u_1 x_1 y_j x_2 u_2.$$

Thus we can reach the same sentential form with G and $\widehat{G}$. If (6.1) is used again later, we can repeat the argument. It follows then, by induction on the number of times the production is applied, that

$$S \overset{*}{\Rightarrow}_{\widehat{G}} w.$$

Therefore, if $w \in L\left(G\right)$, then $w \in L\left(\widehat{G}\right)$.

By similar reasoning, we can show that if $w \in L\left(\widehat{G}\right)$, then $w \subset L\left(G\right)$, completing the proof. ∎

Theorem 6.1 is a simple and quite intuitive substitution rule: A production $A \to x_1 B x_2$ can be eliminated from a grammar if we put in its place the set of productions in which B is replaced by all strings it derives in one step. In this result, it is necessary that A and B be different variables. The case when $A = B$ is partially addressed in Exercises 22 and 23 at the end of this section.

Example 6.1   Consider $G = (\{A, B\}, \{a, b, c\}, A, P)$ with productions

$$A \rightarrow a \,|aaA|\, abBc,$$
$$B \rightarrow abbA | b.$$

Using the suggested substitution for the variable B, we get the grammar $\widehat{G}$ with productions

$$A \rightarrow a \,|aaA|\, ababbAc | abbc,$$
$$B \rightarrow abbA | b.$$

The new grammar $\widehat{G}$ is equivalent to G. The string $aaabbc$ has the derivation

$$A \Rightarrow aaA \Rightarrow aaabBc \Rightarrow aaabbc$$

in G, and the corresponding derivation

$$A \Rightarrow aaA \Rightarrow aaabbc$$

in $\widehat{G}$.

Notice that, in this case, the variable B and its associated productions are still in the grammar even though they can no longer play a part in any derivation. We will see shortly how such unnecessary productions can be removed from a grammar.

Removing Useless Productions

One invariably wants to remove productions from a grammar that can never take part in any derivation. For example, in the grammar whose entire production set is

$$S \rightarrow aSb \,|\lambda|\, A,$$
$$A \rightarrow aA,$$

the production $S \rightarrow A$ clearly plays no role, as A cannot be transformed into a terminal string. While A can occur in a string derived from S, this can never lead to a sentence. Removing this production leaves the language unaffected and is a simplification by any definition.

Definition 6.1

Let $G = (V, T, S, P)$ be a context-free grammar. A variable $A \in V$ is said to be **useful** if and only if there is at least one $w \in L(G)$ such that

$$S \stackrel{*}{\Rightarrow} xAy \stackrel{*}{\Rightarrow} w, \tag{6.2}$$

with x, y in $(V \cup T)^*$. In words, a variable is useful if and only if it occurs in at least one derivation. A variable that is not useful is called **useless**. A production is useless if it involves any useless variable.

Example 6.2 A variable may be useless because there is no way of getting a terminal string from it. The case just mentioned is of this kind. Another reason a variable may be useless is shown in the next grammar. In a grammar with start symbol S and productions

$$S \to A,$$
$$A \to aA | \lambda,$$
$$B \to bA,$$

the variable B is useless and so is the production $B \to bA$. Although B can derive a terminal string, there is no way we can achieve $S \stackrel{*}{\Rightarrow} xBy$. ∎

This example illustrates the two reasons why a variable is useless: either because it cannot be reached from the start symbol or because it cannot derive a terminal string. A procedure for removing useless variables and productions is based on recognizing these two situations. Before we present the general case and the corresponding theorem, let us look at another example.

Example 6.3 Eliminate useless symbols and productions from $G = (V, T, S, P)$, where $V = \{S, A, B, C\}$ and $T = \{a, b\}$, with P consisting of

$$S \to aS | A | C,$$
$$A \to a,$$
$$B \to aa,$$
$$C \to aCb.$$

Figure 6.1

First, we identify the set of variables that can lead to a terminal string. Because $A \to a$ and $B \to aa$, the variables A and B belong to this set. So does S, because $S \Rightarrow A \Rightarrow a$. However, this argument cannot be made for C, thus identifying it as useless. Removing C and its corresponding productions, we are led to the grammar G_1 with variables $V_1 = \{S, A, B\}$, terminals $T = \{a\}$, and productions

$$S \to aS|A,$$
$$A \to a,$$
$$B \to aa.$$

Next we want to eliminate the variables that cannot be reached from the start variable. For this, we can draw a **dependency graph** for the variables. Dependency graphs are a way of visualizing complex relationships and are found in many applications. For context-free grammars, a dependency graph has its vertices labeled with variables, with an edge between vertices C and D if and only if there is a production form

$$C \to xDy.$$

A dependency graph for V_1 is shown in Figure 6.1. A variable is useful only if there is a path from the vertex labeled S to the vertex labeled with that variable. In our case, Figure 6.1 shows that B is useless. Removing it and the affected productions and terminals, we are led to the final answer $\widehat{G} = \left(\widehat{V}, \widehat{T}, S, \widehat{P}\right)$ with $\widehat{V} = \{S, A\}$, $\widehat{T} = \{a\}$, and productions

$$S \to aS|A,$$
$$A \to a.$$

The formalization of this process leads to a general construction and the corresponding theorem.

Theorem 6.2   Let $G = (V, T, S, P)$ be a context-free grammar. Then there exists an equivalent grammar $\widehat{G} = \left(\widehat{V}, \widehat{T}, S, \widehat{P}\right)$ that does not contain any useless variables or productions.

Proof: The grammar $\widehat{G}$ can be generated from G by an algorithm consisting of two parts. In the first part we construct an intermediate grammar $G_1 = (V_1, T_2, S, P_1)$ such that V_1 contains only variables A for which

$$A \overset{*}{\Rightarrow} w \in T^*$$

is possible. The steps in the algorithm are:

1. Set V_1 to $\varnothing$.

2. Repeat the following step until no more variables are added to V_1.

   For every $A \in V$ for which P has a production of the form

   $$A \to x_1 x_2 \cdots x_n, \text{ with all } x_i \text{ in } V_1 \cup T,$$

   add A to V_1.

3. Take P_1 as all the productions in P whose symbols are all in $(V_1 \cup T)$.

   Clearly this procedure terminates. It is equally clear that if $A \in V_1$, then $A \overset{*}{\Rightarrow} w \in T^*$ is a possible derivation with G_1. The remaining issue is whether every A for which $A \overset{*}{\Rightarrow} w = ab\cdots$ is added to V_1 before the procedure terminates. To see this, consider any such A and look at the partial derivation tree corresponding to that derivation (Figure 6.2). At level k, there are only terminals, so every variable A_i at level $k - 1$ will be added to V_1 on the first pass through Step 2 of the algorithm. Any variable at level $k - 2$ will then be added to V_1 on the second pass through Step 2. The third time through Step 2, all variables at level $k - 3$ will be added, and so on. The algorithm cannot terminate while there are variables in the tree that are not yet in V_1. Hence A will eventually be added to V_1.

   In the second part of the construction, we get the final answer $\widehat{G}$ from G_1. We draw the variable dependency graph for G_1 and from it find all

Figure 6.2

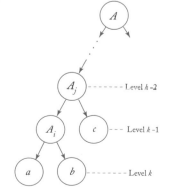

variables that cannot be reached from S. These are removed from the variable set, as are the productions involving them. We can also eliminate any terminal that does not occur in some useful production. The result is the grammar $\widehat{G} = \left(\widehat{V}, \widehat{T}, S, \widehat{P} \right)$.

Because of the construction, $\widehat{G}$ does not contain any useless symbols or productions. Also, for each $w \in L(G)$ we have a derivation

$$S \stackrel{*}{\Rightarrow} xAy \stackrel{*}{\Rightarrow} w.$$

Since the construction of $\widehat{G}$ retains A and all associated productions, we have everything needed to make the derivation

$$S \stackrel{*}{\Rightarrow}_{\widehat{G}} xAy \stackrel{*}{\Rightarrow}_{\widehat{G}} w.$$

The grammar $\widehat{G}$ is constructed from G by the removal of productions, so that $\widehat{P} \subseteq P$. Consequently $L\left(\widehat{G}\right) \subseteq L(G)$. Putting the two results together, we see that G and $\widehat{G}$ are equivalent. ∎

Removing λ-Productions

One kind of production that is sometimes undesirable is one in which the right side is the empty string.

Definition 6.2

Any production of a context-free grammar of the form

$$A \rightarrow \lambda$$

is called a λ-**production**. Any variable A for which the derivation

$$A \stackrel{*}{\Rightarrow} \lambda \tag{6.3}$$

is possible is called **nullable**.

A grammar may generate a language not containing λ, yet have some λ-productions or nullable variables. In such cases, the λ-productions can be removed.

Example 6.4   Consider the grammar

$$S \rightarrow aS_1b,$$
$$S_1 \rightarrow aS_1b|\lambda.$$

This grammar generates the λ-free language $\{a^nb^n : n \geq 1\}$. The λ-production $S_1 \rightarrow \lambda$ can be removed after adding new productions obtained by substituting λ for S_1 where it occurs on the right. Doing this we get the grammar

$$S \rightarrow aS_1b|ab,$$
$$S_1 \rightarrow aS_1b|ab.$$

We can easily show that this new grammar generates the same language as the original one.

In more general situations, substitutions for λ-productions can be made in a similar, although more complicated, manner.

Theorem 6.3   Let G be any context-free grammar with λ not in $L(G)$. Then there exists an equivalent grammar $\widehat{G}$ having no λ-productions.

Proof: We first find the set V_N of all nullable variables of G, using the following steps.

1. For all productions $A \rightarrow \lambda$, put A into V_N.

2. Repeat the following step until no further variables are added to V_N. For all productions

$$B \rightarrow A_1A_2 \cdots A_n,$$

where $A_1, A_2, ..., A_n$ are in V_N, put B into V_N.

Once the set V_N has been found, we are ready to construct $\widehat{P}$. To do so, we look at all productions in P of the form

$$A \rightarrow x_1x_2 \cdots x_m, m \geq 1,$$

where each $x_i \in V \cup T$. For each such production of P, we put into $\widehat{P}$ that production as well as all those generated by replacing nullable variables with λ in all possible combinations. For example, if x_i and x_j are both nullable, there will be one production in $\widehat{P}$ with x_i replaced with λ, one in which x_j is replaced with λ, and one in which both x_i and x_j are replaced with λ.

There is one exception: if all x_i are nullable, the production $A \to \lambda$ is not put into $\widehat{P}$.

The argument that this grammar $\widehat{G}$ is equivalent to G is straightforward and will be left to the reader. ■

Example 6.5   Find a context-free grammar without λ-productions equivalent to the grammar defined by

$$S \to ABaC,$$
$$A \to BC,$$
$$B \to b|\lambda,$$
$$C \to D|\lambda,$$
$$D \to d.$$

From the first step of the construction in Theorem 6.3, we find that the nullable variables are A, B, C. Then, following the second step of the construction, we get

$$S \to ABaC\,|BaC|\,AaC\,|ABa|\,aC\,|Aa|\,Ba|a,$$
$$A \to B\,|C|\,BC,$$
$$B \to b,$$
$$C \to D,$$
$$D \to d.$$

Removing Unit-Productions

As we see from Theorem 6.2, productions in which both sides are a single variable are at times undesirable.

Definition 6.3

Any production of a context-free grammar of the form

$$A \to B,$$

where $A, B \in V$ is called a **unit-production**.

To remove unit-productions, we use the substitution rule discussed in Theorem 6.1. As the construction in the next theorem shows, this can be done if we proceed with some care.

Theorem 6.4

Let $G = (V, T, S, P)$ be any context-free grammar without λ-productions. Then there exists a context-free grammar $\widehat{G} = \left(\widehat{V}, \widehat{T}, S, \widehat{P}\right)$ that does not have any unit-productions and that is equivalent to G.

Proof: Obviously, any unit-production of the form $A \to A$ can be removed from the grammar without effect, and we need only consider $A \to B$, where A and B are different variables. At first sight, it may seem that we can use Theorem 6.1 directly with $x_1 = x_2 = \lambda$ to replace

$$A \to B$$

with

$$A \to y_1 \,|y_2|\cdots|y_n.$$

But this will not always work; in the special case

$$A \to B,$$
$$B \to A,$$

the unit-productions are not removed. To get around this, we first find, for each A, all variables B such that

$$A \overset{*}{\Rightarrow} B. \tag{6.4}$$

We can do this by drawing a dependency graph with an edge (C, D) whenever the grammar has a unit-production $C \to D$; then (6.4) holds whenever there is a walk between A and B. The new grammar $\widehat{G}$ is generated by first putting into $\widehat{P}$ all non-unit productions of P. Next, for all A and B satisfying (6.4), we add to $\widehat{P}$

$$A \to y_1 \,|y_2|\cdots|y_n,$$

where $B \to y_1 \,|y_2|\cdots|y_n$ is the set of all rules in $\widehat{P}$ with B on the left. Note that since $B \to y_1 \,|y_2|\cdots|y_n$ is taken from $\widehat{P}$, none of the y_i can be a single variable, so that no unit-productions are created by the last step.

To show that the resulting grammar is equivalent to the original one we can follow the same line of reasoning as in Theorem 6.1. ∎

Figure 6.3

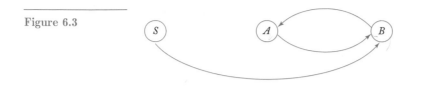

Example 6.6   Remove all unit-productions from

$$S \rightarrow Aa|B,$$
$$B \rightarrow A|bb,$$
$$A \rightarrow a|bc|B.$$

The dependency graph for the unit-productions is given in Figure 6.3; we see from it that $S \overset{*}{\Rightarrow} A$, $S \overset{*}{\Rightarrow} B$, $B \overset{*}{\Rightarrow} A$, and $A \overset{*}{\Rightarrow} B$. Hence, we add to the original non-unit productions

$$S \rightarrow Aa,$$
$$A \rightarrow a|bc,$$
$$B \rightarrow bb,$$

the new rules

$$S \rightarrow a|bc|bb,$$
$$A \rightarrow bb,$$
$$B \rightarrow a|bc,$$

to obtain the equivalent grammar

$$S \rightarrow a|bc|bb|Aa,$$
$$A \rightarrow a|bb|bc,$$
$$B \rightarrow a|bb|bc.$$

Note that the removal of the unit-productions has made B and the associated productions useless.

We can put all these results together to show that grammars for context-free languages can be made free of useless productions, λ-productions, and unit-productions.

Theorem 6.5   Let L be a context-free language that does not contain λ. Then there exists a context-free grammar that generates L and that does not have any useless productions, λ-productions, or unit-productions.

Proof: The procedures given in Theorems 6.2, 6.3, and 6.4 remove these kinds of productions in turn. The only point that needs consideration is that the removal of one type of production may introduce productions of another type; for example, the procedure for removing λ-productions can create new unit-productions. Also, Theorem 6.4 requires that the grammar have no λ-productions. But note that the removal of unit-productions does not create λ-productions (Exercise 15 at the end of this section), and the removal of useless productions does not create λ-productions or unit-productions (Exercise 16 at the end of this section). Therefore, we can remove all undesirable productions using the following sequence of steps:

1. Remove λ-productions

2. Remove unit-productions

3. Remove useless productions

The result will then have none of these productions, and the theorem is proved. ∎

EXERCISES

1. Complete the proof of Theorem 6.1 by showing that

$$S \overset{*}{\Rightarrow}_{\widehat{G}} w$$

implies

$$S \overset{*}{\Rightarrow}_{G} w.$$

2. In Example 6.1, show a derivation tree for the string $ababbbac$, using both the original and the modified grammar.

3. Show that the two grammars

$$S \rightarrow abAB|ba,$$
$$A \rightarrow aaa,$$
$$B \rightarrow aA|bb$$

and

$$S \rightarrow abAaA\,|abAbb|\,ba,$$
$$A \rightarrow aaa$$

are equivalent.

4. In Theorem 6.1, why is it necessary to assume that A and B are different variables?

5. Eliminate all useless productions from the grammar

$$S \rightarrow aS | AB,$$
$$A \rightarrow bA,$$
$$B \rightarrow AA.$$

What language does this grammar generate?

6. Eliminate useless productions from

$$S \rightarrow a | aA | B | C,$$
$$A \rightarrow aB | \lambda,$$
$$B \rightarrow Aa,$$
$$C \rightarrow cCD,$$
$$D \rightarrow ddd.$$

7. Eliminate all λ-productions from

$$S \rightarrow AaB | aaB,$$
$$A \rightarrow \lambda,$$
$$B \rightarrow bbA | \lambda.$$

8. Remove all unit-productions, all useless productions, and all λ-productions from the grammar

$$S \rightarrow aA | aBB,$$
$$A \rightarrow aaA | \lambda,$$
$$B \rightarrow bB | bbC,$$
$$C \rightarrow B.$$

What language does this grammar generate? **S**

9. Eliminate all unit productions from the grammar in Exercise 7.

10. Complete the proof of Theorem 6.3.

11. Complete the proof of Theorem 6.4.

12. Use the construction in Theorem 6.3 to remove λ-productions from the grammar in Example 5.4. What language does the resulting grammar generate?

13. Suppose that G is a context free grammar for which $\lambda \in L(G)$. Show that if we apply the construction in Theorem 6.3, we obtain a new grammar $\widehat{G}$ such that $L\left(\widehat{G}\right) = L(G) - \{\lambda\}$.

14. Give an example of a situation in which the removal of λ-productions introduces previously nonexistent unit-productions. **S**

15. Let G be a grammar without λ-productions, but possibly with some unit-productions. Show that the construction of Theorem 6.4 does not then introduce any λ-productions.

16. Show that if a grammar has no λ-productions and no unit-productions, then the removal of useless productions by the construction of Theorem 6.2 does not introduce any such productions. **S**

17. Justify the claim made in the proof of Theorem 6.1 that the variable B can be replaced as soon as it appears.

18. Suppose that a context-free grammar $G = (V, T, S, P)$ has a production of the form

$$A \rightarrow xy,$$

where $x, y \in (V \cup T)^{1}$. Prove that if this rule is replaced by

$$A \rightarrow By,$$
$$B \rightarrow x,$$

where $B \notin V$, then the resulting grammar is equivalent to the original one.

19. Consider the procedure suggested in Theorem 6.2 for the removal of useless productions. Reverse the order of the two parts, first eliminating variables that cannot be reached from S, then removing those that do not yield a terminal string. Does the new procedure still work correctly? If so, prove it. If not, give a counterexample.

20. It is possible to define the term simplification precisely by introducing the concept of **complexity** of a grammar. This can be done in many ways; one of them is through the length of all the strings giving the production rules. For example, we might use

$$complexity(G) = \sum_{A \rightarrow v \in P} \{1 + |v|\}.$$

Show that the removal of useless productions always reduces the complexity in this sense. What can you say about the removal of λ-productions and unit-productions?

21. A context-free grammar G is said to be minimal for a given language L if $complexity(G) \leq complexity\left(\widehat{G}\right)$ for any $\widehat{G}$ generating L. Show by example that the removal of useless productions does not necessarily produce a minimal grammar. **Ⓢ**

★22. Prove the following result. Let $G = (V, T, S, P)$ be a context-free grammar. Divide the set of productions whose left sides are some given variable (say, A), into two disjoint subsets

$$A \rightarrow Ax_1 \,|Ax_2|\cdots|Ax_n,$$

and

$$A \rightarrow y_1 \,|y_2|\cdots|y_m,$$

where x_i, y_i are in $(V \cup T)^*$, but A is not a prefix of any y_i. Consider the grammar $\widehat{G} = \left(V \cup \{Z\}, T, S, \widehat{P}\right)$, where $Z \notin V$ and $\widehat{P}$ is obtained by replacing all productions that have A on the left by

$$A \rightarrow y_i|y_iZ, \quad i = 1, 2, ..., m,$$
$$Z \rightarrow x_i|x_iZ, \quad i = 1, 2, ..., n.$$

Then $L(G) = L\left(\widehat{G}\right)$.

23. Use the result of the preceding exercise to rewrite the grammar

$$A \rightarrow Aa \,|aBc| \lambda$$
$$B \rightarrow Bb|bc$$

so that it no longer has productions of the form $A \rightarrow Ax$ or $B \rightarrow Bx$.

★24. Prove the following counterpart of Exercise 22. Let the set of productions involving the variable A on the left be divided into two disjoint subsets

$$A \rightarrow x_1 A \,|x_2A|\cdots|x_n A$$

and

$$A \rightarrow y_1 \,|y_2|\cdots|y_m$$

where A is not a suffix of any y_i. Show that the grammar obtained by replacing these productions with

$$A \rightarrow y_i|Zy_i, \quad i = 1, 2, ..., m$$
$$Z \rightarrow x_i|Zx_i, \quad i = 1, 2, ..., n$$

is equivalent to the original grammar.

6.2 Two Important Normal Forms

There are many kinds of normal forms we can establish for context-free grammars. Some of these, because of their wide usefulness, have been studied extensively. We consider two of them briefly.

Chomsky Normal Form

One kind of normal form we can look for is one in which the number of symbols on the right of a production are strictly limited. In particular, we can ask that the string on the right of a production consist of no more than two symbols. One instance of this is the **Chomsky normal form.**

Definition 6.4

A context-free grammar is in Chomsky normal form if all productions are of the form

$$A \to BC,$$

or

$$A \to a,$$

where A, B, C are in V, and a is in T.

Example 6.7   The grammar

$$S \to AS|a,$$
$$A \to SA|b$$

is in Chomsky normal form. The grammar

$$S \to AS|AAS,$$
$$A \to SA|aa$$

is not; both productions $S \to AAS$ and $A \to aa$ violate the conditions of Definition 6.4.

Theorem 6.6   Any context-free grammar $G = (V, T, S, P)$ with $\lambda \notin L(G)$ has an equivalent grammar $\widehat{G} = \left(\widehat{V}, \widehat{T}, S, \widehat{P}\right)$ in Chomsky normal form.

Proof: Because of Theorem 6.5, we can assume without loss of generality that G has no λ-productions and no unit-productions. The construction of $\widehat{G}$ will be done in two steps.

Step 1: Construct a grammar $G_1 = (V_1, T, S, P_1)$ from G by considering all productions in P in the form

$$A \rightarrow x_1 x_2 \cdots x_n, \tag{6.5}$$

where each x_i is a symbol either in V or T. If $n = 1$ then x_1 must be a terminal since we have no unit-productions. In this case, put the production into P_1. If $n \geq 2$, introduce new variables B_a for each $a \in T$. For each production of P in the form (6.5) we put into P_1 the production

$$A \rightarrow C_1 C_2 \cdots C_n,$$

where

$$C_i = x_i \text{ if } x_i \text{ is in } V,$$

and

$$C_i = B_a \text{ if } x_i = a.$$

For every B_a we also put into P_1 the production

$$B_a \rightarrow a.$$

This part of the algorithm removes all terminals from productions whose right side has length greater than one, replacing them with newly introduced variables. At the end of this step we have a grammar G_1 all of whose productions have the form

$$A \rightarrow a, \tag{6.6}$$

or

$$A \rightarrow C_1 C_2 \cdots C_n, \tag{6.7}$$

where $C_i \in V_1$.

It is an easy consequence of Theorem 6.1 that

$$L(G_1) = L(G).$$

Step 2: In the second step, we introduce additional variables to reduce the length of the right sides of the productions where necessary. First we put all productions of the form (6.6) as well as all the productions of the form (6.7) with $n = 2$ into $\widehat{P}$. For $n > 2$, we introduce new variables $D_1, D_2, \ldots$ and put into $\widehat{P}$ the productions

$$A \rightarrow C_1 D_1,$$
$$D_1 \rightarrow C_2 D_2,$$
$$\vdots$$
$$D_{n-2} \rightarrow C_{n-1} C_n.$$

Obviously, the resulting grammar $\widehat{G}$ is in Chomsky normal form. Repeated applications of Theorem 6.1 will show that $L(G_1) = L\left(\widehat{G}\right)$, so that

$$L\left(\widehat{G}\right) = L(G).$$

This somewhat informal argument can easily be made more precise. We will leave this to the reader. ■

Example 6.8   Convert the grammar with productions

$$S \rightarrow ABa,$$
$$A \rightarrow aab,$$
$$B \rightarrow Ac,$$

to Chomsky normal form.

As required by the construction of Theorem 6.6, the grammar does not have any λ-productions or any unit-productions.

In Step 1, we introduce new variables B_a, B_b, B_c and use the algorithm to get

$$S \rightarrow ABB_a,$$
$$A \rightarrow B_a B_a B_b,$$
$$B \rightarrow AB_c,$$
$$B_a \rightarrow a,$$
$$B_b \rightarrow b,$$
$$B_c \rightarrow c.$$

In the second step, we introduce additional variables to get the first two productions into normal form and we get the final result

$$S \to AD_1,$$
$$D_1 \to BB_a,$$
$$A \to B_aD_2,$$
$$D_2 \to B_aB_b,$$
$$B \to AB_c,$$
$$B_a \to a,$$
$$B_b \to b,$$
$$B_c \to c.$$

Greibach Normal Form

Another useful grammatical form is the **Greibach normal form.** Here we put restrictions not on the length of the right sides of a production, but on the positions in which terminals and variables can appear. Arguments justifying Greibach normal form are a little complicated and not very transparent. Similarly, constructing a grammar in Greibach normal form equivalent to a given context-free grammar is tedious. We therefore deal with this matter very briefly. Nevertheless, Greibach normal form has many theoretical and practical consequences.

Definition 6.5

A context-free grammar is said to be in Greibach normal form if all productions have the form

$$A \to ax,$$

where $a \in T$ and $x \in V^*$.

If we compare this with Definition 5.4, we see that the form $A \to ax$ is common to both Greibach normal form and s-grammars, but Greibach normal form does not carry the restriction that the pair (A, a) occur at most once. This additional freedom gives Greibach normal form a generality not possessed by s-grammars.

If a grammar is not in Greibach normal form, we may be able to rewrite it in this form with some of the techniques encountered above. Here are two simple examples.

Example 6.9   The grammar

$$S \rightarrow AB,$$
$$A \rightarrow aA \,|bB|\, b,$$
$$B \rightarrow b$$

is not in Greibach normal form. However, using the substitution given by Theorem 6.1, we immediately get the equivalent grammar

$$S \rightarrow aAB \,|bBB|\, bB,$$
$$A \rightarrow aA \,|bB|\, b,$$
$$B \rightarrow b,$$

which is in Greibach normal form.

Example 6.10   Convert the grammar

$$S \rightarrow abSb|aa,$$

into Greibach normal form.

Here we can use a device similar to the one introduced in the construction of Chomsky normal form. We introduce new variables A and B that are essentially synonyms for a and b, respectively. Substituting for the terminals with their associated variables leads to the equivalent grammar

$$S \rightarrow aBSB|aA,$$
$$A \rightarrow a,$$
$$B \rightarrow b,$$

which is in Greibach normal form.

In general, though, neither the conversion of a given grammar to Greibach normal form nor the proof that this can always be done are simple matters. We introduce Greibach normal form here because it will simplify the technical discussion of an important result in the next chapter. However, from a conceptual viewpoint, Greibach normal form plays no further role in our discussion, so we only quote the following general result without proof.

Theorem 6.7

For every context-free grammar G with $\lambda \notin L(G)$, there exists an equivalent grammar $\widehat{G}$ in Greibach normal form.

EXERCISES

1. Provide the details of the proof of Theorem 6.6.

2. Convert the grammar $S \rightarrow aSb|ab$ into Chomsky normal form.

3. Transform the grammar $S \rightarrow aSaA|A, A \rightarrow abA|b$ into Chomsky normal form.

4. Transform the grammar with productions

$$S \rightarrow abAB,$$
$$A \rightarrow bAB|\lambda,$$
$$B \rightarrow BAa\,|A|\,\lambda,$$

into Chomsky normal form.

5. Convert the grammar

$$S \rightarrow AB|aB$$
$$A \rightarrow aab|\lambda$$
$$B \rightarrow bbA$$

into Chomsky normal form. **S**

6. Let $G = (V, T, S, P)$ be any context-free grammar without any λ-productions or unit-productions. Let k be the maximum number of symbols on the right of any production in P. Show that there is an equivalent grammar in Chomsky normal form with no more than $(k-1)|P| + |T|$ production rules.

7. Draw the dependency graph for the grammar in Exercise 4.

8. A linear language is one for which there exists a linear grammar (for a definition, see Example 3.13). Let L be any linear language not containing λ. Show that there exists a grammar $G = (V, T, S, P)$ all of whose productions have one of the forms

$$A \rightarrow aB,$$
$$A \rightarrow Ba,$$
$$A \rightarrow a,$$

where $a \in T, A, B \in V$, such that $L = L(G)$. **S**

9. Show that for every context-free grammar $G = (V, T, S, P)$ there is an equivalent one in which all productions have the form

$$A \to aBC,$$

or

$$A \to \lambda,$$

where $a \in \Sigma \cup \{\lambda\}, A, B, C \in V$. ⓢ

10. Convert the grammar

$$S \to aSb|bSa|a|b$$

into Greibach normal form.

11. Convert the following grammar into Greibach normal form.

$$S \quad \to aSb|ab.$$

12. Convert the grammar

$$S \to ab\,|aS|\,aaS$$

into Greibach normal form. ⓢ

13. Convert the grammar

$$S \to ABb|a,$$
$$A \to aaA|B,$$
$$B \to bAb$$

into Greibach normal form.

14. Can every linear grammar be converted to a form in which all productions look like $A \to ax$, where $a \in T$ and $x \in V \cup \{\lambda\}$?

15. A context-free grammar is said to be in two-standard form if all production rules satisfy the following pattern

$$A \to aBC,$$
$$A \to aB,$$
$$A \to a,$$

where $A, B, C \in V$ and $a \in T$.

Convert the grammar $G = (\{S, A, B, C\}, \{a, b\}, S, P)$ with P given as

$$S \to aSA,$$
$$A \to bABC,$$
$$B \to b,$$
$$C \to aBC,$$

into two-standard form. ⓢ

★16. Two-standard form is general; for any context-free grammar G with $\lambda \notin L(G)$, there exists an equivalent grammar in two-standard form. Prove this.

6.3 A Membership Algorithm for Context-Free Grammars*

In Section 5.2, we claimed, without any elaboration, that membership and parsing algorithms for context-free grammars exist that require approximately $|w|^3$ steps to parse a string w. We are now in a position to justify this claim. The algorithm we will describe here is called the CYK algorithm, after its originators J. Cocke, D. H. Younger, and T. Kasami. The algorithm works only if the grammar is in Chomsky normal form and succeeds by breaking one problem into a sequence of smaller ones in the following way. Assume that we have a grammar $G = (V, T, S, P)$ in Chomsky normal form and a string

$$w = a_1 a_2 \cdots a_n.$$

We define substrings

$$w_{ij} = a_i \cdots a_j,$$

and subsets of V

$$V_{ij} = \left\{ A \in V : A \overset{*}{\Rightarrow} w_{ij} \right\}.$$

Clearly, $w \in L(G)$ if and only if $S \in V_{1n}$.

To compute V_{ij}, observe that $A \in V_{ii}$ if and only if G contains a production $A \to a_i$. Therefore, V_{ii} can be computed for all $1 \leq i \leq n$ by inspection of w and the productions of the grammar. To continue, notice that for $j > i$, A derives w_{ij} if and only if there is a production $A \to BC$, with $B \overset{*}{\Rightarrow} w_{ik}$ and $C \overset{*}{\Rightarrow} w_{k+1j}$ for some k with $i \leq k, k < j$. In other words,

$$V_{ij} = \bigcup_{k \in \{i, i+1, \dots, j-1\}} \{A : A \to BC, \text{ with } B \in V_{ik}, C \in V_{k+1, j}\}. \quad (6.8)$$

An inspection of the indices in (6.8) shows that it can be used to compute all the V_{ij} if we proceed in the sequence

1. Compute $V_{11}, V_{22}, \dots, V_{nn}$

2. Compute $V_{12}, V_{23}, \dots, V_{n-1, n}$

3. Compute $V_{13}, V_{24}, \dots, V_{n-2, n}$

and so on.

Example 6.11   Determine whether the string $w = aabbb$ is in the language generated by the grammar

$$S \rightarrow AB,$$
$$A \rightarrow BB|a,$$
$$B \rightarrow AB|b,$$

First note that $w_{11} = a$, so V_{11} is the set of all variables that immediately derive a, that is, $V_{11} = \{A\}$. Since $w_{22} = a$, we also have $V_{22} = \{A\}$ and, similarly,

$$V_{11} = \{A\}, V_{22} = \{A\}, V_{33} = \{B\}, V_{44} = \{B\}, V_{55} = \{B\}.$$

Now we use (6.8) to get

$$V_{12} = \{A : A \rightarrow BC, B \in V_{11}, C \in V_{22}\}.$$

Since $V_{11} = \{A\}$ and $V_{22} = \{A\}$, the set consists of all variables that occur on the left side of a production whose right side is AA. Since there are none, V_{12} is empty. Next,

$$V_{23} = \{A : A \rightarrow BC, B \in V_{22}, C \in V_{33}\},$$

so the required right side is AB, and we have $V_{23} = \{S, B\}$. A straightforward argument along these lines then gives

$$V_{12} = \varnothing, V_{23} = \{S, B\}, V_{34} = \{A\}, V_{45} = \{A\},$$
$$V_{13} = \{S, B\}, V_{24} = \{A\}, V_{35} = \{S, B\},$$
$$V_{14} = \{A\}, V_{25} = \{S, B\},$$
$$V_{15} = \{S, B\},$$

so that $w \in L(G)$.

The CYK algorithm, as described here, determines membership for any language generated by a grammar in Chomsky normal form. With some additions to keep track of how the elements of V_{ij} are derived, it can be converted into a parsing method. To see that the CYK membership algorithm requires On^3 steps, notice that exactly $n(n+1)/2$ sets of V_{ij} have to be computed. Each involves the evaluation of at most n terms in (6.8), so the claimed result follows.

EXERCISES

1. Use the CYK algorithm to determine whether the strings *aabb*, *aabba*, and *abbbb* are in the language generated by the grammar in Example 6.11.

2. Use the CYK algorithm to find a parsing of the string *aab*, using the grammar of Example 6.11. **S**

3. Use the approach employed in Exercise 2 to show how the CYK membership algorithm can be made into a parsing method.

★★ 4. Use the result in Exercise 3 to write a computer program for parsing with any context-free grammar in Chomsky normal form.

Chapter 7

Pushdown
Automata

The description of context-free languages by means of context-free grammars is convenient, as illustrated by the use of BNF in programming language definition. The next question is whether there is a class of automata that can be associated with context-free languages. As we have seen, finite automata cannot recognize all context-free languages. Intuitively, we understand that this is because finite automata have strictly finite memories, whereas the recognition of a context-free language may require storing an unbounded amount of information. For example, when scanning a string from the language $L = \{a^n b^n : n \geq 0\}$, we must not only check that all a's precede the first b, we must also count the number of a's. Since n is unbounded, this counting cannot be done with a finite memory. We want a machine that can count without limit. But as we see from other examples, such as $\{ww^R\}$, we need more than unlimited counting ability: we need the ability to store and match a sequence of symbols in reverse order. This suggests that we might try a stack as a storage mechanism, allowing unbounded storage that is restricted to operating like a stack. This gives us a class of machines called **pushdown automata (pda).**

Figure 7.1

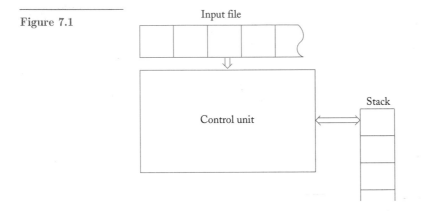

In this chapter, we explore the connection between pushdown automata and context-free languages. We first show that if we allow pushdown automata to act nondeterministically, we get a class of automata that accepts exactly the family of context-free languages. But we will also see that here there is no longer an equivalence between the deterministic and nondeterministic versions. The class of deterministic pushdown automata defines a new family of languages, the deterministic context-free languages, forming a proper subset of the context-free languages. Since this is an important family for the treatment of programming languages, we conclude the chapter with a brief introduction to the grammars associated with deterministic context-free languages.

7.1 Nondeterministic Pushdown Automata

A schematic representation of a pushdown automaton is given in Figure 7.1. Each move of the control unit reads a symbol from the input file, while at the same time changing the contents of the stack through the usual stack operations. Each move of the control unit is determined by the current input symbol as well as by the symbol currently on top of the stack. The result of the move is a new state of the control unit and a change in the top of the stack. In our discussion, we will restrict ourselves to pushdown automata acting as accepters.

Definition of a Pushdown Automaton

Formalizing this intuitive notion gives us a precise definition of a pushdown automaton.

Definition 7.1

A **nondeterministic pushdown accepter (npda)** is defined by the septuple

$$M = (Q, \Sigma, \Gamma, \delta, q_0, z, F),$$

where

Q is a finite set of internal states of the control unit,
Σ is the input alphabet,
Γ is a finite set of symbols called the **stack alphabet,**
$\delta : Q \times (\Sigma \cup \{\lambda\}) \times \Gamma \rightarrow$ finite subsets of $Q \times \Gamma^*$ is the transition function,
$q_0 \in Q$ is the initial state of the control unit,
$z \in \Gamma$ is the **stack start symbol,**
$F \subseteq Q$ is the set of final states.

The complicated formal appearance of the domain and range of δ merits a closer examination. The arguments of δ are the current state of the control unit, the current input symbol, and the current symbol on top of the stack. The result is a set of pairs (q, x), where q is the next state of the control unit and x is a string which is put on top of the stack in place of the single symbol there before. Note that the second argument of δ may be λ, indicating that a move that does not consume an input symbol is possible. We will call such a move a λ-transition. Note also that δ is defined so that it needs a stack symbol; no move is possible if the stack is empty. Finally, the requirement that the range of δ be a finite subset is necessary because $Q \times \Gamma^*$ is an infinite set and therefore has infinite subsets. While an npda may have several choices for its moves, this choice must be restricted to a finite set of possibilities.

Example 7.1

Suppose the set of transition rules of an npda contains

$$\delta (q_1, a, b) = \{(q_2, cd), (q_3, \lambda)\}.$$

If at any time the control unit is in state q_1, the input symbol read is a, and the symbol on top of the stack is b, then one of two things can happen: (1) the control unit goes into state q_2 and the string cd replaces b on top of the stack, or (2) the control unit goes into state q_3 with the symbol b removed from the top of the stack. In our notation we assume that the insertion of a string into a stack is done symbol by symbol, starting at the right end of the string.

Example 7.2　Consider an npda with

$$Q = \{q_0, q_1, q_2, q_3\},$$
$$\Sigma = \{a, b\},$$
$$\Gamma = \{0, 1\},$$
$$z = 0,$$
$$F = \{q_3\},$$

and

$$\delta(q_0, a, 0) = \{(q_1, 10), (q_3, \lambda)\},$$
$$\delta(q_0, \lambda, 0) = \{(q_3, \lambda)\},$$
$$\delta(q_1, a, 1) = \{(q_1, 11)\},$$
$$\delta(q_1, b, 1) = \{(q_2, \lambda)\},$$
$$\delta(q_2, b, 1) = \{(q_2, \lambda)\},$$
$$\delta(q_2, \lambda, 0) = \{(q_3, \lambda)\}.$$

What can we say about the action of this automaton?

First, notice that transitions are not specified for all possible combinations of input and stack symbols. For instance, there is no entry given for $\delta(q_0, b, 0)$. The interpretation of this is the same that we used for nondeterministic finite automata: an unspecified transition is to the null set and represents a dead configuration for the npda.

The crucial transitions are

$$\delta(q_1, a, 1) = \{(q_1, 11)\},$$

which adds a 1 to the stack when an a is read, and

$$\delta(q_2, b, 1) = \{(q_2, \lambda)\},$$

which removes a 1 when a b is encountered. These two steps count the number of a's and match that count against the number of b's. The control unit is in state q_1 until the first b is encountered at which time it goes into state q_2. This assures that no b precedes the last a. After analyzing the remaining transitions, we see that the npda will end in the final state q_3 if and only if the input string is in the language

$$L = \{a^n b^n : n \geq 0\} \cup \{a\}.$$

As an analogy with finite automata, we might say that the npda accepts the above language. Of course, before making such a claim, we must define what we mean by an npda accepting a language.

To simplify the discussion, we introduce a convenient notation for describing the successive configurations of an npda during the processing of a string. The relevant factors at any time are the current state of the control unit, the unread part of the input string, and the current contents of the stack. Together these completely determine all the possible ways in which the npda can proceed. The triplet

$$(q, w, u),$$

where q is the state of the control unit, w is the unread part of the input string, and u is the stack contents (with the leftmost symbol indicating the top of the stack) is called an **instantaneous description** of a pushdown automaton. A move from one instantaneous description to another will be denoted by the symbol $\vdash$; thus

$$(q_1, aw, bx) \vdash (q_2, w, yx)$$

is possible if and only if

$$(q_2, y) \in \delta(q_1, a, b).$$

Moves involving an arbitrary number of steps will be denoted by $\vdash^*$. On occasions where several automata are under consideration we will use $\vdash_M$ to emphasize that the move is made by the particular automaton M.

The Language Accepted by a Pushdown Automaton

Definition 7.2

Let $M = (Q, \Sigma, \Gamma, \delta, q_0, z, F)$ be a nondeterministic pushdown automaton. The language accepted by M is the set

$$L(M) = \left\{ w \in \Sigma^* : (q_0, w, z) \vdash_M^* (p, \lambda, u), p \in F, u \in \Gamma^* \right\}.$$

In words, the language accepted by M is the set of all strings that can put M into a final state at the end of the string. The final stack content u is irrelevant to this definition of acceptance.

Example 7.3   Construct an npda for the language

$$L = \left\{ w \in \{a, b\}^* : n_a(w) = n_b(w) \right\}.$$

As in Example 7.2, the solution to this problem involves counting the number of a's and b's, which is easily done with a stack. Here we need not even worry about the order of the a's and b's. We can insert a counter symbol, say 0, into the stack whenever an a is read, then pop one counter symbol from the stack when a b is found. The only difficulty with this is that if there is a prefix of w with more b's than a's, we will not find a 0 to use. But this is easy to fix; we can use a negative counter symbol, say 1, for counting the b's that are to be matched against a's later. The complete solution is an npda $M = (\{q_0, q_f\}, \{a, b\}, \{0, 1, z\}, \delta, q_0, z, \{q_f\})$, with δ given as

$$\delta(q_0, \lambda, z) = \{(q_f, z)\},$$
$$\delta(q_0, a, z) = \{(q_0, 0z)\},$$
$$\delta(q_0, b, z) = \{(q_0, 1z)\},$$
$$\delta(q_0, a, 0) = \{(q_0, 00)\},$$
$$\delta(q_0, b, 0) = \{(q_0, \lambda)\},$$
$$\delta(q_0, a, 1) = \{(q_0, \lambda)\},$$
$$\delta(q_0, b, 1) = \{(q_0, 11)\}.$$

In processing the string $baab$, the npda makes the moves

$$(q_0, baab, z) \vdash (q_0, aab, 1z) \vdash (q_0, ab, z)$$
$$\vdash (q_0, b, 0z) \vdash (q_0, \lambda, z) \vdash (q_f, \lambda, z)$$

and hence the string is accepted.

Example 7.4   To construct an npda for accepting the language

$$L = \left\{ ww^R : w \in \{a, b\}^+ \right\},$$

we use the fact that the symbols are retrieved from a stack in the reverse order of their insertion. When reading the first part of the string, we push consecutive symbols on the stack. For the second part, we compare the current input symbol with the top of the stack, continuing as long as the two match. Since symbols are retrieved from the stack in reverse of the order in which they were inserted, a complete match will be achieved if and only if the input is of the form ww^R.

An apparent difficulty with this suggestion is that we do not know the middle of the string, that is, where w ends and w^R starts. But the nondeterministic nature of the automaton helps us with this; the npda correctly guesses where the middle is and switches states at that point. A solution to the problem is given by $M = (Q, \Sigma, \Gamma, \delta, q_0, z, F)$, where

$$Q = \{q_0, q_1, q_2\},$$
$$\Sigma = \{a, b\},$$
$$\Gamma = \{a, b, z\},$$
$$F = \{q_2\}.$$

The transition function can be visualized as having several parts: a set to push w on the stack,

$$\delta\left(q_0, a, a\right) = \left\{\left(q_0, aa\right)\right\},$$
$$\delta\left(q_0, b, a\right) = \left\{\left(q_0, ba\right)\right\},$$
$$\delta\left(q_0, a, b\right) = \left\{\left(q_0, ab\right)\right\},$$
$$\delta\left(q_0, b, b\right) = \left\{\left(q_0, bb\right)\right\},$$
$$\delta\left(q_0, a, z\right) = \left\{\left(q_0, az\right)\right\},$$
$$\delta\left(q_0, b, z\right) = \left\{\left(q_0, bz\right)\right\},$$

a set to guess the middle of the string, where the npda switches from state q_0 to q_1,

$$\delta\left(q_0, \lambda, a\right) = \left\{\left(q_1, a\right)\right\},$$
$$\delta\left(q_0, \lambda, b\right) = \left\{\left(q_1, b\right)\right\},$$

a set to match w^R against the contents of the stack,

$$\delta\left(q_1, a, a\right) = \left\{\left(q_1, \lambda\right)\right\},$$
$$\delta\left(q_1, b, b\right) = \left\{\left(q_1, \lambda\right)\right\},$$

and finally

$$\delta\left(q_1, \lambda, z\right) = \left\{\left(q_2, z\right)\right\},$$

to recognize a successful match.

The sequence of moves in accepting $abba$ is

$$(q_0, abba, z) \vdash (q_0, bba, az) \vdash (q_0, ba, baz)$$
$$\vdash (q_1, ba, baz) \vdash (q_1, a, az) \vdash (q_1, \lambda, z) \vdash (q_2, z).$$

The nondeterministic alternative for locating the middle of the string is taken at the third move. At that stage, the pda has the instantaneous descriptions (q_0, ba, baz) and has two choices for its next move. One is to use $\delta\left(q_0, b, b\right) = \left\{\left(q_0, bb\right)\right\}$ and make the move

$$(q_0, baa, baz) \vdash (q_0, a, bbaz),$$

the second is the one used above, namely $\delta\left(q_0, \lambda, b\right) = \left\{\left(q_1, b\right)\right\}$. Only the latter leads to acceptance of the input.

Exercises

√1. Find a pda with fewer than four states that accepts the same language as the pda in Example 7.2.

2. Prove that the pda in Example 7.4 does not accept any string not in $\{ww^R\}$.
   S

3. Construct npda's that accept the following regular languages.

   (a) $L_1 = L(aaa^*b)$

   (b) $L_1 = L(aab^*aba^*)$

   (c) the union of L_1 and L_2

   (d) $L_1 - L_2$

√4. Construct npda's that accept the following languages on $\Sigma = \{a, b, c\}$.

   (a) $L = \{a^n b^{2n} : n \geq 0\}$ **S**

   (b) $L = \{wcw^R : w \in \{a, b\}^*\}$

   (c) $L = \{a^n b^m c^{n+m} : n \geq 0, m \geq 0\}$

   (d) $L = \{a^n b^{n+m} c^m : n \geq 0, m \geq 1\}$

   (e) $L = \{a^3 b^n c^n : n \geq 0\}$

   (f) $L = \{a^n b^m : n \leq m \leq 3n\}$ **S**

   (g) $L = \{w : n_a(w) = n_b(w) + 1\}$

   (h) $L = \{w : n_a(w) = 2n_b(w)\}$

   (i) $L = \{w : n_a(w) + n_b(w) = n_c(w)\}$

   (j) $L = \{w : 2n_a(w) \leq n_b(w) \leq 3n_a(w)\}$

   (k) $L = \{w : n_a(w) < n_b(w)\}$

5. Construct an npda that accepts the language $L = \{a^n b^m : n \geq 0, n \neq m\}$.

6. Find an npda on $\Sigma = \{a, b, c\}$ that accepts the language

$$L = \left\{w_1 c w_2 : w_1, w_2 \in \{a, b\}^*, w_1 \neq w_2^R\right\}.$$

7. Find an npda for the concatenation of $L(a^*)$ and the language in Exercise 6.

8. Find an npda for the language $L = \{ab(ab)^n b(ba)^n : n \geq 0\}$.

9. Is it possible to find a dfa that accepts the same language as the pda

$$M = (\{q_0, q_1\}, \{a, b\}, \{z\}, q_0, \{q_1\}),$$

with

$$\delta(q_0, a, z) = \{(q_1, z)\},$$
$$\delta(q_0, b, z) = \{(q_0, z)\},$$
$$\delta(q_1, a, z) = \{(q_1, z)\},$$
$$\delta(q_1, b, z) = \{(q_0, z)\}? \quad \text{S}$$

10. What language is accepted by the pda

$$M - (\{q_0, q_1, q_2, q_3, q_4, q_5\}, \{a, b\}, \{0, 1, n\}, q_0, \{q_5\}),$$

with

$$\delta(q_0, b, z) = \{(q_1, 1z)\},$$
$$\delta(q_1, b, 1) = \{(q_1, 11)\},$$
$$\delta(q_2, a, 1) = \{(q_3, \lambda)\},$$
$$\delta(q_3, a, 1) = \{(q_4, \lambda)\},$$
$$\delta(q_4, a, z) = \{(q_4, z), (q_5, z)\}?$$

11. What language is accepted by the npda $M = (\{q_0, q_1, q_2\}, \{a, b\}, \{a, b, z\}, \delta, q_0, z, \{q_2\})$ with transitions

$$\delta(q_0, a, z) = \{(q_1, a), (q_2, \lambda)\},$$
$$\delta(q_1, b, a) = \{(q_1, b)\},$$
$$\delta(q_1, b, b) = \{(q_1, b)\},$$
$$\delta(q_1, a, b) = \{(q_2, \lambda)\}. \quad \text{S}$$

12. What language is accepted by the npda in Example 7.3 if we use $F = \{q_0, q_f\}$?

13. What language is accepted by the npda in Exercise 11 above if we use $F = \{q_0, q_1, q_2\}$?

14. Find an npda with no more than two internal states that accepts the language $L(aa^*ba^*)$. **S**

15. Suppose that in Example 7.2 we replace the given value of $\delta(q_2, \lambda, 0)$ with

$$\delta(q_2, \lambda, 0) = \{(q_0, \lambda)\}.$$

What is the language accepted by this new pda?

16. We can define a restricted npda as one that can increase the length of the stack by at most one symbol in each move, changing Definition 7.1 so that

$$\delta: Q \times (\Sigma \cup \{\lambda\}) \times \Gamma \rightarrow 2^{Q \times (\Gamma\Gamma \cup \Gamma \cup \{\lambda\})}.$$

The interpretation of this is that the range of δ consists of sets of pairs of the form $(q_i, ab), (q_i, a)$, or (q_i, λ). Show that for every npda M there exists such a restricted npda $\widehat{M}$ such that $L(M) = L(\widehat{M})$. **S**

17. An alternative to Definition 7.2 for language acceptance is to require the stack to be empty when the end of the input string is reached. Formally, an npda M is said to accept the language $N(M)$ by empty stack if

$$N(M) = \left\{ w \in \Sigma^* : (q_0, w, z) \overset{*}{\vdash}_M (p, \lambda, \lambda) \right\},$$

where p is any element in Q. Show that this notion is effectively equivalent to Definition 7.2, in the sense that for any npda M there exists an npda $\widehat{M}$ such that $L(M) = N\left(\widehat{M}\right)$, and vice versa.

7.2 Pushdown Automata and Context-Free Languages

In the examples of the previous section, we saw that pushdown automata exist for some of the familiar context-free languages. This is no accident. There is a general relation between context-free languages and nondeterministic pushdown accepters that is established in the next two major results. We will show that for every context-free language there is an npda that accepts it, and conversely, that the language accepted by any npda is context-free.

Pushdown Automata for Context-Free Languages

We first show that for every context-free language there is an npda that accepts it. The underlying idea is to construct an npda that can, in some way, carry out a leftmost derivation of any string in the language. To simplify the argument a little, we assume that the language is generated by a grammar in Greibach normal form.

The pda we are about to construct will represent the derivation by keeping the variables in the right part of the sentential form on its stack, while the left part, consisting entirely of terminals, is identical with the input read. We begin by putting the start symbol on the stack. After that, to simulate the application of a production $A \rightarrow ax$, we must have the variable A on top of the stack and the terminal a as the input symbol. The variable on the stack is removed and replaced by the variable string x. What δ should be to achieve this is easy to see. Before we present the general argument, let us look at a simple example.

◁**Example 7.5**   Construct a pda that accepts the language generated by grammar with productions

$$S \rightarrow aSbb \mid a.$$

We first transform the grammar into Greibach normal form, changing the productions to

$$S \rightarrow aSA|a,$$
$$A \rightarrow bB,$$
$$B \rightarrow b.$$

The corresponding automaton will have three states $\{q_0, q_1, q_2\}$, with initial state q_0 and final state q_2. First, the start symbol S is put on the stack by

$$\delta(q_0, \lambda, z) = \{(q_1, Sz)\}.$$

The production $S \rightarrow aSA$ will be simulated in the pda by removing S from the stack and replacing it with SA, while reading a from the input. Similarly, the rule $S \rightarrow a$ should cause the pda to read an a while simply removing S. Thus, the two productions are represented in the pda by

$$\delta(q_1, a, S) = \{(q_1, SA), (q_1, \lambda)\}.$$

In an analogous manner, the other productions give

$$\delta(q_1, b, A) = \{(q_1, B)\},$$
$$\delta(q_1, b, B) = \{(q_1, \lambda)\}.$$

The appearance of the stack start symbol on top of the stack signals the completion of the derivation and the pda is put into its final state by

$$\delta(q_1, \lambda, z) = \{(q_2, \lambda)\}.$$

The construction of this example can be adapted to other cases, leading to a general result.

Theorem 7.1

For any context-free language L, there exists an npda M such that

$$L = L(M).$$

Proof: If L is a λ-free context-free language, there exists a context-free grammar in Greibach normal form for it. Let $G = (V, T, S, P)$ be such a grammar. We then construct an npda which simulates leftmost derivations in this grammar. As suggested, the simulation will be done so that the unprocessed part of the sentential form is in the stack, while the terminal prefix of any sentential form matches the corresponding prefix of the input string.

Specifically, the npda will be

$$M = (\{q_0, q_1, q_f\}, T, V \cup \{z\}, \delta, q_0, z, \{q_f\}),$$

where $z \notin V$. Note that the input alphabet of M is identical with the set of terminals of G and that the stack alphabet contains the set of variables of the grammar.

The transition function will include

$$\delta(q_0, \lambda, z) = \{(q_1, Sz)\}, \tag{7.1}$$

so that after the first move of M, the stack contains the start symbol S of the derivation. (The stack start symbol z is a marker to allow us to detect the end of the derivation.) In addition, the set of transition rules is such that

$$(q_1, u) \in \delta(q_1, a, A), \tag{7.2}$$

whenever

$$A \rightarrow au$$

is in P. This reads input a and removes the variable A from the stack, replacing it with u. In this way it generates the transitions that allow the pda to simulate all derivations. Finally, we have

$$\delta(q_1, \lambda, z) = \{(q_f, z)\}, \tag{7.3}$$

to get M into a final state.

To show that M accepts any $w \in L(G)$, consider the partial leftmost derivation

$$S \overset{*}{\Rightarrow} a_1 a_2 \cdots a_n A_1 A_2 \cdots A_m$$
$$\Rightarrow a_1 a_2 \cdots a_n b B_1 \cdots B_k A_2 \cdots A_m.$$

If M is to simulate this derivation, then after reading $a_1 a_2 \cdots a_n$, the stack must contain $A_1 A_2 \cdots A_m$. To take the next step in the derivation, G must have a production

$$A_1 \rightarrow b B_1 \cdots B_k.$$

But the construction is such that then M has a transition rule in which

$$(q_1, B_1 \cdots B_k) \in \delta(q_1, b, A_1),$$

so that the stack now contains $B_1 \cdots B_k A_2 \cdots A_m$ after having read $a_1 a_2 \cdots a_n b$.

A simple induction argument on the number of steps in the derivation then shows that if

$$S \overset{*}{\Rightarrow} w,$$

then

$$(q_1, w, Sz) \overset{*}{\vdash} (q_1, \lambda, z).$$

Using (7.1) and (7.3) we have

$$(q_0, w, z) \vdash (q_1, w, Sz) \overset{*}{\vdash} (q_1, \lambda, z) \vdash (q_f, \lambda, z),$$

so that $L(G) \subseteq L(M)$.

To prove that $L(M) \subseteq L(G)$, let $w \in L(M)$. Then by definition

$$(q_0, w, z) \overset{*}{\vdash} (q_f, \lambda, u).$$

But there is only one way to get from q_0 to q_1 and only one way from q_1 to q_f. Therefore, we must have

$$(q_1, w, Sz) \overset{*}{\vdash} (q_1, \lambda, z).$$

Now let us write $w = a_1 a_2 a_3 \cdots a_n$. Then the first step in

$$(q_1, a_1 a_2 a_3 \cdots a_n, Sz) \overset{*}{\vdash} (q_1, \lambda, z) \tag{7.4}$$

must be a rule of the form (7.2) to get

$$(q_1, a_1 a_2 a_3 \cdots a_n, Sz) \vdash (q_1, a_2 a_3 \cdots a_n, u_1 z).$$

But then the grammar has a rule of the form $S \to a_1 u_1$, so that

$$S \Rightarrow a_1 u_1.$$

Repeating this, writing $u_1 = A u_2$, we have

$$(q_1, a_2 a_3 \cdots a_n, A u_2 z) \vdash (q_1, a_3 \cdots a_n, u_3 u_2 z),$$

implying that $A \to a_2 u_3$ is in the grammar and that

$$S \overset{*}{\Rightarrow} a_1 a_2 u_3 u_2.$$

This makes it quite clear at any point the stack contents (excluding z) are identical with the unmatched part of the sentential form, so that (7.4) implies

$$S \overset{*}{\Rightarrow} a_1 a_2 \cdots a_n.$$

In consequence, $L(M) \subseteq L(G)$, completing the proof if the language does not contain λ.

If $\lambda \in L$, we add to the constructed npda the transition

$$\delta(q_0, \lambda, z) = \{(q_f, z)\}$$

so that the empty string is also accepted. ∎

Example 7.6   Consider the grammar

$$S \rightarrow aA,$$
$$A \rightarrow aABC \,|bB|\, a,$$
$$B \rightarrow b,$$
$$C \rightarrow c.$$

Since the grammar is already in Greibach normal form, we can use the construction in the previous theorem immediately. In addition to rules

$$\delta\left(q_0, \lambda, z\right) = \{(q_1, Sz)\}$$

and

$$\delta\left(q_1, \lambda, z\right) = \{(q_f, z)\},$$

the pda will also have transition rules

$$\delta\left(q_1, a, S\right) = \{(q_1, A)\},$$
$$\delta\left(q_1, a, A\right) = \{(q_1, ABC),(q_1, \lambda)\},$$
$$\delta\left(q_1, b, A\right) = \{(q_1, B)\},$$
$$\delta\left(q_1, b, B\right) = \{(q_1, \lambda)\},$$
$$\delta\left(q_1, c, C\right) = \{(q_1, \lambda)\}.$$

The sequence of moves made by M in processing $aaabc$ is

$$(q_0, aaabc, z) \vdash (q_1, aaabc, Sz)$$
$$\vdash (q_1, aabc, Az)$$
$$\vdash (q_1, abc, ABCz)$$
$$\vdash (q_1, bc, BCz)$$
$$\vdash (q_1, c, Cz)$$
$$\vdash (q_1, \lambda, z)$$
$$\vdash (q_f, \lambda, z).$$

This corresponds to the derivation

$$S \Rightarrow aA \Rightarrow aaABC \Rightarrow aaaBC \Rightarrow aaabC \Rightarrow aaabc.$$

In order to simplify the arguments, the proof in Theorem 7.1 assumed that the grammar was in Greibach normal form. It is not necessary to do this; we can make a similar and only slightly more complicated construction from a general context-free grammar. For example, for productions of the form

$$A \rightarrow Bx,$$

we remove A from the stack and replace it with Bx, but consume no input symbol. For productions of the form

$$A \rightarrow abCx,$$

we must first match the ab in the input against a similar string in the stack and then replace A with Cx. We leave the details of the construction and the associated proof as an exercise.

Context-Free Grammars for Pushdown Automata

The converse of Theorem 7.1 is also true. The construction involved readily suggests itself: reverse the process in Theorem 7.1 so that the grammar simulates the moves of the pda. This means that the content of the stack should be reflected in the variable part of the sentential form, while the processed input is the terminal prefix of the sentential form. Quite a few details are needed to make this work.

To keep the discussion as simple as possible, we will assume that the npda in question meets the following requirements:

1. It has a single final state q_f that is entered if and only if the stack is empty;

2. All transitions must have the form $\delta (q_i, a, A) = \{c_1, c_2, ..., c_n\}$, where

$$c_i = (q_j, \lambda), \tag{7.5}$$

or

$$c_i = (q_j, BC). \tag{7.6}$$

That is, each move either increases or decreases the stack content by a single symbol.

These restrictions may appear to be very severe, but they are not. It can be shown that for any npda there exists an equivalent one having properties 1 and 2. This equivalence was explored partially in Exercises 16 and 17 in Section 7.1. Here we need to explore it further, but again we will leave the arguments as an exercise (see Exercise 16 at the end of this section). Taking this as given, we now construct a context-free grammar for the language accepted by the npda.

As stated, we want the sentential form to represent the content of the stack. But the configuration of the npda also involves an internal state, and this has to be remembered in the sentential form as well. It is hard to see how this can be done, and the construction we give here is a little tricky.

Suppose for the moment that we can find a grammar whose variables are of the form $(q_i A q_j)$ and whose productions are such that

$$(q_i A q_j) \overset{*}{\Rightarrow} v,$$

if and only if the npda erases A from the stack while reading v and going from state q_i to state q_j. "Erasing" here means that A and its effects (i.e., all the successive strings by which it is replaced) are removed from the stack, bringing the symbol originally below A to the top. If we can find such a grammar, and if we choose $(q_0 z q_f)$ as its start symbol, then

$$(q_0 z q_f) \overset{*}{\Rightarrow} w,$$

if and only if the npda removes z (creating an empty stack) while reading w and going from q_0 to q_f. But this is exactly how the npda accepts w. Therefore, the language generated by the grammar will be identical to the language accepted by the npda.

To construct a grammar that satisfies these conditions, we examine the different types of transitions that can be made by the npda. Since (7.5) involves an immediate erasure of A, the grammar will have a corresponding production

$$(q_i A q_j) \rightarrow a.$$

Productions of type (7.6) generate the set of rules

$$(q_i A q_k) \rightarrow a (q_j B q_l) (q_l C q_k),$$

where q_k and q_l take on all possible values in Q. This is due to the fact that to erase A we first replace it with BC, while reading an a and going from state q_i to q_j. Subsequently, we go from q_j to q_l, erasing B, then from q_l to q_k, erasing C.

In the last step, it may seem that we have added too much, as there may be some states q_l that cannot be reached from q_j while erasing B. This is true, but this does not affect the grammar. The resulting variables $(q_j B q_l)$ are useless variables and do not affect the language accepted by the grammar.

Finally, as start variable we take $(q_0 z q_f)$, where q_f is the single final state of the npda.

Example 7.7 Consider the npda with transitions

$$\delta (q_0, a, z) = \{(q_0, Az)\},$$
$$\delta (q_0, a, A) = \{(q_0, A)\},$$
$$\delta (q_0, b, A) = \{(q_1, \lambda)\},$$
$$\delta (q_1, \lambda, z) = \{(q_2, \lambda)\}.$$

Using q_0 as initial state and q_2 as the final state, the npda satisfies condition 1 above, but not 2. To satisfy the latter, we introduce a new state q_3 and an intermediate step in which we first remove the A from the stack, then replace it in the next move. The new set of transition rule is

$$\delta (q_0, a, z) = \{(q_0, Az)\},$$
$$\delta (q_3, \lambda, z) = \{(q_0, Az)\},$$
$$\delta (q_0, a, A) = \{(q_3, \lambda)\},$$
$$\delta (q_0, b, A) = \{(q_1, \lambda)\},$$
$$\delta (q_1, \lambda, z) = \{(q_2, \lambda)\}.$$

The last three transitions are of the form (7.5) so that they yield the corresponding productions

$$(q_0 A q_3) \rightarrow a, \quad (q_0 A q_1) \rightarrow b, \quad (q_1 z q_2) \rightarrow \lambda.$$

From the first two transitions we get the set of productions.

$$(q_0 z q_0) \rightarrow a(q_0 A q_0)(q_0 z q_0)|a(q_0 A q_1)(q_1 z q_0)|$$
$$a(q_0 A q_2)(q_2 z q_0)|a(q_0 A q_3)(q_3 z q_0),$$
$$(q_0 z q_1) \rightarrow a(q_0 A q_0)(q_0 z q_1)|a(q_0 A q_1)(q_1 z q_1)|$$
$$a(q_0 A q_2)(q_2 z q_1)|a(q_0 A q_3)(q_3 z q_1),$$
$$(q_0 z q_2) \rightarrow a(q_0 A q_0)(q_0 z q_2)|a(q_0 A q_1)(q_1 z q_2)|$$
$$a(q_0 A q_2)(q_2 z q_2)|a(q_0 A q_3)(q_3 z q_2),$$
$$(q_0 z q_3) \rightarrow a(q_0 A q_0)(q_0 z q_3)|a(q_0 A q_1)(q_1 z q_3)|$$
$$a(q_0 A q_2)(q_2 z q_3)|a(q_0 A q_3)(q_3 z q_3),$$

$$(q_3 z q_0) \rightarrow (q_0 A q_0)(q_0 z q_0)|(q_0 A q_1)(q_1 z q_0)|(q_0 A q_2)(q_2 z q_0)|(q_0 A q_3)(q_3 z q_0),$$
$$(q_3 z q_1) \rightarrow (q_0 A q_0)(q_0 z q_1)|(q_0 A q_1)(q_1 z q_1)|(q_0 A q_2)(q_2 z q_1)|(q_0 A q_3)(q_3 z q_1),$$
$$(q_3 z q_2) \rightarrow (q_0 A q_0)(q_0 z q_2)|(q_0 A q_1)(q_1 z q_2)|(q_0 A q_2)(q_2 z q_2)|(q_0 A q_3)(q_3 z q_2),$$
$$(q_3 z q_3) \rightarrow (q_0 A q_0)(q_0 z q_3)|(q_0 A q_1)(q_1 z q_3)|(q_0 A q_2)(q_2 z q_3)|(q_0 A q_3)(q_3 z q_3).$$

The start variable will be $(q_0 z q_2)$. The string aab is accepted by the pda, with successive configurations

$$(q_0, aab, z) \vdash (q_0, ab, Az)$$
$$\vdash (q_3, b, z)$$
$$\vdash (q_0, b, Az)$$
$$\vdash (q_1, \lambda, z)$$
$$\vdash (q_2, \lambda, \lambda).$$

The corresponding derivation with G is

$$(q_0 z q_2) \Rightarrow a (q_0 A q_3)(q_3 z q_2)$$
$$\Rightarrow aa (q_3 z q_2)$$
$$\Rightarrow aa (q_0 A q_1)(q_1 z q_2)$$
$$\Rightarrow aab (q_1 z q_2)$$
$$\Rightarrow aab.$$

The steps in the proof of the following theorem will be easier to understand if you notice the correspondence between the successive instantaneous descriptions of the pda and the sentential forms in the derivation. The first q_i in the leftmost variable of every sentential form is the current state of the pda, while the sequence of middle symbols is the same as the stack content. Although the construction yields a rather complicated grammar, it can be applied to any pda whose transition rules satisfy the given conditions. This forms the basis for the proof of the general result.

Theorem 7.2   If $L = L(M)$ for some npda M, then L is a context-free language.

Proof: Assume that $M = (Q, \Sigma, \Gamma, \delta, q_0, z, \{q_f\})$ satisfies conditions 1 and 2 above. We use the suggested construction to get the grammar $G = (V, T, S, P)$, with $T = \Sigma$ and V consisting of elements of the form $(q_i c q_j)$. We will show that the grammar so obtained is such that for all $q_i, q_j, \in Q, A \in \Gamma, X \in \Gamma^*, u, v \in \Sigma^*$,

$$(q_i, uv, AX) \overset{*}{\vdash} (q_j, v, X) \tag{7.7}$$

implies that

$$(q_i A q_j) \overset{*}{\Rightarrow} u,$$

and vice versa.

The first part is to show that, whenever the npda is such that the symbol A and its effects can be removed from the stack while reading u and going from state q_i to q_j, then the variable $(q_i A q_j)$ can derive u. This is not hard to see since the grammar was explicitly constructed to do this. We only need an induction on the number of moves to make this precise.

For the converse, consider a single step in the derivation such as

$$(q_i A q_k) \Rightarrow a \, (q_j B q_l) \, (q_l C q_k).$$

Using the corresponding transition for the npda

$$\delta \, (q_i, a, A) = \{(q_j, BC), ...\}, \tag{7.8}$$

we see that the A can be removed from the stack, BC put on, reading a, with the control unit going from state q_i to q_j. Similarly, if

$$(q_i A q_j) \Rightarrow a, \tag{7.9}$$

then there must be a corresponding transition

$$\delta \, (q_i, a, A) = \{(q_j, \lambda)\} \tag{7.10}$$

whereby the A can be popped off the stack. We see from this that the sentential forms derived from $(q_i A q_j)$ define a sequence of possible configurations of the npda by which (7.7) can be achieved.

Notice that $(q_i A q_j) \Rightarrow a \, (q_j B q_l) \, (q_l C q_k)$ might be possible for some $(q_j B q_l) \, (q_l C q_k)$ for which there is no corresponding transition of the form (7.8) or (7.10). But, in that case, at least one of the variables on the right will be useless. For all sentential forms leading to a terminal string, the argument given holds.

If we now apply the conclusion to

$$(q_0, w, z) \vdash^* (q_f, \lambda, \lambda),$$

we see that this can be so if and only if

$$(q_0 z q_f) \overset{*}{\Rightarrow} w.$$

Consequently $L(M) = L(G)$. ∎

EXERCISES

1. Show that the pda constructed in Example 7.5 accepts the string $aaabbbb$ that is in the language generated by the given grammar.

2. Prove that the pda in Example 7.5 accepts the language $L = \{a^{n+1}b^{2n} : n \geq 0\}$.

3. Construct an npda that accepts the language generated by the grammar

$$S \rightarrow aSbb|aab. \ \text{\small S}$$

4. Construct an npda that accepts the language generated by the grammar $S \rightarrow aSSS|ab.$ **S**

5. Construct an npda corresponding to the grammar

$$S \rightarrow aABB|aAA,$$
$$A \rightarrow aBB|a,$$
$$B \rightarrow bBB|A.$$

6. Construct an npda that will accept the language generated by the grammar $G = (\{S, A\}, \{a, b\}, S, P)$, with productions $S \rightarrow AA\,|a, A \rightarrow SA|\,b.$

7. Show that Theorems 7.1 and 7.2 imply the following. For every npda M, there exists an npda $\widehat{M}$ with at most three states, such that $L(M) = L\left(\widehat{M}\right).$ **S**

8. Show how the number of states of $\widehat{M}$ in the above exercise can be reduced to two.

9. Find an npda with two states for the language $L = \left\{a^n b^{n+1} : n \geq 0\right\}.$ **S**

10. Find an npda with two states that accepts $L = \left\{a^n b^{2n} : n \geq 1\right\}.$

11. Show that the npda in Example 7.7 accepts $L(aa^*b).$ **S**

12. Show that the grammar in Example 7.7 generates the language $L(aa^*b).$

13. In Example 7.7, show that the variables $(q_0 B q_0)$ and $(q_0 z q_1)$ are useless.

14. Use the construction in Theorem 7.1 to find an npda for the language Example 7.5, Section 7.1.

15. Find a context-free grammar that generates the language accepted by the npda $M = (\{q_0, q_1\}, \{a, b\}, \{A, z\}, \delta, q_0, z, \{q_1\})$, with transitions

$$\delta(q_0, a, z) = \{(q_0, Az)\},$$
$$\delta(q_0, b, A) = \{(q_0, AA)\},$$
$$\delta(q_0, a, A) = \{(q_1, \lambda)\}.$$

16. Show that for every npda there exists an equivalent one satisfying conditions 1 and 2 in the preamble to Theorem 7.2.

17. Give full details of the proof of Theorem 7.2.

18. Give a construction by which an arbitrary context-free grammar can be used in the proof of Theorem 7.1.

7.3 Deterministic Pushdown Automata and Deterministic Context-Free Languages

A **deterministic pushdown accepter** (**dpda**) is a pushdown automaton that never has a choice in its move. This can be achieved by a modification of Definition 7.1.

Definition 7.3

A pushdown automaton $M = (Q, \Sigma, \Gamma, \delta, q_0, z, F)$ is said to be deterministic if it is an automaton as defined in Definition 7.1, subject to the restrictions that, for every $q \in Q, a \in \Sigma \cup \{\lambda\}$ and $b \in \Gamma$,

1. $\delta(q, a, b)$ contains at most one element,

2. if $\delta(q, \lambda, b)$ is not empty, then $\delta(q, c, b)$ must be empty for every $c \in \Sigma$.

The first of these conditions simply requires that for any given input symbol and any stack top, at most one move can be made. The second condition is that when a λ-move is possible for some configuration, no input-consuming alternative is available.

It is interesting to note the difference between this definition and the corresponding definition of a deterministic finite automaton. The domain of the transition function is still as in Definition 7.1 rather than $Q \times \Sigma \times \Gamma$ because we want to retain λ-transitions. Since the top of the stack plays a role in determining the next move, the presence of λ-transitions does not automatically imply nondeterminism. Also, some transitions of a dpda may be to the empty set, that is, undefined, so there may be dead configurations. This does not affect the definition; the only criterion for determinism is that at all times at most one possible move exists.

Definition 7.4

A language L is said to be a **deterministic context-free language** if and only if there exists a dpda M such that $L = L(M)$.

Example 7.8　The language

$$L = \{a^n b^n : n \geq 0\}$$

is a deterministic context-free language. The pda $M = (\{q_0, q_1, q_2\}, \{a, b\},$ $\{0, 1\}, \delta, q_0, 0, \{q_0\})$ with

$$\delta(q_0, a, 0) = \{(q_1, 10)\},$$
$$\delta(q_1, a, 1) = \{(q_1, 11)\},$$
$$\delta(q_1, b, 1) = \{(q_2, \lambda)\},$$
$$\delta(q_2, b, 1) = \{(q_2, \lambda)\},$$
$$\delta(q_2, \lambda, 0) = \{(q_0, \lambda)\},$$

accepts the given language. It satisfies the conditions of Definition 7.4 and is therefore deterministic.

Look now at Example 7.4. The npda there is not deterministic because

$$\delta(q_0, a, a) = \{(q_0, aa)\}$$

and

$$\delta(q_0, \lambda, a) = \{(q_1, a)\}$$

violate condition 2 of Definition 7.3. This, of course, does not imply that the language $\{ww^R\}$ itself is nondeterministic, since there is the possibility of an equivalent dpda. But it is known that the language is indeed not deterministic. From this and the next example we see that, in contrast to finite automata, deterministic and nondeterministic pushdown automata are not equivalent. There are context-free languages that are not deterministic.

Example 7.9　Let

$$L_1 = \{a^n b^n : n \geq 0\}$$

and

$$L_2 = \{a^n b^{2n} : n \geq 0\}.$$

An obvious modification of the argument that L_1 is a context-free language shows that L_2 is also context-free. The language

$$L = L_1 \cup L_2$$

is context-free as well. This will follow from a general theorem to be presented in the next chapter, but can easily be made plausible at this point. Let $G_1 = (V_1, T, S_1, P_1)$ and $G_2 = (V_2, T, S_2, P_2)$ be context-free grammars such that $L_1 = L(G_1)$ and $L_2 = L(G_2)$. If we assume that V_1 and V_2 are disjoint and that $S \notin V_1 \cup V_2$, then, combining the two, grammar $G = (V_1 \cup V_2 \cup \{S\}, T, S, P)$, where

$$P = P_1 \cup P_2 \cup \{S \rightarrow S_1 | S_2\},$$

generates $L_1 \cup L_2$. This should be fairly clear at this point, but the details of the argument will be deferred until Chapter 8. Accepting this, we see that L is context-free. But L is not a deterministic context free language. This seems reasonable, since the pda has either to match one b or two against each a, and so has to make an initial choice whether the input is in L_1 or in L_2. There is no information available at the beginning of the string by which the choice can be made deterministically. Of course, this sort of argument is based on a particular algorithm we have in mind; it may lead us to the correct conjecture, but does not prove anything. There is always the possibility of a completely different approach that avoids an initial choice. But it turns out that there is not, and L is indeed nondeterministic. To see this we first establish the following claim. If L were a deterministic context-free language, then

$$\widehat{L} = L \cup \{a^n b^n c^n : n \geq 0\}$$

would be a context-free language. We show the latter by constructing an npda $\widehat{M}$ for $\widehat{L}$, given a dpda M for L.

The idea behind the construction is to add to the control unit of M a similar part in which transitions caused by the input symbol b are replaced with similar ones for input c. This new part of the control unit may be entered after M has read $a^n b^n$. Since the second part responds to c^n in the same way as the first part does to b^n, the process that recognizes $a^n b^{2n}$ now also accepts $a^n b^n c^n$. Figure 7.2 describes the construction graphically; a formal argument follows.

Let $M = (Q, \Sigma, \Gamma, \delta, q_0, z, F)$ with

$$Q = \{q_0, q_1, ..., q_n\}.$$

Then consider $\widehat{M} = \left(\widehat{Q}, \Sigma, \Gamma, \delta \cup \widehat{\delta}, z, \widehat{F}\right)$ with

$$\widehat{Q} = Q \cup \{\widehat{q}_0, \widehat{q}_1, ..., \widehat{q}_n\},$$
$$\widehat{F} = F \cup \{\widehat{q}_i : q_i \in F\},$$

and $\widehat{\delta}$ constructed from δ by including

$$\widehat{\delta}(q_f, \lambda, s) = \{(\widehat{q}_f, s)\},$$

Figure 7.2

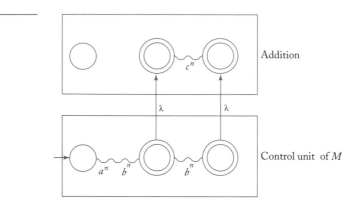

for all $q_f \in F, s \in \Gamma$, and

$$\widehat{\delta} \left(\widehat{q}_i, c, s \right) = \left\{ \left(\widehat{q}_j, u \right) \right\},$$

for all

$$\delta \left(q_i, b, s \right) = \left\{ \left(q_j, u \right) \right\},$$

$q_i \in Q, s \in \Gamma, u \in \Gamma^*$. For M to accept $a^n b^n$ we must have

$$\left(q_0, a^n b^n, z \right) \overset{*}{\vdash}_M \left(q_i, \lambda, u \right),$$

with $q_i \in F$. Because M is deterministic, it must also be true that

$$\left(q_0, a^n b^{2n}, z \right) \overset{*}{\vdash}_M \left(q_i, b^n, u \right),$$

so that for it to accept $a^n b^{2n}$ we must further have

$$\left(q_i, b^n, u \right) \overset{*}{\vdash}_M \left(q_j, \lambda, u_1 \right),$$

for some $q_j \in F$. But then, by construction

$$\left(\widehat{q}_i, c^n, u \right) \overset{*}{\vdash}_{\widehat{M}} \left(\widehat{q}_j, \lambda, u_1 \right),$$

so that $\widehat{M}$ will accept $a^n b^n c^n$. It remains to be shown that no strings other than those in $\widehat{L}$ are accepted by $\widehat{M}$; this is considered in several exercises at the end of this section. The conclusion is that $\widehat{L} = L \left(\widehat{M} \right)$, so that $\widehat{L}$ is context-free. But we will show in the next chapter (Example 8.1) that $\widehat{L}$ is not context-free. Therefore, our assumption that L is a deterministic context-free language must be false.

EXERCISES

1. Show that $L = \{a^n b^{2n} : n \geq 0\}$ is a deterministic context-free language.

2. Show that $L = \{a^n b^m : m \geq n + 2\}$ is deterministic.

3. Is the language $L = \{a^n b^n : n \geq 1\} \cup \{b\}$ deterministic?

4. Is the language $L = \{a^n b^n : n \geq 1\} \cup \{a\}$ in Example 7.2 deterministic? **S**

5. Show that the pushdown automaton in Example 7.3 is not deterministic, but that the language in the example is nevertheless deterministic.

6. For the language L in Exercise 1, show that L^* is a deterministic context-free language.

7. Give reasons why one might conjecture that the following language is not deterministic.

$$L = \left\{ a^n b^m c^k : n = m \text{ or } m = k \right\}$$

8. Is the language $L = \{a^n b^m : n = m \text{ or } n = m + 2\}$ deterministic?

9. Is the language $\left\{ w c w^R : w \in \{a, b\}^* \right\}$ deterministic? **S**

10. While the language in Exercise 9 is deterministic, the closely related language $L = \left\{ w w^R : w \in \{a, b\}^* \right\}$ is known to be nondeterministic. Give arguments that make this statement plausible.

11. Show that $L = \{w \in \{a, b\}^* : n_a(w) \neq n_b(w)\}$ is a deterministic context-free language. **S**

12. Show that $\widehat{M}$ in Example 7.9 does not accept $a^n b^n c^k$ for $k \neq n$.

13. Show that $\widetilde{M}$ in Example 7.9 does not accept any string not in $L(a^* b^* c^*)$.

14. Show that $\widehat{M}$ in Example 7.9 does not accept $a^n b^{2n} c^k$ with $k > 0$. Show also that it does not accept $a^n b^m c^k$ unless $m = n$ or $m = 2n$.

15. Show that every regular language is a deterministic context-free language. **S**

16. Show that if L_1 is deterministic context-free and L_2 is regular, then the language $L_1 \cup L_2$ is deterministic context-free. **S**

17. Show that under the conditions of Exercise 16, $L_1 \cap L_2$ is a deterministic context-free language.

18. Give an example of a deterministic context-free language whose reverse is not deterministic.

7.4 Grammars for Deterministic Context-Free Languages*

The importance of deterministic context-free languages lies in the fact that they can be parsed efficiently. We can see this intuitively by viewing the pushdown automaton as a parsing device. Since there is no backtracking involved, we can easily write a computer program for it, and we may expect that it will work efficiently. Since there may be λ-transitions involved, we cannot immediately claim that this will yield a linear-time parser, but it puts us on the right track nevertheless. To pursue this, let us see what grammars might be suitable for the description of deterministic context-free languages. Here we enter a topic important in the study of compilers, but somewhat peripheral to our interests. We will provide only a brief introduction to some important results, referring the reader to books on compilers for a more thorough treatment.

Suppose we are parsing top-down, attempting to find the leftmost derivation of a particular sentence. For the sake of discussion, we use the approach illustrated in Figure 7.3. We scan the input w from left to right, while developing a sentential form whose terminal prefix matches the prefix of w up to the currently scanned symbol. To proceed in matching consecutive symbols, we would like to know exactly which production rule is to be applied at each step. This would avoid backtracking and give us an efficient parser. The question then is whether there are grammars that allow us to do this. For a general context-free grammar, this is not the case, but if the form of the grammar is restricted, we can achieve our goal.

As first case, take the s-grammars introduced in Definition 5.4. From the discussion there, it is clear that at every stage in the parsing we know exactly which production has to be applied. Suppose that $w = w_1 w_2$ and that we have developed the sentential form $w_1 A x$. To get the next symbol of the sentential form matched against the next symbol in w, we simply look at the leftmost symbol of w_2, say a. If there is no rule $A \rightarrow a y$ in the grammar, the string w does not belong to the language. If there is such a rule, the parsing can proceed. But in this case there is only one such rule, so there is no choice to be made.

Figure 7.3

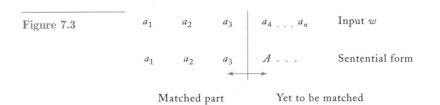

Although s-grammars are useful, they are too restrictive to capture all aspects of the syntax of programming languages. We need to generalize the idea so that it becomes more powerful without losing its essential property for parsing. One type of grammar is called an **LL grammar.** In an LL grammar we still have the property that we can, by looking at a limited part of the input (consisting of the scanned symbol plus a finite number of symbols following it), predict exactly which production rule must be used. The term LL is standard usage in books on compilers; the first L stands for the fact that the input is scanned from left to right; the second L indicates that leftmost derivations are constructed. Every s-grammar is an LL grammar, but the concept is more general.

Example 7.10	The grammar

$$S \rightarrow aSb|ab$$

is not an s-grammar, but it is an LL grammar. In order to determine which production is to be applied, we look at two consecutive symbols of the input string. If the first is an a and the second a b, we must apply the production $S \rightarrow ab$. Otherwise, the rule $S \rightarrow aSb$ must be used.

We say that a grammar is an $LL(k)$ grammar if we can uniquely identify the correct production, given the currently scanned symbol and a "look-ahead" of the next $k-1$ symbols. The above is an example of an $LL(2)$ grammar.

Example 7.11	The grammar

$$S \rightarrow SS\,|aSb|\,ab$$

generates the positive closure of the language in Example 7.10. As remarked in Example 5.4, this is the language of properly nested parenthesis structures. The grammar is not an $LL(k)$ grammar for any k.

To see why this is so, look at the derivation of strings of length greater than two. To start, we have available two possible productions $S \rightarrow SS$ and $S \rightarrow aSb$. The scanned symbol does not tell us which is the right one. Suppose we now use a look-ahead and consider the first two symbols, finding that they are aa. Does this allow us to make the right decision? The answer is still no, since what we have seen could be a prefix of a number of strings, including both $aabb$ or $aabbab$. In the first case, we must start with $S \rightarrow aSb$, while in the second it is necessary to use $S \rightarrow SS$. The grammar is therefore not an $LL(2)$ grammar. In a similar fashion, we can see that no matter how many look-ahead symbols we have, there are always some situations that cannot be resolved.

This observation about the grammar does not imply that the language is not deterministic or that no LL grammar for it exists. We can find an LL grammar for the language if we analyze the reason for the failure of the original grammar. The difficulty lies in the fact that we cannot predict how many repetitions of the basic pattern $a^n b^n$ there are until we get to the end of the string, yet the grammar requires an immediate decision. Rewriting the grammar avoids this difficulty. The grammar

$$S \to aSbS | \lambda$$

is an LL-grammar nearly equivalent to the original grammar.

To see this, consider the leftmost derivation of $w = abab$. Then

$$S \Rightarrow aSbS \Rightarrow abS \Rightarrow abaSbS \Rightarrow ababS \Rightarrow abab.$$

We see that we never have any choice. When the input symbol examined is a, we must use $S \to aSbS$, when the symbol is b or if we are at the end of the string, we must use $S \to \lambda$.

But the problem is not yet completely solved because the new grammar can generate the empty string. We fix this by introducing a new start variable S_0 and a production to ensure that some nonempty string is generated. The final result

$$S_0 \to aSbS$$
$$S \to aSbS | \lambda$$

is then an LL-grammar equivalent to the original grammar. ∎

While this informal description of LL grammars is adequate for understanding simple examples, we need a more precise definition if any rigorous results are to be developed. We conclude our discussion with such a definition.

Definition 7.5

Let $G = (V, T, S, P)$ be a context-free grammar. If for every pair of left-most derivations

$$S \overset{*}{\Rightarrow} w_1 A x_1 \Rightarrow w_1 y_1 x_1 \overset{*}{\Rightarrow} w_1 w_2,$$
$$S \overset{*}{\Rightarrow} w_1 A x_2 \Rightarrow w_1 y_2 x_2 \overset{*}{\Rightarrow} w_1 w_3,$$

with $w_1, w_2, w_3 \in T^*$, the equality of the k leftmost symbols of w_2 and w_3 implies $y_1 = y_2$, then G is said to be an $LL(k)$ grammar. (If $|w_2|$ or $|w_3|$ is less than k, then k is replaced by the smaller of these.)

The definition makes precise what has already been indicated. If at any stage in the leftmost derivation $(w_1 A x)$ we know the next k symbols of the input, the next step in the derivation is uniquely determined (as expressed by $y_1 = y_2$).

The topic of LL grammars is an important one in the study of compilers. A number of programming languages can be defined by LL grammars, and many compilers have been written using LL parsers. But LL grammars are not sufficiently general to deal with all deterministic context-free languages. Consequently, there is interest in other, more general deterministic grammars. Particularly important are the so-called LR grammars, which also allow efficient parsing, but can be viewed as constructing the derivation tree from the bottom up. There is a great deal of material on this subject that can be found in books on compilers (e.g., Hunter 1981) or books specifically devoted to parsing methods for formal languages (such as Aho and Ullman 1972).

EXERCISES

1. Show that the second grammar in Example 7.11 is an LL grammar and that it is equivalent to the original grammar.

2. Show that the grammar for $L = \{w : n_a(w) = n_b(w)\}$ given in Example 1.13 is not an LL grammar. Ⓢ

3. Find an LL grammar for the language in Exercise 2.

4. Construct an LL grammar for the language $L(a^*ba) \cup L(abbb^*)$. Ⓢ

5. Show that any LL grammar is unambiguous.

6. Show that if G is an $LL(k)$ grammar, then $L(G)$ is a deterministic context-free language.

7. Show that a deterministic context-free language is never inherently ambiguous. Ⓢ

8. Let G be a context-free grammar in Greibach normal form. Describe an algorithm which, for any given k, determines whether or not G is an $LL(k)$ grammar.

9. Give LL grammars for the following languages, assuming $\Sigma = \{a, b, c\}$.

   (a) $L = \{a^n b^m c^{n\,|\,m} : n \geq 0, m \geq 0\}$ Ⓢ

   (b) $L = \{a^{n+2} b^m c^{n+m} : n \geq 0, m \geq 0\}$

   (c) $L = \{a^n b^{n+2} c^m : n \geq 0, m > 1\}$

   (d) $L = \{w : n_a(w) < n_b(w)\}$

   (e) $L = \{w : n_a(w) + n_b(w) \neq n_c(w)\}$

Chapter 8

Properties of Context-Free Languages

The family of context-free languages occupies a central position in a hierarchy of formal languages. On the one hand, context-free languages include important but restricted language families such as regular and deterministic context-free languages. On the other hand, there are broader language families of which context-free languages are a special case. To study the relationship between language families and to exhibit their similarities and differences, we investigate characteristic properties of the various families. As in Chapter 4, we look at closure under a variety of operations, algorithms for determining properties of members of the family, and structural results such as pumping lemmas. These all provide us with a means of understanding relations between the different families as well as for classifying specific languages in an appropriate category.

8.1 Two Pumping Lemmas

The pumping lemma given in Theorem 4.8 is an effective tool for showing that certain languages are not regular. Similar pumping lemmas are known for other language families. Here we will discuss two such results, one for context-free languages in general, the other for a restricted type of context-free language.

A Pumping Lemma for Context-Free Languages

Theorem 8.1

Let L be an infinite context-free language. Then there exists some positive integer m such that any $w \in L$ with $|w| \geq m$ can be decomposed as

$$w = uvxyz, \tag{8.1}$$

with

$$|vxy| \leq m, \tag{8.2}$$

and

$$|vy| \geq 1, \tag{8.3}$$

such that

$$uv^i xy^i z \in L, \tag{8.4}$$

for all $i = 0, 1, 2, \dots$. This is known as the pumping lemma for context-free languages.

Proof: Consider the language $L - \{\lambda\}$, and assume that we have for it a grammar G without unit-productions or λ-productions. Since the length of the string on the right side of any production is bounded, say by k, the length of the derivation of any $w \in L$ must be at least $|w|/k$. Therefore, since L is infinite, there exist arbitrarily long derivations and corresponding derivation trees of arbitrary height.

Consider now such a high derivation tree and some sufficiently long path from the root to a leaf. Since the number of variables in G is finite, there must be some variable that repeats on this path, as shown schematically in Figure 8.1. Corresponding to the derivation tree in Figure 8.1, we have the derivation

$$S \overset{*}{\Rightarrow} uAz \overset{*}{\Rightarrow} uvAyz \overset{*}{\Rightarrow} uvxyz,$$

where u, v, x, y, and z are all strings of terminals. From the above we see that $A \overset{*}{\Rightarrow} vAy$ and $A \overset{*}{\Rightarrow} x$, so all the strings $uv^i xy^i z$, $i = 0, 1, 2, \dots$, can be generated by the grammar and are therefore in L. Furthermore, in the

Figure 8.1
Derivation tree for
a long string.

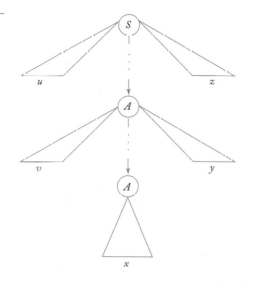

derivations $A \overset{*}{\Rightarrow} vAy$ and $A \overset{*}{\Rightarrow} x$, we can assume that no variable repeats (otherwise, we just use the repeating variable as A). Therefore, the lengths of the strings v, x, and y depend only on the productions of the grammar and can be bounded independently of w so that (8.2) holds. Finally, since there are no unit productions and no λ productions, v and y cannot both be empty strings, giving (8.3).

This completes the argument that (8.1) to (8.4) hold. ■

This pumping lemma is useful in showing that a language does not belong to the family of context-free languages. Its application is typical of pumping lemmas in general; they are used negatively to show that a given language does not belong to some family. As in Theorem 4.8, the correct argument can be visualized as a game against an intelligent opponent. But now the rules make it a little more difficult for us. For regular languages, the substring xy whose length is bounded by m starts at the left end of w. Therefore the substring y that can be pumped is within m symbols of the beginning of w. For context-free languages, we only have a bound on $|vxy|$. The substring u that precedes vxy can be arbitrarily long. This gives additional freedom to the adversary, making arguments involving Theorem 8.1 a little more complicated.

Example 8.1　Show that the language

$$L = \{a^n b^n c^n : n \geq 0\}$$

is not context-free.

Once the adversary has chosen m, we pick the string $a^m b^m c^m$, which is in L. The adversary now has several choices. If he chooses vxy to contain only a's, then the pumped string will obviously not be in L. If he chooses a string containing an equal number of a's and b's, then the pumped string $a^k b^k c^m$ with $k \neq m$ can be generated, and again we have generated a string not in L. In fact, the only way the adversary could stop us from winning is to pick vxy so that vy has the same number of a's, b's, and c's. But this is not possible because of restriction (8.2). Therefore, L is not context-free.

If we try the same argument on the language $L = \{a^n b^n\}$, we fail, as we must, since the language is context-free. If we pick any string in L, such as $w = a^m b^m$, the adversary can pick $v = a^k$ and $y = b^k$. Now, no matter what i we choose, the resulting pumped string w_i is in L. Remember, though, that this does not prove that L is context-free; all we can say is that we have been unable to get any conclusion from the pumping lemma. That L is context-free must come from some other argument, such as the construction of a context-free grammar.

The argument also justifies a claim made in Example 7.9 and allows us to close a gap in that example. The language

$$\widehat{L} = \{a^n b^n\} \cup \{a^n b^{2n}\} \cup \{a^n b^n c^n\}$$

is not context-free. The string $a^m b^m c^m$ is in $\widehat{L}$, but the pumped result is not.

■

Example 8.2   Consider the language

$$L = \{ww : w \in \{a, b\}^*\}.$$

Although this language appears to be very similar to the context-free language of Example 5.1, it is not context-free.

Consider the string

$$a^m b^m a^m b^m.$$

There are many ways in which the adversary can now pick vxy, but for all of them we have a winning countermove. For example, for the choice in Figure 8.2, we can use $i = 0$ to get a string of the form

$$a^k b^j a^m b^m, k < m \text{ or } j < m,$$

which is not in L. For other choices by the adversary, similar arguments can be made. We conclude that L is not context-free.

■

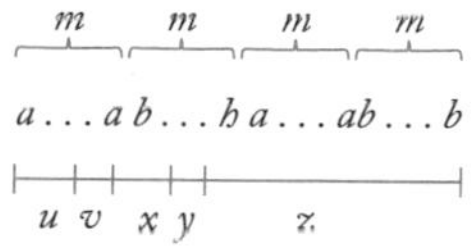

Figure 8.2

Example 8.3

Show that the language

$$L = \{a^{n!} : n \geq 0\}$$

L does not include λ.

is not context-free.

In Example 4.11 we showed that this language is not regular. However, for a language over an alphabet with a single symbol, there is little difference between Theorem 8.1 and the pumping lemma for regular languages. In either case, the strings to be pumped consist entirely of a's, and whatever new string can be generated by Theorem 8.1 can also be generated by Theorem 4.8. Therefore, we can use essentially the same arguments as in Example 4.11 to show that L is not context-free.

Example 8.4

Show that the language

$$L = \{a^n b^j : n = j^2\}$$

is not context-free.

Given m in Theorem 8.1, we pick as our string $a^{m^2} b^m$. The adversary now has several choices. The only one that requires much thought is the one shown in Figure 8.3. Pumping i times will yield a new string with $m^2 + (i-1)k_1$ a's and $m + (i-1)k_2$ b's. If the adversary takes $k_1 \neq 0$, $k_2 \neq 0$, we can pick $i = 0$. Since

$$(m - k_2)^2 \leq (m-1)^2$$
$$= m^2 - 2m + 1$$
$$< m^2 - k_1,$$

the result is not in L. If the opponent picks $k_1 = 0$, $k_2 \neq 0$ or $k_1 \neq 0$, $k_2 = 0$, then again with $i = 0$, the pumped string is not in L. We can conclude from this that L is not a context-free language.

Figure 8.3

A Pumping Lemma for Linear Languages

We previously made a distinction between linear and nonlinear context-free grammars. We now make a similar distinction between languages.

Definition 8.1

A context-free language L is said to be linear if there exists a linear context-free grammar G such that $L = L(G)$.

Clearly, every linear language is context-free, but we have not yet established whether or not the converse is true.

Example 8.5

The language $L = \{a^n b^n : n \geq 0\}$ is a linear language. A linear grammar for it is given in Example 1.10. The grammar given in Example 1.12 for the language $L = \{w : n_a(w) = n_b(w)\}$ is not linear, so the second language is not necessarily linear.

Of course, just because a specific grammar is not linear does not imply that the language generated by it is not linear. If we want to prove that a language is not linear, we must show that there exists no equivalent linear grammar. We approach this in the usual way, establishing structural properties for linear languages, then showing that some context-free languages do not have a required property.

Theorem 8.2

Let L be an infinite linear language. Then there exists some positive integer m, such that any $w \in L$, with $|w| \geq m$ can be decomposed as $w = uvxyz$ with

$$|uvyz| \leq m, \tag{8.5}$$

$$|vy| \geq 1, \tag{8.6}$$

such that

$$uv^i xy^i z \in L, \tag{8.7}$$

for all $i = 0, 1, 2, \dots$.

Note that the conclusions of this theorem differ from those of Theorem 8.1, since (8.2) is replaced by (8.5). This implies that the strings v and y to be pumped must now be located within m symbols of the left and right ends of w, respectively. The middle string x can be of arbitrary length.

Proof: Our reasoning follows the proof of Theorem 8.1. Since the language is linear, there exists some linear grammar G for it. To use the argument in Theorem 8.1, we also need to claim that G contains no unit-productions and no λ-productions. An examination of the proofs of Theorem 6.3 and Theorem 6.4 will show that removing λ-productions and unit-productions does not destroy the linearity of the grammar. We can therefore assume that G has the required property.

Consider now the derivation tree as shown in Figure 8.1. Because the grammar is linear, variables can appear only on the path from S to the first A, on the path from the first A to the second one, and on the path from the second A to some leaf of the tree. Since there are only a finite number of variables on the path from S to the first A, and since each of these generates a finite number of terminals, u and z must be bounded. By a similar argument, v and y are bounded, so (8.5) follows.

The rest of the argument is as in Theorem 8.1. ∎

Example 8.6   The language

$$L = \{w : n_a(w) = n_b(w)\}$$

is not linear.

To show this, assume that the language is linear and apply Theorem 8.2 to the string

$$w = a^m b^{2m} a^m.$$

Inequality (8.7) shows that in this case the strings u, v, y, z must all consist entirely of a's. If we pump this string, we get $a^{m+k} b^{2m} a^{m+l}$, with either $k \geq 1$ or $l \geq 1$, a result that is not in L. This contradiction of Theorem 8.2 proves that the language is not linear.

This example answers the general question raised on the relation between the families of context-free and linear languages. The family of linear languages is a proper subset of the family of context-free languages.

EXERCISES

1. Use reasoning similar to that in Example 4.11 to give a complete proof that the language in Example 8.3 is not context-free.

2. Show that the language $L = \{a^n : n \text{ is a prime number}\}$ is not context-free.

3. Show that $L = \{ww^R w : w \in \{a, b\}^*\}$ is not a context-free language. $\textbf{\large S}$

4. Show that $L = \{w \in \{a, b, c\}^* : n_a^2(w) + n_b^2(w) = n_c^2(w)\}$ is not context-free.

5. Is the language $L = \{a^n b^m : n = 2^m\}$ context-free?

6. Show that the language $L = \{a^{n^2} : n \geq 0\}$ is not context-free.

7. Show that the following languages on $\Sigma = \{a, b, c\}$ are not context-free.

    (a) $L = \{a^n b^j : n \leq j^2\}$ $\textbf{\large S}$

    (b) $L = \{a^n b^j : n \geq (j - 1)^3\}$

    (c) $L = \{a^n b^j c^k : k = jn\}$

    (d) $L = \{a^n b^j c^k : k > n, k > j\}$

    (e) $L = \{a^n b^j c^k : n < j, n \leq k \leq j\}$

    (f) $L = \{w : n_a(w) < n_b(w) < n_c(w)\}$ (S)

    (g) $L = \{w : n_a(w) / n_b(w) = n_c(w)\}$

    (h) $L = \{w \in \{a, b, c\}^* : n_a(w) + n_b(w) = 2n_c(w)\}$.

8. Determine whether or not the following languages are context-free.

    (a) $L = \{a^n w w^R a^n : n \geq 0, w \in \{a, b\}^*\}$

    (b) $L = \{a^n b^j a^n b^j : n \geq 0, j \geq 0\}$ $\textbf{\large S}$

    (c) $L = \{a^n b^j a^j b^n : n \geq 0, j \geq 0\}$

    (d) $L = \{a^n b^j a^k b^l : n + j \leq k + l\}$

    (e) $L = \{a^n b^j a^k b^l : n \leq k, j \leq l\}$

    (f) $L = \{a^n b^n c^j : n \leq j\}$

9. In Theorem 8.1, find a bound for m in terms of the properties of the grammar G.

10. Determine whether or not the following language is context-free.

$$L = \{w_1 c w_2 : w_1, w_2 \in \{a, b\}^*, w_1 \neq w_2\} \textbf{\large S}$$

11. Show that the language $L = \{a^n b^n a^m b^m : n \geq 0, m \geq 0\}$ is context-free but not linear.

12. Show that the following language is not linear.

$$L = \{w : n_a(w) \geq n_b(w)\} \quad \text{ⓢ}$$

13. Show that the language $L = \{w \in \{a, b, c\}^* : n_a(w) + n_b(w) = n_c(w)\}$ is context-free, but not linear.

14. Determine whether or not the language $L = \{a^n b^j : j \leq n \leq 2j - 1\}$ is linear.

15. Determine whether or not the language in Example 5.12 is linear. ⓢ

16. In Theorem 8.2, find a bound on m in terms of the properties of the grammar G.

17. Justify the claim made in Theorem 8.2 that for any linear language (not containing λ) there exists a linear grammar without λ-productions and unit-productions.

18. Consider the set of all strings a/b, where a and b are positive decimal integers such that $a < b$. The set of strings then represents all possible decimal fractions. Determine whether or not this is a context-free language.

★19. Show that the complement of the language in Exercise 6 is not context-free.

20. Is the following language context-free?

$$L = \{a^{nm} : n \text{ and } m \text{ are prime numbers}\} \quad \text{ⓢ}$$

8.2 Closure Properties and Decision Algorithms for Context-Free Languages

In Chapter 4 we looked at closure under certain operations and algorithms to decide on the properties of the family of regular languages. On the whole, the questions raised there had easy answers. When we ask the same questions about context-free languages, we encounter more difficulties. First, closure properties that hold for regular languages do not always hold for context-free languages. When they do, the arguments needed to prove them are often quite complicated. Second, many intuitively simple and important questions about context-free languages cannot be answered. This statement may seem at first surprising and will need to be elaborated as we proceed. In this section, we provide only a sample of some of the most important results.

Closure of Context-Free Languages

Theorem 8.3

The family of context-free languages is closed under union, concatenation, and star-closure.

Proof: Let L_1 and L_2 be two context-free languages generated by the context-free grammars $G_1 = (V_1, T_1, S_1, P_1)$ and $G_2 = (V_2, T_2, S_2, P_2)$, respectively. We can assume without loss of generality that the sets V_1 and V_2 are disjoint.

Consider now the language $L(G_3)$, generated by the grammar

$$G_3 = (V_1 \cup V_2 \cup \{S_3\}, T_1 \cup T_2, S_3, P_3),$$

where S_3 is a variable not in $V_1 \cup V_2$. The productions of G_3 are all the productions of G_1 and G_2, together with an alternative starting production that allows us to use one or the other grammars. More precisely,

$$P_3 = P_1 \cup P_2 \cup \{S_3 \rightarrow S_1 | S_2\}.$$

Obviously, G_3 is a context-free grammar, so that $L(G_3)$ is a context-free language. But it is easy to see that

$$L(G_3) = L_1 \cup L_2. \tag{8.8}$$

Suppose for instance that $w \in L_1$. Then

$$S_3 \Rightarrow S_1 \overset{*}{\Rightarrow} w$$

is a possible derivation in grammar G_3. A similar argument can be made for $w \in L_2$. Also, if $w \in L(G_3)$ then either

$$S_3 \Rightarrow S_1 \tag{8.9}$$

or

$$S_3 \Rightarrow S_2 \tag{8.10}$$

must be the first step of the derivation. Suppose (8.9) is used. Since sentential forms derived from S_1 have variables in V_1, and V_1 and V_2 are disjoint, the derivation

$$S_1 \overset{*}{\Rightarrow} w$$

can involve productions in P_1 only. Hence w must be in L_1. Alternatively, if (8.10) is used first, then w must be in L_2 and it follows that $L(G_3)$ is the union of L_1 and L_2.

Next, consider

$$G_4 = (V_1 \cup V_2 \cup \{S_4\}, T_1 \cup T_2, S_4, P_4).$$

Here again S_4 is a new variable and

$$P_4 = P_1 \cup P_2 \cup \{S_4 \rightarrow S_1 S_2\}.$$

Then

$$L(G_4) = L(G_1) L(G_2)$$

follows easily.

Finally, consider $L(G_5)$ with

$$G_5 = (V_1 \cup \{S_5\}, T_1, S_5, P_5),$$

where S_5 is a new variable and

$$P_5 = P_1 \cup \{S_5 \rightarrow S_1 S_5 | \lambda\}.$$

Then

$$L(G_5) = L(G_1)^*.$$

Thus we have shown that the family of context-free languages is closed under union, concatenation, and star-closure. ∎

Theorem 8.4   The family of context-free languages is not closed under intersection and complementation.

Proof: Consider the two languages

$$L_1 = \{a^n b^n c^m : n \geq 0, m \geq 0\}$$

and

$$L_2 = \{a^n b^m c^m : n \geq 0, m \geq 0\}.$$

There are several ways one can show that L_1 and L_2 are context-free. For instance, a grammar for L_1 is

$$S \rightarrow S_1 S_2,$$
$$S_1 \rightarrow a S_1 b | \lambda,$$
$$S_2 \rightarrow c S_2 | \lambda.$$

Alternatively, we note that L_1 is the concatenation of two context-free languages, so it is context-free by Theorem 8.3. But

$$L_1 \cap L_2 = \{a^n b^n c^n : n \geq 0\},$$

which we have already shown not to be context-free. Thus, the family of context-free languages is not closed under intersection.

The second part of the theorem follows from Theorem 8.3 and the set identity

$$L_1 \cap L_2 = \overline{\overline{L_1} \cup \overline{L_2}}.$$

If the family of context-free languages were closed under complementation, then the right side of the above expression would be a context-free language for any context-free L_1 and L_2. But this contradicts what we have just shown, that the intersection of two context-free languages is not necessarily context-free. Consequently, the family of context-free languages is not closed under complementation. ∎

While the intersection of two context-free languages may produce a language that is not context-free, the closure property holds if one of the languages is regular.

Theorem 8.5

Let L_1 be a context-free language and L_2 be a regular language. Then $L_1 \cap L_2$ is context-free.

Proof: Let $M_1 = (Q, \Sigma, \Gamma, \delta_1, q_0, z, F_1)$ be an npda which accepts L_1 and $M_2 = (P, \Sigma, \delta_2, p_0, F_2)$ be a dfa that accepts L_2. We construct a pushdown automaton $\widehat{M} = \left(\widehat{Q}, \Sigma, \Gamma, \widehat{\delta}, \widehat{q_0}, z, \widehat{F}\right)$ which simulates the parallel action of M_1 and M_2: whenever a symbol is read from the input string, $\widehat{M}$ simultaneously executes the moves of M_1 and M_2. To this end we let

$$\widehat{Q} = Q \times P,$$
$$\widehat{q_0} = (q_0, p_0),$$
$$\widehat{F} = F_1 \times F_2,$$

and define $\widehat{\delta}$ such that

$$((q_k, p_l), x) \in \widehat{\delta}((q_i, p_j), a, b),$$

if and only if

$$(q_k, x) \in \delta_1(q_i, a, b),$$

and

$$\delta_2(p_j, a) = p_l.$$

In this, we also require that if $a = \lambda$, then $p_j = p_l$. In other words, the states of $\widehat{M}$ are labeled with pairs (q_i, p_j), representing the respective states in which M_1 and M_2 can be after reading a certain input string. It is a straightforward induction argument to show that

$$((q_0, p_0), w, z) \vdash^*_{\widehat{M}} ((q_r, p_s), x),$$

with $q_r \in F_1$ and $p_s \in F_2$ if and only if

$$(q_0, w, z) \vdash^*_{M_1} (q_r, x),$$

and

$$\delta^* (p_0, w) = p_s.$$

Therefore, a string is accepted by $\widehat{M}$ if and only if it is accepted by M_1 and M_2, that is, if it is in $L(M_1) \cap L(M_2) = L_1 \cap L_2$. ∎

The property addressed by this theorem is called closure under **regular intersection**. Because of the result of the theorem, we say that the family of context-free languages is closed under regular intersection. This closure property is sometimes useful for simplifying arguments in connection with specific languages.

Example 8.7   Show that the language

$$L = \{a^n b^n : n \geq 0, n \neq 100\}$$

is context-free.

It is possible to prove this claim by constructing a pda or a context-free grammar for the language, but the process is tedious. We can get a much neater argument with Theorem 8.5.

Let

$$L_1 = \{a^{100} b^{100}\}.$$

Then, because L_1 is finite, it is regular. Also, it is easy to see that

$$L = \{a^n b^n : n \geq 0\} \cap \overline{L_1}.$$

Therefore, by the closure of regular languages under complementation and the closure of context-free languages under regular intersection, the desired result follows.

Example 8.8   Show that the language

$$L = \left\{ w \in \{a, b, c\}^* : n_a\left(w\right) = n_b\left(w\right) = n_c\left(w\right) \right\}$$

is not context-free.

The pumping lemma can be used for this, but again we can get a much shorter argument using closure under regular intersection. Suppose that L were context-free. Then

$$L \cap L\left(a^* b^* c^*\right) = \{a^n b^n c^n : n \geq 0\}$$

would also be context-free. But we already know that this is not so. We conclude that L is not context-free.

    Closure properties of languages play an important role in the theory of formal languages and many more closure properties for context-free languages can be established. Some additional results are explored in the exercises at the end of this section.

Some Decidable Properties of Context-Free Languages

By putting together Theorems 5.2 and 6.6, we have already established the existence of a membership algorithm for context-free languages. This is of course an essential feature of any language family useful in practice. Other simple properties of context-free languages can also be determined. For the purpose of this discussion, we assume that the language is described by its grammar.

Theorem 8.6   Given a context-free grammar $G = (V, T, S, P)$, there exists an algorithm for deciding whether or not $L\left(G\right)$ is empty.

Proof: For simplicity, assume that $\lambda \notin L\left(G\right)$. Slight changes have to be made in the argument if this is not so. We use the algorithm for removing useless symbols and productions. If S is found to be useless, then $L\left(G\right)$ is empty; if not, then $L\left(G\right)$ contains at least one element. ■

Theorem 8.7   Given a context-free grammar $G = (V, T, S, P)$, there exists an algorithm for determining whether or not $L\left(G\right)$ is infinite.

Proof: We assume that G contains no λ-productions, no unit-productions, and no useless symbols. Suppose the grammar has a repeating variable in the sense that there exists some $A \in V$ for which there is a derivation

$$A \overset{*}{\Rightarrow} xAy.$$

Since G is assumed to have no λ-productions and no unit-productions, x and y cannot be simultaneously empty. Since A is neither nullable nor a useless symbol, we have

$$S \overset{*}{\Rightarrow} uAv \overset{*}{\Rightarrow} w$$

and

$$A \overset{*}{\Rightarrow} z,$$

where, u, v, and z are in T^*. But then

$$S \overset{*}{\Rightarrow} uAv \overset{*}{\Rightarrow} ux^n Ay^n v \overset{*}{\Rightarrow} ux^n zy^n v$$

is possible for all n, so that $L(G)$ is infinite.

If no variable can ever repeat, then the length of any derivation is bounded by $|V|$. In that case, $L(G)$ is finite.

Thus, to get an algorithm for determining whether $L(G)$ is finite, we need only to determine whether the grammar has some repeating variables. This can be done simply by drawing a dependency graph for the variables in such a way that there is an edge (A, B) whenever there is a corresponding production

$$A \to xBy.$$

Then any variable that is at the base of a cycle is a repeating one. Consequently, the grammar has a repeating variable if and only if the dependency graph has a cycle.

Since we now have an algorithm for deciding whether a grammar has a repeating variable, we have an algorithm for determining whether or not $L(G)$ is infinite. ∎

Somewhat surprisingly, other simple properties of context-free languages are not so easily dealt with. As in Theorem 4.7, we might look for an algorithm to determine whether two context-free grammars generate the same language. But it turns out that there is no such algorithm. For the moment, we do not have the technical machinery for properly defining the meaning of "there is no algorithm," but its intuitive meaning is clear. This is an important point to which we will return later.

EXERCISES

1. Is the complement of the language in Example 8.8 context-free? **S**

2. Consider the language L_1 in Theorem 8.4. Show that this language is linear.

3. Show that the family of context-free languages is closed under homomorphism.

4. Show that the family of linear languages is closed under homomorphism.

5. Show that the family of context-free languages is closed under reversal. **ⓢ**

6. Which of the language families we have discussed are not closed under reversal?

7. Show that the family of context-free languages is not closed under difference in general, but is closed under regular difference, that is, if L_1 is context-free and L_2 is regular, then $L_1 - L_2$ is context-free.

8. Show that the family of deterministic context-free languages is closed under regular difference.

9. Show that the family of linear languages is closed under union, but not closed under concatenation. **ⓢ**

10. Show that the family of linear languages is not closed under intersection.

11. Show that the family of deterministic context-free languages is not closed under union and intersection.

12. Give an example of a context-free language whose complement is not context-free.

★ 13. Show that if L_1 is linear and L_2 is regular, then $L_1 L_2$ is a linear language. **ⓢ**

14. Show that the family of unambiguous context-free languages is not closed under union.

15. Show that the family of unambiguous context-free languages is not closed under intersection. **ⓢ**

16. Let L be a deterministic context-free language and define a new language $L_1 = \{w : aw \in L, a \in \Sigma\}$. Is it necessarily true that L_1 is a deterministic context-free language?

17. Show that the language $L = \{a^n b^n : n \geq 0, n \text{ is not a multiple of 5}\}$ is context-free.

18. Show that the following language is context-free.

$$L = \{w \in \{a, b\}^* : n_a(w) = n_b(w), w \text{ does not contain a substring } aab\}$$

19. Is the family of deterministic context-free languages closed under homomorphism?

20. Give the details of the inductive argument in Theorem 8.5.

21. Give an algorithm which, for any given context-free grammar G, can determine whether or not $\lambda \in L(G)$. **ⓢ**

22. Show that there exists an algorithm to determine whether the language generated by some context-free grammar contains any words of length less than some given number n.

23. Let L_1 be a context-free language and L_2 be regular. Show that there exists an algorithm to determine whether or not L_1 and L_2 have a common element.

Chapter 9

Turing
Machines

I n the foregoing discussion, we have encountered some fundamental ideas, in particular the concepts of regular and context-free languages and their association with finite automata and pushdown acceptors. Our study has revealed that the regular languages form a proper subset of the context-free languages, and therefore, that pushdown automata are more powerful than finite automata. We also saw that context-free languages, while fundamental to the study of programming languages, are limited in scope. This was made clear in the last chapter, where our results showed that some simple languages, such as $\{a^n b^n c^n\}$ and $\{ww\}$, are not context-free. This prompts us to look beyond context-free languages and investigate how one might define new language families that include these examples. To do so, we return to the general picture of an automaton. If we compare finite automata with pushdown automata, we see that the nature of the temporary storage creates the difference between them. If there is no storage, we have a finite automaton; if the storage is a stack, we have the more powerful pushdown automaton. Extrapolating from this observation, we can expect to discover even more powerful language families if we give the automaton more flexible storage. For example, what would happen if, in the general scheme of Figure 1.3, we used two stacks, three stacks, a queue, or some other storage device? Does each storage device define a new kind of automaton and through it a new language family? This approach raises a large number of questions, most of which turn out to be uninteresting. It is more instructive to ask a more ambitious question and consider how far the concept of an automaton can be pushed. What can we say about the most powerful of automata and the limits of computation? This leads to the fundamental concept of a **Turing machine** and, in turn, to a precise definition of the idea of a mechanical or algorithmic computation.

We begin our study with a formal definition of a Turing machine, then develop some feeling for what is involved by doing some simple programs. Next we argue that, while the mechanism of a Turing machine is quite rudimentary, the concept is broad enough to cover very complex processes. The discussion culminates in the **Turing thesis**, which maintains that any computational process, such as those carried out by present-day computers, can be done on a Turing machine.

9.1 The Standard Turing Machine

Although we can envision a variety of automata with complex and sophisticated storage devices, a Turing machine's storage is actually quite simple. It can be visualized as a single, one-dimensional array of cells, each of which can hold a single symbol. This array extends indefinitely in both directions and is therefore capable of holding an unlimited amount of information. The information can be read and changed in any order. We will call such a storage device a **tape** because it is analogous to the magnetic tapes used in actual computers.

Definition of a Turing Machine

A Turing machine is an automaton whose temporary storage is a tape. This tape is divided into cells, each of which is capable of holding one symbol. Associated with the tape is a **read-write head** that can travel right or left on the tape and that can read and write a single symbol on each move. To deviate slightly from the general scheme of Chapter 1, the automaton that we use as a Turing machine will have neither an input file nor any special output mechanism. Whatever input and output is necessary will be done on the machine's tape. We will see later that this modification of our general model in Section 1.2 is of little consequence. We could retain the input file and a specific output mechanism without affecting any of the conclusions we are about to draw, but we leave them out because the resulting automaton is a little easier to describe.

Figure 9.1

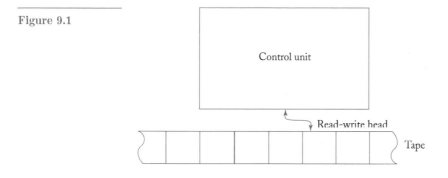

A diagram giving an intuitive visualization of a Turing machine is shown in Figure 9.1. Definition 9.1 makes the notion precise.

Definition 9.1

A Turing machine M is defined by

$$M = (Q, \Sigma, \Gamma, \delta, q_0, \square, F),$$

where

Q is the set of internal states,
Σ is the input alphabet,
Γ is a finite set of symbols called the **tape alphabet**,
δ is the transition function,
$\square \in \Gamma$ is a special symbol called the **blank**,
$q_0 \in Q$ is the initial state,
$F \subseteq Q$ is the set of final states.

In the definition of a Turing machine, we assume that $\Sigma \subseteq \Gamma - \{\square\}$, that is, that the input alphabet is a subset of the tape alphabet, not including the blank. Blanks are ruled out as input for reasons that will become apparent shortly. The transition function δ is defined as

$$\delta : Q \times \Gamma \rightarrow Q \times \Gamma \times \{L, R\}.$$

In general, δ is a partial function on $Q \times \Gamma$; its interpretation gives the principle by which a Turing machine operates. The arguments of δ are the current state of the control unit and the current tape symbol being read. The result is a new state of the control unit, a new tape symbol,

Figure 9.2
The situation
(a) before the move
and (b) after the
move.

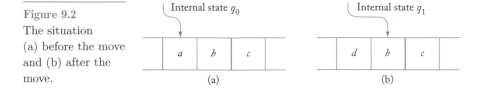

Internal state q_0

	a	b	c	

(a)

Internal state q_1

	d	b	c	

(b)

which replaces the old one, and a move symbol, L or R. The move symbol indicates whether the read-write head moves left or right one cell after the new symbol has been written on the tape.

Example 9.1　Figure 9.2 shows the situation before and after the move caused by the transition

$$\delta\left(q_0, a\right) = \left(q_1, d, R\right).$$

We can think of a Turing machine as a rather simple computer. It has a processing unit, which has a finite memory, and in its tape, it has a secondary storage of unlimited capacity. The instructions that such a computer can carry out are very limited: it can sense a symbol on its tape and use the result to decide what to do next. The only actions the machine can perform are to rewrite the current symbol, to change the state of the control, and to move the read-write head. This small instruction set may seem inadequate for doing complicated things, but this is not so. Turing machines are quite powerful in principle. The transition function δ defines how this computer acts, and we often call it the "program" of the machine.

As always, the automaton starts in the given initial state with some information on the tape. It then goes through a sequence of steps controlled by the transition function δ. During this process, the contents of any cell on the tape may be examined and changed many times. Eventually, the whole process may terminate, which we achieve in a Turing machine by putting it into a **halt state**. A Turing machine is said to halt whenever it reaches a configuration for which δ is not defined; this is possible because δ is a partial function. In fact, we will assume that no transitions are defined for any final state, so the Turing machine will halt whenever it enters a final state.

Figure 9.3
A sequence of
moves.

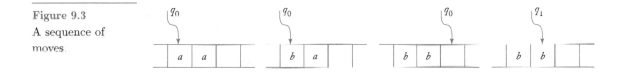

Example 9.2   Consider the Turing machine defined by

$$Q = \{q_0, q_1\},$$
$$\Sigma = \{a, b\},$$
$$\Gamma = \{a, b, \square\},$$
$$F = \{q_1\},$$

and

$$\delta(q_0, a) = (q_0, b, R),$$
$$\delta(q_0, b) = (q_0, b, R),$$
$$\delta(q_0, \square) = (q_1, \square, L).$$

If this Turing machine is started in state q_0 with the symbol a under the read-write head, the applicable transition rule is $\delta(q_0, a) = (q_0, b, R)$. Therefore the read-write head will replace the a with a b, then move right on the tape. The machine will remain in state q_0. Any subsequent a will also be replaced with a b, but b's will not be modified. When the machine encounters the first blank, it will move left one cell, then halt in final state q_1.

Figure 9.3 shows several stages of the process for a simple initial configuration. ∎

Example 9.3   Take Q, Σ, Γ as defined in the previous example, but let F be empty. Define δ by

$$\delta(q_0, a) = (q_1, a, R),$$
$$\delta(q_0, b) = (q_1, b, R),$$
$$\delta(q_0, \square) = (q_1, \square, R),$$
$$\delta(q_1, a) = (q_0, a, L),$$
$$\delta(q_1, b) = (q_0, b, L),$$
$$\delta(q_1, \square) = (q_0, \square, L).$$

To see what happens here, we can trace a typical case. Suppose that the tape initially contains $ab...$, with the read-write head on the a. The machine then reads the a, but does not change it. Its next state is q_1 and the read-write head moves right, so that it is now over the b. This symbol is also read and left unchanged. The machine goes back into state q_0 and the read-write head moves left. We are now back exactly in the original state, and the sequence of moves starts again. It is clear from this that the machine, whatever the initial information on its tape, will run forever, with the read-write head moving alternately right then left, but making no modifications to the tape. This is an instance of a Turing machine that does not halt. As an analogy with programming terminology, we say that the Turing machine is in an **infinite loop**.

Since one can make several different definitions of a Turing machine, it is worthwhile to summarize the main features of our model, which we will call a **standard Turing machine**:

1. The Turing machine has a tape that is unbounded in both directions, allowing any number of left and right moves.

2. The Turing machine is deterministic in the sense that δ defines at most one move for each configuration.

3. There is no special input file. We assume that at the initial time the tape has some specified content. Some of this may be considered input. Similarly, there is no special output device. Whenever the machine halts, some or all of the contents of the tape may be viewed as output.

These conventions were chosen primarily for the convenience of subsequent discussion. In Chapter 10, we will look at other versions of Turing machines and discuss their relation to our standard model.

To exhibit the configurations of a Turing machine, we use the idea of an instantaneous description. Any configuration is completely determined by the current state of the control unit, the contents of the tape, and the position of the read-write head. We will use the notation in which

$$x_1 q x_2$$

or

$$a_1 a_2 \cdots a_{k-1} q a_k a_{k+1} \cdots a_n$$

is the instantaneous description of a machine in state q with the tape depicted in Figure 9.4. The symbols $a_1, ..., a_n$ show the tape contents, while q defines the state of the control unit. This convention is chosen so that

Figure 9.4

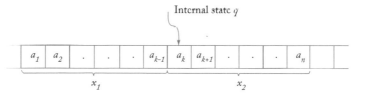

the position of the read-write head is over the cell containing the symbol immediately following q.

The instantaneous description gives only a finite amount of information to the right and left of the read-write head. The unspecified part of the tape is assumed to contain all blanks; normally such blanks are irrelevant and are not shown explicitly in the instantaneous description. If the position of blanks is relevant to the discussion, however, the blank symbol may appear in the instantaneous description. For example, the instantaneous description $q\square w$ indicates that the read-write head is on the cell to the immediate left of the first symbol of w and that this cell contains a blank.

Example 9.4

The pictures drawn in Figure 9.3 correspond to the sequence of instantaneous descriptions $q_0 aa$, $bq_0 a$, $bbq_0\square$, $bq_1 b$.

A move from one configuration to another will be denoted by $\vdash$. Thus, if

$$\delta(q_1, c) = (q_2, e, R),$$

then the move

$$abq_1 cd \vdash abeq_2 d$$

is made whenever the internal state is q_1, the tape contains $abcd$, and the read-write head is on the c. The symbol $\overset{*}{\vdash}$ has the usual meaning of an arbitrary number of moves. Subscripts, such as $\vdash_M$, are used in arguments to distinguish between several machines.

Example 9.5

The action of the Turing machine in Figure 9.3 can be represented by

$$q_0 aa \vdash bq_0 a + bbq_0\square \vdash bq_1 b$$

or

$$q_0 aa \overset{*}{\vdash} bq_1 b.$$

For further discussion, it is convenient to summarize the various observations just made in a formal way.

Definition 9.2

Let $M = (Q, \Sigma, \Gamma, \delta, q_0, \square, F)$ be a Turing machine. Then any string $a_1 \cdots a_{k-1} q_1 a_k a_{k+1} \cdots a_n$, with $a_i \in \Gamma$ and $q_1 \in Q$, is an instantaneous description of M. A move

$$a_1 \cdots a_{k-1} q_1 a_k a_{k+1} \cdots a_n \vdash a_1 \cdots a_{k-1} b q_2 a_{k+1} \cdots a_n$$

is possible if and only if

$$\delta\left(q_1, a_k\right) = \left(q_2, b, R\right).$$

A move

$$a_1 \cdots a_{k-1} q_1 a_k a_{k+1} \cdots a_n \vdash a_1 \cdots q_2 a_{k-1} b a_{k+1} \cdots a_n$$

is possible if and only if

$$\delta\left(q_1, a_k\right) = \left(q_2, b, L\right).$$

M is said to halt starting from some initial configuration $x_1 q_i x_2$ if

$$x_1 q_i x_2 \overset{*}{\vdash} y_1 q_j a y_2$$

for any q_j and a, for which $\delta\left(q_j, a\right)$ is undefined. The sequence of configurations leading to a halt state will be called a **computation**.

Example 9.3 shows the possibility that a Turing machine will never halt, proceeding in an endless loop from which it cannot escape. This situation plays a fundamental role in the discussion of Turing machines, so we use a special notation for it. We will represent it by

$$x_1 q x_2 \overset{*}{\vdash} \infty,$$

indicating that, starting from the initial configuration $x_1 q x_2$, the machine never halts.

Turing Machines as Language Accepters

Turing machines can be viewed as accepters in the following sense. A string w is written on the tape, with blanks filling out the unused portions. The machine is started in the initial state q_0 with the read-write head positioned on the leftmost symbol of w. If, after a sequence of moves, the Turing machine enters a final state and halts, then w is considered to be accepted.

Definition 9.3

Let $M = (Q, \Sigma, \Gamma, \delta, q_0, \Box, F)$ be a Turing machine. Then the language accepted by M is

$$L(M) = \left\{ w \in \Sigma^+ : q_0 w \overset{*}{\vdash} x_1 q_f x_2 \text{ for some } q_f \in F, x_1, x_2 \in \Gamma^* \right\}.$$

This definition indicates that the input w is written on the tape with blanks on either side. The reason for excluding blanks from the input now becomes clear: it assures us that all the input is restricted to a well-defined region of the tape, bracketed by blanks on the right and left. Without this convention, the machine could not limit the region in which it must look for the input; no matter how many blanks it saw, it could never be sure that there was not some nonblank input somewhere else on the tape.

Definition 9.3 tells us what must happen when $w \in L(M)$. It says nothing about the outcome for any other input. When w is not in $L(M)$, one of two things can happen: the machine can halt in a nonfinal state or it can enter an infinite loop and never halt. Any string for which M does not halt is by definition not in $L(M)$.

Example 9.6 For $\Sigma = \{0, 1\}$, design a Turing machine that accepts the language denoted by the regular expression 00^*.

This is an easy exercise in Turing machine programming. Starting at the left end of the input, we read each symbol and check that it is a 0. If it is, we continue by moving right. If we reach a blank without encountering anything but 0, we terminate and accept the string. If the input contains a 1 anywhere, the string is not in $L(00^*)$, and we halt in a nonfinal state. To keep track of the computation, two internal states $Q = \{q_0, q_1\}$ and one final state $F = \{q_1\}$ are sufficient. As transition function we can take

$$\delta(q_0, 0) = (q_0, 0, R),$$
$$\delta(q_0, \Box) = (q_1, \Box, R).$$

As long as a 0 appears under the read-write head, the head will move to the right. If at any time a 1 is read, the machine will halt in the nonfinal state q_0, since $\delta(q_0, 1)$ is undefined. Note that the Turing machine also halts in a final state if started in state q_0 on a blank. We could interpret this as acceptance of λ, but for technical reasons the empty string is not included in Definition 9.3.

The recognition of more complicated languages is more difficult. Since Turing machines have a primitive instruction set, the computations that we can program easily in a higher level language are often cumbersome on a Turing machine. Still, it is possible, and the concept is easy to understand, as the next examples illustrate.

Example 9.7   For $\Sigma = \{a, b\}$, design a Turing machine that accepts

$$L = \{a^n b^n : n \geq 1\}.$$

Intuitively, we solve the problem in the following fashion. Starting at the leftmost a, we check it off by replacing it with some symbol, say x. We then let the read-write head travel right to find the leftmost b, which in turn is checked off by replacing it with another symbol, say y. After that, we go left again to the leftmost a, replace it with an x, then move to the leftmost b and replace it with y, and so on. Traveling back and forth this way, we match each a with a corresponding b. If after some time no a's or b's remain, then the string must be in L.

Working out the details, we arrive at a complete solution for which

$$
\begin{aligned}
Q &= \{q_0, q_1, q_2, q_3, q_4\}, \\
F &= \{q_4\}, \\
\Sigma &= \{a, b\}, \\
\Gamma &= \{a, b, x, y, \square\}.
\end{aligned}
$$

The transitions can be broken into several parts. The set

$$
\begin{aligned}
\delta(q_0, a) &= (q_1, x, R), \\
\delta(q_1, a) &= (q_1, a, R), \\
\delta(q_1, y) &= (q_1, y, R), \\
\delta(q_1, b) &= (q_2, y, L),
\end{aligned}
$$

replaces the leftmost a with an x, then causes the read-write head to travel right to the first b, replacing it with a y. When the y is written, the machine enters a state q_2, indicating that an a has been successfully paired with a b.

The next set of transitions reverses the direction until an x is encountered, repositions the read-write head over the leftmost a, and returns control to the initial state.

$$\delta\left(q_2, y\right) = \left(q_2, y, L\right),$$
$$\delta\left(q_2, a\right) = \left(q_2, a, L\right),$$
$$\delta\left(q_2, x\right) = \left(q_0, x, R\right).$$

We are now back in the initial state q_0, ready to deal with the next a and b.

After one pass through this part of the computation, the machine will have carried out the partial computation

$$q_0 aa \cdots abb \cdots b \overset{*}{\vdash} xq_0a \cdots ayb \cdots b,$$

so that a single a has been matched with a single b. After two passes, we will have completed the partial computation

$$q_0 aa \cdots abb \cdots b \overset{*}{\vdash} xxq_0 \cdots ayy \cdots b,$$

and so on, indicating that the matching process is being carried out properly.

When the input is a string $a^n b^n$, the rewriting continues this way, stopping only when there are no more a's to be erased. When looking for the leftmost a, the read-write head travels left with the machine in state q_2. When an x is encountered, the direction is reversed to get the a. But now, instead of finding an a it will find a y. To terminate, a final check is made to see if all a's and b's have been replaced (to detect input where an a follows a b). This can be done by

$$\delta\left(q_0, y\right) = \left(q_3, y, R\right),$$
$$\delta\left(q_3, y\right) = \left(q_3, y, R\right),$$
$$\delta\left(q_3, \square\right) = \left(q_4, \square, R\right).$$

If we input a string not in the language, the computation will halt in a nonfinal state. For example, if we give the machine a string $a^n b^m$, with $n > m$, the machine will eventually encounter a blank in state q_1. It will halt because no transition is specified for this case. Other input not in the language will also lead to a nonfinal halting state (see Exercise 3 at the end of this section).

The particular input $aabb$ gives the following successive instantaneous descriptions

$$a_q aabb \vdash xq_1 abb \vdash xaq_1 bb \vdash xq_2 ayb$$
$$\vdash q_2 xayb \vdash xq_0 ayb \vdash xxq_1 yb$$
$$\vdash xxyq_1 b \vdash xxq_2 yy \vdash xq_2 xyy$$
$$\vdash xxq_0 yy \vdash xxyq_3 y \vdash xxyq_3 \square$$
$$\vdash xxyy \square q_4 \square.$$

At this point the Turing machine halts in a final state, so the string $aabb$ is accepted.

You are urged to trace this program with several more strings in L, as well as with some not in L.

Example 9.8   Design a Turing machine that accepts

$$L = \{a^n b^n c^n : n \geq 1\}.$$

The ideas used to Example 9.7 are easily carried over to this case. We match each a, b, and c by replacing them in order by x, y, z, respectively. At the end, we check that all original symbols have been rewritten. Although conceptually a simple extension of the previous example, writing the actual program is tedious. We leave it as a somewhat lengthy, but straightforward exercise. Notice that even though $\{a^n b^n\}$ is a context-free language and $\{a^n b^n c^n\}$ is not, they can be accepted by Turing machines with very similar structures.

One conclusion we can draw from this example is that a Turing machine can recognize some languages that are not context-free, a first indication that Turing machines are more powerful than pushdown automata.

Turing Machines as Transducers

We have had little reason so far to study transducers; in language theory, accepters are quite adequate. But as we will shortly see, Turing machines are not only interesting as language accepters, they provide us with a simple abstract model for digital computers in general. Since the primary purpose of a computer is to transform input into output, it acts as a transducer. If we want to model computers using Turing machines, we have to look at this aspect more closely.

The input for a computation will be all the nonblank symbols on the tape at the initial time. At the conclusion of the computation, the output will be whatever is then on the tape. Thus, we can view a Turing machine transducer M as an implementation of a function f defined by

$$\widehat{w} = f(w),$$

provided that

$$q_0 w \overset{*}{\vdash}_M q_f \widehat{w},$$

for some final state q_f.

Definition 9.4

A function f with domain D is said to be **Turing-computable** or just **computable** if there exists some Turing machine $M = (Q, \Sigma, \Gamma, \delta, q_0, \square, F)$ such that

$$q_0 w \overset{*}{\vdash}_M q_f f(w), \qquad q_f \in F,$$

for all $w \in D$.

As we will shortly claim, all the common mathematical functions, no matter how complicated, are Turing-computable. We start by looking at some simple operations, such as addition and arithmetic comparison.

Example 9.9 Given two positive integers x and y, design a Turing machine that computes $x + y$.

We first have to choose some convention for representing positive integers. For simplicity, we will use unary notation in which any positive integer x is represented by $w(x) \in \{1\}^+$, such that

$$|w(x)| = x.$$

We must also decide how x and y are placed on the tape initially and how their sum is to appear at the end of the computation. We will assume that $w(x)$ and $w(y)$ are on the tape in unary notation, separated by a single 0, with the read-write head on the leftmost symbol of $w(x)$. After the computation, $w(x + y)$ will be on the tape followed by a single 0, and the read-write head will be positioned at the left end of the result. We therefore want to design a Turing machine for performing the computation

$$q_0 w(x) 0 w(y) \overset{*}{\vdash} q_f w(x + y) 0,$$

where q_f is a final state. Constructing a program for this is relatively simple. All we need to do is to move the separating 0 to the right end of $w(y)$, so that the addition amounts to nothing more than the coalescing of the two strings. To achieve this, we construct $M = (Q, \Sigma, \Gamma, \delta, q_0, \square, F)$, with

$$Q = \{q_0, q_1, q_2, q_3, q_4\},$$
$$F = \{q_4\},$$
$$\delta(q_0, 1) = (q_0, 1, R),$$
$$\delta(q_0, 0) = (q_1, 1, R),$$
$$\delta(q_1, 1) = (q_1, 1, R),$$
$$\delta(q_1, \square) = (q_2, \square, L),$$
$$\delta(q_2, 1) = (q_3, 0, L),$$
$$\delta(q_3, 1) = (q_3, 1, L),$$
$$\delta(q_3, \square) = (q_4, \square, R).$$

Note that in moving the 0 right we temporarily create an extra 1, a fact that is remembered by putting the machine into state q_1. The transition $\delta(q_2, 1) = (q_3, 0, R)$ is needed to remove this at the end of the computation. This can be seen from the sequence of instantaneous descriptions for adding 111 to 11:

$$q_0 111011 \vdash 1q_0 11011 \vdash 11q_0 1011 \vdash 111q_0 011$$
$$\vdash 1111q_1 11 \vdash 11111q_1 1 \vdash 111111q_1 \square$$
$$\vdash 11111q_2 1 \vdash 1111q_3 10$$
$$\overset{*}{\vdash} q_3 \square 111110 \vdash q_4 111110.$$

Unary notation, although cumbersome for practical computations, is very convenient for programming Turing machines. The resulting programs are much shorter and simpler than if we had used another representation, such as binary or decimal.

◼

Adding numbers is one of the fundamental operations of any computer, one that plays a part in the synthesis of more complicated instructions. Other basic operations are copying strings and simple comparisons. These can also be done easily on a Turing machine.

Example 9.10   Design a Turing machine that copies strings of 1's. More precisely, find a machine that performs the computation

$$q_0 w \overset{*}{\vdash} q_f ww,$$

for any $w \in \{1\}^+$.

To solve the problem, we implement the following intuitive process:

1. Replace every 1 by an x.

2. Find the rightmost x and replace it with 1.

3. Travel to the right end of the current nonblank region and create a 1 there.

4. Repeat Steps 2 and 3 until there are no more x's.

A Turing machine version of this is

$$\delta\left(q_0, 1\right) = \left(q_0, x, R\right),$$
$$\delta\left(q_0, \square\right) = \left(q_1, \square, L\right),$$
$$\delta\left(q_1, x\right) = \left(q_2, 1, R\right),$$
$$\delta\left(q_2, 1\right) = \left(q_2, 1, R\right),$$
$$\delta\left(q_2, \square\right) = \left(q_1, 1, L\right),$$
$$\delta\left(q_1, 1\right) = \left(q_1, 1, L\right),$$
$$\delta\left(q_1, \square\right) = \left(q_3, \square, R\right),$$

where q_3 is the only final state. This may be a little hard to see at first, so let us trace the program with the simple string 11. The computation performed in this case is

$$q_0 11 \vdash xq_0 1 \vdash xxq_0\square \vdash xq_1 x$$
$$\vdash x1q_2\square \vdash xq_1 11 \vdash q_1 x11$$
$$\vdash 1q_2 11 \vdash 11q_2 1 \vdash 111q_2\square$$
$$\vdash 11q_1 11 \vdash 1q_1 111$$
$$\vdash q_1 1111 \vdash q_1\square 1111 \vdash q_3 1111.$$

Example 9.11 Let x and y be two positive integers represented in unary notation. Construct a Turing machine that will halt in a final state q_y if $x \geq y$, and that will halt in a nonfinal state q_n if $x < y$. More specifically, the machine is to perform the computation

$$q_0 w\left(x\right) 0 w\left(y\right) \overset{*}{\vdash} q_y w\left(x\right) 0 w\left(y\right), \qquad \text{if } x \geq y,$$
$$q_0 w\left(x\right) 0 w\left(y\right) \overset{*}{\vdash} q_n w\left(x\right) 0 w\left(y\right), \qquad \text{if } x < y.$$

To solve this problem, we can use the idea in Example 9.7 with some minor modifications. Instead of matching a's and b's, we match each 1 on the left of the dividing 0 with the 1 on the right. At the end of the matching, we will have on the tape either

$$xx \cdots 110xx \cdots x\square$$

or

$$xx \cdots xx0xx \cdots x11\square,$$

depending on whether $x > y$ or $y > x$. In the first case, when we attempt to match another 1, we encounter the blank at the right of the working space. This can be used as a signal to enter the state q_y. In the second case, we still find a 1 on the right when all 1's on the left have been replaced. We use this to get into the other state q_n. The complete program for this is straightforward and is left as an exercise.

This example makes the important point that a Turing machine can be programmed to make decisions based on arithmetic comparisons. This kind of simple decision is common in the machine language of computers, where alternate instruction streams are entered, depending on the outcome of an arithmetic operation.

EXERCISES

★★ 1. Write a Turing machine simulator in some higher-level programming language. Such a simulator should accept as input the description of any Turing machine, together with an initial configuration, and should produce as output the result of the computation.

2. Design a Turing machine with no more than three states that accepts the language $L\left(a\left(a+b\right)^{*}\right)$. Assume that $\Sigma = \{a, b\}$. Is it possible to do this with a two-state machine? **Ⓢ**

3. Determine what the Turing machine in Example 9.7 does when presented with the inputs aba and $aaabbbb$.

4. Is there any input for which the Turing machine in Example 9.7 goes into an infinite loop?

5. What language is accepted by the machine $M = (\{q_0, q_1, q_2, q_3\}, \{a, b\},$ $\{a, b, \square\}, \delta, q_0, \square, \{q_3\})$ with

$$\delta(q_0, a) = (q_1, a, R),$$
$$\delta(q_0, b) = (q_2, b, R),$$
$$\delta(q_1, b) = (q_1, b, R),$$
$$\delta(q_1, \square) = (q_3, \square, R),$$
$$\delta(q_2, b) = (q_2, b, R),$$
$$\delta(q_2, a) = (q_3, a, R).$$

6. What happens in Example 9.10 if the string w contains any symbol other than 1?

7. Construct Turing machines that will accept the following languages on $\{a, b\}$.

   (a) $L - L(aba^*b)$ **Ⓢ**

   (b) $L = \{w : |w| \text{ is even}\}$ **Ⓢ**

   (c) $L = \{w : |w| \text{ is a multiple of 3}\}$

   (d) $L = \{a^n b^m : n \geq 1, n \neq m\}$

   (e) $L = \{w : n_a(w) = n_b(w)\}$

   (f) $L - \{a^n b^m a^{n+m} : n \geq 0, m \geq 1\}$

   (g) $L = \{a^n b^n a^n b^n : n \geq 0\}$

   (h) $L = \{a^n b^{2n} : n \geq 1\}$

   For each problem, write out δ in complete detail, then check your answers by tracing several test examples.

8. Design a Turing machine that accepts the language

$$L = \{ww : w \in \{a, b\}^+\}.$$

9. Construct a Turing machine to compute the function

$$f(w) = w^R,$$

   where $w \in \{0, 1\}^+$.

10. Design a Turing machine that finds the middle of a string of even length. Specifically, if $w = a_1 a_2 ... a_n a_{n+1} ... a_{2n}$, with $a_i \in \Sigma$, the Turing machine should produce $\widehat{w} = a_1 a_2 ... a_n c a_{n+1} ... a_{2n}$, where $c \in \Gamma - \Sigma$. **Ⓢ**

11. Design Turing machines to compute the following functions for x and y positive integers represented in unary.

   (a) $f(x) = 3x$

   (b) $f(x, y) = x - y, \qquad x > y$
   $$= 0, \qquad\qquad x \leq y$$

(c) $f(x, y) = 2x + 3y$

(d) $f(x) = \frac{x}{2}$,   if x is even

   $= \frac{x+1}{2}$,   if x is odd

(e) $f(x) = x \bmod 5$

(f) $f(x) = \lfloor \frac{x}{2} \rfloor$, where $\lfloor \frac{x}{2} \rfloor$ denotes the largest integer less than or equal to $\frac{x}{2}$.

12. Design a Turing machine with $\Gamma = \{0, 1, \square\}$ that, when started on any cell containing a blank or a 1, will halt if and only if its tape has a 0 somewhere on it. Ⓢ

13. Write out a complete solution for Example 9.8.

14. Give the sequence of instantaneous descriptions that the Turing machine in Example 9.10 goes through when presented with the input 111. What happens when this machine is started with 110 on its tape?

15. Give convincing arguments that the Turing machine in Example 9.10 does in fact carry out the indicated computation.

16. Complete all the details in Example 9.11.

17. Suppose that in Example 9.9 we had decided to represent x and y in binary. Write a Turing machine program for doing the indicated computation in this representation.

18. Sketch how Example 9.9 could be solved if x and y were represented in decimal.

19. You may have noticed that all the examples in this section had only one final state. Is it generally true that for any Turing machine, there exists another one with only one final state that accepts the same language? Ⓢ

20. Definition 9.2 excludes the empty string from any language accepted by a Turing machine. Modify the definition so that languages that contain λ may be accepted.

9.2 Combining Turing Machines for Complicated Tasks

We have shown explicitly how some important operations found in all computers can be done on a Turing machine. Since, in digital computers, such primitive operations are the building blocks for more complex instructions, let us see how these basic operations can also be put together on a Turing machine. To demonstrate how Turing machines can be combined, we follow a practice common in programming. We start with a high-level description, then refine it successively until the program is in the actual language with which we are working. We can describe Turing machines several ways at a high level; block diagrams or pseudocode are the two approaches we will use

Figure 9.5

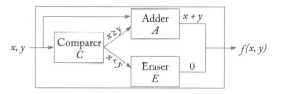

Figure 9.5

most frequently in subsequent discussions. In a block diagram, we encapsule computations in boxes whose function is described, but whose interior details are not shown. By using such boxes, we implicitly claim that they can actually be constructed. As a first example, we combine the machines in Examples 9.9 and 9.11.

Example 9.12

Design a Turing machine that computes the function

$$f(x, y) = x + y, \qquad \text{if } x \geq y,$$
$$= 0, \qquad \text{if } x < y.$$

For the sake of discussion, assume that x and y are positive integers in unary representation. The value zero will be represented by 0, with the rest of the tape blank.

The computation of $f(x, y)$ can be visualized at a high level by means of the diagram in Figure 9.5. The diagram shows that we first use a comparing machine, like that in Example 9.11, to determine whether or not $x \geq y$. If so, the comparer sends a start signal to the adder, which then computes $x + y$. If not, an erasing program is started that changes every 1 to a blank.

In subsequent discussions, we will often use such high-level, black-diagram representations of Turing machines. It is certainly quicker and clearer than the corresponding extensive set of δ's. Before we accept this high-level view, we must justify it. What, for example is meant by saying that the comparer sends a start signal to the adder? There is nothing in Definition 9.1 that offers that possibility. Nevertheless, it can be done in a straightforward way.

The program for the comparer C is written as suggested in Example 9.11, using a Turing machine having states indexed with C. For the adder, we use the idea in Example 9.9, with states indexed with A. For the eraser E, we construct a Turing machine having states indexed with E. The computations to be done by C are

$$q_{C,0} w(x) 0 w(y) \overset{*}{\vdash} q_{A,0} w(x) 0 w(y), \qquad \text{if } x \geq y,$$

and

$$q_{C,0} w(x) 0 w(y) \overset{*}{\vdash} q_{E,0} w(x) 0 w(y), \qquad \text{if } x < y.$$

If we take $q_{A,0}$ and $q_{E,0}$ as the initial states of A and E, respectively, we see that C starts either A or E.

The computations performed by the adder will be

$$q_{A,0} w(x) 0 w(y) \overset{*}{\vdash} q_{A,f} w(x+y) 0,$$

and that of the eraser E will be

$$q_{E,0} w(x) 0 w(y) \overset{*}{\vdash} q_{E,f} 0.$$

The result is a single Turing machine that combines the action of C, A, and E as indicated in Figure 9.5.

Another useful, high-level view of Turing machines is one involving pseudocode. In computer programming, pseudocode is a way of outlining a computation using descriptive phrases whose meaning we claim to understand. While this description is not usable on the computer, we assume that we can translate it into the appropriate language when needed. One simple kind of pseudocode is exemplified by the idea of a macroinstruction, which is a single-statement shorthand for a sequence of lower level statements. We first define the macroinstruction in terms of the lower level language. We then use the macroinstruction in a program with the assumption that the relevant low-level code is substituted for each occurrence of the macroinstruction. This idea is very useful in Turing machine programming.

Example 9.13   Consider the macroinstruction

$$\textit{if } a \text{ then } q_j \text{ else } q_k,$$

with the following interpretation. If the Turing machine reads an a, then regardless of its current state, it is to go into state q_j without changing the tape content or moving the read-write head. If the symbol read is not an a, the machine is to go into state q_k without changing anything.

To implement this macroinstruction requires several relatively obvious steps of a Turing machine.

$$\begin{aligned}
\delta(q_i, a) &= (q_{j0}, a, R) &&\text{for all } q_i \in Q, \\
\delta(q_i, b) &= (q_{k0}, b, R) &&\text{for all } q_i \in Q \text{ and all } b \in \Gamma - \{a\}, \\
\delta(q_{j0}, c) &= (q_j, c, L) &&\text{for all } c \in \Gamma, \\
\delta(q_{k0}, c) &= (q_k, c, L) &&\text{for all } c \in \Gamma.
\end{aligned}$$

The states q_{j0} and q_{k0} are new states, introduced to take care of complications arising from the fact that in a standard Turing machine the read-write head changes position in each move. In the macroinstruction, we want to change the state, but leave the read-write head where it is. We let the head move right, but put the machine into a state q_{j0} or q_{k0}. This indicates that a left move must be made before entering the desired state q_j or q_k.

Going a step further, we can replace macroinstructions with subprograms. Normally, a macroinstruction is replaced by actual code at each occurrence, whereas a subprogram is a single piece of code that is invoked repeatedly whenever needed. Subprograms are fundamental to high-level programming languages, but they can also be used with Turing machines. To make this plausible, let us outline briefly how a Turing machine can be used as a subprogram that can be invoked repeatedly by another Turing machine. This requires a new feature: the ability to store information on the calling program's configuration so the configuration can be recreated on return from the subprogram. For example, say machine A in state q_i invokes machine B. When B is finished, we would like to resume program A in state q_i, with the read-write head (which may have moved during B's operation) in its original place. At other times, A may call B from state q_j, in which case control should return to this state. To solve the control transfer problem, we must be able to pass information from A to B and vice versa, be able to recreate A's configuration when it recovers control from B, and to assure that the temporarily suspended computations of A are not affected by the execution of B. To solve this, we can divide the tape into several regions as shown in Figure 9.6.

Before A calls B, it writes the information needed by B (e.g., A's current state, the arguments for B) on the tape in some region T. A then passes control to B by making a transition to the start state of B. After transfer, B will use T to find its input. The workspace for B is separate from T and from the workspace for A, so no interference can occur. When B is finished, it will return relevant results to region T, where A will expect to find it. In this way, the two programs can interact in the required fashion. Note that this is very similar to what actually happens in a real computer when a subprogram is called.

Figure 9.6

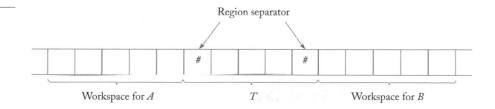

Figure 9.7

We can now program Turing machines in pseudocode, provided that we know (in theory at least) how to translate this pseudocode into an actual Turing machine program.

Example 9.14 Design a Turing machine that multiplies two positive integers in unary notation.

A multiplication machine can be constructed by combining the ideas we encountered in adding and copying. Let us assume that the initial and final tape contents are to be as indicated in Figure 9.7. The process of multiplication can then be visualized as a repeated copying of the multiplicand y for each 1 in the multiplier x, whereby the string y is added the appropriate number of times to the partially computed product. The following pseudocode shows the main steps of the process.

1. Repeat the following steps until x contains no more 1's.

   Find a 1 in x and replace it with another symbol a.

   Replace the leftmost 0 by $0y$.

2. Replace all a's with 1's.

Although this pseudocode is sketchy, the idea is simple enough that there should be no doubt that it can be done.

In spite of the descriptive nature of these examples, it is not too far-fetched to conjecture that Turing machines, while rather primitive in principle, can be combined in many ways to make them quite powerful. Our examples were not general and detailed enough for us to claim that we have proved anything, but it should be plausible at this point that Turing machines can do some quite complicated things.

EXERCISES

1. Write out the complete solution to Example 9.14.

2. Establish a convention for representing positive and negative integers in unary notation. With your convention, sketch the construction of a subtracter for computing $x - y$.

3. Using adders, subtracters, comparers, copiers, or multipliers, draw block diagrams for Turing machines that compute the functions

   (a) $f(n) = n(n+1)$, **S**

   (b) $f(n) = n^5$,

   (c) $f(n) = 2^n$,

   (d) $f(n) = n!$,

   (e) $f(n) = n^{n!}$,

   for all positive integers n.

4. Use a block diagram to sketch the implementation of a function f defined for all $w_1, w_2, w_3 \in \{1\}^+$ by

$$f(w_1, w_2, w_3) = i,$$

   where i is such that $|w_i| = \max(|w_1|, |w_2|, |w_3|)$ if no two w have the same length, and $i = 0$ otherwise.

5. Provide a "high-level" description for Turing machines that accept the following languages on $\{a, b\}$. For each problem, define a set of appropriate macroinstructions that you feel are reasonably easy to implement. Then use them for the solution.

   (a) $L = \{ww^R\}$

   (b) $L = \{w_1 w_2 : w_1 \neq w_2 : |w_1| = |w_2|\}$

   (c) The complement of the language in part (a) **S**

   (d) $L = \{a^n b^m : m = n^2, n \geq 1\}$

   (e) $L = \{a^n : n \text{ is a prime number}\}$

6. Suggest a method for representing rational numbers on a Turing machine, then sketch a method for adding and subtracting such numbers.

7. Sketch the construction of a Turing machine that can perform the addition and multiplication of positive integers x and y given in the usual decimal notation.

8. Give an implementation of the macroinstruction

$$\text{searchright}(a, q_i, q_j),$$

   which indicates that the machine is to search its tape to the right of the current position for the first occurrence of the symbol a. If an a is encountered before a blank, the machine is to go into state q_i, otherwise it is to go into state q_j. **S**

9. Use the macroinstruction in the previous exercise to design a Turing machine on $\Sigma = \{a, b\}$ that accepts the language $L(ab^*ab^*a)$.

10. Use the macroinstruction searchright in Exercise 8 to create a Turing machine program that replaces the symbol immediately to the left of the leftmost a by a blank. If the input contains no a, replace the rightmost nonblank symbol by a b.

9.3 Turing's Thesis

The preceding discussion not only shown how a Turing machine can be constructed from simpler parts, but also illustrates a negative aspect of working with such low-level automata. While it takes very little imagination or ingenuity to translate a block diagram or pseudocode into the corresponding Turing machine program, actually doing it is time consuming, error prone, and adds little to our understanding. The instruction set of a Turing machine is so restricted that any argument, solution, or proof for a nontrivial problem is quite tedious.

We now face a dilemma: we want to claim that Turing machines can perform not only the simple operations for which we have provided explicit programs, but more complex processes as well, describable by block diagrams or pseudocode. To defend such claims against challenge, we should show the relevant programs explicitly. But doing so is unpleasant and distracting, and ought to be avoided if possible. Somehow, we would like to find a way of carrying out a reasonably rigorous discussion of Turing machines without having to write lengthy, low-level code. There is unfortunately no completely satisfactory way of getting out of the predicament; the best we can do is to reach a reasonable compromise. To see how we might achieve such a compromise, we turn to a somewhat philosophical issue.

We can draw some simple conclusions from the examples in the previous section. The first is that Turing machines appear to be more powerful than pushdown automata (for a comment on this, see Exercise 2 at the end of this section). In Example 9.8, we sketched the construction of a Turing machine for a language which is not context-free and for which, consequently, no pushdown automaton exists. Examples 9.9, 9.10, and 9.11 show that Turing machines can do some simple arithmetic operations, perform string manipulations, and make some simple comparisons. The discussion also illustrates how primitive operations can be combined to solve more complex problems, how several Turing machines can be composed, and how one program can act as a subprogram for another. Since very complex operations can be built this way, we might suspect that a Turing machine begins to approach a typical computer in power.

Suppose we were to make the conjecture that, in some sense, Turing machines are equal in power to a typical digital computer? How could we defend or refute such a hypothesis? To defend it, we could take a sequence of increasingly more difficult problems and show how they are solved by some Turing machine. We might also take the machine language instruction set of a specific computer and design a Turing machine that can perform all the instructions in the set. This would undoubtedly tax our patience, but it ought to be possible in principle if our hypothesis is correct. Still, while every success in this direction would strengthen our conviction of the truth of the hypothesis, it would not lead to a proof. The difficulty lies in the fact that we don't know exactly what is meant by "a typical digital computer" and that we have no means for making a precise definition.

We can also approach the problem from the other side. We might try to find some procedure for which we can write a computer program, but for which we can show that no Turing machine can exist. If this were possible, we would have a basis for rejecting the hypothesis. But no one has yet been able to produce a counterexample; the fact that all such tries have been unsuccessful must be taken as circumstantial evidence that it cannot be done. Every indication is that Turing machines are in principle as powerful as any computer.

Arguments of this type led A. M. Turing and others in the mid-1930's to the celebrated conjecture called the **Turing thesis**. This hypothesis states that any computation that can be carried out by mechanical means can be performed by some Turing machine.

This is a sweeping statement, so it is important to keep in mind what Turing's thesis is. It is not something that can be proved. To do so, we would have to define precisely the term "mechanical means." This would require some other abstract model and leave us no further ahead than before. The Turing thesis is more properly viewed as a definition of what constitutes a mechanical computation: a computation is mechanical if and only if it can be performed by some Turing machine.

If we take this attitude and regard the Turing thesis simply as a definition, we raise the question as to whether this definition is sufficiently broad. Is it far-reaching enough to cover everything we now do (and conceivably might do in the future) with computers? An unequivocal "yes" is not possible, but the evidence in its favor is very strong. Some arguments for accepting the Turing thesis as the definition of a mechanical computation are

1. Anything that can be done on any existing digital computer can also be done by a Turing machine.

2. No one has yet been able to suggest a problem, solvable by what we intuitively consider an algorithm, for which a Turing machine program cannot be written.

3. Alternative models have been proposed for mechanical computation, but none of them are more powerful than the Turing machine model.

These arguments are circumstantial, and Turing's thesis cannot be proved by them. In spite of its plausibility, Turing's thesis is still an assumption. But viewing Turing's thesis simply as an arbitrary definition misses an important point. In some sense, Turing's thesis plays the same role in computer science as do the basis laws of physics and chemistry. Classical physics, for example, is based largely on Newton's laws of motion. Although we call them laws, they do not have logical necessity; rather, they are plausible models that explain much of the physical world. We accept them because the conclusions we draw from them agree with our experience and our observations. Such laws cannot be proved to be true, although they can possibly be invalidated. If an experimental result contradicts a conclusion based on the laws, we might begin to question their validity. On the other hand, repeated failure to invalidate a law strengthens our confidence in it. This is the situation for Turing's thesis, so we have some reason for considering it a basic law of computer science. The conclusions we draw from it agree with what we know about real computers, and so far, all attempts to invalidate it have failed. There is always the possibility that someone will come up with another definition that will account for some subtle situations not covered by Turing machines but which still fall within the range of our intuitive notion of mechanical computation. In such an eventuality, some of our subsequent discussions would have to be modified significantly. However, the likelihood of this happening seems to be very small.

Having accepted Turing's thesis, we are in a position to give a precise definition of an algorithm.

Definition 9.5

An algorithm for a function $f : D \to R$ is a Turing machine M, which given as input any $d \in D$ on its tape, eventually halts with the correct answer $f(d) \in R$ on its tape. Specifically, we can require that

$$q_0 d \overset{*}{\vdash}_M q_f f(d), q_f \in F,$$

for all $d \in D$.

Identifying an algorithm with a Turing machine program allows us to prove rigorously such claims as "there exists an algorithm . . ." or "there is no algorithm. . . ." However, to construct explicitly an algorithm for even relatively simple problems is a very lengthy undertaking. To avoid such unpleasant prospects, we can appeal to Turing's thesis and claim that anything we can do on any computer can also be done on a Turing machine.

Consequently, we could substitute "Pascal program" for "Turing machine" in Definition 9.5. This would ease the burden of exhibiting algorithms considerably. Actually, as we have already done, we will go one step further and accept verbal descriptions or block diagrams as algorithms on the assumption that we could write a Turing machine program for them if we were challenged to do so. This greatly simplifies the discussion, but it obviously leaves us open to criticism. While "Pascal program" is well defined, "clear verbal description" is not, and we are in danger of claiming the existence of nonexistent algorithms. But this danger is more than offset by the fact that we can keep the discussion simple and intuitively clear, and that we can give concise descriptions for some rather complex processes. The reader who has any doubt of the validity of these claims can dispel them by writing a suitable program in some programming language.

EXERCISES

★★ 1. Consider the set of machine language instructions for a computer of your choice. Sketch how the various instructions in this set could be carried out by a Turing machine.

2. In the above discussion, we stated at one point that Turing machines appear to be more powerful than pushdown automata. Since the tape of a Turing machine can always be made to behave like a stack, it would seem that we can actually claim that a Turing machine is more powerful. What important factor is not taken into account in this argument? **S**

★★ 3. There are a number of enjoyable articles on Turing machines in the popular literature. A good one is a paper in *Scientific American*, May 1984, by J. E. Hopcroft, titled "Turing Machines." This paper talks about the ideas we have introduced here and also gives some of the historical context in which the work of Turing and others was done. Get a copy of this article and read it, then write a brief review of it.

Chapter 10

Other Models of
Turing Machines

Our definition of a standard Turing machine is not the only possible one; there are alternative definitions that could serve equally well. The conclusions we can draw about the power of a Turing machine are largely independent of the specific structure chosen for it. In this chapter we look at several variations, showing that the standard Turing machine is equivalent, in a sense we will define, to other, more complicated models.

If we accept Turing's thesis, we expect that complicating the standard Turing machine by giving it a more complex storage device will not have any effect on the power of the automaton. Any computation that can be performed on such a new arrangement will still fall under the category of a mechanical computation and, therefore, can be done by a standard model. It is nevertheless instructive to study more complex models, if for no other reason than that an explicit demonstration of the expected result will demonstrate the power of the Turing machine and thereby increase our confidence in Turing's thesis. Many variations on the basic model of Definition 9.1 are possible. For example, we can consider Turing machines with more than one tape or with tapes that extend in several dimensions.

We will consider variants that will be useful in subsequent discussions.

We also look at nondeterministic Turing machines and show that they are no more powerful than deterministic ones. This is unexpected, since Turing's thesis covers only mechanical computations and does not address the clever guessing implicit in nondeterminism. Another issue that is not immediately resolved by Turing's thesis is that of one machine executing different programs at different times. This leads to the idea of a "reprogrammable" or "universal" Turing machine.

Finally, in preparation for later chapters, we look at linear bounded automata. These are Turing machines that have an infinite tape, but that can make use of the tape only in a restricted way.

10.1 Minor Variations on the Turing Machine Theme

We first consider some relatively minor changes in Definition 9.1 and investigate whether these changes make any difference in the general concept. Whenever we change a definition, we introduce a new type of automata and raise the question whether these new automata are in any real sense different from those we have already encountered. What do we mean by an essential difference between one class of automata and another? Although there may be clear differences in their definitions, these differences may not have any interesting consequences. We have seen an example of this in the case of deterministic and nondeterministic finite automata. These have quite different definitions, but they are equivalent in the sense that they both are identified exactly with the family of regular languages. Extrapolating from this, we can define equivalence or nonequivalence for classes of automata in general.

Equivalence of Classes of Automata

Whenever we define equivalence for two automata or classes of automata, we must carefully state what is to be understood by this equivalence. For the rest of this chapter, we follow the precedence established for nfa's and dfa's and define equivalence with respect to the ability to accept languages.

Definition 10.1

Two automata are equivalent if they accept the same language. Consider two classes of automata C_1 and C_2. If for every automaton M_1 in C_1 there is an automaton M_2 in C_2 such that

$$L(M_1) = L(M_2),$$

we say that C_2 is at least as powerful as C_1. If the converse also holds and for every M_2 in C_2 there is an M_1 in C_1 such that $L(M_1) = L(M_2)$, we say that C_1 and C_2 are equivalent.

There are many ways to establish the equivalence of automata. The construction of Theorem 2.2 does this for dfa's and nfa's. For demonstrating the equivalence in connection with Turing's machines, we often use the important technique of **simulation**.

Let M be an automaton. We say that another automaton $\widehat{M}$ can simulate a computation of M, if $\widehat{M}$ can mimic the computation of M in the following manner. Let $d_0, d_1, \ldots$ be the sequence of instantaneous descriptions of the computation of M, that is

$$d_0 \vdash_M d_1 \vdash_M \cdots \vdash_M d_n \cdots.$$

Then $\widehat{M}$ simulates this computation if it carries out a computation analogous to that of M,

$$\widehat{d_0} \overset{*}{\vdash}_{\widehat{M}} \widehat{d_1} \overset{*}{\vdash}_{\widehat{M}} \cdots \overset{*}{\vdash}_{\widehat{M}} \widehat{d_n} \cdots,$$

where $\hat{d}_0, \hat{d}_1, \ldots$ are instantaneous descriptions, such that each of them is associated with a unique configuration of M. In other words, if we know the computation carried out by $\widehat{M}$, we can determine from it exactly what computations M would have done, given the corresponding starting configuration.

Note that the simulation of a single move $d_i \vdash_M d_{i+1}$ of M may involve several moves of $\widehat{M}$. The intermediate configurations in $\hat{d}_i \overset{*}{\vdash}_{\widehat{M}} \hat{d}_{i+1}$ may not correspond to any configuration of M, but this does not affect anything if we can tell which configurations of $\widehat{M}$ are relevant. As long as we can determine from the computation of $\widehat{M}$ what M would have done, the simulation is proper. If $\widehat{M}$ can simulate every computation of M, we say that $\widehat{M}$ can simulate M. It should be clear that if $\widehat{M}$ can simulate M, then matters can be arranged so that M and $\widehat{M}$ accept the same language, and the two automata are equivalent. To demonstrate the equivalence of two classes of automata, we show that for every machine in one class, there is a machine in the second class capable of simulating it.

Turing Machines with a Stay-Option

In our definition of a standard Turing machine, the read-write head must move either to the right or to the left. Sometimes it is convenient to provide a third option, to have the read-write head stay in place after rewriting the cell content. Thus, we can define a Turing machine with stay-option by replacing δ in Definition 9.1 by

$$\delta : Q \times \Gamma \to Q \times \Gamma \times \{L, R, S\}$$

with the interpretation that S signifies no movement of the read-write head. This option does not extend the power of the automaton.

Theorem 10.1

The class of Turing machines with stay-option is equivalent to the class of standard Turing machines.

Proof: Since a Turing machine with stay-option is clearly an extension of the standard model, it is obvious that any standard Turing machine can be simulated by one with a stay-option.

To show the converse, let $M = (Q, \Sigma, \Gamma, \delta, q_0, \Box, F)$ be a Turing machine with stay-option to be simulated by a standard Turing machine $\widehat{M} = \left(\widehat{Q}, \Sigma, \Gamma, \widehat{\delta}, \widehat{q}_0, \Box, \widehat{F}\right)$. For each move of M, the simulating machine $\widehat{M}$ does the following. If the move of M does not involve the stay-option, the simulating machine performs one move, essentially identical to the move to be simulated. If S is involved in the move of M, then $\widehat{M}$ will make two moves: the first rewrites the symbol and moves the read-write head right; the second moves the read-write head left, leaving the tape contents unaltered. The simulating machine can be constructed by M by defining $\widehat{\delta}$ as follows: For each transition

$$\delta\left(q_i, a\right) = \left(q_j, b, L \text{ or } R\right),$$

we put into $\widehat{\delta}$

$$\widehat{\delta}\left(\widehat{q}_i, a\right) = \left(\widehat{q}_j, b, L \text{ or } R\right).$$

For each S-transition

$$\delta\left(q_i, a\right) = \left(q_j, b, S\right),$$

we put into $\widehat{\delta}$ the corresponding transitions

$$\widehat{\delta}\left(\widehat{q}_i, a\right) = \left(\widehat{q}_{js}, b, R\right),$$

and

$$\widehat{\delta}\left(\widehat{q}_{js}, c\right) = \left(\widehat{q}_j, c, L\right),$$

for all $c \in \Gamma$.

It is reasonably obvious that every computation of M has a corresponding computation of $\widehat{M}$, so that $\widehat{M}$ can simulate M. ∎

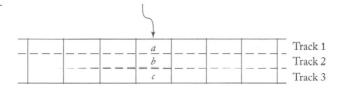

Simulation is a standard technique for showing the equivalence of automata, and the formalism we have described makes it possible, as shown in the above theorem, to talk about the process precisely and prove theorems about equivalence. In our subsequent discussion, we use the notion of simulation frequently, but we generally make no attempt to describe everything in a rigorous and detailed way. Complete simulations with Turing machines are often cumbersome. To avoid this, we keep our discussion descriptive, rather than in theorem-proof form. The simulations are given only in broad outline, but it should not be hard to see how they can be made rigorous. The reader will find it instructive to sketch each simulation in some higher level language or in pseudocode.

Before introducing other models, we make one remark on the standard Turing machine. It is implicit in Definition 9.1 that each tape symbol can be a composite of characters rather than just a single one. This can be made more explicit by drawing an expanded version of Figure 9.1 (Figure 10.1), in which the tape symbols are triplets from some simpler alphabet.

In the picture, we have divided each cell of the tape into three parts, called **tracks**, each containing one member of the triplet. Based on this visualization, such an automaton is sometimes called a Turing machine with **multiple tracks**, but such a view in no way extends Definition 9.1, since all we need to do is make Γ an alphabet in which each symbol is composed of several parts.

However, other Turing machine models involve a change of definition, so the equivalence with the standard machine has to be demonstrated. Here we look at two such models, which are sometimes used as the standard definition. Some variants that are less common are explored in the exercises at the end of this section.

Turing Machines with Semi-Infinite Tape

Many authors do not consider the model in Figure 9.1 as standard, but use one with a tape that is unbounded only in one direction. We can visualize this as a tape that has a left boundary (Figure 10.2). This Turing machine is otherwise identical to our standard model, except that no left move is permitted when the read-write head is at the boundary.

It is not difficult to see that this restriction does not affect the power of the machine. To simulate a standard Turing machine M by a machine $\widehat{M}$ with a semi-infinite tape, we use the arrangement shown in Figure 10.3.

Figure 10.2

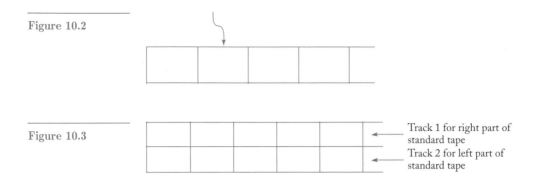

Figure 10.3

Track 1 for right part of standard tape

Track 2 for left part of standard tape

The simulating machine $\widehat{M}$ has a tape with two tracks. On the upper one, we keep the information to the right of some reference point on M's tape. The reference point could be, for example, the position of the read-write head at the start of the computation. The lower track contains the left part of M's tape in reverse order. $\widehat{M}$ is programmed so that it will use information on the upper track only as long as M's read-write head is to the right of the reference point, and work on the lower track as M moves into the left part of its tape. The distinction can be made by partitioning the state set of $\widehat{M}$ into two parts, say Q_U and Q_L: the first to be used when working on the upper track, the second to be used on the lower one. Special end markers # are put on the left boundary of the tape to facilitate switching from one track to the other. For example, assume that the machine to be simulated and the simulating machine are in the respective configurations shown in Figure 10.4 and that the move to be simulated is generated by

$$\delta\left(q_i, a\right) = \left(q_j, c, L\right).$$

The simulating machine will first move via the transition

$$\widehat{\delta}\left(\widehat{q}_i, (a, b)\right) = \left(\widehat{q}_j, (c, b), L\right),$$

where $\widehat{q}_i \in Q_U$. Because $\widehat{q}_i$ belongs to Q_U, only information in the upper track is considered at this point. Now, the simulating machine sees $(\#, \#)$

Figure 10.4
(a) Machine to be simulated.
(b) Simulating machine.

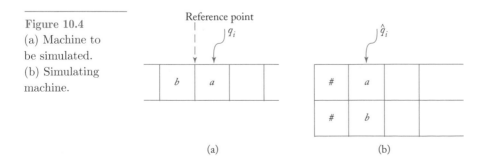

(a)   (b)

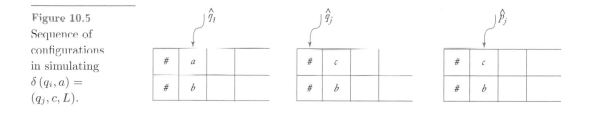

Figure 10.5
Sequence of
configurations
in simulating
$\delta(q_i, a) =$
(q_j, c, L).

in state $\widehat{q}_j \in Q_U$. It next uses a transition

$$\widehat{\delta}\left(\widehat{q}_j, (\#, \#)\right) - \left(\widehat{p}_j, (\#, \#), R\right),$$

with $\widehat{p}_j \in Q_L$, putting it into the configuration shown in Figure 10.5. Now the machine is in a state from Q_L and will work on the lower track. Further details of the simulation are straightforward.

The Off-Line Turing Machine

The general definition of an automaton in Chapter 1 contained an input file as well as temporary storage. In Definition 9.1 we discarded the input file for reasons of simplicity, claiming that this made no difference to the Turing machine concept. We now expand on this claim.

If we put the input file back into the picture, we get what is known as an **off-line Turing machine**. In such a machine, each move is governed by the internal state, what is currently read from the input file, and what is seen by the read-write head. A schematic representation of an off-line machine is shown in Figure 10.6. A formal definition of an off-line Turing machine is easily made, but we will leave this as an exercise. What we

Figure 10.6

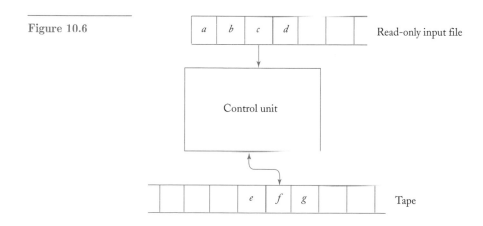

Figure 10.7

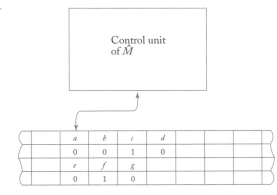

want to do briefly is to indicate why the class of off-line Turing machines is equivalent to the class of standard machines.

First, the behavior of any standard Turing machine can be simulated by some off-line model. All that needs to be done by the simulating machine is to copy the input from the input file to the tape. Then it can proceed in the same way as the standard machine.

The simulation of an off-line machine M by a standard machine $\widehat{M}$ requires a lengthier description. A standard machine can simulate the computation of an off-line machine by using the four-track arrangement shown in Figure 10.7. In that picture, the tape contents shown represent the specific configuration of Figure 10.6. Each of the four tracks of $\widehat{M}$ plays a specific role in the simulation. The first track has the input, the second marks the position at which the input is read, the third represents the tape of M, and the fourth shows the position of M's read-write head.

The simulation of each move of M requires a number of moves of $\widehat{M}$. Starting from some standard position, say the left end, and with the relevant information marked by special end markers, $\widehat{M}$ searches track 2 to locate the position at which the input file of M is read. The symbol found in the corresponding cell on track 1 is remembered by putting the control unit of $\widehat{M}$ into a state chosen for this purpose. Next, track 4 is searched for the position of the read-write head of M. With the remembered input and the symbol on track 3, we now know that M is to do. This information is again remembered by $\widehat{M}$ with an appropriate internal state. Next, all four tracks of $\widehat{M}$'s tape are modified to reflect the move of M. Finally, the read-write head of $\widehat{M}$ returns to the standard position for the simulation of the next move.

EXERCISES

1. Give a formal definition of a Turing machine with a semi-infinite tape. Then

prove that the class of Turing machines with semi-infinite tape is equivalent to the class of standard Turing machines.

2. Give a formal definition of an off-line Turing machine.

3. Give convincing arguments that any language accepted by an off-line Turing machine is also accepted by some standard machine.

4. Consider a Turing machine that, on any particular move, can either change the tape symbol or move the read-write head, but not both.

   (a) Give a formal definition of such a machine.

   (b) Show that the class of such machines is equivalent to the class of standard Turing machines. **ⓢ**

5. Consider a model of a Turing machine in which each move permits the read-write head to travel more than one cell to the left or right, the distance and direction of travel being one of the arguments of δ. Give a precise definition of such an automaton and sketch a simulation of it by a standard Turing machine.

6. A nonerasing Turing machine is one that cannot change a nonblank symbol to a blank. This can be achieved by the restriction that if

$$\delta\left(q_i, a\right) = \left(q_j, \Box, L \text{ or } R\right),$$

then a must be $\Box$. Show that no generality is lost by making such a restriction. **ⓢ**

7. Consider a Turing machine that cannot write blanks; that is, for all $\delta\left(q_i, a\right) = \left(q_j, b, L \text{ or } R\right)$, b must be in $\Gamma - \{\Box\}$. Show how such a machine can simulate a standard Turing machine.

8. Suppose we make the requirement that a Turing machine can halt only in a final state, that is, we ask that $\delta\left(q, a\right)$ be defined for all pairs (q, a) with $a \in \Gamma$ and $q \notin F$. Does this restrict the power of the Turing machine?

9. Suppose we make the restriction that a Turing machine must always write a symbol different from the one it reads, that is, if

$$\delta\left(q_i, a\right) = \left(q_j, b, L \text{ or } R\right),$$

then a and b must be different. Does this limitation reduce the power of the automaton? **ⓢ**

10. Consider a version of the standard Turing machine in which transitions can depend not only on the cell directly under the read-write head, but also on the cells to the immediate right and left. Make a formal definition of such a machine, then sketch its simulation by a standard Turing machine.

11. Consider a Turing machine with a different decision process in which transitions are made if the current tape symbol is not one of a specified set. For example

$$\delta\left(q_i, \{a, b\}\right) = \left(q_j, c, R\right)$$

will allow the indicated move if the current tape symbol is neither a nor b. Formalize this concept and show that this modification is equivalent to a standard Turing machine. Ⓢ

10.2 Turing Machines with More Complex Storage

The storage device of a standard Turing machine is so simple that one might think it possible to gain power by using more complicated storage devices. But this is not the case as we now illustrate with two examples.

Multitape Turing Machines

A multitape Turing machine is a Turing machine with several tapes, each with its own independently controlled read-write head (Figure 10.8).

The formal definition of a multitape Turing machine goes beyond Definition 9.1, since it requires a modified transition function. Typically, we define an n-tape machine by $M = (Q, \Sigma, \Gamma, \delta, q_0, \Box, F)$, where $Q, \Sigma, \Gamma, q_0, F$ are as in Definition 9.1, but where

$$\delta : Q \times \Gamma^n \rightarrow Q \times \Gamma^n \times \{L, R\}^n$$

specifies what happens on all the tapes. For example, if $n = 2$, with a current configuration shown in Figure 10.8, then

$$\delta(q_0, a, e) = (q_1, x, y, L, R)$$

is interpreted as follows. The transition rule can be applied only if the machine is in state q_0 and the first read-write head sees an a and the second an e. The symbol on the first tape will then be replaced with an x and its read-write head will move to the left. At the same time, the symbol on

Figure 10.8

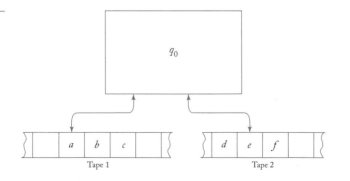

Figure 10.9

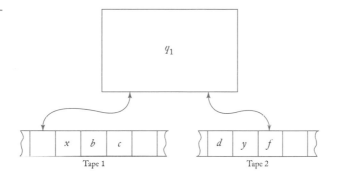

the second tape is rewritten as y and the read-write head moves right. The control unit then changes its state to q_1 and the machine goes into the new configuration shown in Figure 10.9.

To show the equivalence between multitape and standard Turing machines, we argue that any given multitape Turing machine M can be simulated by a standard Turing machine $\widehat{M}$ and, conversely, that any standard Turing machine can be simulated by a multitape one. The second part of this claim needs no elaboration, since we can always elect to run a multitape machine with only one of its tapes doing useful work. The simulation of a multitape machine by one with a single tape is a little more complicated, but conceptually straightforward.

Consider, for example, the two-tape machine in the configuration depicted in Figure 10.10. The simulating single-tape machine will have four

Figure 10.10

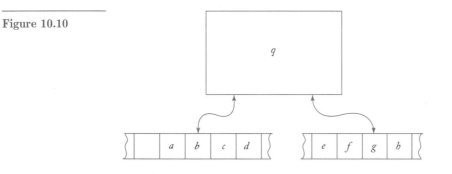

Figure 10.11

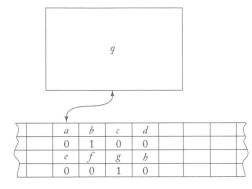

tracks (Figure 10.11). The first track represents the contents of tape 1 of M. The nonblank part of the second track has all zeros, except for a single 1 marking the position of M's read-write head. Tracks 3 and 4 play a similar role for tape 2 of M. Figure 10.11 makes it clear that, for the relevant configurations of $\widehat{M}$ (that is, the ones that have the indicated form), there is a unique corresponding configuration of M.

The representation of a multitape machine by a single-tape machine is similar to that used in the simulation of an off-line machine. The actual steps in the simulation are also much the same, the only difference being that there are more tapes to consider. The outline given for the simulation of off-line machines carries over to this case with minor modifications and suggests a procedure by which the transition function $\widehat{\delta}$ of $\widehat{M}$ can be constructed from the transition function δ of M. While it is not difficult to make the construction precise, it takes a lot of writing. Certainly, the computations of $\widehat{M}$ given the appearance of being lengthy and elaborate, but this has no bearing on the conclusion. Whatever can be done of M can also be done on $\widehat{M}$.

It is important to keep in mind the following point. When we claim that a Turing machine with multiple tapes is no more powerful than a standard one, we are making a statement only about what can be done by these machines, particularly, what languages can be accepted.

Example 10.1   Consider the language $\{a^n b^n\}$. In Example 9.7, we described a laborious method by which this language can be accepted by a Turing machine with one tape. Using a two-tape machine makes the job much easier. Assume that an initial string $a^n b^m$ is written on tape 1 at the beginning of the computation. We then read all the a's, copying them onto tape 2. When we reach the end of the a's, we match the b's on tape 1 against the copied a's on tape 2. This way, we can determine whether there are an equal number of a's and b's without repeated back-and-forth movement of the read-write head.

Remember that the various models of Turing machines are considered equivalent only with respect to their ability to do things, not with respect to ease of programming or any other efficiency measure we might consider. We will return to this important point in Chapter 14.

Multidimensional Turing Machines

A multidimensional Turing machine is one in which the tape can be viewed as extending infinitely in more than one dimension. A diagram of a two-dimensional Turing machine is shown in Figure 10.12.

The formal definition of a two-dimensional Turing machine involves a transition function δ of the form

$$\delta : Q \times \Gamma \to Q \times \Gamma \times \{L, R, U, D\},$$

where U and D specify movement of the read-write head up and down, respectively.

To simulate this machine on a standard Turing machine, we can use the two-track model depicted in Figure 10.13. First, we associate on ordering or address with the cells of the two-dimensional tape. This can be done in a number of ways, for example, in the two-dimensional fashion indicated in Figure 10.12. The two-track tape of the simulating machine will use one track to store cell contents and the other one to keep the associated address. In the scheme of Figure 10.12, the configuration in which cell $(1, 2)$ contains a and cell $(10, -3)$ contains b is shown in Figure 10.13. Note one complication: the cell address can involve arbitrarily large integers, so the address track cannot use a fixed-size field to store addresses. Instead, we must use a variable field-size arrangement, using some special symbols to delimit the fields, as shown in the picture.

Let us assume that, at the start of the simulation of each move, the read-write head of the two-dimensional machine M and the read-write head of the simulating machine $\widehat{M}$ are always on corresponding cells. To simulate a move, the simulating machine $\widehat{M}$ first computes the address of the cell to

Figure 10.12

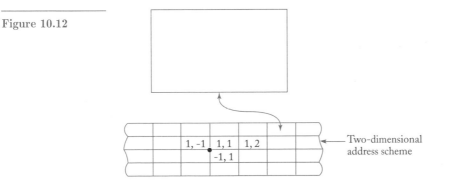

Two-dimensional address scheme

Figure 10.13

	a				b						
1	#	2	#	1	0	#	-	3	#		

which M is to move. Using the two-dimensional address scheme, this is a simple computation. Once the address is computed, $\widehat{M}$ finds the cell with this address on track 2 and then changes the cell contents to account for the move of M. Again, given M, there is a straightforward construction for $\widehat{M}$.

EXERCISES

The purpose of much of our discussion of Turing machines is to lend credence to Turing's thesis by showing how seemingly more complex situations can be simulated on a standard Turing machine. Unfortunately, detailed simulations are very tedious and conceptually uninteresting. In the exercises below, describe the simulations in just enough depth to show that the details can be worked out.

1. A multihead Turing machine can be visualized as a Turing machine with a single tape and a single control unit but with multiple, independent read-write heads. Give a formal definition of a multihead Turing machine, and then show how such a machine can be simulated with a standard Turing machine. Ⓢ

2. Give a formal definition of a multihead-multitape Turing machine. Then show how such a machine can be simulated by a standard Turing machine.

3. Give a formal definition of a Turing machine with a single tape but multiple control units, each with a single read-write head. Show how such a machine can be simulated with a multitape machine.

★ 4. A **queue automaton** is an automaton in which the temporary storage is a queue. Assume that such a machine is an on-line machine, that is, it has no input file, with the string to be processed placed in the queue prior to the start of the computation. Give a formal definition of such an automaton, then investigate its power in relation to Turing machines. Ⓢ

★ 5. Show that for every Turing machine there exists an equivalent standard Turing machine with no more than six states.

6. Reduce the number of required states in Exercise 5 as far as you can (Hint: the smallest possible number is three).

★ 7. A counter is a stack with an alphabet of exactly two symbols, a stack start symbol and a counter symbol. Only the counter symbol can be put on the stack or removed from it. A **counter automaton** is a deterministic automaton with one or more counters as storage. Show that any Turing machine can be simulated using a counter automaton with four counters.

8. Show that every computation that can be done by a standard Turing machine can be done by a multitape machine with a stay-option and at most two states. Ⓢ

9. Write out a detailed program for the computation in Example 10.1.

10.3 Nondeterministic Turing Machines

While Turing's thesis makes it plausible that the specific tape structure is immaterial to the power of the Turing machine, the same cannot be said of nondeterminism. Since nondeterminism involves an element of choice and so has a nonmechanistic flavor, an appeal to Turing's thesis is inappropriate. We must look at the effect of nondeterminism in more detail if we want to argue that nondeterminism adds nothing to the power of a Turing machine. Again we resort to simulation, showing that nondeterministic behavior can be handled deterministically.

Definition 10.2

A nondeterministic Turing machine is an automaton as given by Definition 9.1, except that δ is now a function

$$\delta : Q \times \Gamma \to 2^{Q \times \Gamma \times \{L, R\}}.$$

As always when nondeterminism is involved, the range of δ is a set of possible transitions, any of which can be chosen by the machine.

Example 10.2   If a Turing machine has transitions specified by

$$\delta(q_0, a) = \{(q_1, b, R), (q_2, c, L)\}$$

it is nondeterministic. The moves

$$q_0 aaa \vdash b q_1 aa$$

and

$$q_0 aaa \vdash q_2 \square caa$$

are both possible.

Since it is not clear what role nondeterminism plays in computing functions, nondeterministic automata are usually viewed as accepters. A nondeterministic Turing machine is said to accept w if there is any possible sequence of moves such that

$$q_0 w \overset{*}{\vdash} x_1 q_f x_2,$$

with $q_f \in F$. A nondeterministic machine may have moves available that lead to a nonfinal state or to an infinite loop. But, as always with nondeterminism, these alternatives are irrelevant; all we are interested in is the existence of some sequence of moves leading to acceptance.

To show that a nondeterministic Turing machine is no more powerful than a deterministic one, we need to provide a deterministic equivalent for the nondeterminism. We have already alluded to one. Nondeterminism can be viewed as a deterministic backtracking algorithm, and a deterministic machine can simulate a nondeterministic one as long as it can handle the bookkeeping involved in the backtracking. To see how this can be done simply, let us consider an alternative view of nondeterminism, one which is useful in many arguments: a nondeterministic machine can be seen as one that has the ability to replicate itself whenever necessary. When more than one move is possible, the machine produces as many replicas as needed and gives each replica the task of carrying out one of the alternatives.

This view of nondeterminism may seem particularly nonmechanistic. Unlimited replication is certainly not within the power of present-day computers. Nevertheless, the process can be simulated by a deterministic Turing machine. Consider a Turing machine with a two-dimensional tape (Figure 10.14). Each pair of horizontal tracks represents one machine; the top track containing the machine's tape, the bottom one for indicating its internal state and the position of the read-write head. Whenever a new machine is to be created, two new tracks are started with the appropriate information. Figure 10.15 represents the initial configuration of the machine in Example 10.2 and its successor configurations. The simulating machine searches all active tracks; they are bracketed with special markers and so can always be found. It then carries out the indicated moves, activating new machines as needed. Quite a few details have to be resolved before we can claim to have a reasonable outline of the simulation, but we will leave this to the reader.

Figure 10.14

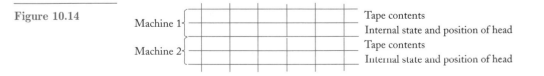

Machine 1 — Tape contents / Internal state and position of head
Machine 2 — Tape contents / Internal state and position of head

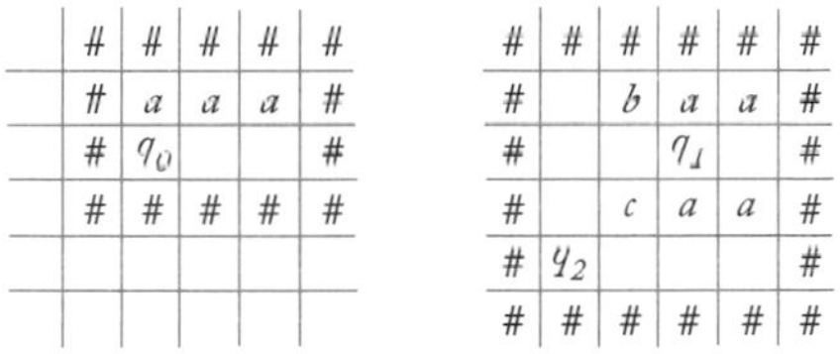

Figure 10.15
Simulation of a
nondeterministic
move.

#	#	#	#	#
#	a	a	a	#
#	q_0			#
#	#	#	#	#

#	#	#	#	#	#
#		b	a	a	#
#			q_1		#
#		c	a	a	#
#	q_2				#
#	#	#	#	#	#

Based on this simulation, our conclusion is that for every nondeterministic Turing machine there exists an equivalent deterministic one. Because of its importance, we state this formally.

Theorem 10.2   The class of deterministic Turing machines and the class of nondeterministic Turing machines are equivalent.

Proof: Use the construction suggested above to show that any nondeterministic Turing machine can be simulated by a deterministic one.   ∎

EXERCISES

1. Discuss in detail the simulation of a nondeterministic Turing machine by a deterministic one. Indicate explicitly how new machines are created, how active machines are identified, and how machines that halt are removed from further consideration.

2. Show how a two-dimensional nondeterministic Turing machine can be simulated by a deterministic machine.

3. Write a program for a nondeterministic Turing machine that accepts the language

$$L = \left\{ ww : w \in \{a, b\}^+ \right\}.$$

    Contrast this with a deterministic solution.   Ⓢ

4. Outline how one would write a program for a nondeterministic Turing machine to accept the language

$$L = \left\{ ww^R w : w \in \{a, b\}^+ \right\}.$$

5. Write a simple program for a nondeterministic Turing machine that accepts the language

$$L = \left\{ xww^R y : x, y, w \in \{a, b\}^+, |x| \geq |y| \right\}.$$

    How would you solve this problem deterministically?

6. Design a nondeterministic Turing machine that accepts the language

$$L = \{a^n : n \text{ is not a prime number}\}. \quad \text{⑤}$$

★ 7. A two-stack automaton is a nondeterministic pushdown automaton with two independent stacks. To define such an automaton, we modify Definition 7.1 so that

$$\delta : Q \times (\Sigma \cup \{\lambda\}) \times \Gamma \times \Gamma \to \text{ finite subsets of } Q \times \Gamma^* \times \Gamma^*.$$

A move depends on the tops of the two stacks and results in new values being pushed on these two stacks. Show that the class of two-stack automata is equivalent to the class of Turing machines. ⑤

10.4 A Universal Turing Machine

Consider the following argument against Turing's thesis: "A Turing machine as presented in Definition 9.1 is a special purpose computer. Once δ is defined, the machine is restricted to carrying out one particular type of computation. Digital computers, on the other hand, are general purpose machines that can be programmed to do different jobs at different times. Consequently, Turing machines cannot be considered equivalent to general purpose digital computers."

This objection can be overcome by designing a reprogrammable Turing machine, called a **universal Turing machine**. A universal Turing machine M_u is an automaton that, given as input the description of any Turing machine M and a string w, can simulate the computation of M on w. To construct such an M_u, we first choose a standard way of describing Turing machines. We may, without loss of generality, assume that

$$Q = \{q_1, q_2, ..., q_n\},$$

with q_1 the initial state, q_2 the single final state, and

$$\Gamma = \{a_1, a_2, ..., a_m\},$$

where a_1 represents the blank. We then select an encoding in which q_1 is represented by 1, q_2 is represented by 11, and so on. Similarly, a_1 is encoded as 1, a_2 as 11, etc. The symbol 0 will be used as a separator between the 1's. With the initial and final state and the blank defined by this convention, any Turing machine can be described completely with δ only. The transition function is encoded according to this scheme, with the arguments and result in some prescribed sequence. For example, $\delta(q_1, a_2) = (q_2, a_3, L)$ might appear as

$$\cdots 1\,0\,1\,1\,0\,1\,1\,0\,1\,1\,1\,0\,1\,0 \cdots.$$

Figure 10.16

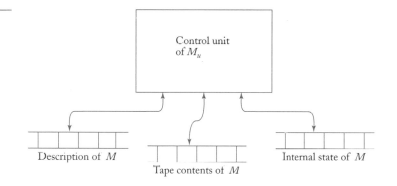

It follows from this that any Turing machine has a finite encoding as a string on $\{0,1\}^{\dagger}$, and that, given any encoding of M, we can decode it uniquely. Some strings will not represent any Turing machine (e.g., the strong 00011), but we can easily spot these, so they are of no concern.

A universal Turing machine M_u then has an input alphabet that includes $\{0,1\}$ and the structure of a multitape machine, as shown in Figure 10.16.

For any input M and w, tape 1 will keep an encoded definition of M. Tape 2 will contain the tape contents of M, and tape 3 the internal state of M. M_u looks first at the contents of tapes 2 and 3 to determine the configuration of M. It then consults tape 1 to see what M would do in this configuration. Finally, tapes 2 and 3 will be modified to reflect the result of the move.

It is within reason to construct an actual universal Turing machine (see, for example, Denning, Dennis, and Qualitz 1978), but the process is uninteresting. We prefer instead to appeal to Turing's hypothesis. The implementation clearly can be done using some programming language; in fact, the program suggested in Exercise 1, Section 9.1 is a realization of a universal Turing machine in a higher level language. Therefore, we expect that it can also be done by a standard Turing machine. We are then justified in claiming the existence of a Turing machine that, given any program, can carry out the computations specified by that program and that is therefore a proper model for a general purpose computer.

The observation that every Turing machine can be represented by a string of 0's and 1's has important implications. But before we explore these implications, we need to review some results from set theory.

Some sets are finite, but most of the interesting sets (and languages) are infinite. For infinite sets, we distinguish between sets that are **countable** and sets that are **uncountable**. A set is said to be countable if its elements can be put into a one-to-one correspondence with the positive integers. By this we mean that the elements of the set can be written in some order, say, $x_1, x_2, x_3, ...$, so that every element of the set has some finite index. For example, the set of all even integers can be written in the order $0, 2, 4, ...$

Figure 10.17

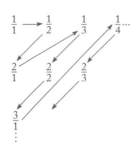

Since any positive integer $2n$ occurs in position $n + 1$, the set is countable. This should not be too surprising, but there are more complicated examples, some of which may seem counterintuitive. Take the set of all quotients of the form p/q, where p and q are positive integers. How should we order this set to show that it is countable? We cannot write

$$\frac{1}{1}, \frac{1}{2}, \frac{1}{3}, \frac{1}{4}, \ldots$$

because then $\frac{2}{3}$ would never appear. This does not imply that the set is uncountable; in this case, there is a clever way of ordering the set to show that it is in fact countable. Look at the scheme depicted in Figure 10.17, and write down the element in the order encountered following the arrows. This gives us

$$\frac{1}{1}, \frac{1}{2}, \frac{2}{1}, \frac{1}{3}, \frac{2}{2}, \ldots$$

Here the element $\frac{2}{3}$ occurs in the eighth place, and every element has some place in the sequence. The set is therefore countable.

We see from this example that we can prove that a set is countable if we can produce a method by which its elements can be written in some sequence. We call such a method an **enumeration procedure**. Since an enumeration procedure is some kind of mechanical process, we can use a Turing machine model to define it formally.

Definition 10.3

Let S be a set of strings on some alphabet Σ. Then an enumeration procedure for S is a Turing machine that can carry out the sequence of steps

$$q_0 \square \overset{*}{\vdash} q_s x_1 \ \# \ s_1 \overset{*}{\vdash} q_s x_2 \ \# \ s_2 \ldots,$$

with $x_i \in \Gamma^* - \{\#\}, s_i \in S$, in such a way that any s in S is produced in a finite number of steps. The state q_s is a state signifying membership in S; that is, whenever q_s is entered, the string following $\#$ must be in S.

Not every set is countable. As we will see in the next chapter, there are some uncountable sets. But any set for which an enumeration procedure exists is countable because the enumeration gives the required sequence.

Strictly speaking, an enumeration procedure cannot be called an algorithm, since it will not terminate when S is infinite. Nevertheless, it can be considered a meaningful process, because it produces well-defined and predictable results.

Example 10.3

Let $\Sigma = \{a, b, c\}$. We can show that the $S = \Sigma^{!}$ is countable if we can find an enumeration procedure that produces its elements in some order, say in the order in which they would appear in a dictionary. However, the order used in dictionaries is not suitable without modification. In a dictionary, all words beginning with a are listed before the string b. But when there are an infinite number of a words, we will never reach b, thus violating the condition of Definition 10.3 that any given string be listed after a finite number of steps.

Instead, we can use a modified order, in which we take the length of the string as the first criterion, followed by an alphabetic ordering of all equal-length strings. This is an enumeration procedure that produces the sequence

$$a, b, c, aa, ab, ac, ba, bb, bc, ca, cb, cc, aaa, \ldots.$$

As we will have several uses for such an ordering we will call it the **proper order**.

An important consequence of the above discussion is that Turing machines are countable.

Theorem 10.3

The set of all Turing machines, although infinite, is countable.

Proof: We can encode each Turing machine using 0 and 1. With this encoding, we then construct the following enumeration procedure.

1. Generate the next string in $\{0, 1\}^{+}$ in proper order.

2. Check the generated string to see if it defines a Turing machine. If so, write it on the tape in the form required by Definition 10.3. If not, ignore the string.

3. Return to Step 1.

Since every Turing machine has a finite description, any specific machine will eventually be generated by this process. ∎

The particular ordering of Turing machines depends on the encoding we use; if we use a different encoding, we must expect a different ordering. This is of no consequence, however, and shows that the ordering itself is unimportant. What matters is the existence of some ordering.

EXERCISES

1. Sketch an algorithm that examines a string in $\{0,1\}^+$ to determine whether or not it represents an encoded Turing machine.

2. Give a complete encoding, using the suggested method, for the Turing machine with

$$\delta(q_1, a_1) = (q_1, a_1, R),$$
$$\delta(q_1, a_2) = (q_3, a_1, L),$$
$$\delta(q_3, a_1) = (q_2, a_2, L).$$

3. Sketch a Turing machine program that enumerates the set $\{0,1\}^+$ in proper order. **ⓢ**

4. What is the index of $0^i 1^j$ in Exercise 3?

5. Design a Turing machine that enumerates the following set in proper order.

$$L = \{a^n b^n : n \geq 1\}$$

6. For Example 10.3, find a function $f(w)$ that gives for each w its index in the proper ordering.

7. Show that the set of all triplets, (i, j, k) with i, j, k positive integers, is countable.

8. Suppose that S_1 and S_2 are countable sets. Show that then $S_1 \cup S_2$ and $S_1 \times S_2$ are also countable. **ⓢ**

9. Show that the Cartesian product of a finite number of countable sets is countable.

10.5 Linear Bounded Automata

While it is not possible to extend the power of the standard Turing machine by complicating the tape structure, it is possible to limit it by restricting the way in which the tape can be used. We have already seen an example of this with pushdown automata. A pushdown automaton can be regarded as a nondeterministic Turing machine with a tape that is restricted to being used like a stack. We can also restrict the tape usage in other ways; for example, we might permit only a finite part of the tape to be used as work space. It can be shown that this leads us back to finite automata (see

Exercise 3 at the end of this section), so we need not pursue this. But there is a way of limiting tape use that leads to a more interesting situation: we allow the machine to use only that part of the tape occupied by the input. Thus, more space is available for long input strings than for short ones, generating another class of machines, the **linear bounded automata** (or **lba**).

A linear bounded automaton, like a standard Turing machine, has an unbounded tape, but how much of the tape can be used is a function of the input. In particular, we restrict the usable part of the tape to exactly the cells taken by the input. To enforce this, we can envision the input as bracketed by two special symbols, the **left-end marker** ([) and the **right-end marker** (]). For an input w, the initial configuration of the Turing machine is given by the instantaneous description $q_0 [w]$. The end markers cannot be rewritten, and the read-write head cannot move to the left of [or to the right of]. We sometimes say that the read-write head "bounces" off the end markers.

Definition 10.4

A linear bounded automaton is a nondeterministic Turing machine $M = (Q, \Sigma, \Gamma, \delta, q_0, \Box, F)$, as in Definition 10.2, subject to the restriction that Σ must contain two special symbols [and], such that $\delta(q_i, [)$ can contain only elements of the form $(q_j, [, R)$, and $\delta(q_i,])$ can contain only elements of the form $(q_j,], L)$.

Definition 10.5

A string w is accepted by a linear bounded automaton if there is a possible sequence of moves

$$q_0 [w] \overset{*}{\vdash} [x_1 q_f x_2]$$

for some $q_f \in F, x_1, x_2 \in \Gamma^*$. The language accepted by the lba is the set of all such accepted strings.

Note that in this definition a linear bounded automaton is assumed to be nondeterministic. This is not just a matter of convenience but essential to the discussion of lba's. While one can define deterministic lba's, it is not known whether they are equivalent to the nondeterministic version. For some exploration of this, see Exercise 8 at the end of this section.

| Example 10.4 | The language |

$$L = \{a^n b^n c^n : n \geq 1\}$$

is accepted by some linear bounded automaton. This follows from the discussion in Example 9.8. The computation outlined there does not require space outside the original input, so it can be carried out by a linear bounded automaton.

| Example 10.5 | Find a linear bounded automaton that accepts the language |

$$L = \left\{ a^{n!} : n \geq 0 \right\}.$$

One way to solve the problem is to divide the number of a's successively by $2, 3, 4, \ldots$, until we can either accept or reject the string. If the input is in L, eventually there will be a single a left; if not, at some point a nonzero remainder will arise. We sketch the solution to point out one tacit implication of Definition 10.4. The tape of a linear bounded automaton may be multitrack, and the extra tracks can be used as scratch space. For this problem, we can use a two-track tape. The first track contains the number of a's left during the process of division, and the second track contains the current divisor (Figure 10.18). The actual solution is fairly simple. Using the divisor on the second track, we divide the number of a's on the first track, say by removing all symbols except those at multiples of the divisor. After this, we increment the divisor by one, and continue until we either find a nonzero remainder or are left with a single a.

The last two examples suggest that linear bounded automata are more powerful than pushdown automata, since neither of the languages are context-free. To prove such a conjecture, we still have to show that any context-free language can be accepted by a linear bounded automaton. We will do this later in a somewhat roundabout way; a more direct approach is suggested in Exercises 5 and 6 at the end of this section. It is not so easy to make a conjecture on the relation between Turing machines and linear bounded automata. Problems like Example 10.5 are invariably solvable by a linear bounded automaton, since an amount of scratch space proportional

| Figure 10.18 |

[	a	a	a	a	a	a	]	a's to be examined
[	a	a	a				]	Current divisor

to the length of the input is available. In fact, it is quite difficult to come up with a concrete and explicitly defined language that cannot be accepted by any linear bounded automaton. In Chapter 11 we will show that the class of linear bounded automata is less powerful than the class of unrestricted Turing machines, but a demonstration of this requires a lot more work.

EXERCISES

1. Give details for the solution of Example 10.5.

2. Find a solution for Example 10.5 that does not require a second track as scratch space. **S**

3. Consider an off-line Turing machine in which the input can be read only once, moving left to right, and not rewritten. On its work tape, it can use at most n extra cells for work space, where n is fixed for all inputs. Show that such a machine is equivalent to a finite automaton.

4. Find linear bounded automata for the following languages.

   (a) $L = \{a^n : n = m^2, m \geq 1\}$

   (b) $L = \{a^n : n$ is a prime number$\}$

   (c) $L = \{a^n : n$ is not a prime number$\}$

   (d) $L = \{ww : w \in \{a, b\}^+\}$

   (e) $L = \{w^n : w \in \{a, b\}^+, n \geq 1\}$ **S**

   (f) $L = \{www^R : w \in \{a, b\}^+\}$

5. Find an lba for the complement of the language in Example 10.5, assuming that $\Sigma = \{a, b\}$.

6. Show that for every context-free language there exists an accepting pda, such that the number of symbols in the stack never exceeds the length of the input string by more than one. **S**

7. Use the observation in the above exercise to show that any context-free language not containing λ is accepted by some linear bounded automaton.

8. To define a deterministic linear bounded automaton, we can use Definition 10.4, but require that the Turing machine be deterministic. Examine your solutions to Exercise 4. Are the solutions all deterministic linear bounded automata? If not, try to find solutions that are.

Chapter 11

A Hierarchy of
Formal Languages
and Automata

W e now return our attention to our main interest, the study of formal languages. Our immediate goal will be to examine the languages associated with Turing machines and some of their restrictions. Because Turing machines can perform any kind of algorithmic computation, we expect to find that the family of languages associated with them is quite broad. It includes not only regular and context-free languages, but also the various examples we have encountered that lie outside these families. The nontrivial question is whether there are *any* languages that are not accepted by some Turing machine. We will answer this question first by showing that there are more languages than Turing machines, so that there must be some languages for which there are no Turing machines. The proof is short and elegant, but nonconstructive, and gives little insight into the problem. For this reason, we will establish the existence of languages not recognizable by Turing machines through more explicit examples that actually allow us to identify one such language. Another avenue of investigation will be to look at the relation between Turing machines and certain types of grammars and to establish a connection between these grammars and regular and context-free grammars. This leads to a hierarchy of grammars and through it to a method for classifying language families. Some set-theoretic diagrams illustrate the relationships between various language families clearly.

Strictly speaking, many of the arguments in this chapter are valid only for languages that do not include the empty string. This restriction arises from the fact that Turing machines, as we have defined them, cannot accept the empty string. To avoid having to rephrase the definition or having to add a repeated disclaimer, we make the tacit assumption that the languages discussed in this chapter, unless otherwise stated, do not contain λ. It is a trivial matter to restate everything so that λ is included, but we will leave this to the reader.

11.1 Recursive and Recursively Enumerable Languages

We start with some terminology for the languages associated with Turing machines. In doing so, we must make the important distinction between languages for which there exists an accepting Turing machine and languages for which there exists a membership algorithm. Because a Turing machine does not necessarily halt on input that it does not accept, the first does not imply the second.

Definition 11.1

A language L is said to be **recursively enumerable** if there exists a Turing machine that accepts it.

This definition implies only that there exists a Turing machine M, such that, for every $w \in L$,

$$q_0 w \overset{*}{\vdash}_M x_1 q_f x_2,$$

with q_f a final state. The definition says nothing about what happens for w not in L; it may be that the machine halts in a nonfinal state or that it never halts and goes into an infinite loop. We can be more demanding and ask that the machine tell us whether or not any given input is in its language.

Definition 11.2

A language L on Σ is said to be **recursive** if there exists a Turing machine M that accepts L and that halts on every w in Σ^+. In other words, a language is recursive if and only if there exists a membership algorithm for it.

If a language is recursive, then there exists an easily constructed enumeration procedure. Suppose that M is a Turing machine that determines membership in a recursive language L. We first construct another Turing machine, say $\widehat{M}$, that generates all strings in Σ^+ in proper order, let us say $w_1, w_2, \ldots$. As these strings are generated, they become the input to M, which is modified so that it writes strings on its tape only if they are in L.

That there is also an enumeration procedure for every recursively enumerable language is not as easy to see. We cannot use the above argument as it stands, because if some w_j is not in L, the machine M, when started with w_j on its tape, may never halt and therefore never get to the strings in L that follow w_j in the enumeration. To make sure that this does not happen, the computation is performed in a different way. We first get $\widehat{M}$ to generate w_1 and let M execute one move on it. Then we let $\widehat{M}$ generate w_2 and let M execute one move on w_2, followed by the second move on w_1. After this, we generate w_3 and do one step on w_3, the second step on w_2, the third step on w_1, and so on. The order of performance is depicted in Figure 11.1. From this, it is clear that M will never get into an infinite loop. Since any $w \in L$ is generated by $\widehat{M}$ and accepted by M in a finite number of steps, every string in L is eventually produced by M.

It is easy to see that every language for which an enumeration procedure exists is recursively enumerable. We simply compare the given input string against successive strings generated by the enumeration procedure. If $w \in L$, we will eventually get a match, and the process can be terminated.

Definitions 11.1 and 11.2 give us very little insight into the nature of either recursive or recursively enumerable languages. These definitions attach names to language families associated with Turing machines, but shed

Figure 11.1

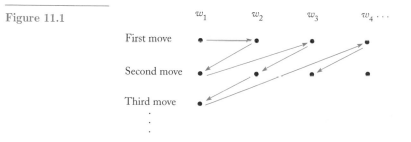

no light on the nature of representative languages in these families. Nor do they tell us much about the relationships between these languages or their connection to the language families we have encountered before. We are therefore immediately faced with question such as "Are there languages that are recursively enumerable but not recursive?" and "Are there languages, describable somehow, that are not recursively enumerable?" While we will be able to supply some answers, we will not be able to produce very explicit examples to illustrate these questions, especially the second one.

Languages That Are Not Recursively Enumerable

We can establish the existence of languages that are not recursively enumerable in a variety of ways. One is very short and uses a very fundamental and elegant result of mathematics.

Theorem 11.1   Let S be an infinite countable set. Then its powerset 2^s is not countable.

Proof: Let $S = \{s_1, s_2, s_3, ...\}$. Then any element t of 2^s can be represented by a sequence of 0's and 1's, with a 1 in position i if and only if s_i is in t. For example, the set $\{s_2, s_3, s_6\}$ is represented by 01100100..., while $\{s_1, s_3, s_5, ...\}$ is represented by 10101.... Clearly, any element of 2^S can be represented by such a sequence, and any such sequence represents a unique element of 2^S. Suppose that 2^S were countable; then its elements could be written in some order, say $t_1, t_2, ...$, and we could enter these into a table, as shown in Figure 11.2. In this table, take the elements in the main diagonal, and complement each entry, that is, replace 0 with 1, and vice versa. In the example in Figure 11.2, the elements are 1100..., so we get 0011... as the result. The new sequence represents some element of 2^S, say t_i for some i. But it cannot be t_1 because it differs from t_1 through s_1. For the same

Figure 11.2

$$
\begin{array}{cccccc}
t_1 & \boxed{1} & 0 & 0 & 0 & 0 & \cdots \\
t_2 & 1 & \boxed{1} & 0 & 0 & 0 & \cdots \\
t_3 & 1 & 1 & \boxed{0} & 1 & 0 & \cdots \\
t_4 & 1 & 1 & 0 & \boxed{0} & 1 & \cdots \\
\end{array}
$$

reason it cannot be t_2, t_3, or any other t_i. This contradiction creates a logical impasse that can be removed only by throwing out the assumption that 2^S is countable. ∎

This kind of argument, because it involves a manipulation of the diagonal elements of a table, is called **diagonalization**. The technique is attributed to the mathematician G. F. Cantor, who used it to demonstrate that the set of real numbers is not countable. In the next few chapters, we will see a similar argument in several contexts. Theorem 11.1 is diagonalization in its purest form.

As an immediate consequence of this result, we can show that, in some sense, there are fewer Turing machines than there are languages, so that there must be some languages that are not recursively enumerable.

Theorem 11.2 For any nonempty Σ, there exist languages that are not recursively enumerable.

Proof: A language is a subset of Σ^*, and every such subset is a language. Therefore the set of all languages is exactly 2^{Σ^*}. Since Σ^* is infinite, Theorem 11.1 tells us that the set of all languages on Σ is not countable. But the set of all Turing machines can be enumerated, so the set of all recursively enumerable languages is countable. By Exercise 16 at the end of this section, this implies that there must be some languages on Σ that are not recursively enumerable. ∎

This proof, although short and simple, is in many ways unsatisfying. It is completely nonconstructive and, while it tells us of the existence of some languages that are not recursively enumerable, it gives us no feeling at all for what these languages might look like. In the next set of results, we investigate the conclusion more explicitly.

A Language That Is Not Recursively Enumerable

Since every language that can be described in a direct algorithmic fashion can be accepted by a Turing machine and hence is recursively enumerable, the description of a language that is not recursively enumerable must be indirect. Nevertheless, it is possible. The argument involves a variation on the diagonalization theme.

Theorem 11.3 There exists a recursively enumerable language whose complement is not recursively enumerable.

Proof: Let $\Sigma = \{a\}$, and consider the set of all Turing machines with this input alphabet. By Theorem 10.3, this set is countable, so we can associate an order $M_1, M_2, ...$ with its elements. For each Turing machine M_i, there is an associated recursively enumerable language $L(M_i)$. Conversely, for each recursively enumerable language on Σ, there is some Turing machine that accepts it.

We now consider a new language L defined as follows. For each $i \geq 1$, the string a^i is in L if and only if $a^i \in L(M_i)$. It is clear that the language L is well defined, since the statement $a^i \in L(M_i)$, and hence $a^i \in L$, must either be true or false. Next, we consider the complement of L,

$$\overline{L} = \left\{ a^i : a^i \notin L(M_i) \right\}, \tag{11.1}$$

which is also well defined but, as we will show, is not recursively enumerable.

We will show this by contradiction, starting from the assumption that $\overline{L}$ is recursively enumerable. If this is so, then there must be some Turing machine, say M_k, such that

$$\overline{L} = L(M_k). \tag{11.2}$$

Consider the string a^k. Is it in L or in $\overline{L}$? Suppose that $a^k \in \overline{L}$. By (11.2) this implies that

$$a^k \in L(M_k).$$

But (11.1) now implies that

$$a^k \notin \overline{L}.$$

Conversely, if we assume that a^k is in L, then $a^k \notin \overline{L}$ and (11.2) implies that

$$a^k \notin L(M_k).$$

But then from (11.1) we get that

$$a^k \in \overline{L}.$$

The contradiction is inescapable, and we must conclude that our assumption that $\overline{L}$ is recursively enumerable is false.

To complete the proof of the theorem as stated, we must still show that L is recursively enumerable. We can use for this the known enumeration procedure for Turing machines. Given a^i, we first find i by counting the number of a's. We then use the enumeration procedure for Turing machines to find M_i. Finally, we give its description along with a^i to a universal Turing machine M_u that simulates the action of M on a^i. If a^i is in L, the computation carried out by M_u will eventually halt. The combined effect of this is a Turing machine that accepts every $a^i \in L$. Therefore, by Definition 11.1, L is recursively enumerable. ∎

The proof of this theorem explicitly exhibits, through (11.1), a well-defined language that is not recursively enumerable. This is not to say that there is an easy, intuitive interpretation of $\overline{L}$; it would be difficult to exhibit more than a few trivial members of this language. Nevertheless, $\overline{L}$ is properly defined.

A Language That Is Recursively Enumerable But Not Recursive

Next, we show there are some languages that are recursively enumerable but not recursive. Again, we need do so in a rather roundabout way. We begin by establishing a subsidiary result.

Theorem 11.4   If a language L and its complement L are both recursively enumerable, then both languages are recursive. If L is recursive, then $\overline{L}$ is also recursive, and consequently both are recursively enumerable.

Proof: If L and $\overline{L}$ are both recursively enumerable, then there exist Turing machines M and $\widehat{M}$ that serve as enumeration procedures for L and $\overline{L}$, respectively. The first will produce $w_1, w_2, \ldots$ in L, the second $\widehat{w}_1, \widehat{w}_2, \ldots$ in $\overline{L}$. Suppose now we are given any $w \in \Sigma^+$. We first let M generate w_1 and compare it with w. If they are not the same, we let $\widehat{M}$ generate $\widehat{w}_1$ and compare again. If we need to continue, we next let M generate w_2, then $\widehat{M}$ generate $\hat{w}_2$, and so on. Any $w \in \Sigma^+$ will be generated either by M or $\widehat{M}$, so eventually we will get a match. If the matching string is produced by M, w belongs to L, otherwise it is in $\overline{L}$. The process is a membership algorithm for both L and $\overline{L}$, so they are both recursive.

For the converse, assume that L is recursive. Then there exists a membership algorithm for it. But this becomes a membership algorithm for $\overline{L}$ by simply complementing its conclusion. Therefore $\overline{L}$ is recursive. Since any recursive language is recursively enumerable, the proof is completed. ∎

From this, we conclude directly that the family of recursively enumerable languages and the family of recursive languages are not identical. The language L in Theorem 11.3 is in the first but not in the second family.

Theorem 11.5   There exists a recursively enumerable language that is not recursive; that is, the family of recursive languages is a proper subset of the family of recursively enumerable languages.

Proof: Consider the language L of Theorem 11.3. This language is recursively enumerable, but its complement is not. Therefore, by Theorem 11.4, it is not recursive, giving us the looked-for example. ∎

We conclude from this that there are indeed well-defined languages for which one cannot construct a membership algorithm.

EXERCISES

1. Prove that the set of all real numbers is not countable.

2. Prove that the set of all languages that are not recursively enumerable is not countable. **S**

3. Let L be a finite language. Show that then L^+ is recursively enumerable. Suggest an enumeration procedure for L^+.

4. Let L be a context-free language. Show that L^+ is recursively enumerable and suggest an enumeration procedure for it.

5. Show that, if a language is not recursively enumerable, its complement cannot be recursive.

6. Show that the family of recursively enumerable languages is closed under union. **S**

7. Is the family of recursively enumerable languages closed under intersection?

8. Show that the family of recursive languages is closed under union and intersection.

9. Show that the families of recursively enumerable and recursive languages are closed under reversal.

10. Is the family of recursive languages closed under concatenation?

11. Prove that the complement of a context-free language must be recursive. **S**

12. Let L_1 be recursive and L_2 recursively enumerable. Show that $L_2 - L_1$ is necessarily recursively enumerable.

13. Suppose that L is such that there exists a Turing machine that enumerates the elements of L in proper order. Show that this means that L is recursive.

14. If L is recursive, is it necessarily true that L^+ is also recursive? **S**

15. Choose a particular encoding for Turing machines, and with it, find one element of the language $\overline{L}$ in Theorem 11.3.

16. Let S_1 be a countable set, S_2 a set that is not countable, and $S_1 \subset S_2$. Show that S_2 must then contain an infinite number of elements that are not in S_1.

17. In Exercise 16, show that in fact $S_2 - S_1$ cannot be countable.

18. Why does the argument in Theorem 11.1 fail when S is finite? **S**

19. Show that the set of all irrational numbers is not countable.

11.2 Unrestricted Grammars

To investigate the connection between recursively enumerable languages and grammars, we return to the general definition of a grammar in Chapter 1. In Definition 1.1 the production rules were allowed to take any form, but various restrictions were later made to get specific grammar types. If we take the general form and impose no restrictions, we get unrestricted grammars.

Definition 11.3

A grammar $G = (V, T, S, P)$ is called **unrestricted** if all the productions are of the form

$$u \rightarrow v,$$

where u is in $(V \cup T)^+$ and v is in $(V \cup T)^*$.

In an unrestricted grammar, essentially no conditions are imposed on the productions. Any number of variables and terminals can be on the left or right, and these can occur in any order. There is only one restriction: λ is not allowed as the left side of a production.

As we will see, unrestricted grammars are much more powerful than restricted forms like the regular and context-free grammars we have studied so far. In fact, unrestricted grammars correspond to the largest family of languages so we can hope to recognize by mechanical means; that is, unrestricted grammars generate exactly the family of recursively enumerable languages. We show this in two parts; the first is quite straightforward, but the second involves a lengthy construction.

Theorem 11.6

Any language generated by an unrestricted grammar is recursively enumerable.

Proof: The grammar in effect defines a procedure for enumerating all strings in the language systematically. For example, we can list all w in L such that

$$S \Rightarrow w,$$

that is, w is derived in one step. Since the set of the productions of the grammar is finite, there will be a finite number of such strings. Next, we list all w in L that can be derived in two steps

$$S \Rightarrow x \Rightarrow w,$$

and so on. We can simulate these derivations on a Turing machine and, therefore, have an enumeration procedure for the language. Hence it is recursively enumerable. ∎

This part of the correspondence between recursively enumerable languages and unrestricted grammars is not surprising. The grammar generates strings by a well-defined algorithmic process, so the derivations can be done on a Turing machine. To show the converse, we describe how any Turing machine can be mimicked by an unrestricted grammar.

We are given a Turing machine $M = (Q, \Sigma, \Gamma, \delta, q_0, \square, F)$ and want to produce a grammar G such that $L(G) = L(M)$. The idea behind the construction is relatively simple, but its implementation becomes notationally cumbersome.

Since the computation of the Turing machine can be described by the sequence of instantaneous descriptions

$$q_0 w \overset{*}{\vdash} x q_f y, \tag{11.3}$$

we will try to arrange it so that the corresponding grammar has the property that

$$q_0 w \overset{*}{\Rightarrow} x q_f y, \tag{11.4}$$

if and only if (11.3) holds. This is not hard to do; what is more difficult to see is how to make the connection between (11.4) and what we really want, namely,

$$S \overset{*}{\Rightarrow} w$$

for all w satisfying (11.3). To achieve this, we construct a grammar which, in broad outline, has the following properties:

1. S can derive $q_0 w$ for all $w \in \Sigma^+$.

2. (11.4) is possible if and only if (11.3) holds.

3. When a string $x q_f y$ with $q_f \in F$ is generated, the grammar transforms this string into the original w.

The complete sequence of derivations is then

$$S \stackrel{*}{\Rightarrow} q_0 w \stackrel{*}{\Rightarrow} x q_f y \stackrel{*}{\Rightarrow} w. \tag{11.5}$$

The third step in the above derivation is the troublesome one. How can the grammar remember w if it is modified during the second step? We solve this by encoding strings so that the coded version originally has two copies of w. The first is saved, while the second is used in the steps in (11.4). When a final configuration is entered, the grammar erases everything except the saved w.

To produce two copies of w and to handle the state symbol of M (which eventually has to be removed by the grammar), we introduce variables V_{ab} and V_{aib} for all $a \in \Sigma \cup \{\sqcup\}$, $b \in \Gamma$, and all i such that $q_i \subset Q$. The variable V_{ab} encodes the two symbols a and b, while V_{aib} encodes a and b as well as the state q_i.

The first step in (11.5) can be achieved (in the encoded form) by

$$S \rightarrow V_{\square\square} S \,|\, S V_{\square\square} \,|\, T, \tag{11.6}$$

$$T \rightarrow T V_{aa} \,|\, V_{a0a}, \tag{11.7}$$

for all $a \in \Sigma$. These productions allow the grammar to generate an encoded version of any string $q_0 w$ with an arbitrary number of leading and trailing blanks.

For the second step, for each transition

$$\delta\left(q_i, c\right) = \left(q_j, d, R\right)$$

of M, we put into the grammar productions

$$V_{aic} V_{pq} \rightarrow V_{ad} V_{pjq}, \tag{11.8}$$

for all $a, p \in \Sigma \cup \{\sqcap\}$, $q \in \Gamma$. For each

$$\delta\left(q_i, c\right) = \left(q_j, d, L\right)$$

of M, we include in G

$$V_{pq} V_{aic} \rightarrow V_{pjq} V_{ad}, \tag{11.9}$$

for all $a, p \in \Sigma \cup \{\square\}$, $q \in \Gamma$.

If in the second step, M enters a final state, the grammar must then get rid of everything except w, which is saved in the first indices of the V's. Therefore, for every $q_j \in F$, we include productions

$$V_{ajb} \rightarrow a, \tag{11.10}$$

for all $a \in \Sigma \cup \{\Box\}$, $b \in \Gamma$. This creates the first terminal in the string, which then causes a rewriting in the rest by

$$cV_{ab} \rightarrow ca, \tag{11.11}$$

$$V_{ab}c \rightarrow ac, \tag{11.12}$$

for all $a, c \in \Sigma \cup \{\Box\}$, $b \in \Gamma$. We need one more special production

$$\Box \rightarrow \lambda. \tag{11.13}$$

This last production takes care of the case when M moves outside that part of the tape occupied by the input w. To make things work in this case, we must first use (11.6) and (11.7) to generate

$$\Box \ldots \Box q_0 w \Box \ldots \Box,$$

representing all the tape region used. The extraneous blanks are removed at the end by (11.13).

The following example illustrates this complicated construction. Carefully check each step in the example to see what the various productions do and why they are needed.

Example 11.1   Let $M = (Q, \Sigma, \Gamma, \delta, q_0, \Box, F)$ be a Turing machine with

$$Q = \{q_0, q_1\},$$
$$\Gamma = \{a, b, \Box\},$$
$$\Sigma = \{a, b\},$$
$$F = \{q_1\},$$

and

$$\delta(q_0, a) = (q_0, a, R),$$
$$\delta(q_0, \Box) = (q_1, \Box, L).$$

This machine accepts $L(aa^*)$.

Consider now the computation

$$q_0aa \vdash aq_0a \vdash aaq_0\Box \vdash aq_1a\Box \tag{11.14}$$

which accepts the string aa. To derive this string with G, we first use rules of the form (11.6) and (11.7) to get the appropriate starting string,

$$S \Rightarrow SV_{\Box\Box} \Rightarrow TV_{\Box\Box} \Rightarrow TV_{aa}V_{\Box\Box} \Rightarrow V_{a0a}V_{aa}V_{\Box\Box}.$$

The last sentential form is the starting point for the part of the derivation that mimics the computation of the Turing machine. It contains the original input $aa\square$ in the sequence of first indices and the initial instantaneous description $q_0aa\square$ in the remaining indices. Next, we apply

$$V_{a0a}V_{aa} \to V_{aa}V_{a0a},$$

and

$$V_{a0a}V_{\sqcup\sqcup} \to V_{aa}V_{\square 0\square},$$

which are specific instances of (11.8), and

$$V_{aa}V_{\square 0\square} \to V_{a1a}V_{\square\square}$$

coming from (11.9). Then the next steps in the derivation are

$$V_{a0a}V_{aa}V_{\square\square} \Rightarrow V_{aa}V_{a0a}V_{\square\square} \Rightarrow V_{aa}V_{aa}V_{\square 0\square} \Rightarrow V_{aa}V_{a1a}V_{\square\square}.$$

The sequence of first indices remains the same, always remembering the initial input. The sequence of the other indices is

$$0aa\square, a0a\square, aa0\square, a1a\square,$$

which is equivalent to the sequence of instantaneous descriptions in (11.14).
Finally, (11.10) to (11.13) are used in the last steps

$$V_{aa}V_{a1a}V_{\square\square} \Rightarrow V_{aa}aV_{\square\square} \Rightarrow V_{aa}a\square \Rightarrow aa\square \Rightarrow aa.$$

The construction described in (11.6) to (11.13) is the basis of the proof of the following result.

Theorem 11.7   For every recursively enumerable language L, there exists an unrestricted grammar G, such that $L = L(G)$.

Proof: The construction described guarantees that if

$$x \vdash y,$$

then

$$e(x) \Rightarrow e(y),$$

where $c(x)$ denotes the encoding of a string according to the given convention. By an induction on the number of steps, we can then show that

$$e(q_0w) \overset{*}{\Rightarrow} e(y),$$

if and only if

$$q_0 w \overset{*}{\vdash} y.$$

We also must show that we can generate every possible starting configuration and that w is properly reconstructed if and only if M enters a final configuration. The details, which are not too difficult, are left as an exercise. ■

These two theorems establish what we set out to do. They show that the family of languages associated with unrestricted grammars is identical with the family of recursively enumerable languages.

EXERCISES

1. What language does the unrestricted grammar

$$S \to S_1 B$$
$$S_1 \to aS_1 b$$
$$bB \to bbbB$$
$$aS_1 b \to aa$$
$$B \to \lambda$$

derive? **Ⓢ**

2. What difficulties would arise if we allowed the empty string as the left side of a production in an unrestricted grammar?

3. Consider a variation on grammars in which the starting point for any derivation can be a finite set of strings, rather than a single variable. Formalize this concept, then investigate how such grammars relate to the unrestricted grammars we have used here. **Ⓢ**

4. In Example 11.1, prove that the constructed grammar cannot generate any sentence with a b in it.

5. Give the details of the proof of Theorem 11.7.

6. Construct a Turing machine for $L\left(01\left(01\right)^*\right)$, then find an unrestricted grammar for it using the construction in Theorem 11.7. Give a derivation for 0101 using the resulting grammar.

7. Show that for every unrestricted grammar there exists an equivalent unrestricted grammar, all of whose productions have the form

$$u \to v,$$

with $u, v \in \left(V \cup T\right)^+$ and $|u| \le |v|$, or

$$A \to \lambda,$$

with $A \in V$. **Ⓢ**

8. Show that the conclusion of Exercise 7 still holds if we add the further conditions $|u| \leq 2$ and $|v| \leq 2$.

9. Some authors give a definition of unrestricted grammars that is not quite the same as our Definition 11.3. In this alternate definition, the productions of an unrestricted grammar are required to be of the form

$$x \to y,$$

where

$$x \in (V \cup T)^* V (V \cup T)^*,$$

and

$$y \in (V \cup T)^*.$$

The difference is that here the left side must have at least one variable.

Show that this alternate definition is basically the same as the one we use, in the sense that for every grammar of one type, there is an equivalent grammar of the other type.

11.3 Context-Sensitive Grammars and Languages

Between the restricted, context-free grammars and the general, unrestricted grammars, a great variety of "somewhat restricted" grammars can be defined. Not all cases yield interesting results; among the ones that do, the context-sensitive grammars have received considerable attention. These grammars generate languages associated with a restricted class of Turing machines, linear bounded automata, which we introduced in Section 10.5.

Definition 11.4

A grammar $G = (V, T, S, P)$ is said to be **context-sensitive** if all productions are of the form

$$x \to y,$$

where $x, y \in (V \cup T)^+$ and

$$|x| \leq |y|. \tag{11.15}$$

This definition shows clearly one aspect of this type of grammar; it is **noncontracting**, in the sense that the length of successive sentential forms can never decrease. It is less obvious why such grammars should be called context-sensitive, but it can be shown (see, for example, Salomaa 1973) that all such grammars can be rewritten in a normal form in which all productions are of the form

$$xAy \rightarrow xvy.$$

This is equivalent to saying that the production

$$A \rightarrow v$$

can be applied only in the situation where A occurs in a context of the string x on the left and the string y on the right. While we use the terminology arising from this particular interpretation, the form itself is of little interest to us here, and we will rely entirely on Definition 11.4.

Context-Sensitive Languages and Linear Bounded Automata

As the terminology suggests, context-sensitive grammars are associated with a language family with the same name.

Definition 11.5

A language L is said to be context-sensitive if there exists a context-sensitive grammar G, such that $L = L(G)$ or $L = L(G) \cup \{\lambda\}$.

In this definition, we reintroduce the empty string. Definition 11.4 implies that $x \rightarrow \lambda$ is not allowed, so that a context-sensitive grammar can never generate a language containing the empty string. Yet, every context-free language without λ can be generated by a special case of a context-sensitive grammar, say by one in Chomsky or Greibach normal form, both of which satisfy the conditions of Definition 11.4. By including the empty string in the definition of a context-sensitive language (but not in the grammar), we can claim that the family of context-free languages is a subset of the family of context-sensitive languages.

Example 11.2   The language $L = \{a^n b^n c^n : n \geq 1\}$ is a context-sensitive language. We show this by exhibiting a context-sensitive grammar for the language. One such grammar is

$$S \rightarrow abc \,|\, aAbc,$$
$$Ab \rightarrow bA,$$
$$Ac \rightarrow Bbcc,$$
$$bB \rightarrow Bb,$$
$$aB \rightarrow aa \,|\, aaA.$$

We can see how this works by looking at a derivation of $a^3 b^3 c^3$.

$$S \Rightarrow aAbc \Rightarrow abAc \Rightarrow abBbcc$$
$$\Rightarrow aBbbcc \Rightarrow aaAbbcc \Rightarrow aabAbcc$$
$$\Rightarrow aabbAcc \Rightarrow aabbBbccc$$
$$\Rightarrow aabBbbccc \Rightarrow aaBbbbccc$$
$$\Rightarrow aaabbbccc.$$

The solution effectively uses the variables A and B as messengers. An A is created on the left, travels to the right to the first c, where it creates another b and c. It then sends the messenger B back to the left in order to create the corresponding a. The process is very similar to the way one might program a Turing machine to accept the language L. ∎

Since the language in the above example is not context-free, we see that the family of context-free languages is a proper subset of the family of context-sensitive languages. Example 11.2 also shows that it is not an easy matter to find a context-sensitive grammar even for relatively simple examples. Often the solution is most easily obtained by starting with a Turing machine program, then finding an equivalent grammar for it. A few examples will show that, whenever the language is context-sensitive, the corresponding Turing machine has predictable space requirements; in particular, it can be viewed as a linear bounded automaton.

Theorem 11.8   For every context-sensitive language L not including λ, there exists some linear bounded automaton M such that $L = L(M)$.

Proof: If L is context-sensitive, then there exists a context-sensitive grammar for $L - \{\lambda\}$. We show that derivations in this grammar can be simulated by a linear bounded automaton. The linear bounded automaton will have two tracks, one containing the input string w, the other containing the sentential forms derived using G. A key point of this argument is that no possible sentential form can have length greater than $|w|$. Another point to notice is that a linear bounded automaton is, by definition, nondeterministic. This is necessary in the argument, since we can claim that the correct production can always be guessed and that no unproductive alternatives have to be pursued. Therefore, the computation described in Theorem 11.6 can be carried out without using space except that originally occupied by w; that is, it can be done by a linear bounded automaton. ∎

Theorem 11.9   If a language L is accepted by some linear bounded automaton M, then there exists a context-sensitive grammar that generates L.

Proof: The construction here is similar to that in Theorem 11.7. All productions generated in Theorem 11.7 are noncontracting except (11.13),

$$\square \to \lambda.$$

But this production can be omitted. It is necessary only when the Turing machine moves outside the bounds of the original input, which is not the case here. The grammar obtained by the construction without this unnecessary production is noncontracting, completing the argument. ∎

Relation Between Recursive and Context-Sensitive Languages

Theorem 11.9 tells us that every context-sensitive language is accepted by some Turing machine and is therefore recursively enumerable. Theorem 11.10 follows easily from this.

Theorem 11.10   Every context-sensitive language L is recursive.

Proof: Consider the context-sensitive language L with an associated context-sensitive grammar G, and look at a derivation of w

$$S \Rightarrow x_1 \Rightarrow x_2 \Rightarrow \cdots \Rightarrow x_n \Rightarrow w.$$

We can assume without any loss of generality that all sentential forms in a single derivation are different; that is, $x_i \neq x_j$ for all $i \neq j$. The crux of our argument is that the number of steps in any derivation is a bounded function of $|w|$. We know that

$$|x_j| \leq |x_{j+1}|,$$

because G is noncontracting. The only thing we need to add is that there exist some m, depending only on G and w, such that

$$|x_j| < |x_{j+m}|,$$

for all j, with $m = m(|w|)$ a bounded function of $|V \cup T|$ and $|w|$. This follows because the finiteness of $|V \cup T|$ implies that there are only a finite number of strings of a given length. Therefore, the length of a derivation of $w \in L$ is at most $|w| \, m(|w|)$.

This observation gives us immediately a membership algorithm for L. We check all derivations of length up to $|w| \, m(|w|)$. Since the set of productions of G is finite, there are only a finite number of these. If any of them give w, then $w \subset L$, otherwise it is not. ■

Theorem 11.11   There exists a recursive language that is not context-sensitive.

Proof: Consider the set of all context-sensitive grammars on $T = \{a, b\}$. We can use a convention in which each grammar has a variable set of the form

$$V = \{V_0, V_1, V_2, ...\}.$$

Every context-sensitive grammar is completely specified by its productions; we can think of them as written as a single string

$$x_1 \rightarrow y_1; x_2 \rightarrow y_2; \ldots ; x_m \rightarrow y_m.$$

To this string we now apply the homomorphism

$$h(a) = 010,$$
$$h(b) = 01^2 0,$$
$$h(\rightarrow) = 01^3 0,$$
$$h(;) = 01^4 0,$$
$$h(V_i) = 01^{i+5} 0.$$

Thus, any context-sensitive grammar can be represented uniquely by a string from $L\left((011^*0)^*\right)$. Furthermore, the representation is invertible in the sense that, given any such string, there is at most one context-sensitive grammar corresponding to it.

Let us introduce a proper ordering on $\{0, 1\}^+$, so we can write strings in the order w_1, w_2, etc. A given string w_j may not define a context-sensitive grammar; if it does, call the grammar G_j. Next, we define a language L by

$$L = \{w_i : w_i \text{ defines a context-sensitive grammar } G_i \text{ and } w_i \notin L(G_i)\}.$$

L is well defined and is in fact recursive. To see this, we construct a membership algorithm. Given w_i, we check it to see if it defines a context-sensitive grammar G_i. If not, then $w_i \notin L$. If the string does define a grammar, then $L(G_i)$ is recursive, and we can use the membership algorithm of Theorem 11.10 to find out if $w_i \in L(G_i)$. If it is not, then w_i belongs to L.

But L is not context-sensitive. If it were, there would exist some w_j such that $L = L(G_j)$. We can then ask if w_j is in $L(G_j)$. If we assume that $w_j \in L(G_j)$, then by definition w_j is not in L. But $L = L(G_j)$, so we have a contradiction. Conversely, if we assume that $w_j \notin L(G_j)$, then by definition $w_j \in L$ and we have another contradiction. We must therefore conclude that L is not context-sensitive. ∎

The result in Theorem 11.11 indicates that linear bounded automata are indeed less powerful than Turing machines, since they accept only a proper subset of the recursive languages. It follows from the same result that linear bounded automata are more powerful than pushdown automata. Context-free languages, being generated by context-free grammars, are a subset of the context-sensitive languages. As various examples show, they are a proper subset. Because of the essential equivalence of linear bounded automata and context-sensitive languages on one hand, and pushdown automata and context-free languages on the other, we see that any language accepted by a pushdown automaton is also accepted by some linear bounded automaton, but that there are languages accepted by some linear bounded automata for which there are no pushdown automata.

EXERCISES

★ 1. Find context-sensitive grammars for the following languages.

    (a) $L = \{a^{n+1}b^n c^{n-1} : n \geq 1\}$.

    (b) $L = \{a^n b^n a^{2n} : n \geq 1\}$

    (c) $L = \{a^n b^m c^n d^m : n \geq 1, m \geq 1\}$ Ⓢ

    (d) $L = \{ww : w \in \{a,b\}^+\}$

★ 2. Find context-sensitive grammars for the following languages.

    (a) $L = \{w : n_a(w) = n_b(w) = n_c(w)\}$

    (b) $L = \{w : n_a(w) = n_b(w) < n_c(w)\}$

3. Show that the family of context-sensitive languages is closed under union.

4. Show that the family of context-sensitive languages is closed under reversal. Ⓢ

5. For m in Theorem 11.10, give explicit bounds for m as a function of $|w|$ and $|V \cup T|$.

6. Without explicitly constructing it, show that there exists a context-free grammar for the language $L = \{wuw : w, u \in \{a, b\}^+\}$ **ⓢ**

11.4 The Chomsky Hierarchy

We have now encountered a number of language families, among them the recursively enumerable languages (L_{RE}), the context-sensitive languages (L_{CS}), the context-free languages (L_{CF}), and the regular languages (L_{REG}). One way of exhibiting the relationship between these families is by the **Chomsky hierarchy**. Noam Chomsky, a founder of formal language theory, provided an initial classification into four language types, type 0 to type 3. This original terminology has persisted and one finds frequent references to it, but the numeric types are actually different names for the language families we have studied. Type 0 languages are those generated by unrestricted grammars, that is, the recursively enumerable languages. Type 1 consists of the context-sensitive languages, type 2 consists of the context-free languages and type 3 consists of the regular languages. As we have seen, each language family of type i is a proper subset of the family of type $i-1$. A diagram (Figure 11.3) exhibits the relationship clearly. Figure 11.3 shows the original Chomsky hierarchy. We have also met several other language families that can be fitted into this picture. Including the families of deterministic context-free languages (L_{DCF}), and recursive languages (L_{REC}), we arrive at the extended hierarchy shown in Figure 11.4.

Other language families can be defined and their place in Figure 11.4 studied, although their relationships do not always have the neatly nested structure of Figures 11.3 and 11.4. In some instances, the relationships are not completely understood.

Figure 11.3

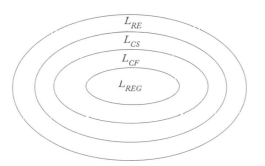

Figure 11.4

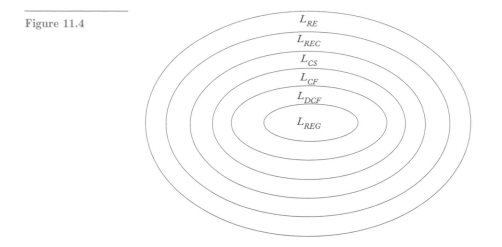

Example 11.3 We have previously introduced the context-free language

$$L = \{w : n_a(w) = n_b(w)\}$$

and shown that it is deterministic, but not linear. On the other hand, the language

$$L = \{a^n b^n\} \cup \{a^n b^{2n}\}$$

is linear, but not deterministic. This indicates that the relationship between regular, linear, deterministic context-free, and nondeterministic context-free languages is as shown in Figure 11.5.

Figure 11.5

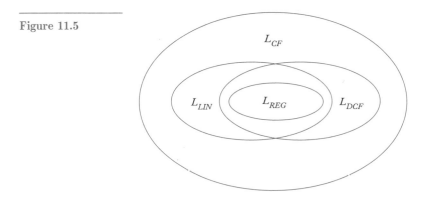

There is still an unresolved issue. We introduced the concept of a deterministic linear bounded automaton in Exercise 8, Section 10.5. We can now ask the question we asked in connection with other automata: What role does nondeterminism play here? Unfortunately, there is no easy answer. At this time, it is not known whether the family of languages accepted by deterministic linear bounded automata is a proper subset of the context-sensitive languages.

To summarize, we have explored the relationships between several language families and their associated automata. In doing so, we established a hierarchy of languages and classified automata by their power as language acceptors. Turing machines are more powerful than linear bounded automata. These in turn are more powerful than pushdown automata. At the bottom of the hierarchy are finite accepters, with which we began our study.

EXERCISES

1. Collect examples given in this book that demonstrate that all the subset relations depicted in Figure 11.4 are indeed proper ones.

2. Find two examples (excluding the one in Example 11.3) of languages that are linear but not deterministic context-free.

3. Find two examples (excluding the one in Example 11.3) of languages that are deterministic context-free but not linear.

Chapter 12

Limits of Algorithmic Computation

Having talked about what Turing machines can do, we now look at what they cannot do. Although Turing's thesis leads us to believe that there are few limitations to the power of a Turing machine, we have claimed on several occasions that there could not exist any algorithms for the solution of certain problems. Now we make more explicit what we mean by this claim. Some of the results came about quite simply; if a language is nonrecursive, then by definition there is no membership algorithm for it. If this were all there was to this issue, it would not be very interesting; nonrecursive languages have little practical value. But the problem goes deeper. For example, we have stated (but not yet proved) that there exists no algorithm to determine whether a context-free grammar is unambiguous. This question is clearly of practical significance in the study of programming languages.

We first define the concept of **decidability** and **computability** to pin down what we mean when we say that something cannot be done by a Turing machine. We then look at several classical problems of this type, among them the well-known halting problem for Turing machines. From this follow a number of related problems for Turing machines and recursively enumerable languages. After this, we look at some questions relating to context-free languages. Here we find quite a few important problems for which, unfortunately, there are no algorithms.

12.1 Some Problems That Cannot Be Solved by Turing Machines

The argument that the power of mechanical computations is limited is not surprising. Intuitively we know that many vague and speculative questions require special insight and reasoning well beyond the capacity of any computer that we can now construct or even plausibly foresee. What is more interesting to computer scientists is that there are questions that can be clearly and simply stated, with an apparent possibility of an algorithmic solution, but which are known to be unsolvable by any computer.

Computability and Decidability

In Definition 9.4, we stated that a function f on a certain domain is said to be computable if there exists a Turing machine that computes the value of f for all arguments in its domain. A function is uncomputable if no such Turing machine exists. There may be a Turing machine that can compute f on part of its domain, but we call the function computable only if there is a Turing machine that computes the function on the whole of its domain. We see from this that, when we classify a function as computable or not computable, we must be clear on what its domain is.

Our concern here will be the somewhat simplified setting where the result of a computation is a simple "yes" or "no." In this case, we talk about a problem being **decidable** or **undecidable**. By a *problem* we will understand a set of related statements, each of which must be either true or false. For example, we consider the statement "For a context-free grammar G, the language $L(G)$ is ambiguous." For some G this is true, for others it is false, but clearly we must have one or the other. The problem is to decide whether the statement is true for any G we are given. Again, there is an underlying domain, the set of all context-free grammars. We say that a problem is decidable if there exists a Turing machine that gives the correct answer for every statement in the domain of the problem.

When we state decidability or undecidability results, we must always know what the domain is, because this may affect the conclusion. The problem may be decidable on some domain but not on another. Specifically, a single instance of a problem is always decidable, since the answer is either true or false. In the first case, a Turing machine that always answers "true" gives the correct answer, while in the second case one that always answers "false" is appropriate. This may seem like a facetious answer, but it emphasizes an important point. The fact that we do not know what the correct answer is makes no difference, what matters is that there exists some Turing machine that does give the correct response.

The Turing Machine Halting Problem

We begin with some problems that have some historical significance and that at the same time give us a starting point for developing later results. The best known of these is the Turing machine **halting problem**. Simply stated, the problem is: given the description of a Turing machine M and an input w, does M, when started in the initial configuration $q_0 w$, perform a computation that eventually halts? Using an abbreviated way of talking about the problem, we ask whether M applied to w, or simply (M, w), halts or does not halt. The domain of this problem is to be taken as the set of all Turing machines and all w; that is, we are looking for a single Turing machine that, given the description of an arbitrary M and w, will predict whether or not the computation of M applied to w will halt.

We cannot find the answer by simulating the action of M on w, say by performing it on a universal Turing machine, because there is no limit on the length of the computation. If M enters an infinite loop, then no matter how long we wait, we can never be sure that M is in fact in a loop. It may simply be a case of a very long computation. What we need is an algorithm that can determine the correct answer for any M and w by performing some analysis on the machine's description and the input. But as we now show, no such algorithm exists.

For subsequent discussion, it is convenient to have a precise idea of what we mean by the halting problem; for this reason, we make a specific definition of what we stated somewhat loosely above.

Definition 12.1

Let w_M be a string that describes a Turing machine $M = (Q, \Sigma, \Gamma, \delta, q_0, \square, F)$, and let w be a string in M's alphabet. We will assume that w_M and w are encoded as a string of 0's and 1's, as suggested in Section 10.4. A solution of the halting problem is a Turing machine H, which for any w_M and w performs the computation

$$q_0 w_M w \overset{*}{\vdash} x_1 q_y x_2,$$

if M applied to w halts, and

$$q_0 w_M w \overset{*}{\vdash} y_1 q_n y_2,$$

if M applied to w does not halt. Here q_y and q_n are both final states of H.

Theorem 12.1   There does not exist any Turing machine H that behaves as required by Definition 12.1. The halting problem is therefore undecidable.

Proof: We assume the contrary, namely, that there exists an algorithm, and consequently some Turing machine H, that solves the halting problem. The input to H will be the string $w_M w$. The requirement is then that, given any $w_M w$, the Turing machine H will halt with either a yes or no answer. We achieve this by asking that H halt in one of two corresponding final states, say, q_y or q_n. The situation can be visualized by a block diagram like Figure 12.1. The intent of this diagram is to indicate that, if M is started in state q_0 with input $w_M w$, it will eventually halt in state q_y or q_n. As required by Definition 12.1, we want H to operate according to the following rules:

$$q_0 w_M w \vdash_H^* x_1 q_y x_2,$$

if M applied to w halts, and

$$q_0 w_M w \vdash_H^* y_1 q_n y_2,$$

if M applied to w does not halt.

Next, we modify H to produce a Turing machine H' with the structure shown in Figure 12.2. With the added states in Figure 12.2 we want to convey that the transitions between state q_y and the new states q_a and q_b are to be made, regardless of the tape symbol, in such a way that the tape remains unchanged. The way this is done is straightforward. Comparing H and H' we see that, in situations where H reaches q_y and halts, the modified machine H' will enter an infinite loop. Formally, the action of H' is described by

$$q_0 w_M w \vdash_{H'}^* \infty,$$

if M applied to w halts, and

$$q_0 w_M w \vdash_{H'}^* y_1 q_n y_2,$$

if M applied to w does not halt.

Figure 12.1

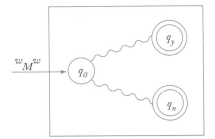

Figure 12.2

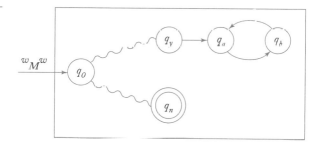

From H' we construct another Turing machine $\widehat{H}$. This new machine takes as input w_M and copies it, ending in its initial state q_0. After that, it behaves exactly like H'. Then the action of $\widehat{H}$ is such that

$$q_0 w_M \overset{*}{\vdash}_{\widehat{H}} q_0 w_M w_M \overset{*}{\vdash}_{\widehat{H}} \infty,$$

if M applied to w_M halts, and

$$q_0 w_M \overset{*}{\vdash}_{\widehat{H}} q_0 w_M w_M \overset{*}{\vdash}_{\widehat{H}} y_1 q_n y_2,$$

if M applied to w_M does not halt.

Now $\widehat{H}$ is a Turing machine, so it has a description in $\{0,1\}^*$, say, $\widehat{w}$. This string, in addition to being the description of $\widehat{H}$, also can be used as input string. We can therefore legitimately ask what would happen if $\widehat{H}$ is applied to $\widehat{w}$. From the above, identifying M with $\widehat{H}$, we get

$$q_0 \widehat{w} \overset{*}{\vdash}_{\widehat{H}} \infty,$$

if $\widehat{H}$ applied to $\widehat{w}$ halts, and

$$q_0 \widehat{w} \overset{*}{\vdash}_{\widehat{H}} y_1 q_n y_2,$$

if $\widehat{H}$ applied to $\widehat{w}$ does not halt. This is clearly nonsense. The contradiction tells us that our assumption of the existence of H, and hence the assumption of the decidability of the halting problem, must be false. ■

One may object to Definition 12.1, since we required that, to solve the halting problem, H had to start and end in very specific configurations. It is, however, not hard to see that these somewhat arbitrarily chosen conditions play only a minor role in the argument, and that essentially the same reasoning could be used with any other starting and ending configurations. We have tied the problem to a specific definition for the sake of the discussion, but this does not affect the conclusion.

It is important to keep in mind what Theorem 12.1 says. It does not preclude solving the halting problem for specific cases; often we can tell by an analysis of M and w whether or not the Turing machine will halt. What the theorem says is that this cannot always be done; there is no algorithm that can make a correct decision for all w_M and w.

The arguments for proving Theorem 12.1 were given because they are classical and of historical interest. The conclusion of the theorem is actually implied in previous results as the following argument shows.

Theorem 12.2

If the halting problem were decidable, then every recursively enumerable language would be recursive. Consequently, the halting problem is undecidable.

Proof: To see this, let L be a recursively enumerable language on Σ, and let M be a Turing machine that accepts L. Let H be the Turing machine that solves the halting problem. We construct from this the following procedure:

1. Apply H to $w_M w$. If H says "no," then by definition w is not in L.

2. If H says "yes," then apply M to w. But M must halt, so it will eventually tell us whether w is in L or not.

This constitutes a membership algorithm, making L recursive. But we already know that there are recursively enumerable languages that are not recursive. The contradiction implies that H cannot exist, that is, that the halting problem is undecidable. ∎

The simplicity with which the halting problem can be obtained from Theorem 11.5 is a consequence of the fact that the halting problem and the membership problem for recursively enumerable languages are nearly identical. The only difference is that in the halting problem we do not distinguish between halting in a final and nonfinal state, whereas in the membership problem we do. The proofs of Theorems 11.5 (via Theorem 11.3) and 12.1 are closely related, both being a version of diagonalization.

Reducing One Undecidable Problem to Another

The above argument, connecting the halting problem to the membership problem, illustrates the very important technique of reduction. We say that a problem A is **reduced** to a problem B if the decidability of A follows from the decidability of B. Then, if we know that A is undecidable, we can conclude that B is also undecidable. Let us do a few examples to illustrate this idea.

Example 12.1

The **state-entry problem** is as follows. Given any Turing machine $M = (Q, \Sigma, \Gamma, \delta, q_0, \square, F)$ and any $q \in Q$, $w \in \Sigma^+$, decide whether or not the state q is ever entered when M is applied to w. This problem is undecidable.

To reduce the halting problem to the state-entry problem, suppose that we have an algorithm A that solves the state-entry problem. We could then use it to solve the halting problem. For example, given any M and w, we first modify M to get $\widehat{M}$ in such a way that $\widehat{M}$ halts in state q if and only if M halts. We can do this simply by looking at the transition function δ of M. If M halts, it does so because some $\delta(q_i, a)$ is undefined. To get $\widehat{M}$, we change every such undefined δ to

$$\delta(q_i, a) = (q, a, R),$$

where q is a final state. We apply the state-entry algorithm A to $\left(\widehat{M}, q, w\right)$. If A answers yes, that is, the state q is entered, then (M, w) halts. If A says no, then (M, w) does not halt.

Thus, the assumption that the state-entry problem is decidable gives us an algorithm for the halting problem. Because the halting problem is undecidable, the state-entry problem must also be undecidable.

Example 12.2   The **blank-tape halting problem** is another problem to which the halting problem can be reduced. Given a Turing machine M, determine whether or not M halts if started with a blank tape. This is undecidable.

To show how this reduction is accomplished, assume that we are given some M and some w. We first construct from M a new machine M_w that starts with a blank tape, writes w on it, then positions itself in a configuration $q_0 w$. After that, M_w acts like M. Clearly M_w will halt on a blank tape if and only if M halts on w.

Suppose now that the blank-tape halting problem were decidable. Given any (M, w), we first construct M_w, then apply the blank-tape halting problem algorithm to it. The conclusion tells us whether M applied to w will halt. Since this can be done for any M and w, an algorithm for the blank-tape halting problem can be converted into an algorithm for the halting problem. Since the latter is known to be undecidable, the same must be true for the blank-tape halting problem.

The construction in the arguments of these two examples illustrates an approach common in establishing undecidability results. A block diagram often helps us visualize the process. The construction in Example 12.2 is summarized in Figure 12.3. In that diagram, we first use an algorithm that transforms (M, w) into M_w; such an algorithm clearly exists. Next, we use the algorithm for solving the blank-tape halting problem, which we assume exists. Putting the two together yields an algorithm for the halting problem. But this is impossible, and we can conclude that A cannot exist.

Figure 12.3
Algorithm for
halting problem.

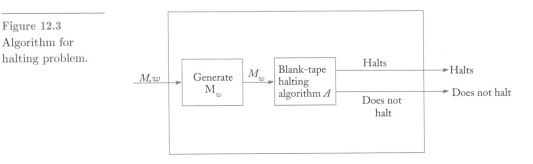

A decision problem is effectively a function with a range $\{0, 1\}$, that is, a true or false answer. We can look also at more general functions to see if they are computable; to do so, we follow the established method and reduce the halting problem (or any other problem known to be undecidable) to the problem of computing the function in question. Because of Turing's thesis, we expect that functions encountered in practical circumstances will be computable, so for examples of uncomputable functions we must look a little further. Most examples of uncomputable functions are associated with attempts to predict the behavior of Turing machines.

Example 12.3   Let $\Gamma = \{0, 1, \square\}$. Consider the function $f(n)$ whose value is the maximum number of moves that can be made by any n-state Turing machine that halts when started with a blank tape. This function, as it turns out, is not computable.

Before we set out to demonstrate this, let us make sure that $f(n)$ is defined for all n. Notice first that there are only a finite number of Turing machines with n states. This is because Q and Γ are finite, so δ has a finite domain and range. This in turn implies that there are only a finite number of different δ's and therefore a finite number of different n-state Turing machines.

Of all of the n-state machines, there are some that always halt, for example machines that have only final states and therefore make no moves. Some of the n-state machines will not halt when started with a blank tape, but they do not enter the definition of f. Every machine that does halt will execute a certain number of moves; of these, we take the largest to give $f(n)$.

Take any Turing machine M and positive number m. It is easy to modify M to produce $\widehat{M}$ in such a way that the latter will always halt with one of two answers: M applied to a blank tape halts in no more than m moves, or M applied to a blank tape makes more than m moves. All we have to do for this is to have M count its moves and terminate when this count exceeds m. Assume now that $f(n)$ is computable by some Turing

Figure 12.4
Algorithm for
blank-tape halting
problem.

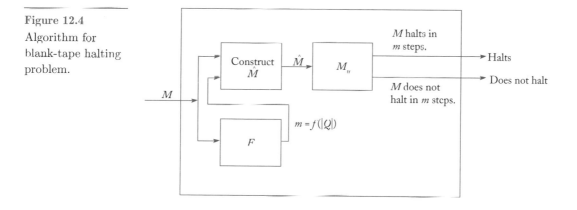

machine F. We can then put $\widehat{M}$ and F together as shown in Figure 12.4. First we compute $f(|Q|)$, where Q is the state set of M. This tells us the maximum number of moves that M can make if it is to halt. The value we get is then used as m to construct $\widehat{M}$ as outlined, and a description of $\widehat{M}$ is given to a universal Turing machine for execution. This tells us whether M applied to a blank tape halts or does not halt in less than $f(|Q|)$ steps. If we find that M applied to a blank tape makes more than $f(|Q|)$ moves, then because of the definition of f, the implication is that M never halts. Thus we have a solution to the blank tape halting problem. The impossibility of the conclusion forces us to accept that f is not computable.

EXERCISES

1. Describe in detail how H in Theorem 12.1 can be modified to produce H'.

2. Suppose we change Definition 12.1 to require that $q_0 w_M w \overset{*}{\vdash} q_y w$ or $q_0 w_M w \overset{*}{\vdash} q_n w$, depending on whether M applied to w halts or not. Reexamine the proof of Theorem 12.1 to show that this difference in the definition does not affect the proof in any significant way.

3. Show that the following problem is undecidable. Given any Turing machine M, $a \in \Gamma$, and $w \in \Sigma^+$, determine whether or not the symbol a is ever written when M is applied to w. **S**

4. In the general halting problem, we ask for an algorithm that gives the correct answer for any M and w. We can relax this generality, for example, by looking for an algorithm that works for all M but only a single w. We say that such a problem is decidable if for every w there exists a (possibly different) algorithm that determines whether or not (M, w) halts. Show that even in this restricted setting the problem is undecidable.

5. Show that there is no algorithm to decide whether or not an arbitrary Turing machine halts on all input.

6. Consider the question: "Does a Turing machine in the course of a computation revisit the starting cell (i.e. the cell under the read-write head at the beginning of the computation)?" Is this a decidable question?

7. Show that there is no algorithm for deciding if any two Turing machines M_1 and M_2 accept the same language. ⓢ

8. How is the conclusion of Exercise 7 affected if M_2 is a finite automaton?

9. Is the halting problem solvable for deterministic pushdown automata; that is, given a pda as in Definition 7.2, can we always predict whether or not the automaton will halt on input w?

10. Let M be any Turing machine and x and y two possible instantaneous descriptions of it. Show that the problem of determining whether or not

$$x \stackrel{*}{\vdash}_M y$$

    is undecidable. ⓢ

11. In Example 12.3, give the values of $f(1)$ and $f(2)$.

12. Show that the problem of determining whether a Turing machine halts on any input is undecidable.

13. Let B be the set of all Turing machines that halt when started with a blank tape. Show that this set is recursively enumerable, but not recursive. ⓢ

14. Consider the set of all n-state Turing machines with tape alphabet $\Gamma = \{0, 1, \square\}$. Give an expression for $m(n)$, the number of distinct Turing machines with this Γ.

15. Let $\Gamma = \{0, 1, \square\}$ and let $b(n)$ be the maximum number of tape cells examined by any n-state Turing machine that halts when started with a blank tape. Show that $b(n)$ is not computable.

16. Determine whether or not the following statement is true: Any problem whose domain is finite is decidable. ⓢ

12.2 Undecidable Problems for Recursively Enumerable Languages

We have determined that there is no membership algorithm for recursively enumerable languages. The lack of an algorithm to decide on some property is not an exceptional state of affairs for recursively enumerable languages, but rather is the general rule. As we now show, there is little we can say about these languages. Recursively enumerable languages are so general that, in essence, any question we ask about them is undecidable. Invariably, when we ask a question about recursively enumerable languages, we find that there is some way of reducing the halting problem to this question. We give here some examples to show how this is done and from these examples derive an indication of the general situation.

Theorem 12.3 Let G be an unrestricted grammar. Then the problem of determining whether or not

$$L(G) = \varnothing$$

is undecidable.

Proof: We will reduce the membership problem for recursively enumerable languages to this problem. Suppose we are given a Turing machine M and some string w. We can modify M as follows. M first saves its input on some special part of its tape. Then, whenever it enters a final state, it checks its saved input and accepts it if and only if it is w. We can do this by changing δ in a simple way, creating for each w a machine M_w such that

$$L(M_w) = L(M) \cap \{w\}.$$

Using Theorem 11.7, we then construct a corresponding grammar G_w. Clearly, the construction leading from M and w to G_w can always be done. Equally clear is that $L(G_w)$ is nonempty if and only if $w \in L(M)$.

Assume now that there exists an algorithm A for deciding whether or not $L(G) = \varnothing$. If we let T denote an algorithm by which we generate G_w, then we can put T and A together as shown in Figure 12.5. Figure 12.5 is a Turing machine which for any M and w tells us whether or not w is in $L(M)$. If such a Turing machine existed, we would have a membership algorithm for any recursively enumerable language, in direct contradiction to a previously established result. We conclude therefore that the stated problem "$L(G) = \varnothing$" is not decidable. ∎

Figure 12.5
Membership algorithm.

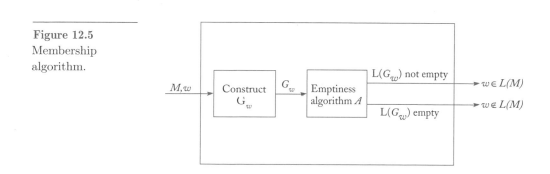

Theorem 12.4

Let M be any Turing machine. Then the question of whether or not $L(M)$ is finite is undecidable.

Proof: Consider the halting problem (M, w). From M we construct another Turing machine $\widehat{M}$ that does the following. First, the halting states of M are changed so that if any one is reached, all input is accepted by $\widehat{M}$. This can be done by having any halting configuration go to a final state. Second, the original machine is modified so that the new machine $\widehat{M}$ first generates w on its tape, then performs the same computations as M, using the newly created w and some otherwise unused space. In other words, the moves made by $\widehat{M}$ after it has written w on its tape are the same as would have been made by M had it started in the original configuration $q_0 w$. If M halts in any configuration, then $\widehat{M}$ will halt in a final state.

Therefore, if (M, w) halts, $\widehat{M}$ will reach a final state for all input. If (M, w) does not halt, then $\widehat{M}$ will not halt either and so will accept nothing. In other words, $\widehat{M}$ either accepts the infinite language Σ^+ or the finite language $\varnothing$.

If we now assume the existence of an algorithm A that tells us whether or not $L\left(\widehat{M}\right)$ is finite, we can construct a solution to the halting problem as shown in Figure 12.6. Therefore no algorithm for deciding whether or not $L(M)$ is finite can exist. ∎

Notice that in the proof of Theorem 12.4, the specific nature of the question asked, namely "Is $L(M)$ finite?", is immaterial. We can change the nature of the problem without significantly affecting the argument.

Example 12.4

Show that for an arbitrary Turing machine M with $\Sigma = \{a, b\}$, the problem "$L(M)$ contains two different strings of the same length" is undecidable.

To show this, we use exactly the same approach as in Theorem 12.4, except that when $\widehat{M}$ reaches a halting configuration, it will be modified to accept the two strings a and b. For this, the initial input is saved and at the

Figure 12.6

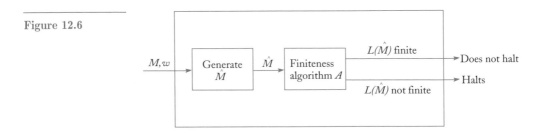

end of the computation compared with a and b, accepting only these two strings. Thus, if (M, w) halts, $\widehat{M}$ will accept two strings of equal length, otherwise $\widehat{M}$ will accept nothing. The rest of the argument then proceeds as in Theorem 12.4.

━━━━━━━━━━━━━━━━━━━━━━━━━━━━━━━━━━━ ■

In exactly the same manner, we can substitute other questions such as "Does $L(M)$ contain any string of length five?" or "Is $L(M)$ regular?" without affecting the argument essentially. These questions, as well as similar questions, are all undecidable. A general result formalizing this is known as **Rice's theorem**. This theorem states that any nontrivial property of a recursively enumerable language is undecidable. The adjective "nontrivial" refers to a property possessed by some but not all recursively enumerable languages. A precise statement and a proof of Rice's theorem can be found in Hopcroft and Ullman (1979).

EXERCISES

1. Show in detail how the machine $\widehat{M}$ in Theorem 12.4 is constructed.

2. Show that the two problems mentioned at the end of the preceding section, namely

    (a) $L(M)$ contains any string of length five,

    (b) $L(M)$ is regular,

    are undecidable.

3. Let M_1 and M_2 be arbitrary Turing machines. Show that the problem "$L(M_1) \subseteq L(M_2)$" is undecidable. **S**

4. Let G be any unrestricted grammar. Does there exist an algorithm for determining whether or not $L(G)^R$ is recursively enumerable?

5. Let G be any unrestricted grammar. Does there exist an algorithm for determining whether or not $L(G) = L(G)^R$?

6. Let G_1 be any unrestricted grammar, and G_2 any regular grammar. Show that the problem

$$L(G_1) \cap L(G_2) = \varnothing$$

    is undecidable. **S**

7. Show that the question in Exercise 6 is undecidable for any fixed G_2, as long as $L(G_2)$ is not empty.

8. For an unrestricted grammar G, show that the question "Is $L(G) = L(G)^*$?" is undecidable. Argue (a) from Rice's Theorem and (b) from first principles. **S**

12.3 The Post Correspondence Problem

The undecidability of the halting problem has many consequences of practical interest, particularly in the area of context-free languages. But in many instances it is cumbersome to work with the halting problem directly, and it is convenient to establish some intermediate results that bridge the gap between the halting problem and other problems. These intermediate results follow from the undecidability of the halting problem, but are more closely related to the problems we want to study and therefore make the arguments easier. One such intermediate result is the **Post correspondence problem**.

The Post correspondence problem can be stated as follows. Given two sequences of n strings on some alphabet Σ, say

$$A = w_1, w_2, ..., w_n$$

and

$$B = v_1, v_2, ..., v_n$$

we say that there exists a Post correspondence solution (PC-solution) for pair (A, B) if there is a nonempty sequence of integers $i, j, ..., k$, such that

$$w_i w_j \cdots w_k = v_i v_j \cdots v_k.$$

The Post correspondence problem is to devise an algorithm that will tell us, for any (A, B), whether or not there exists a PC-solution.

Example 12.5   Let $\Sigma = \{0, 1\}$ and take A and B as

$$w_1 = 11, w_2 = 100, w_3 = 111$$
$$v_1 = 111, v_2 = 001, v_3 = 11$$

For this case, there exists a PC-solution as Figure 12.7 shows.
    If we take

$$w_1 = 00, w_2 = 001, w_3 = 1000$$
$$v_1 = 0, v_2 = 11, v_3 = 011$$

Figure 12.7

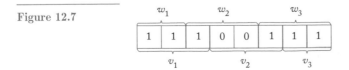

there cannot be any PC-solution simply because any string composed of elements of A will be longer than the corresponding string from B. ∎

In specific instances we may be able to show by explicit construction that a pair (A, B) permits a PC-solution, or we may be able to argue, as we did above, that no such solution can exist. But in general, there is no algorithm for deciding this question under all circumstances. The Post correspondence problem is therefore undecidable.

To show this is a somewhat lengthy process. For the sake of clarity, we break it into two parts. In the first part, we introduce the **modified Post correspondence problem**. We say that the pair (A, B) has a modified Post correspondence solution (MPC-solution) if there exists a sequence of integers $i, j, ..., k$, such that

$$w_1 w_i w_j \cdots w_k = v_1 v_i v_j \cdots v_k.$$

In the modified Post correspondence problem, the first elements of the sequences A and B play a special role. An MPC solution must start with w_1 on the left side and with v_1 on the right side. Note that if there exists an MPC-solution, then there is also a PC-solution, but the converse is not true.

The modified Post correspondence problem is to devise an algorithm for deciding if an arbitrary pair (A, B) admits an MPC-solution. This problem is also undecidable. We will demonstrate the undecidability of the modified Post correspondence problem by reducing a known undecidable problem, the membership problem for recursively enumerable languages, to it. To this end, we introduce the following construction. Suppose we are given an unrestricted grammar $G = (V, T, S, P)$ and a target string w. With these, we create the pair (A, B) as shown in Figure 12.8. In Figure 12.8, the string $FS \Rightarrow$ is to be taken as w_1 and the string F as v_1. The order of the rest of the strings is immaterial.

We want to claim eventually that $w \in L(G)$ if and only if the sets A and B constructed in this way have an MPC-solution. Since this is perhaps not immediately obvious, let us illustrate it with a simple example.

Example 12.6   Let $G = (\{A, B, C\}, \{a, b, c, \}, S, P)$ with productions

$$S \rightarrow aABb|Bbb,$$
$$Bb \rightarrow C,$$
$$AC \rightarrow aac,$$

Figure 12.8

A	B	
$FS \Rightarrow$	F	F is a symbol not in $V \cup T$
a	a	for every $a \in T$
V_i	V_i	for every $V_i \in V$
E	$\Rightarrow wE$	E is a symbol not in $V \cup T$
y_i	x_i	for every $x_i \rightarrow y_i$ in P
$\Rightarrow$	$\Rightarrow$	

and take $w = aaac$. The sequences A and B obtained from the suggested construction are given in Figure 12.9. The string $w = aaac$ is in $L(G)$ and has a derivation

$$S \Rightarrow aABb \Rightarrow aAC \Rightarrow aaac.$$

How this derivation is paralleled by an MPC-solution with the constructed sets can be seen in Figure 12.10, where the first two steps in the derivation are shown. The integers above and below the derivation string show the indices for w and v, respectively, used to create the string.

Figure 12.9

i	w_i	v_i
1	$FS \Rightarrow$	F
2	a	a
3	b	b
4	c	c
5	A	A
6	B	B
7	C	C
8	S	S
9	E	$\Rightarrow aaacE$
10	$aABb$	S
11	Bbb	S
12	C	Bb
13	aac	AC
14	$\Rightarrow$	$\Rightarrow$

Figure 12.10

Figure 12.11

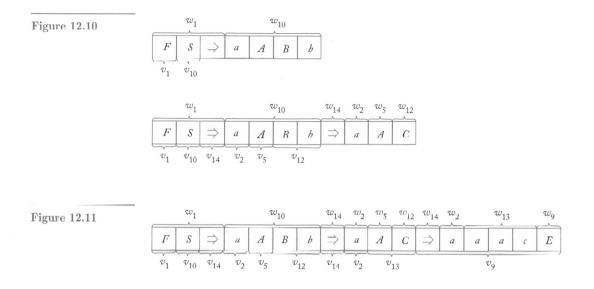

Examine Figure 12.10 carefully to see what is happening. We want to construct an MPC-solution, so we must start with w_1, that is, $FS \Rightarrow$. This string contains S, so to match it we have to use v_{10} or v_{11}. In this instance, we use v_{10}; this brings in w_{10}, leading us to the second string in the partial derivation. Looking at several more steps, we see that the string $w_1 w_i w_j...$ is always longer than the corresponding string $v_1 v_i v_j...$, and that the first is exactly one step ahead in the derivation. The only exception is the last step, where w_9 must be applied to let the v-string catch up. The complete MPC-solution is shown in Figure 12.11. The construction, together with the example, indicate the lines along which the next result is established. ∎

Theorem 12.5

Let $G = (V, T, S, P)$ be any unrestricted grammar, with w any string in T^+. Let (A, B) be the correspondence pair constructed from G and w be the process exhibited in Figure 12.8. Then the pair (A, B) permits an MPC-solution if and only if $w \in L(G)$.

Proof: The proof involves a formal inductive argument based on the outlined reasoning. We will omit the details. ∎

With this result, we can reduce the membership problem for recursively enumerable languages to the modified Post correspondence problem and thereby demonstrate the undecidability of the latter.

Figure 12.12
Membership
algorithm.

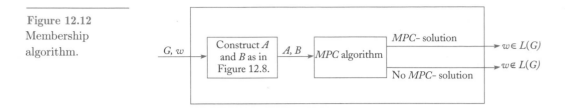

Theorem 12.6 The modified Post correspondence problem is undecidable.

Proof: Given any unrestricted grammar $G = (V, T, S, P)$ and $w \in T^+$, we construct the sets A and B as suggested above. By Theorem 12.5, the pair (A, B) has an MPC-solution if and only if $w \in L(G)$.

Suppose now we assume that the modified Post correspondence problem is decidable. We can then construct an algorithm for the membership problem of G as sketched in Figure 12.12. An algorithm for constructing A from B from G and w clearly exists, but a membership algorithm for G and w does not. We must therefore conclude that there cannot be any algorithm for deciding the modified Post correspondence problem. ∎

With this preliminary work, we are now ready to prove the Post correspondence problem in its original form.

Theorem 12.7 The Post correspondence problem is undecidable.

Proof: We argue that if the Post correspondence problem were decidable, the modified Post correspondence problem would be decidable.

Suppose we are given sequences $A = w_1, w_2, ..., w_n$ and $B = v_1, v_2, ..., v_n$ on some alphabet Σ. We then introduce new symbols $\cent$ and $\S$ and the new sequences

$$C = y_0, y_1, ..., y_{n+1},$$
$$D = z_0, z_1, ..., z_{n+1},$$

defined as follows. For $i = 1, 2, ..., n$

$$y_i = w_{i1} \cent w_{i2} \cent \cdots w_{im_i} \cent,$$
$$z_i = \cent v_{i1} \cent v_{i2} \cent \cdots v_{ir_i},$$

where w_{ij} and v_{ij} denote the jth letter of w_i and v_i, respectively, and $m_i = |w_i|, r_i = |v_i|$. In words, y_i is created from w_i by appending $\cent$ to each

Figure 12.13
MPC algorithm.

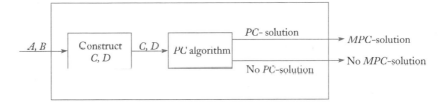

character, while z_i is obtained by prefixing each character of v_i with φ. To complete the definition of C and D, we take

$$y_0 = \varphi y_1,$$
$$y_{n+1} = \S,$$
$$z_0 = z_1,$$
$$z_{n+1} = \varphi\S.$$

Consider now the pair (C, D), and suppose it has a PC-solution. Because of the placement of φ and $\S$, such a solution must have y_0 on the left and y_{n+1} on the right and so must look like

$$\varphi w_{11} \varphi w_{12} \cdots \varphi w_{j1} \varphi \cdots \varphi w_{k1} \cdots \varphi \S = \varphi v_{11} \varphi v_{12} \cdots \varphi v_{j1} \varphi \cdots \varphi v_{k1} \cdots \varphi \S.$$

Ignoring the characters φ and $\S$, we see that this implies

$$w_1 w_j \cdots w_k = v_1 v_j \cdots v_k,$$

so that the pair (A, B) permits an MPC-solution.

We can turn the argument around to show that if there is an MPC-solution for (A, B) then there is a PC-solution for the pair (C, D).

Assume now that the Post correspondence problem is decidable. We can then construct the machine shown in Figure 12.13. This machine clearly decides the modified Post correspondence problem. But the modified Post correspondence problem is undecidable, consequently, we cannot have an algorithm for deciding the Post correspondence problem. ∎

EXERCISES

1. Let $A = \{001, 0011, 11, 101\}$ and $B = \{01, 111, 111, 010\}$. Does the pair (A, B) have a PC-solution? Does it have an MPC-solution? Ⓢ

2. Provide the details of the proof of Theorem 12.5.

3. Show that for $|\Sigma| = 1$, the Post correspondence problem is decidable, that is, there is an algorithm that can decide whether or not (A, B) has a PC-solution for any given (A, B) on a single-letter alphabet. **S**

4. Suppose we restrict the domain of the Post correspondence problem to include only alphabets with exactly two symbols. Is the resulting correspondence problem decidable?

5. Show that the following modifications of the Post correspondence problem are undecidable.

    (a) There is an MPC-solution if there is a sequence of integers such that $w_i w_j \cdots w_k w_1 = v_i v_j \cdots v_k v_1$. **S**

    (b) There is an MPC-solution if there is a sequence of integers such that $w_1 w_2 w_i w_j \cdots w_k = v_1 v_2 v_i v_j \cdots v_k$.

6. The correspondence pair (A, B) is said to have an *even* PC-solution if and only if there exists a nonempty sequence of even integers $i, j, ...k$ such that $w_i w_j \cdots w_k = v_i v_j \cdots v_k$. Show that the problem of deciding whether or not an arbitrary pair (A, B) has an even PC-solution is undecidable.

12.4 Undecidable Problems for Context-Free Languages

The Post correspondence problem is a convenient tool for studying undecidable questions for context-free languages. We illustrate this with a few selected results.

Theorem 12.8   There exists no algorithm for deciding whether any given context-free grammar is ambiguous.

Proof: Consider two sequences of strings $A = (w_1, w_2, ..., w_n)$ and $B = (v_1, v_2, ...v_n)$ over some alphabet Σ. Choose a new set of distinct symbols $a_1, a_2, ..., a_n$, such that

$$\{a_1, a_2, ..., a_n\} \cap \Sigma = \varnothing,$$

and consider the two languages

$$L_A = \{w_i w_j \cdots w_l w_k a_k a_l \cdots a_j a_i\}$$

and

$$L_B = \{v_i v_j \cdots v_l v_k a_k a_l \cdots a_j a_i\}.$$

Now look at the context-free grammar

$$G = (\{S, S_A, S_B\}, \Sigma \cup \{a_1, a_2, ...a_n\}, P, S)$$

where the set of productions P is the union of the two subsets: the first set P_A consists of

$$S \rightarrow S_A,$$
$$S_A \rightarrow w_i S_A a_i | w_i a_i, \qquad i - 1, 2, ..., n,$$

the second set P_B has the productions

$$S \rightarrow S_B,$$
$$S_B \rightarrow v_i S_B a_i | v_i a_i, \qquad i = 1, 2, ..., n.$$

Now take

$$G_A = (\{S, S_A\}, \Sigma \cup \{a_1, a_2, ..., a_n\}, P_A, S)$$

and

$$G_B = (\{S, S_B\}, \Sigma \cup \{a_1, a_2, ..., a_n\}, P_B, S).$$

Then clearly

$$L_A = L(G_A),$$
$$L_B = L(G_B),$$

and

$$L(G) = L_A \cup L_B.$$

It is easy to see that G_A and G_B by themselves are unambiguous. If a given string in $L(G)$ ends with a_i, then its derivation with grammar G_A must have started with $S \Rightarrow w_i S a_i$. Similarly, we can tell at any later stage which rule has to be applied. Thus, if G is ambiguous it must be because there is a w for which there are two derivations

$$S \Rightarrow S_A \Rightarrow w_i S_A a_i \overset{*}{\Rightarrow} w_i w_j \cdots w_k a_k \cdots a_j a_i = w$$

and

$$S \Rightarrow S_B \Rightarrow v_i S_B a_i \overset{*}{\Rightarrow} v_i v_j \cdots v_k a_k \cdots a_j a_i = w.$$

Consequently, if G is ambiguous, then the Post correspondence problem with the pair (A, B) has a solution. Conversely, if G is unambiguous, then the Post correspondence problem cannot have a solution.

If there existed an algorithm for solving the ambiguity problem, we could adapt it to solve the Post correspondence problem as shown in Figure 12.14. But since there is no algorithm for the Post correspondence problem, we conclude that the ambiguity problem is undecidable. ∎

Figure 12.14
PC algorithm.

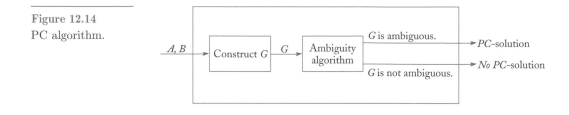

Theorem 12.9   There exists no algorithm for deciding whether or not

$$L(G_1) \cap L(G_2) = \varnothing$$

for arbitrary context-free grammars G_1 and G_2.

Proof: Take as G_1 the grammar G_A and as G_2 the grammar G_B as defined in the proof of Theorem 12.8. Suppose that $L(G_A)$ and $L(G_B)$ have a common element, that is

$$S_A \overset{*}{\Rightarrow} w_i w_j \cdots w_k a_k \cdots a_j a_i$$

and

$$S_B \overset{*}{\Rightarrow} v_i v_j \cdots v_k a_k \cdots a_j a_i.$$

Then the pair (A, B) has a PC-solution. Conversely, if the pair does not have a PC-solution, then $L(G_A)$ and $L(G_B)$ cannot have a common element. We conclude that $L(G_A) \cap L(G_B)$ is nonempty if and only if (A, B) has a PC-solution. This reduction proves the theorem. ∎

There is a variety of other known results along these lines. Some of them can be reduced to the Post correspondence problem, while others are more easily solved by establishing different intermediate results first (see for example Exercises 6 and 7 at the end of this section). We will not give the arguments here, but point to some additional results in the exercises.

That there are many undecidable problems connected with context-free languages seems surprising at first and shows that there are limitations to computations in an area in which we might be tempted to try an algorithmic approach. For example, it would be helpful if we could tell if a programming language defined in BNF is ambiguous, or if two different specifications of a language are in fact equivalent. But the results that have been established tell us that this is not possible, and it would be a waste of time to look for an algorithm for either of these tasks. Keep in mind that this does not rule out the possibility that there may be ways of getting the answer for specific cases or perhaps even most interesting ones. What the undecidability results tell us is that there is no completely general algorithm and that no matter how many different cases a method can handle, there are invariably some situations for which it will break down.

EXERCISES

1. Prove the claim made in Theorem 12.8 that G_A and G_B by themselves are unambiguous.

★ 2. Show that the problem of determining whether or not

$$L(G_1) \subseteq L(G_2)$$

is undecidable for context-free grammars G_1, G_2.

★ 3. Show that, for arbitrary context-free grammars G_1 and G_2, the problem "$L(G_1) \cap L(G_2)$ is context-free" is undecidable.

★ 4. Show that if the language $L(G_A) \cap L(G_B)$ in Theorem 12.8 is regular, then it must be empty. Use this to show that the problem "$L(G)$ is regular" is undecidable for context-free G.

★ 5. Let L_1 be a regular language and G a context-free grammar. Show that the problem "$L_1 \subseteq L(G)$" is undecidable.

★ 6. Let M be any Turing machine. We can assume without loss of generality that every computation involves an even number of moves. For any such computation

$$q_0 w \vdash x_1 \vdash x_2 \vdash \cdots \vdash x_n,$$

we can then construct the string

$$q_0 w \vdash x_1^R \vdash x_2 \vdash x_3^R \vdash \cdots \vdash x_n.$$

This is called a **valid computation**.

Show that for every M we can construct three context-free grammars G_1, G_2, G_3, such that

(a) the set of all valid computations is $L(G_1) \cap L(G_2)$,

(b) the set of all invalid computations (that is, the complement of the set of valid computations) is $L(G_3)$.

★ 7. Use the results of the above exercise to show that "$L(G) = \Sigma^*$" is undecidable over the domain of all context-free grammars G.

★ 8. Let G_1 be a context-free grammar and G_2 a regular grammar. Is the problem

$$L(G_1) \cap L(G_2) = \varnothing$$

decidable?

★ 9. Let G_1 and G_2 be grammars with G_1 regular. Is the problem

$$L(G_1) = L(G_2)$$

decidable when

(a) G_2 is unrestricted,

(b) when G_2 is context-free,

(c) when G_2 is regular?

Chapter 13

Other Models
of Computation

Although Turing machines are the most general models of computation we can construct, they are not the only ones. At various times, other models have been proposed, some of which at first glance seemed to be radically different from Turing machines. Eventually, however, all the models were found to be equivalent. Much of the pioneering work in this area was done in the period between 1930 and 1940 and a number of mathematicians, A. M. Turing among them, contributed to it. The results that were found shed light not only on the concept of a mechanical computation, but on mathematics as a whole.

Turing's work was published in 1936. No commercial computers were available at that time. In fact, the whole idea had been considered only in a very peripheral way. Although Turing's ideas eventually became very important in computer science, his original goal was not to provide a foundation for the study of digital computers. To understand what Turing was trying to do, we must briefly look at the state of mathematics at that time.

With the discovery of differential and integral calculus by Newton and Leibniz in the seventeenth and eighteenth centuries, interest in mathematics increased and the discipline entered an era of explosive growth. A number of different areas were studied, and significant advances were made in almost all of them. By the end of the nineteenth century, the body of mathematical knowledge had become quite large. Mathematicians also had become sufficiently sophisticated to recognize that some logical difficulties had arisen that required a more careful approach. This led to a concern with rigor in reasoning and a consequent examination of the foundations of mathematical knowledge in the process. To see why this was necessary, consider what is involved in a typical proof in just about every book and paper dealing with mathematical subjects. A sequence of plausible claims is made, interspersed with phrases like "it can be seen easily" and "it follows from this." Such phrases are conventional, and what one means by them is that, if challenged to do so, one could give more detailed reasoning. Of course, this is very dangerous, since it is possible to overlook things, use faulty hidden assumptions, or make wrong inferences. Whenever we see arguments like this, we cannot help but wonder if the proof we are given is indeed correct. Often there is no way of telling, and long and involved proofs have been published and found erroneous only after a considerable amount of time. Because of practical limitations, however, this type of reasoning is accepted by most mathematicians. The arguments throw light on the subject and at least increase our confidence that the result is true. But to those demanding complete reliability, they are unacceptable.

One alternative to such "sloppy" mathematics is to formalize as far as possible. We start with a set of assumed givens, called **axioms**, and precisely defined rules for logical inference and deduction. The rules are used in a sequence of steps, each of which takes us from one proven fact to another. The rules must be such that the correctness of their application can be checked in a routine and completely mechanical way. A proposition is considered proven true if we can derive it from the axioms in a finite sequence of logical steps. If the proposition conflicts with another proposition that can be proved to be true, then it is considered false.

Finding such formal systems was a major goal of mathematics at the end of the nineteenth century. Two concerns immediately arose. The first was that the system should be **consistent**. By this we mean that there should not be any proposition that can be proved to be true by one sequence of steps, then shown to be false by another equally valid argument. Consistency is indispensable in mathematics, and anything derived from an inconsistent system would be contrary to all we agree on. A second concern was whether a system is **complete**, by which we mean that any proposition expressible in the system can be proved to be true or false. For some time it was hoped that consistent and complete systems for all of mathematics could be devised thereby opening the door to rigorous but completely mechanical theorem proving. But this hope was dashed by the work of K. Gödel. In his famous **Incompleteness Theorem**, Gödel showed that any interesting consistent system must be incomplete; that is, it must contain some unprovable propositions. Gödel's revolutionary conclusion was published in 1931.

Gödel's work left unanswered the question of whether the unprovable statements could somehow be distinguished from the provable ones, so that there was still some hope that most of mathematics could be made precise with mechanically verifiable proofs. It was this problem that Turing and other mathematicians of the time, particularly A. Church, S. C. Kleene, and E. Post, addressed. In order to study the question, a variety of formal models of computation were established. Prominent among them were the recursive functions of Church and Kleene and Post systems, but there are many other such systems that have been studied. In this chapter we briefly review some of the ideas that arose out of these studies. There is a wealth of material here that we cannot cover. We will give only a very brief presentation, referring the reader to other references for detail. A quite accessible account of recursive functions and Post systems can be found in Denning, Dennis, and Qualitz (1978), while a good discussion of various other rewriting systems is given in Salomaa (1973) and Salomaa (1985).

The models of computation we study here, as well as others that have been proposed, have diverse origins. But it was eventually found that they were all equivalent in their power to carry out computations. The spirit of this observation is generally called **Church's thesis**. This thesis states that all possible models of computation, if they are sufficiently broad, must be equivalent. It also implies that there is an inherent limitation in this and that there are functions that cannot be expressed in any way that gives an explicit method for their computation. The claim is of course very closely related to Turing's thesis, and the combined notion is sometimes called the **Church-Turing thesis**. It provides a general principle for algorithmic computation and, while not provable, gives strong evidence that no more powerful models can be found.

13.1 Recursive Functions

The concept of a function is fundamental to much of mathematics. As summarized in Section 1.1, a function is a rule that assigns to an element of one set, called the **domain** of the function, a unique value in another set, called the **range** of the function. This is very broad and general and immediately raises the question of how we can explicitly represent this association. There are many ways in which functions can be defined. Some of them we use frequently, while others are less common.

We are all familiar with functional notation in which we write expressions like

$$f(n) = n^2 + 1.$$

This defines the function f by means of a recipe for its computation: given any value for the argument n, multiply that value by itself, and then add one. Since the function is defined in this explicit way, we can compute its values in a strictly mechanical fashion. To complete the definition of f, we also must specify its domain. If, for example, we take the domain to be the set of all integers, then the range of f will be some subset of the set of positive integers.

Since many very complicated functions can be specified this way, we may well ask to what extent the notation is universal. If a function is defined (that is, we know the relation between the elements of its domain and its range), can it be expressed in such a functional form? To answer the question, we must first clarify what the permissible forms are: for this we introduce some basic functions, together with rules for building from them some more complicated ones.

Primitive Recursive Functions

To keep the discussion simple, we will consider only functions of one or two variables, whose domain is either I, the set of all non-negative integers, or $I \times I$, and whose range is in I. In this setting, we start with the basic functions:

1. The **zero function** $z(x) = 0$, for all $x \in I$.

2. The **successor function** $s(x)$, whose value is the integer next in sequence to x, that is, in the usual notation, $s(x) = x + 1$.

3. The **projector functions**

$$p_k(x_1, x_2) = x_k, \qquad k = 1, 2.$$

There are two ways of building more complicated functions from these:

1. **Composition**, by which we construct

$$f(x, y) = h(g_1(x, y), g_2(x, y))$$

from defined functions g_1, g_2, h.

2. **Primitive recursion**, by which a function can be defined recursively through

$$f(x, 0) = g_1(x),$$
$$f(x, y + 1) = h(g_2(x, y), f(x, y)),$$

from defined functions g_1, g_2, and h.

We illustrate how this works by showing how the basic operations of integer arithmetic can be constructed in this fashion.

| Example 13.1 | Addition of integers x and y can be implemented with the function $add\,(x,y)$, defined by |

$$add\,(x,0) = x,$$
$$add\,(x,y+1) = add\,(x,y) + 1.$$

To add 2 and 3, we apply these rules successively:

$$\begin{aligned}
add\,(3,2) &= add\,(3,1) + 1 \\
&= (add\,(3,0) + 1) + 1 \\
&= (3+1) + 1 \\
&= 4 + 1 = 5.
\end{aligned}$$

| Example 13.2 | Using the add function defined in Example 13.1, we can now define multiplication by |

$$mult\,(x,0) = 0,$$
$$mult\,(x,y+1) = add\,(x, mult\,(x,y)).$$

Formally, the second step is an application of primitive recursion, in which h is identified with the add function, and $g_2\,(x,y)$ is the projector function $p_1\,(x,y)$.

| Example 13.3 | Substraction is not quite so obvious. First, we must define it, taking into account that negative numbers are not permitted in our system. A kind of subtraction is defined from usual subtraction by |

$$x \overset{\cdot}{-} y = x - y \text{ if } x \geq y,$$
$$x \overset{\cdot}{-} y = 0 \text{ if } x < y.$$

The operator $\overset{\cdot}{-}$ is sometimes called the **monus**; it defines subtraction so that its range is I.

Now we define the predecessor function

$$pred\,(0) = 0,$$
$$pred\,(y + 1) = y,$$

and from it, the subtracting function

$$subtr\,(x, 0) = x,$$
$$subtr\,(x, y + 1) = pred\,(subtr\,(x, y)).$$

To prove that $5-3 = 2$, we reduce the proposition by applying the definitions a number of times:

$$
\begin{aligned}
subtr\,(5, 3) &= pred\,(subtr\,(5, 2)) \\
&= pred\,(pred\,(subtr\,(5, 1))) \\
&= pred\,(pred\,(pred\,(subtr\,(5, 0)))) \\
&= pred\,(pred\,(pred\,(5))) \\
&= pred\,(pred\,(4)) \\
&= pred\,(3) \\
&= 2.
\end{aligned}
$$

In much the same way, we can define integer division, but we will leave the demonstration of it as an exercise. If we accept this as given, we see that the basic arithmetic operations are all constructible by the elementary processes described. With the algebraic operations precisely defined, other more complicated ones can now be constructed, and very complex computations built from the simple ones. We call functions that can be constructed in such a manner primitive recursive.

Definition 13.1

A function is called **primitive recursive** if and only if it can be constructed from the basic functions z, s, p_k, by successive composition and primitive recursion.

Note that if g_1, g_2, and h are total functions, then f defined by composition and primitive recursion is also a total function. It follows from this that every primitive recursive function is a total function on I or $I \times I$.

The expressive power of primitive recursive functions is considerable, and most common functions are primitive recursive. However, not all functions are in this class, as the following argument shows.

Theorem 13.1

Let F denote the set of all functions from I to I. Then there is some function in F that is not primitive recursive.

Proof: Every primitive recursive function can be described by a finite string that indicates how it is defined. Such strings can be encoded and arranged in standard order. Therefore, the set of all primitive recursive functions is countable.

Suppose now that the set of all functions is also countable. We can then write all functions in some order, say, $f_1, f_2, \dots$. We next construct a function g defined as

$$g(i) = f_i(i) + 1, \qquad i = 1, 2, \dots.$$

Clearly, g is well defined and is therefore in F, but equally clearly, g differs from every f_i in the diagonal position. This contradiction proves that F cannot be countable.

Combining these two observations proves that there must be some function in F that is not primitive recursive. ∎

Actually, this goes even further; not only are there functions that are not primitive recursive, there are in fact computable functions that are not primitive recursive.

Theorem 13.2

Let C be the set of all total computable functions from I to I. Then there is some function in C that is not primitive recursive.

Proof: By the argument of the previous theorem, the set of all primitive recursive functions is countable. Let us denote the functions in this set as $r_1, r_2, \dots$ and define a function g by

$$g(i) = r_i(i) + 1.$$

By construction, the function g differs from every r_i and is therefore not primitive recursive. But clearly g is computable, proving the theorem. ∎

The nonconstructive proof that there are computable functions that are not primitive recursive is a fairly simple exercise in diagonalization. The actual construction of an example of such a function is a much more complicated matter. We will give here one example that looks quite simple; however, the demonstration that it is not primitive recursive is quite lengthy.

Ackermann's Function

Ackermann's function is a function from $I \times I$ to I, defined by

$$A(0, y) = y + 1,$$
$$A(x, 0) = A(x - 1, 1),$$
$$A(x, y + 1) = A(x - 1, A(x, y)).$$

It is not hard to see that A is a total, computable function. In fact, it is quite elementary to write a recursive computer program for its computation. But in spite of its apparent simplicity, Ackermann's function is not primitive recursive.

Of course, we cannot argue directly from the definition of A. Even though this definition is not in the form required for a primitive recursive function, it is possible that an appropriate alternative definition could exist. The situation here is similar to the one we encountered when we tried to prove that a language was not regular or not context-free. We need to appeal to some general property of the class of all primitive recursive functions and show that Ackermann's function violates this property. For primitive recursive functions, one such property is the growth rate. There is a limit to how fast a primitive recursive function can grow as $i \to \infty$, and Ackermann's function violates this limit. That Ackermann's function grows very rapidly is easily demonstrated; see, for example, Exercises 9 to 11 at the end of this section. How this is related to the limit of growth for primitive recursive functions is made precise in the following theorem. Its proof, which is tedious and technical, will be omitted.

Theorem 13.3 Let f be any primitive recursive function. Then there exists some integer n such that

$$f(i) < A(n, i),$$

for all $i = n, n + 1, \ldots$.

Proof: For the details of the argument, see Denning, Dennis, and Qualitz (1978, p. 534). ∎

If we accept this result, it follows easily that Ackermann's function is not primitive recursive.

Theorem 13.4 Ackermann's function is not primitive recursive.

Proof: Consider the function

$$g(i) = A(i, i).$$

If A were primitive recursive, then so would g. But then, according to Theorem 13.3, there exists an n such that

$$g(i) < A(n, i),$$

for all i. If we now pick $i = n$, we get the contradiction

$$\begin{aligned} g(n) &= A(n, n) \\ &< A(n, n), \end{aligned}$$

proving that A cannot be primitive recursive. ∎

μ-Recursive Functions

To extend the idea of recursive functions to cover Ackermann's function and other computable functions, we must add something to the rules by which such functions can be constructed. One way is to introduce the μ or **minimalization** operator, defined by

$$\mu y(g(x, y)) = \text{ smallest } y \text{ such that } g(x, y) = 0.$$

In this definition, we assume that g is a total function.

Example 13.4   Let

$$g(x, y) = x + y - 3,$$

which is a total function. If $x \leq 3$, then

$$y = 3 - x$$

is the result of the minimalization, but if $x > 3$, then there is no $y \in I$ such that $x + y - 3 = 0$. Therefore,

$$\begin{aligned} \mu y(g(x, y)) &= 3 - x, &&\text{for } x \leq 3 \\ &= \text{undefined, for } x > 3. \end{aligned}$$

We see from this that even though $g(x, y)$ is a total function, $\mu y(g(x, y))$ may only be partial.

As the above example shows, the minimalization operation opens the possibility of defining partial functions recursively. But it turns out that it also extends the power to define total functions so as to include all computable functions. Again, we merely quote the major result with references to the literature where the details may be found.

Definition 13.2

A function is said to be μ-recursive if it can be constructed from the basis functions by a sequence of applications of the μ-operator and the operations of composition and primitive recursion.

Theorem 13.5   A function is μ-recursive if and only if it is computable.

Proof: For a proof, see Denning, Dennis, and Qualitz (1978, Chapter 13).   ■

The μ-recursive functions therefore give us another model for algorithmic computation.

EXERCISES

1. Use the definitions in Examples 13.1 and 13.2 to prove that $3 + 4 = 7$ and $2 * 3 = 6$.

2. Define the function

$$greater\,(x, y) = 1 \text{ if } x > y$$
$$= 0 \text{ if } x \leq y$$

Show that this function is primitive recursive. Ⓢ

3. Consider the function

$$equals\,(x, y) = 1 \quad \text{if } x = y,$$
$$= 0 \quad \text{if } x \neq y.$$

Show that this function is primitive recursive.

4. Let f be defined by

$$f\,(x, y) = x \quad \text{if } x \neq y,$$
$$= 0 \quad \text{if } x = y.$$

Show that this function is primitive recursive.

★ 5. Integer division can be defined by two functions *div* and *rem*:

$$div\,(x, y) = n,$$

where n is the largest integer such that $x \geq ny$, and

$$rem\,(x, y) = x - ny.$$

Show that the functions *div* and *rem* are primitive recursive.

6. Show that

$$f\,(n) = 2^n$$

is primitive recursive.

7. Show that the function

$$g\,(x, y) = x^y$$

is primitive recursive. **S**

8. Write a computer program for computing Ackermann's function. Use it to evaluate $A\,(2, 5)$ and $A\,(3, 3)$.

9. Prove the following for the Ackermann function.

(a) $A\,(1, y) = y + 2$ **S**

(b) $A\,(2, y) = 2y + 3$ **S**

(c) $A\,(3, y) = 2^{y+3} - 3$

10. Use Exercise 9 to compute $A\,(4, 1)$ and $A\,(4, 2)$.

11. Give a general expression for $A\,(4, y)$.

12. Show the sequence of recursive calls in the computation of $A\,(5, 2)$.

13. Show that Ackermann's function is a total function in $I \times I$.

14. Try to use the program constructed for Exercise 8 to evaluate $A\,(5, 5)$. Can you explain what you observe?

15. For each g below, compute $\mu y\,(g\,(x, y))$, and determine its domain.

(a) $g\,(x, y) = xy$

(b) $g\,(x, y) = 2^x + y \dot- 3$ **S**

(c) $g\,(x, y) = $ integer part of $(x - 1)\,/\,(y + 1)$

(d) $g\,(x, y) = x \bmod(y + 1)$

16. The definition of *pred* in Example 13.3, although intuitively clear, does not strictly adhere to the definition of a primitive recursive function. Show how the definition can be rewritten so that it has the correct form.

13.2 Post Systems

A Post system looks very much like an unrestricted grammar, consisting of an alphabet and some production rules by which successive strings can be derived. But there are significant differences in the way in which the productions are applied.

Definition 13.3

A Post system Π is defined by

$$\Pi = (C, V, A, P),$$

where

> C is a finite set of constants, consisting of two disjoint sets C_N, called the **nonterminal constants**, and C_T, the set of **terminal constants**,
>
> V is a finite set of variables,
>
> A is a finite set from C^*, called the **axioms**,
>
> P is a finite set of productions.

The productions in a Post system must satisfy certain restrictions. They must be of the form

$$x_1 V_1 x_2 \cdots V_n x_{n+1} \rightarrow y_1 W_1 y_2 \cdots W_m y_{m+1}, \tag{13.1}$$

where x_i, $y_i \in C^*$, and V_i, $W_i \in V$, subject to the requirement that any variable can appear at most once on the left, so that

$$V_i \neq V_j \text{ for } i \neq j,$$

and that each variable on the right must appear on the left, that is

$$\bigcup_{i=1}^{m} W_i \subseteq \bigcup_{i=1}^{n} V_i.$$

Suppose we have a string of terminals of the form $x_1 w_1 x_2 w_2 \cdots w_n x_{n+1}$, where the substrings x_1, $x_2 \cdots$ match the corresponding strings in (13.1) and $w_i \in C^*$. We can then make the identification $w_1 - V_1$, $w_2 = V_2, ...,$ and substitute these values for the W's on the right of (13.1). Since every

W is some V_i that occurs on the left, it is assigned a unique value, and we get the new string $y_1 w_i y_2 w_j \cdots y_{m+1}$. We write this as

$$x_1 w_1 x_2 w_2 \cdots x_{n+1} \Rightarrow y_1 w_i y_2 w_j \cdots y_{m+1}.$$

As for a grammar, we can now talk about the language derived by a Post system.

Definition 13.4

The language generated by the Post system $\Pi = (C, V, A, P)$ is

$$L(\Pi) = \left\{ w \in C_T^* : w_0 \overset{*}{\Rightarrow} w \text{ for some } w_0 \in A \right\}.$$

Example 13.5   Consider the Post system with

$$C_T = \{a, b\},$$
$$C_N = \emptyset,$$
$$V = \{V_1\},$$
$$A = \{\lambda\},$$

and production

$$V_1 \to a V_1 b.$$

This allows the derivation

$$\lambda \Rightarrow ab \Rightarrow aabb.$$

In the first step, we apply (13.1) with the identification $x_1 = \lambda$, $V_1 = \lambda$, $x_2 = \lambda$, $y_1 = a$, $W_1 = V_1$, and $y_2 = b$. In the second step, we re-identify $V_1 = ab$, leaving everything else the same. If you continue with this, you will quickly convince yourself that the language generated by this particular Post system is $\{a^n b^n : n \geq 0\}$.

Example 13.6   Consider the Post system with

$$C_T = \{1, +, =\},$$
$$C_N = \emptyset,$$
$$V = \{V_1, V_2, V_3\},$$
$$A = \{1 + 1 = 11\},$$

and productions

$$V_1 + V_2 = V_3 \rightarrow V_1 1 + V_2 = V_3 1,$$
$$V_1 + V_2 = V_3 \rightarrow V_1 + V_2 1 = V_3 1.$$

The system allows the derivation

$$1 + 1 = 11 \Rightarrow 11 + 1 = 111$$
$$\Rightarrow 11 + 11 = 1111.$$

Interpreting the strings of 1's as unary representations of integers, the derivation can be written as

$$1 + 1 = 2 \Rightarrow 2 + 1 = 3 \Rightarrow 2 + 2 = 4.$$

The language generated by this Post system is the set of all identities of integer additions, such as $2 + 2 = 4$, derived from the axiom $1 + 1 = 2$.

Example 13.6 illustrates in a simple manner the original intent of Post systems as a mechanism for rigorously proving mathematical statements from a set of axioms. It also shows the inherent awkwardness of such a completely rigorous approach and why it is rarely used. But Post systems, even though they are cumbersome for proving complicated theorems, are general models for computation, as the next theorem shows.

Theorem 13.6   A language is recursively enumerable if and only if there exists some Post system that generates it.

Proof: The arguments here are relatively simple and we sketch them briefly. First, since a derivation by a Post system is completely mechanical, it can be carried out on a Turing machine. Therefore, any language generated by a Post system is recursively enumerable.

For the converse, remember that any recursively enumerable language is generated by some unrestricted grammar G, having productions all of the form

$$x \rightarrow y,$$

with $x, y \in (V \cup T)^*$. Given any unrestricted grammar G, we create a Post system $\Pi = (V_\Pi, C, A, P_\Pi)$, where $V_\Pi = \{V_1, V_2\}, C_N = V, C_T = T, A = \{S\}$, and with productions

$$V_1 x V_2 \rightarrow V_1 y V_2,$$

for every production $x \rightarrow y$ of the grammar. It is then an easy matter to show that a w can be generated by the Post system Π if and only if it is in the language generated by G. ∎

EXERCISES

1. For $\Sigma = \{a, b, c\}$, find a Post system that generates the following languages.

   (a) $L(a^* b + a b^* c)$

   (b) $L = \{ww\}$ **S**

   (c) $L = \{a^n b^n c^n\}$

2. Find a Post system that generates

$$L = \left\{ ww^R : w \in \{a, b\}^* \right\}.$$

3. For $\Sigma = \{a\}$, what language does the Post system with axiom $\{a\}$ and the following production generate?

$$V_1 \rightarrow V_1 V_1 \quad \text{S}$$

4. What language does the Post system in Exercise 3 generate if the axiom set is $\{a, ab\}$?

5. Find a Post system for proving the identities of integer multiplication, starting from the axiom $1 * 1 = 1$. **S**

6. Give the details of the proof of Theorem 13.6.

7. What language does the Post system with

$$V \rightarrow aVV$$

   and axiom set $\{ab\}$ generate?

8. A restricted Post system is one on which every production $x \rightarrow y$ satisfies, in addition to the usual requirements, the further restriction that the number of variable occurrences on the right and left is the same, i.e., $n = m$ in (13.1). Show that for every language L generated by some Post system, there exists a restricted Post system to generates L.

█13.3█ Rewriting Systems

The various grammars we have studied have a number of things in common with Post systems: They are all based on some alphabet from which one string can be obtained from another. Even a Turing machine can be viewed this way, since its instantaneous description is a string that completely defines its configuration. The program is then just a set of rules for producing one such string from a previous one. These observations can be formalized in the concept of a **rewriting system**. Generally, a rewriting system consists of an alphabet Σ and a set of rules or productions by which a string in Σ^+ can produce another. What distinguishes one rewriting system from another is the nature of Σ and restrictions for the application of the productions.

The idea is quite broad and allows any number of specific cases in addition to the ones we have already encountered. Here we briefly introduce some less well-known ones that are interesting and also provide general models for computation. For details, see Salomaa (1973) and Salomaa (1985).

Matrix Grammars

Matrix grammars differ from the grammars we have previously studied (which are often called **phrase-structure grammars**) in how the productions can be applied. For matrix grammars, the set of productions consists of subsets $P_1, P_2, ..., P_n$, each of which is an ordered sequence

$$x_1 \to y_1, x_2 \to y_2, ...$$

Whenever the first production of some set P_i is applied, we must next apply the second one to the string just created, then the third one, and so on. We cannot apply the first production of P_i unless all other productions in this set can also be applied.

Example 13.7   Consider the matrix grammar

$$P_1 : S \to S_1 S_2,$$
$$P_2 : S_1 \to a S_1, S_2 \to b S_2 c,$$
$$P_3 : S_1 \to \lambda, S_2 \to \lambda.$$

A derivation with this grammar is

$$S \Rightarrow S_1 S_2 \Rightarrow a S_1 b S_2 c \Rightarrow a a S_1 b b S_2 c c \Rightarrow a a b b c c.$$

Note that whenever the first rule of P_2 is used to create an a, the second one also has to be used, producing a corresponding b and c. This makes it easy to see that the set of terminal strings generated by this matrix grammar is

$$L = \{a^n b^n c^n : n \geq 0\}.$$

Matrix grammars contain phrase-structure grammars as a special case in which each P_i contains exactly one production. Also, since matrix grammars represent algorithmic processes, they are governed by Church's thesis. We conclude from this that matrix grammars and phrase-structure grammars have the same power as models of computation. But, as Example 13.7 shows, sometimes the use of a matrix grammar gives a much simpler solution than we can achieve with an unrestricted phrase-structure grammar.

Markov Algorithms

A Markov algorithm is a rewriting system whose productions

$$x \rightarrow y$$

are considered ordered. In a derivation, the first applicable production must be used. Furthermore, the leftmost occurrence of the substring x must be replaced by y. Some of the productions may be singled out as terminal productions; they will be shown as

$$x \rightarrow .y.$$

A derivation starts with some string $w \in \Sigma$ and continues until either a terminal production is used or until there are no applicable productions.

For language acceptance, a set $T \subseteq \Sigma$ of terminals is identified. Starting with a terminal string, productions are applied until the empty string is produced.

Definition 13.5

Let M be a Markov algorithm with alphabet Σ and terminals T. Then the set

$$L(M) = \left\{ w \in T^* : w \stackrel{*}{\Rightarrow} \lambda \right\}$$

is the language accepted by M.

Example 13.8   Consider the Markov algorithm with $\Sigma = T = \{a, b\}$ and productions

$$ab \rightarrow \lambda,$$
$$ba \rightarrow \lambda.$$

Every step in the derivation annihilates a substring ab or ba, so

$$L(M) = \left\{ w \in \{a, b\}^* : n_a(w) = n_b(w) \right\}.$$

Example 13.9   Find a Markov algorithm for

$$L = \{a^n b^n : n \geq 0\}.$$

An answer is

$$ab \rightarrow S,$$
$$aSb \rightarrow S,$$
$$S \rightarrow \cdot\lambda.$$

If in this last example we take the first two productions and reverse the left and right sides, we get a context-free grammar that generates the language L. In a certain sense, Markov algorithms are simply phrase-structure grammars working backward. This cannot be taken too literally, since it is not clear what to do with the last production. But the observation does provide a starting point for a proof of the following theorem that characterizes the power of Markov algorithms.

Theorem 13.7   A language is recursively enumerable if and only if there exists a Markov algorithm for it.

Proof: See Salomaa (1985, p. 35). ■

L-Systems

The origins of L-systems are quite different from what we might expect. Their developer, A. Lindenmayer, used them to model the growth pattern of certain organisms. L-systems are essentially *parallel* rewriting systems. By this we mean that in each step of a derivation, every symbol has to be rewritten. For this to make sense, the productions of an L-system must be of the form

$$a \rightarrow u, \tag{13.2}$$

where $a \in \Sigma$ and $u \in \Sigma^*$. When a string is rewritten, one such production must be applied to every symbol of the string before the new string is generated.

Example 13.10 Let $\Sigma = \{a\}$ and

$$a \rightarrow aa$$

define an L-system. Starting from the string a, we can make the derivation

$$a \Rightarrow aa \Rightarrow aaaa \Rightarrow aaaaaaaa.$$

The set of strings so derived is clearly

$$L = \left\{a^{2^n} : n \geq 0\right\}.$$

Note again how such special rewriting systems are able to deal with problems that are quite difficult for phrase structure grammars.

It is known that L-systems with productions of the form (13.2) are not sufficiently general to provide for all algorithmic computations. An extension of the idea provides the necessary generalization. In an extended L-system, productions are of the form

$$(x, a, y) \rightarrow u,$$

where $a \in \Sigma$ and $x, y, u \in \Sigma^*$, with the interpretation that a can be replaced by u only if it occurs as part of the string xay. It is known that such extended L-systems are general models of computation. For details, see Salomaa (1985).

EXERCISES

1. Find a matrix grammar for

$$L - \{ww : w \in \{a, b\}^*\}. \quad \text{Ⓢ}$$

2. What language is generated by the matrix grammar

$$P_1 : S \rightarrow S_1 S_2,$$
$$P_2 : S_1 \rightarrow aS_1 b, S_2 \rightarrow bS_2 a,$$
$$P_3 : S_1 \rightarrow \lambda, S_2 \rightarrow \lambda.$$

3. Suppose that in Example 13.7 we change the last group of productions to

$$P_3 : S_1 \rightarrow \lambda, S_2 \rightarrow S.$$

What language is generated by this matrix grammar?

4. Why does the Markov algorithm in Example 13.9 not accept *abab*?

5. Find a Markov algorithm that derives the language $L = \{a^n b^n c^n : n \geq 1\}$.
   Ⓢ

★ 6. Find a Markov algorithm that accepts

$$L = \{a^n b^m a^{nm} : n \geq 1, m \geq 1\}.$$

7. Find an L-system that generates $L(aa^*)$.

8. What is the set of strings generated by the L-system with productions

$$a \rightarrow aa,$$
$$a \rightarrow aaa,$$

when started with the string a? Ⓢ

Chapter 14

An Introduction to Computational Complexity

In studying algorithms and computations, we have so far paid little attention to what actually can be expected when we apply these ideas to real computers. We have been almost exclusively concerned with questions of the existence or nonexistence of algorithms for certain problems. This is an appropriate starting point for a theory but clearly of limited practical significance. For actual computations, we need not only to know that a problem can be solved in principle, but we also must be able to construct algorithms that can be carried out with reasonable efficiency. Problems that can be solved effectively are called **tractable**, a descriptive term that will be given a more precise meaning in this chapter.

In the practical world of software development, efficiency has many facets. Sometimes, we are concerned with the efficient use of the computer's resources, such as processor time and memory space. At other times, we may be more concerned with how quickly software can be created, how effectively it can be maintained, or how reliable it is. At still other times, we may emphasize the efficiency with which a user's problems can be solved. All this is much too complicated to be captured by any abstract theory. All we can do is to focus on some of the more tangible issues and create the

343

appropriate abstract framework for these. Most of the results that have been developed address the space and time efficiency of a computation, leading to the important topic of **complexity theory**. In the study of complexity, the primary concern is the efficiency of a computation as measured by its time and space requirements. We refer to this as the **time-complexity** and the **space-complexity** of algorithms.

Computational complexity theory is an extensive topic, most of which is well outside the scope of this text. There are some results, however, that are simply stated and easily appreciated, and that throw further light on the nature of languages and computations. In this section, we give a brief overview of some complexity results. For the most part, proofs are difficult and we will dispense with them by reference to appropriate sources. Our intent here is to present the flavor of the subject matter and show how it relates to what we know about languages and automata. For this reason we will allow ourselves a great deal of latitude, both in the selection of topics and in the formality of the discussion.

We will limit our discussion here to issues of time-complexity. There are similar results for space-complexity, but time-complexity is a little more accessible.

14.1 Efficiency of Computation

Let us start with a concrete example. Given a list of one thousand integers, we want to sort them in some way, say, in ascending order. Sorting is a simple problem but also one that is very fundamental in computer science. If we now ask the question "How long will it take to do this task?" we see immediately that much more information is needed before we can answer it. Clearly, the number of items in the list plays an important role in how much time will be taken, but there are other factors. There is the question of what computer we use and how we write the program. Also, there are a number of sorting methods so that selection of the algorithm is important. There are probably a few more things you can think of that need to be looked at before you can even make a rough guess of the time requirements. If we have any hope of producing some general picture of sorting, most of these issues have to be ignored, and we must concentrate on those that are most fundamental.

For our discussion of computational complexity, we will make the following simplifying assumptions.

1. The model for our study will be a Turing machine. The exact type of Turing machine to be used will be discussed below.

2. The size of the problem will be denoted by n. For our sorting problem, n is obviously the number of items in the list. Although the size of a

problem is not always so easily characterized, we can generally relate it in some way to a positive integer.

3. In analyzing an algorithm, we are less interested in its performance on a specific case than in its general behavior. We are particularly concerned with how the algorithm behaves when the problem size increases. Because of this, the primary question is with how fast the resource requirements grow as n becomes large.

Our immediate goal will then be to characterize the time requirement of a problem as a function of its size, using a Turing machine as the computer model.

First, we give some meaning to the concept of time for a Turing machine. We think of a Turing machine as making one move per time unit, so the time taken by a computation is the number of moves made. As stated, we want to study how the computational requirements grow with the size of the problem. Normally, in the set of all problems of a given size, there is some variation. Here we are interested only in the worst case that has the highest resource requirements. By saying that a computation has a time-complexity $T(n)$, we mean that the computation for any problem of size n can be completed in no more than $T(n)$ moves on some Turing machine.

After settling on a specific type of Turing machine as a computational model, we could analyze algorithms by writing explicit programs and counting the number of steps involved in solving the problem. But, for a variety of reasons, this is not overly useful. First, the number of operations performed may vary with the small details of the program and so may depend strongly on the programmer. Second, from a practical standpoint, we are interested in how the algorithm performs in the real world, which may differ considerably from how it does on a Turing machine. The best we can hope for is that the Turing machine analysis is representative of the major aspects of the real-life performance, for example, the asymptotic growth rate of the time complexity. Our first attempt at understanding the resource requirements of an algorithm is therefore invariably an *order-of-magnitude* analysis in which we use the O, Θ, and Ω notation introduced in Chapter 1. In spite of the apparent informality of this approach, we often get very useful information.

Example 14.1

Given a set of n numbers $x_1, x_2, ..., x_n$ and a key number x, determine if the set contains x.

Unless the set is organized in some way, the simplest algorithm is just a *linear search* in which we compare x successively against $x_1, x_2, ...,$ until we either find a match or we get to the last element of the set. Since we may find a match on the first comparison or on the last, we cannot predict how much work is involved, but we know that, in the worst case, we have to make n comparisons. We can then say that the time-complexity of this linear search is $O(n)$, or even better, $\Theta(n)$. In making this analysis, we made no specific assumptions about what machine this is run on or how the algorithm is implemented.

EXERCISES

1. Suppose you are given a set of n numbers $x_1, x_2, ..., x_n$ and are asked to determine whether this set contains any duplicates.

   (a) Suggest an algorithm and find an order-of-magnitude expression for its time-complexity.

   (b) Examine if the implementation of the algorithm on a Turing machine affects your conclusions.

2. Repeat Exercise 2, this time determining if the set contains any triplicates. Is the algorithm as efficient as possible?

3. Review how the choice of algorithm affects the efficiency of sorting.

14.2 Turing Machines and Complexity

In Chapter 10 we argued that the various types of Turing machines were equivalent in their power to solve problems. This allowed us to take whatever type was most convenient for an argument and even use programs in higher-level computer languages to avoid some of the tedium involved in using the standard Turing machine model. But when we make complexity an issue, the equivalence between the various types of Turing machines no longer holds.

Example 14.2   In Example 9.4 we constructed a single-tape Turing machine for the language

$$L = \{a^n b^n : n \geq 1\}.$$

A look at that algorithm will show that for $w = a^n b^n$ it takes roughly $2n$ steps to match each a with the corresponding b. Therefore the whole computation takes $O(n^2)$ time.

But, as we later indicated in Example 10.1, with a two-tape machine we can use a different algorithm. We first copy all the a's to the second

Figure 14.1

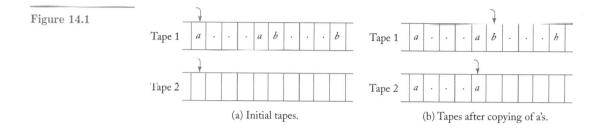

(a) Initial tapes.   (b) Tapes after copying of a's.

tape, then match them against the b's on the first. The situation before and after the copying is shown in Figure 14.1. Both the copying and the matching can be done in $O(n)$ time and we see that a two-tape machine has time-complexity $O(n)$.

Example 14.3   In Sections 5.2 and 6.3 we discussed the membership problem for context-free languages. If we take the length of the input string w as the problem size n, then the exhaustive search method has complexity $O\left(n^{M}\right)$, where M depends on the grammar. The more efficient CYK algorithm has complexity $O\left(n^{3}\right)$. Both these algorithms are deterministic.

A nondeterministic algorithm for this problem proceeds by simply guessing which sequence of productions is applied in the derivation of w. If we work with a grammar that has no unit or λ-productions, the length of the derivation is essentially $|w|$, so we have an $O(n)$ algorithm.

Example 14.4   We now introduce the **satisfiability problem**, which plays an important role in complexity theory.

A logic or boolean constant or variable is one that can take on exactly two values, true or false, which we will denote by 1 and 0, respectively. Boolean operators are then used to combine boolean constants and variables into boolean expressions. The simplest boolean operators are *or*, denoted by $\vee$ and defined by

$$0\vee1 = 1\vee0 = 1\vee1 = 1,$$
$$0\vee0 = 0,$$

and the *and* operation ($\land$) defined by

$$0 \land 0 = 0 \land 1 = 1 \land 0 = 0,$$
$$1 \land 1 = 1.$$

Also needed is *negation*, denoted by a bar, and defined by

$$\overline{0} = 1,$$
$$\overline{1} = 0.$$

We consider now boolean expressions in **conjunction normal form**. In this form, we create expressions from variables $x_1, x_2, ..., x_n$, starting with

$$e = t_i \land t_j \land ... \land t_k. \tag{14.1}$$

The terms $t_i, t_j, ..., t_k$ are created by or-ing together variables and their negation, that is,

$$t_i = s_l \lor s_m \lor ... \lor s_p, \tag{14.2}$$

where each $s_l, s_m, ..., s_p$ stands for some variable or the negation of a variable.

The satisfiability problem is then simply stated: given an expression e in conjunctive normal form, is there an assignment of values to the variables $x_1, x_2, ..., x_n$ that will make the value of e true. For a specific case, look at

$$e_1 = (\overline{x}_1 \lor x_2) \land (x_1 \lor x_3).$$

The assignment $x_1 = 0, x_2 = 1, x_3 = 1$ makes e_1 true so that this expression is satisfiable. On the other hand,

$$e_2 = (x_1 \lor x_2) \land \overline{x}_1 \land \overline{x}_2$$

is not satisfiable because every assignment for the variables x_1 and x_2 will make e_2 false.

A deterministic algorithm for the satisfiability problem is easy to discover. We take all possible values for the variables $x_1, x_2, ..., x_n$ and evaluate the expression. Since there are 2^n such choices, this exhaustive approach has exponential time complexity.

Again, the nondeterministic approach simplifies matters. If e is satisfiable, we guess the value of each x_i and then evaluate e. This is essentially an $O(n)$ algorithm. As in Example 14.3, we have a deterministic exhaustive search algorithm whose complexity is exponential and a linear nondeterministic one. However, unlike the previous example, we do not know of any nonexponential deterministic algorithm.

These examples suggest that complexity questions are affected by the type of Turing machine we use and that the issue of determinism versus nondeterminism is a particularly crucial one. Example 14.1 suggests that algorithms for a multitape machine may be reasonably close to what we might use when we program in a computer language. For this reason, we will use a multitape Turing machine as our model for studying complexity issues.

EXERCISES

For the exercises in this set, assume that the Turing machines involved are all deterministic.

1. Find a linear-time algorithm for membership in $\{ww : w \in \{a, b\}^*\}$ using a two-tape Turing machine. What is the best you could expect on a one-tape machine?

2. Show that any computation that can be performed on a single-tape, off-line Turing machine in time $O(T(n))$ also can be performed on a standard Turing machine in time $O(T(n))$.

3. Show that any computation that can be performed on a standard Turing machine in time $O(T(n))$ also can be performed on a Turing machine with one semi-infinite tape in time $O(T(n))$.

4. Show that any computation that can be performed on a two-tape machine in time $O(T(n))$ can be performed on a standard Turing machine in time $O(T^2(n))$.

5. Rewrite the boolean expression

$$(x_1 \wedge x_2) \vee x_3$$

in conjunctive normal form.

6. Determine whether or not the expression

$$(x_1 \vee \overline{x}_2 \vee x_3) \wedge (x_1 \vee x_2 \vee \overline{x}_3) \wedge (\overline{x}_1 \vee \overline{x}_2 \vee \overline{x}_3)$$

is satisfiable.

7. In Example 14.2 we claimed that the first algorithm had time complexity $O(n^2)$ and the second $O(n)$. Can we be more precise and claim that $T(n) = \Theta(n^2)$ for the first case, and $T(n) = \Theta(n)$ for the second? How this strengthen the argument in Example 14.2?

14.3 Language Families and Complexity Classes

In the Chomsky hierarchy for language classification, we associate language families with classes of automata, where each class of automata is defined by the nature of its temporary storage. Another way of classifying languages is to use a Turing machine of a particular type but consider time complexity a distinguishing factor. To do so, we first define the time complexity of a language.

Definition 14.1

We say that a Turing machine accepts a language L in time $T(n)$ if every w in L with $|w| \leq n$ is accepted in $O(T(n))$ moves. If M is nondeterministic, this implies that for every $w \in L$, there is at least one sequence of moves of length $O(T(|w|))$ that leads to acceptance.

Definition 14.2

A language L is said to be a member of the class $DTIME(T(n))$ if there exists a deterministic multitape Turing machine that accepts L in time $T(n)$.

A language L is said to be a member of the class $NTIME(T(n))$ if there exists a nondeterministic multitape Turing machine that accepts L in time $T(n)$.

Some relations between these complexity classes such as

$$DTIME(T(n)) \subseteq NTIME(T(n)),$$

and

$$T_1(n) = O(T_2(n))$$

implies

$$DTIME(T_1(n)) \subseteq DTIME(T_2(n)),$$

are obvious, but from here the situation gets obscure quickly. What we can say is that as the order of $T(n)$ increases, we take in progressively more languages.

Theorem 14.1 For every integer $k \geq 1$,

$$DTIME\left(n^k\right) \subset DTIME\left(n^{k+1}\right).$$

Proof: This follows from a result in Hopcroft and Ullman (1979, p. 299). ∎

The conclusion we can draw from this is that there are some languages that can be accepted in time n^2 for which there is no linear membership algorithm, that there are languages in $DTIME\left(n^3\right)$ that are not in $DTIME\left(n^2\right)$, and so on. This gives us an infinite number of nested complexity classes. We get even more if we allow exponential time complexity. In fact, there is no limit to this; no matter how rapidly the complexity function $T(n)$ grows, there is always something outside $DTIME\left(T(n)\right)$.

Theorem 14.2 There is no total Turing computable function $f(n)$ such that every recursive language is in $DTIME\left(f(n)\right)$.

Proof: Consider the alphabet $\Sigma = \{0, 1\}$, with all strings in Σ^+ arranged in proper order $w_1, w_2, \dots$. Also, assume that we have a proper ordering for the Turing machines in $M_1, M_2, \dots$.

Assume now that the function $f(n)$ in the statement of the theorem exists. We can then define the language

$$L = \{w_i : M_i \text{ does not accept } w_i \text{ in } f\left(|w_i|\right) \text{ steps}\}. \tag{14.3}$$

We claim that L is recursive. To see this, consider any $w \in L$ and compute first $f(|w|)$. By assuming that f is a total Turing computable function, this is possible. We next find the position i of w in the sequence $w_1, w_2, \dots$. This is also possible because the sequence is in proper order. When we have i, we find M_i and let it operate on w for $f(|w|)$ steps. This will tell us whether or not w is in L, so is recursive.

But we can now show that L is not in $DTIME\left(f(n)\right)$. Suppose it were. Since L is recursive, there is some M_k, such that $L = L(M_k)$. Is w_k in L? If we claim that w_k is in L, then M_k accepts w_k in $f(|w_k|)$ steps. This is because $L \in DTIME\left(f(n)\right)$ and every $w \in L$ is accepted by M_k in time $f(|w|)$. But this contradicts (14.3). Conversely, we get a contradiction if we assume that $w_k \notin L$. The inability to resolve this issue is a typical diagonalization result and leads us to conclude that the original assumption, namely the existence of a computable $f(n)$, must be false. ∎

Theorem 14.1 and 14.2 allow us to make various claims, for example, that there is a language in $DTIME\left(n^4\right)$ that is not in $DTIME\left(n^3\right)$. Although this may be of theoretical interest, it is not clear that such a result has any practical significance. At this point, we have no clue what the characteristics of a language in $DTIME\left(n^4\right)$ might be. We can get a little more insight into the matter if we relate the complexity classification to the languages in the Chomsky hierarchy. We will look at some simple examples that give some of the more obvious results.

Example 14.5　Every regular language can be recognized by a deterministic finite automaton in time proportional to the length of the input. Therefore

$$L_{REG} \subseteq DTIME\left(n\right).$$

But $DTIME\left(n\right)$ includes much more than L_{REG}. We have already established in Example 13.7 that the context-free language $\{a^n b^n : n \geq 0\}$ can be recognized in time $O\left(n\right)$. The argument given there can be used for even more complicated languages.

Example 14.6　The non-context-free language $L = \left\{ww : w \in \{a, b\}^*\right\}$ is in $NTIME\left(n\right)$. This is straightforward, as we can recognize strings in this language by the algorithm

1. Copy the input from the input file to tape 1. Nondeterministically guess the middle of this string.

2. Copy the second part to tape 2.

3. Compare the symbols on tape 1 and tape 2 one by one.

Clearly all of the steps can be done in $O\left(|w|\right)$ time, so $L \in NTIME\left(n\right)$.

Actually, we can show that $L \in DTIME\left(n\right)$ if we can devise an algorithm for finding the middle of a string in $O\left(n\right)$ time. This can be done: we look at each symbol on tape 1, keeping a count on tape 2, but counting only every second symbol. We leave the details as an exercise.

Example 14.7　It follows from Example 14.2 that

$$L_{CF} \subseteq DTIME\left(n^3\right)$$

and

$$L_{CF} \subseteq NTIME\left(n\right).$$

Consider now the family of context-sensitive languages. Exhaustive search parsing is possible here also since at every step only a limited number of productions are applicable. Therefore, every string of length n can be parsed in time n^M, where M depends on the grammar. Note, however, that we cannot claim from this that

$$L_{CS} \subseteq DTIME\left(n^M\right)$$

because we cannot put an upper bound on M.

From these examples we note a trend: as $T(n)$ increases, more and more of the families L_{REG}, L_{CF}, L_{CS} are covered. But the connection between the Chomsky hierarchy and the complexity classes is tenuous and not very clear.

EXERCISES

1. Complete the argument in Example 14.5.
2. Show that $L = \left\{ww^Rw : w \in \{a,b\}^+\right\}$ is in $DTIME(n)$.
3. Show that $L = \left\{www : w \in \{a,b\}^+\right\}$ is in $DTIME(n)$.
4. Show that there are languages that are not in $NTIME(2^n)$.

14.4 The Complexity Classes P and NP

Since the attempt to produce meaningful hierarchies via time-complexities with different growth rates appears to be unproductive, let us ignore some factors that are less important, for example by removing some uninteresting distinctions, such as that between $DTIME\left(n^k\right)$ and $DTIME\left(n^{k+1}\right)$. We can argue that the difference between, say, $DTIME(n)$ and $DTIME\left(n^2\right)$ is not fundamental, since some of it depends on the specific model of Turing machine we have (e.g., how many tapes), and it is not a priori clear which model is most appropriate for a real computer. This leads us to consider the famous complexity class

$$\mathbf{P} = \bigcup_{i>1} DTIME\left(n^i\right).$$

This class includes all languages that are accepted by some deterministic Turing machine in polynomial time, without any regard to the degree of the polynomial. As we have already seen, L_{REG} and L_{CF} are in $\mathbf{P}$.

Since the distinction between deterministic and nondeterministic complexity classes appears to be fundamental, we also introduce

$$\mathbf{NP} = \bigcup_{i>1} NTIME\left(n^i\right).$$

Obviously

$$\mathbf{P} \subseteq \mathbf{NP},$$

but what is not known is if this containment is proper. While it is generally believed that there are some languages in **NP** that are not in **P**, no one has yet found an example of this.

The interest in these complexity classes, particularly in the class **P**, comes from an attempt to distinguish between realistic and unrealistic computations. Certain computations, although theoretically possible, have such high resource requirements that in practice they must be rejected as unrealistic on existing computers, as well as on supercomputers yet to be designed. Such problems are sometimes called **intractable** to indicate that, while in principle computable, there is no realistic hope of a practical algorithm. To understand this better, computer scientists have attempted to put the idea of intractability on a formal basis. One attempt to define the term intractable is made in what is generally called the **Cook-Karp thesis**. In the Cook-Karp thesis, a problem that is in **P** is called tractable, and one that is not is said to be intractable.

Is the Cook-Karp thesis a good way of separating problems we can work with realistically from those we cannot? The answer is not clear-cut. Obviously, any computation that is not in **P** has time complexity that grows faster than any polynomial, and its requirements will increase very quickly with the problem size. Even for a function like $2^{0.1n}$, this will be excessive for large n, say $n \geq 1000$, and we might feel justified in calling a problem with this complexity intractable. But what about problems that are in $DTIME\left(n^{100}\right)$? While the Cook-Karp thesis calls such a problem tractable, one surely cannot do much with it even for small n. The justification for the Cook-Karp thesis seems to lie in the empirical observation that most practical problems in **P** are in $DTIME\left(n\right)$, $DTIME\left(n^2\right)$, or $DTIME\left(n^3\right)$, while those outside this class tend to have exponential complexities. Among practical problems, a clear distinction exists between problems in **P** and those not in **P**.

The study of the relation between the complexity classes **P** and **NP** has generated particular interest among computer scientists. At the root of this is the question whether or not

$$\mathbf{P} = \mathbf{NP}.$$

This is one of the fundamental unsolved problems in the theory of computation. To explore it, computer scientists have introduced a variety of related concepts and questions. One of them is the idea of an **NP**-complete problem. Loosely speaking, an **NP** complete problem is one that is as hard as any **NP** problem and in some sense is equivalent to all of them. What this means has to be explained.

Definition 14.3

A language L_1 is said to be **polynomial-time reducible** to some language L_2 if there exists a deterministic Turing machine by which any w_1 in the alphabet of L_1 can be transformed in polynomial time to a w_2 in the alphabet of L_2 in such a way that $w_1 \in L_1$ if and only if $w_2 \in L_2$.

From this we see that if L_1 is polynomial-time reducible to L_2, and if $L_2 \in \mathbf{P}$, then $L_1 \in \mathbf{P}$. Similarly, if $L_2 \in \mathbf{NP}$, then $L_1 \in \mathbf{NP}$.

Definition 14.4

A language L is said to be **NP**-complete if $L \in \mathbf{NP}$ and if every $L' \in \mathbf{NP}$ is polynomial-time reducible to L.

It follows easily from these definitions that if some L_1 is **NP**-complete and polynomial-time reducible to L_2, then L_2 is also **NP**-complete. The implication of this definition is that if we can find a deterministic polynomial-time algorithm for any **NP**-complete language, then every language in **NP** is also in **P**, that is

$$\mathbf{P} = \mathbf{NP}.$$

This puts **NP**-completeness in a central role for the study of this question.

Example 14.8 The satisfiability problem can be viewed as a language problem. We encode specific instances as a string that is accepted if and only if the expression is satisfiable. This problem is **NP**-complete. The statement that the satisfiability problem is **NP**-complete is known as **Cook's theorem**, a discussion of which can be found in Hopcroft and Ullman (1979).

In addition to the satisfiability problem, a large number of other **NP**-complete problems have been found. For all of them we can find exponential algorithms, but for none of them has anyone discovered a polynomial-time algorithm. These failures lead us to believe that probably

$$\mathbf{P} \neq \mathbf{NP},$$

but until someone produces an actual language in **NP** that is not on **P** or, alternatively, until someone proves that no such language exists, the question remains open.

EXERCISES

1. Prove the statement that if a language L_1 is **NP**-complete and polynomial-time reducible to L_2, then L_2 is also **NP**-complete.

★★ 2. Consult books on complexity theory, and compile a list of problems that are **NP**-complete.

3. Is it possible that the question $\mathbf{P} = \mathbf{NP}$ is undecidable?

Answers

Solutions and Hints for Selected Exercises

Chapter 1

Section 1.1

5. To prove that two sets are equal, we must show that an element is in the first set if and only if it is in the second. Suppose $x \in \overline{S_1 \cup S_2}$. Then $x \notin S_1 \cup S_2$, which means that x cannot be in S_1 or in S_2, that is $x \in \overline{S}_1 \cap \overline{S}_2$. Conversely, if $x \in \overline{S}_1 \cap \overline{S}_2$, then x is not in S_1 and x is not in S_2, that is $x \in \overline{S_1 \cup S_2}$.

6. This can be proven by an induction on the number of sets. Let $Z = S_1 \cup S_2 ... \cup S_n$. Then $S_1 \cup S_2 ... \cup S_n \cup S_{n+1} = Z \cup S_{n+1}$. By the standard DeMorgan's law

$$\overline{Z \cup S_{n+1}} = \overline{Z} \cap \overline{S}_{n+1}.$$

With the inductive assumption, the relation is true for up to n sets, that is,

$$\overline{Z} = \overline{S}_1 \cap \overline{S}_2 \cap ... \cap \overline{S}_n.$$

Therefore

$$\overline{Z \cup S_{n+1}} = \overline{S}_1 \cap \overline{S}_2 \cap ... \cap \overline{S}_n \cap \overline{S}_{n+1},$$

completing the inductive step.

357

8. Suppose $S_1 = S_2$. Then $S_1 \cap \overline{S}_2 = \overline{S_1} \cap S_2 = S_1 \cap \overline{S}_1 = \varnothing$ and the entire expression is the empty set. Suppose now that $S_1 \neq S_2$ and that there is an element x in S_1 but not in S_2. Then $x \in \overline{S}_2$ so that $S_1 \cap \overline{S}_2 \neq \varnothing$. The complete expression can then not be equal to the empty set.

12. If x is in S_1 and x is in S_2, then x is not in $(S_1 \cup S_2) - S_2$. Because of this, a necessary and sufficient condition is that the two sets be disjoint.

15. (c) Since

$$\frac{n!}{n^n} = \frac{n}{n} \frac{n-1}{n} \cdots \frac{2}{n} \frac{1}{n}$$

is the product of factors less than or equal one. Therefore, $n! = O(n^n)$.

27. An argument by contradiction works. Suppose that $2 - \sqrt{2}$ were rational. Then

$$2 - \sqrt{2} = \frac{n}{m}$$

gives

$$\sqrt{2} = \frac{2m - n}{m}$$

contradicting the fact that $\sqrt{2}$ is not rational.

29. By induction. Suppose that every integer less than n can be written as a product of primes. If n is a prime, there is nothing to prove, if not, it can be written as the product

$$n = n_1 n_2$$

where both factors are less than n. By the inductive assumption, they both can be written as the product of primes, and so can n.

Section 1.2

2. Many string identities can be proven by induction. Suppose that $(uv)^R = v^R u^R$ for all $u \in \Sigma^*$ and all v of length n. Take now a string of length $n+1$, say $w = va$. Then

$$
\begin{aligned}
(uw)^R &= (uva)^R \\
&= a\,(uv)^R, \text{ by the definition of the reverse} \\
&= a v^R u^R, \text{ by the inductive assumption} \\
&= w^R u^R.
\end{aligned}
$$

By induction then, the result holds for all strings.

4. Since *abaabaaabaa* can be decomposed into strings ab, aa, baa, ab, aa, each of which is in L, the string is in L^*. Similarly, *baaaaabaa* is in L^*. However, there is no possible decomposition for *baaaaabaaaab*, so this string is not in L^*.

10. (d) We first generate three a's, then add an arbitrary number of a's and b's anywhere.

$$S \rightarrow AaAaAaA$$
$$A \rightarrow aA\,|bA|\,\lambda$$

The first production generates three a's. The second can generate any number of a's and b's in any position. This shows that the grammar can generate any string $w \in \{a, b\}^*$ as long as $n_a(w) \geq 3$.

11.

$$S \Rightarrow aA \Rightarrow abS \Rightarrow abaA \Rightarrow ababS$$

from which we see that

$$L(G) = \{(ab)^n : n \geq 0\}.$$

13. (a) Generate one b, then an equal number of a's and b's, finally as many more b's as needed.

$$S \rightarrow AbA$$
$$A \rightarrow aAb|\lambda$$
$$B \rightarrow bB|\lambda$$

13. (d) The answer is easier to see if you notice that

$$L_4 = \{a^{m+3}b^m : m > 0\}.$$

This leads to the easy solution

$$S \rightarrow aaaA$$
$$A \rightarrow aAb|\lambda$$

14. (b) The problem is simplified if you break it into two cases, $|w| \bmod 3 = 1$ and $|w| \bmod 3 = 2$. The first is covered by

$$S_1 \rightarrow aaaS_1|a,$$

the second by

$$S_2 \rightarrow aaaS_2|aa.$$

The two can be combined into a single grammar by

$$S \rightarrow S_1|S_2.$$

16. (a) We can use the trick and results of Example 1.13. Let L_1 be the language in Example 1.13 and modify that grammar so that the start symbol is S_1. Consider then a string $w \in L$. If this string start with an a, then it has the form $w = aw_1$, where $w_1 \in L_1$. This situation can be taken care of by $S \to aS_1$. If it starts with a b, it can be derived by $S \to S_1S$.

Section 1.3

1.

$$\begin{aligned}
\text{integer} &\to \text{sign magnitude} \\
\text{sign} &\to +\,|-|\,\lambda \\
\text{magnitude} &\to \text{digit} \mid \text{digit magnitude} \\
\text{digit} &\to 0|1|2|3|4|5|6|7|8|9
\end{aligned}$$

This can be considered an ideal version of C, as it puts no limit on the length of an integer. Most real compilers, though, place a limit on the number of digits.

7. The automaton has to remember the input for one time period so that it can be reproduced for output later. Remembering can be done by labeling the state with the appropriate information. The label of the state is then produced as output later.

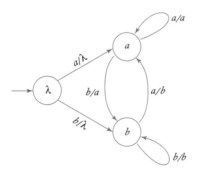

10. We remember input by labeling the states mnemonically. When a set of three bits is done, we produce output and return to the beginning to process the next three bits. The following solution is partial, but the completion should be obvious.

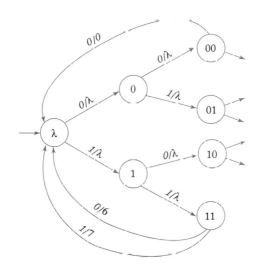

11. In this case, the transducer must remember the two preceding input symbols and make transitions so that the needed information is kept track of.

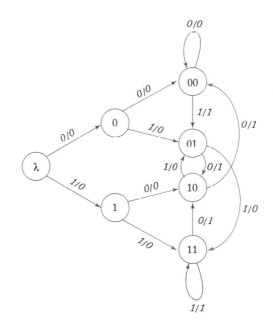

Chapter 2

Section 2.1

2. (c) Break it into three cases each with an accepting state: no a's, one a, two a's, three a's. A fourth a will then send the dfa into a non-accepting trap state. A solution:

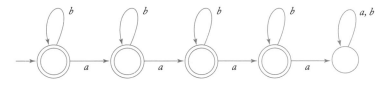

5. (a) The first six symbols are checked. If they are not correct, the string is rejected. If the prefix is correct, we keep track of the last two symbols read, putting the dfa in an accepting state if the suffix is bb.

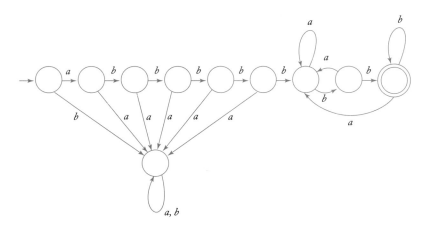

7. (a) Use states labeled with $|w| \bmod 3$. The solution then is quite simple.

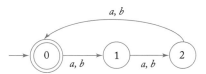

(d) For this we use nine state, with the first part of each label $n_a(w) \bmod 3$, the second part $n_b(w) \bmod 3$. The transitions and the final states are then simple to figure out.

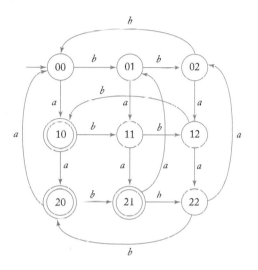

9. (a) Count consecutive zeros, to get the main part of the dfa.

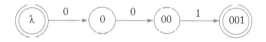

Then put in additional transitions to keep track of consecutive zeros and to trap unacceptable strings.

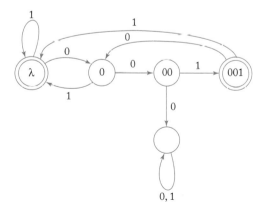

(d) Here we need to remember all combinations of three bits. This requires 8 states plus some start-up. The solution is a little long but not hard. A partial sketch of the solution is below.

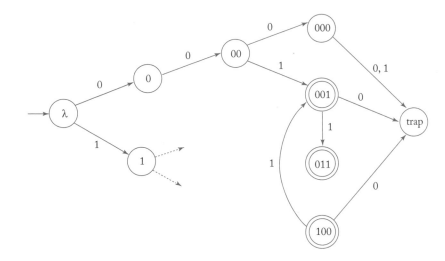

13. The easiest way to solve this problem is to construct a dfa for $L = \{a^n : n = 4\}$, then complement the solution.

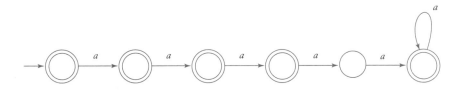

21. (a) By contradiction. Suppose G_M has no cycles in any path from the initial state to any final state. Then every walk has a finite number of steps, and so every accepted string has to be of finite length. But this implies that the language is finite.

(b) Also by contradiction. Assume that G_M has some cycle in a path from the initial state to some accepting state. We can then use the cycle to generate an arbitrarily long walk labeled with an accepted string. But a finite language cannot contain arbitrarily long strings.

24. There are many different solutions. Here is one of them.

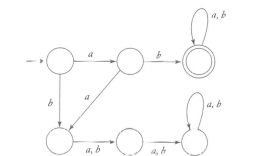

Section 2.2

4. $\delta^* (q_0, a) = \{q_0, q_1, q_2\}, \delta^* (q_1, \lambda) = \{q_0, q_2\}$.

7. A four-state solution is trivial, but it takes a little experimenting to get a three-state one. Here is one answer:

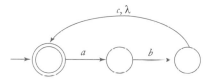

8. No. The string abc has three different symbols and there is no way this can be accepted with fewer than three states.

15. This is the kind of problem in which you just have to try different ways. Probably most of your tries will not work. Here is one that does.

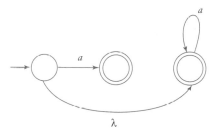

17. Introduce a single starting state p_0. Then add a transition

$$\delta (p_0, \lambda) = Q_0.$$

Next, remove starting state status from Q_0. It is straightforward to see that the new nfa is equivalent to the original one.

20. Introduce a non-accepting trap state and make all undefined transitions to this new state. Solution:

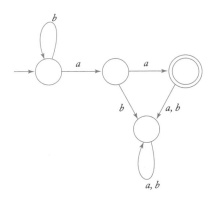

Section 2.3

2. Just follow the procedure nfa_to_dfa. This gives the dfa

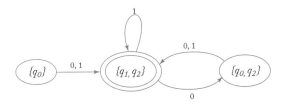

7. Introduce a new final state p_f and for every $q \in F$ add the transitions

$$\delta (q, \lambda) = \{p_f\}.$$

Then make p_f the only final state. It is a simple matter then to argue that if $\delta^* (q_0, w) \in F$ originally, then $\delta^* (q_0, w) = \{p_f\}$ after the modification, so both the original and the modifies nfa's are equivalent.

Since this construction requires λ-transitions, it cannot be made for dfa's. Generally, it is impossible to have only one final state in a dfa, as can be seen by constructing dfa's that accept $\{\lambda, a\}$.

8. Getting an answer requires some thought. One solution is

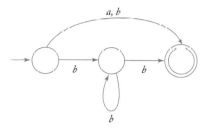

11. Suppose that $L = \{w_1, w_2, ...w_m\}$. Then the nfa

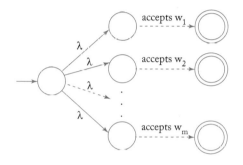

accepts L, so the language is regular.

14. This is not easy to see. The trick is to use a dfa for L and modify it so that it remembers if it has read an even or an odd number of symbols. This can be done by doubling the number of states and adding O or E to the labels. For example, if part of the dfa is

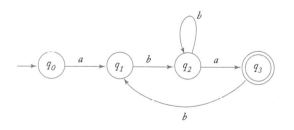

its equivalent becomes

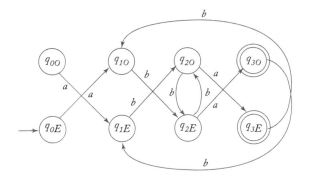

Now replace all transitions from an E state to an O state with λ-transitions.

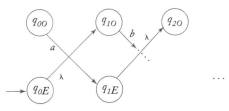

With a few examples you should be able to convince yourself that if the original dfa accepts $a_1 a_2 a_3 a_4$, the new automaton will accept $\lambda a_2 \lambda a_4 ...$, and therefore $even\,(L)$.

15. Suppose we have a dfa that accepts L. We then

(a) identify all states $\overline{Q}$ that can be reached from q_0, reading any two-symbol prefix v, that is

$$\overline{Q} = \{q \in Q : \delta^*\,(q_0, v) = q\}.$$

(b) introduce a new initial state p_0 and add

$$\delta\,(p_0, \lambda) = \overline{Q}.$$

It should not be hard to see that the new nfa accepts $chop2\,(L)$.

Although the construction is plausible, a complete answer requires a proof of the last statement.

Section 2.4

2. (c)

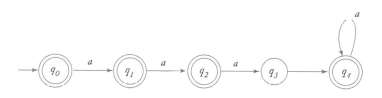

This is minimal for the following reason. $q_3 \notin F$ and $q_4 \in F$, so q_3 and q_4 are distinguishable. Next, $\delta^*(q_2, a) \notin F$ and $\delta^*(q_4, a) \in F$, so q_2 and q_4 are distinguishable. Similarly, $\delta^*(q_1, aa) \notin F$ and $\delta^*(q_3, aa) \in F$, so q_1 and q_3 are distinguishable. Continuing this way, we see that all states are distinguishable and therefore the dfa is minimal.

4. First, remove the inaccessible states q_2 and q_4. Then use the procedure *mark* to find the indistinguishable pairs (q_0, q_1) and (q_3, q_5). This then gives the minimal dfa.

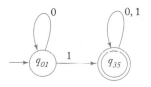

6. By contradiction. Assume that $\widehat{M}$ is not minimal. Then we can construct a smaller dfa $\widetilde{M}$ that accepts $\overline{L}$. In $\widetilde{M}$, complement the final state set to give a dfa for L. But this dfa is smaller than M, contradicting the assumption that M is minimal.

10. By contradiction. Assume that q_b and q_c are indistinguishable. Since q_a and q_b are indistinguishable and indistinguishability is an equivalence relation (Exercise 7), q_a and q_c must be indistinguishable.

Chapter 3

Section 3.1

2. Yes, because $\left((0 + 1)(0 + 1)^*\right)^*$ denotes any string of 0's and 1's. So does $(0 + 1)^*$.

5. (a) Separate into cases $m = 0, 1, 2, 3$. Generate 4 or more a's, followed by the requisite number of b's. Solution: $aaaaa^* (\lambda + b + bb + bbb)$.

(c) The complement of the language in 5(a) is harder to find. A string is not in L if it is of the form $a^n b^m$, with either $n < 4$ or $m > 3$, but this does not completely describe $\overline{L}$. We must also take in the strings in which a b is followed by an a. Solution:

$$(\lambda + a + aa + aaa)\, b^* + a^* bbbbb^* + (a + b)^* ba\, (a + b)^* .$$

9. Split into three cases: $m = 1,\ n \geq 3,\ n \geq 2,\ m \geq 2$, and $n = 1,\ m \geq 3$. Each case has a straightforward solution.

12. Enumerate all cases with $|v| = 2$ to get

$$aa\, (a + b)^* aa + ab\, (a + b)^* ab + ba\, (a + b)^* ba + bb\, (a + b)^* bb.$$

14. (c) You just have to get in each symbol at least once. The term

$$(a + b + c)^* a\, (a + b + c)^* b\, (a + b + c)^* c\, (a + b + c)^*$$

will do this, but is not enough since the a will precede the b, etc. For the complete solution you must generate all permutations of the three symbols, giving six terms that can be added. The answer, although quite long, is conceptually not hard.

15. (c) Create two 0's, interspersed with 1's, then repeat. But don't forget the case when there are no 0's at all. Solution: $(1^*01^*01^*)^* + 1^*$.

16. (a) Create all strings of length three and repeat. A short solution is $((a + b + c)(a + b + c)(a + b + c))^*$.

18. (c) The statement

$$(r_1 + r_2)^* \equiv (r_1{}^* r_2{}^*)^*$$

is true. By the given rules $(r_1 + r_2)^*$ denotes the language $(L(r_1) \cup L(r_2))^*$, that is the set of all strings of arbitrary concatenations of elements of $L(r_1)$ and $L(r_2)$. But $(r_1{}^* r_2{}^*)^*$ denotes $((L(r_1))^* (L(r_2))^*)^*$, which is the same set.

21. The expression for an infinite language must involve at least one starred subexpression, otherwise it can only denote finite strings. If there is one starred subexpression that denotes a non-empty string, then this string can be repeated as often as desired and therefore denote arbitrarily long strings.

23. A closed contour will be generated by an expression r if and only if $n_l(r) = n_r(r)$ and $n_u(r) = n_d(r)$.

25. Notice several things. The bit string must be at least 6 bits long. If it is longer than 6 bits, its value is at least 64, so anything will do. If it is exactly 6 bits, then either the second bit from the left (16) or the third bit from the left (8) must be 1. If you see this, then the solution

$$(111 + 110 + 101)(0 + 1)(0 + 1)(0 + 1) +$$
$$1(0 + 1)(0 + 1)(0 + 1)(1 + 0)(1 + 0)(1 + 0)(1 + 0)^*$$

readily suggests itself.

Section 3.2

3. This can be solved from first principles, without going through the regular expression_to_nfa construction. The latter will of course work, but gives a more complicated answer. Solution:

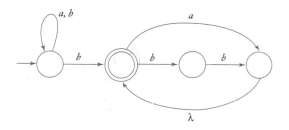

4. (a) Start with

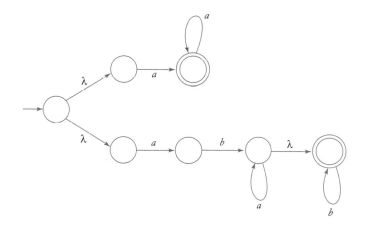

Then use the nfa_to_dfa algorithm in a routine manner.

7. One case is

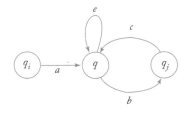

Since there is no path from q_j to q_i, the edges in the general case created by such a path are omitted. The result, gotten by looking at all possible paths, is

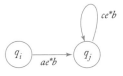

The other case can be analyzed in a similar manner.

8. Removing the middle vertex gives

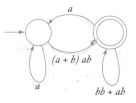

The language accepted then is $L(r)$ where $r = a^*(a+b)ab(bb+ab+ aa^*(a+b)ab)^*$.

10. (b) First, we have to modify the nfa so that it satisfies the conditions imposed by the construction in Theorem 3.2, one of which is $q_0 \notin F$. This is easily done.

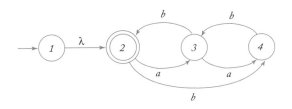

Then remove state 3.

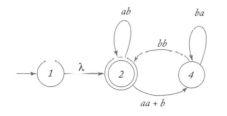

Next, remove state 4.

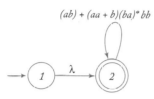

The regular expression then is $r = \left(ab + (aa + b)(ba)^* bb^*\right)^*$.

17. (a) This is a hard problem until you see the trick. Start with a dfa with states $q_0, q_1, ...$, and introduce a "parallel" automaton with states $\overline{q}_0, \overline{q}_1, ...$ Then arrange matters so that the spurious symbol nondeterministically transfers from any state of the original automaton to the corresponding state in the parallel part. For example, if part of the original dfa looks like

then the dfa with its parallel will be an nfa whose corresponding part is

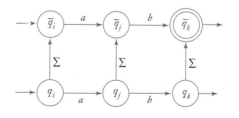

It is not hard to make the argument that the original dfa accepts L if and only if the constructed nfa accepts *insert* (L).

Section 3.3

4. Right linear grammar:

$$S \rightarrow aaA$$
$$A \rightarrow aA|B$$
$$B \rightarrow bbbC$$
$$C \rightarrow bC|\lambda$$

Left linear grammar:

$$S \rightarrow Abbb$$
$$A \rightarrow Ab|B$$
$$B \rightarrow aaC$$
$$C \rightarrow aC|\lambda$$

7. We can show by induction that if w is a sentential form derived with G, then w^R can be derived in the same number of steps by $\widehat{G}$.

Because w is created with left linear derivations, it must have the form $w = Aw_1$, with $A \in V$ and $w_1 \in T^*$. By the inductive assumption $w^R = w_1^R A$ can be derived via $\widehat{G}$. If we now apply $A \rightarrow Bv$, then

$$w \Rightarrow Bvw_1.$$

But $\widehat{G}$ contains the rule $A \rightarrow v^R B$, so we can make the derivation

$$w^R \rightarrow w_1^R v^R B$$
$$= (Bvw_1)^R$$

completing the inductive step.

10. Split this into two cases: (i) n and m are both even and (ii) n and m are both odd. The solution then falls out easily, with

$$S \rightarrow aaS|A$$
$$A \rightarrow bbA|\lambda$$

taking care of case (i).

12. (a) First construct a dfa for L. This is straightforward and gives transitions such as

$$\delta(q_0, a) = q_1, \delta(q_0, b) = q_2$$
$$\delta(q_1, a) = q_0, \delta(q_1, b) = q_3$$
$$\delta(q_2, a) = q_3, \delta(q_2, b) = q_0$$
$$\delta(q_3, a) = q_2, \delta(q_3, b) = q_1$$

with q_0 the initial and final state. Then the construction of Theorem 3.4 gives the answer

$$q_0 \rightarrow aq_1 \, |bq_2| \, \lambda$$
$$q_1 \rightarrow bq_3 | aq_0$$
$$q_2 \rightarrow aq_3 | bq_0$$
$$q_3 \rightarrow aq_2 | bq_1$$

16. Obviously, S_1 is regular as is S_2. We can show that their union is also regular by constructing the following dfa.

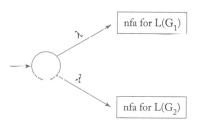

The condition that V_1 and V_2 should be disjoint is essential so that the two nfa's are distinct.

Chapter 4

Section 4.1

2. (a) The construction is straightforward, but tedious. A dfa for $L\left((a+b)\,a^*\right)$ is given by

$$\delta\left(q_0, a\right) = q_1, \quad \delta\left(q_0, b\right) = q_1, \quad \delta\left(q_1, a\right) = q_1, \quad \delta\left(q_1, b\right) = q_t,$$

with q_t a trap state and final state q_1. A dfa for $L\left(baa^*\right)$ is given by

$$\delta\left(p_0, a\right) = p_t, \delta\left(p_0, b\right) = p_1, \delta\left(p_1, a\right) = p_2,$$
$$\delta\left(p_1, b\right) = p_t, \delta\left(p_2, a\right) = p_2, \delta\left(p_2, b\right) = p_t$$

with final state p_2. From this we find

$$\delta\left(\left(q_0, p_0\right), a\right) = \left(q_1, p_t\right), \delta\left(\left(q_0, p_0\right), b\right) = \left(q_1, p_1\right),$$
$$\delta\left(\left(q_1, p_1\right), a\right) = \left(q_1, p_2\right), \delta\left(\left(q_1, p_2\right), a\right) = \left(q_1, p_2\right),$$

etc. When we complete this construction, we see that the only final state is $\left(q_1, p_2\right)$ and that $L\left((a+b)\,a^*\right) \cap L\left(baa^*\right) = baa^*$.

7. Notice that

$$nor\,(L_1, L_2) = \overline{L_1 \cup L_2}.$$

The result then follows from closure under intersection and complementation.

12. The answer is yes. It can be obtained by starting from the set identity

$$L_2 = \big((L_1 \cup L_2) \cap \overline{L_1}\big) \cup (L_1 \cap L_2).$$

The key observation is that since L_1 is finite, $L_1 \cap L_2$ is finite, and therefore regular for all L_2. The rest then follows easily from the known closures under union and complementation.

14. By closure under reversal, L^R is regular. The result then follows from closure under concatenation.

16. Use $L_1 = \Sigma^*$. Then, for any L_2, $L_1 \cup L_2 = \Sigma^*$, which is regular. The given statement would then imply that any L_2 is regular.

18. We can use the following construction. Find all states P such that there is a path from the initial vertex to some element of P, and from that element to a final state. Then make every element of P a final state.

26. Suppose $G_1 = (V_1, T, S_1, P_1)$ and $G_2 = (V_2, T, S_2, P_2)$. Without loss of generality, we can assume that V_1 and V_2 are disjoint. Combine the two grammars and

   (a) Make S the new start symbol and add productions $S \to S_1 | S_2$.
   (b) In P_1, replace every production of the form $A \to x$, with $A \in V_1$ and $x \in T^*$, by $A \to xS_2$.
   (c) In P_1, replace every production of the form $A \to x$, with $A \in V_1$, and $x \in T^*$, by $A \to xS_1$.

Section 4.2

1. Since by Example 4.1 $L_1 - L_2$ is regular, there exists a membership algorithm for it.

2. If $L_1 \subseteq L_2$, then $L_1 \cup L_2 = L_2$. Since $L_1 \cup L_2$ is regular and we have an algorithm for set equality, we also have an algorithm for set inclusion.

5. From the dfa for L, construct the dfa for L^R, using the construction suggested in Theorem 4.2. Then use the equality algorithm in Theorem 4.7.

12. Here you need a little trick. If L contains no even length strings, then

$$L \cap L\big((aa + ab + ba + bb)^*\big) = \varnothing.$$

The left side is regular, so we can use Theorem 4.6.

Section 4.3

2. For the dfa for L to process the middle string v requires a walk in the transition graph of length $|v|$. If this is longer than the number of states in the dfa, there must be a cycle labeled y in this walk. But clearly this cycle can be repeated as often as desired without changing the acceptability of a string.

4. (a) Given m, pick $w = a^m b^m a^{2m}$. The string y must then be a^k and the pumped strings will be

$$w_i = a^{m+(i-1)k} b^m a^{2m}.$$

If we take $i \geq 2$ then $m + (i-1)k > m$, then w_i is not in L.

(e) It does not seem easy to apply the pumping lemma directly, so we proceed indirectly. Suppose that L were regular. Then by the closure of regular languages under complementation, $\overline{L}$ would also be regular. But $\overline{L} = \{w : n_a(w) = n_b(w)\}$ which, as is easily shown, is not regular. By contradiction, L is not regular.

5. (a) Take p to be the smallest prime number greater or equal to m and choose $w = a^p$. Now y is a string of a's of length k, so that

$$w_i = a^{p+(i-1)k}.$$

If we take $i - 1 = p$, then $p + (i-1)k = p(k+1)$ is composite and w_{p+1} is not in the language.

8. The proposition is false. As a counterexample, take $L_1 = \{a^n b^m : n \leq m\}$ and $L_2 = \{a^n b^m : n > m\}$, both of which are non regular. But $L_1 \cup L_2 = L(a^* b^*)$, which is regular.

9. (a) The language is regular. This is most easily seen by splitting the problem into cases such as $l = 0, k = 0, n > 5$, for which one can easily construct regular expressions.

(b) This language is not regular. If we choose $w = aaaaaab^m a^m$, our opponent has several choices. If y consists of only a's, we use $i = 0$ to violate the condition $n > 5$. If the opponent chooses y as consisting of b's, we can then violate the condition $k \leq l$.

11. L is regular. We see this from $L = L_1 \cap L_2^R$ and the known closures for regular languages.

13. (a) The language is regular, since any string that has two consecutive symbols the same is in the language. A regular expression for L is $(a+b)(a+b)^*(aa+bb)(a+b)(a+b)^*$.

(b) The language is not regular. Take $w = (ab)^m aa (ba)^m$. The adversary now has several choices, such as $y = (ab)^k$ or $y = (ab)^k a$. In the first case

$$w_0 = (ab)^{m-k} aa (ba)^m .$$

Since the only possible identification is $ww^R = b^l aab^l$, w_0 is not in L. With the second choice, the length of w_0 is odd, so it cannot be in L either.

15. Take $L_i = a^i b^i$, $i = 0, 1, ...$ For each i, L_i is finite and therefore regular, but the union of all the languages is the non-regular language $L = \{a^n b^n : n \geq 0\}$.

17. No, it is not. As counterexample, take the languages

$$L_i = \left\{ v_i u v_i^R : |v_i| = i \right\} \cup \left\{ v_i v_i^R : |v_i| < i \right\}, i = 0, 1, 2, ...$$

We claim that the union of all the L_i is the set $\{ww^R\}$. To justify this, take any string $z = ww^R$, with $|w| = n$. If $n \geq i$, then $z \in \left\{ v_i u v_i^R : |v_i| = i \right\}$ and therefore in L_i. If $n < i$, then $z \in \left\{ v_i v_i^R : |v_i| < i \right\}$, $i = \{0, 1, 2, ...\}$ and so also in L_i. Consequently, z is in the union of all the L_i.

Conversely, take any string z of length m that is in all of the L_i. If we take i greater than m, z cannot be in $\left\{ v_i u v_i^R : |v_i| = i \right\}$ because it is not long enough. It must therefore be in $\left\{ v_i v_i^R : |v_i| < i \right\}$, so that it has the form ww^R.

As the final step we must show that for each i, L_i is regular. This follows from the fact that for each i there are only a finite number of substrings v_i.

Chapter 5

Section 5.1

4. It is quite obvious that any string generated by this grammar has the same number of a's as b's. To show that the prefix condition $n_a (v) \geq n_b (v)$ holds, we carry out an induction on the length of the derivation. Suppose that for every sentential form derived from S in n steps this condition holds. To get a sentential form in $n + 1$ steps, we can apply $S \to \lambda$ or $S \to SS$. Since neither of these changes the number of a's and b's or the location of those already there, the prefix condition continues to hold. Alternatively, we apply $S \to aSb$. This adds an extra a and an extra b, but since the added a is to the left of the added b, the prefix condition will still be satisfied. Thus, if the prefix condition holds after n steps, it will still hold after $n+1$ steps. Obviously, the prefix condition holds after one step, so we have a basis and the induction succeeds.

7. (a) First, solve the case $n = m + 3$. Then add more b's. This can be done by

$$S \rightarrow aaaA$$
$$A \rightarrow aAb|B$$
$$B \rightarrow Bb|\lambda$$

But this is incomplete since it creates at least three a's. To take care of the cases $n = 0, 1, 2$, we add

$$S \rightarrow \lambda \,|aA| \,aaA$$

(d) This has an unexpectedly simple solution

$$S \rightarrow aSbb\,|aSbbb|\,\lambda.$$

These productions nondeterministically produce either bb or bbb for each generated a.

8. (a) For the first case $n = m$ and k is arbitrary. This can be achieved by

$$S_1 = AC$$
$$A \rightarrow aAb|\lambda$$
$$C \rightarrow Cc|\lambda$$

In the second case, n is arbitrary and $m \le k$. Here we use

$$S_2 \rightarrow BD$$
$$B \rightarrow aB|\lambda$$
$$D \rightarrow bDc|E$$
$$E \rightarrow Ec|\lambda.$$

Finally, we start productions with $S \rightarrow S_1|S_2$.

(e) Split the problem into two cases: $n = k + m$ and $m = k + n$. The first case is solved by

$$S \rightarrow aSc\,|S_1|\,\lambda$$
$$S_1 \rightarrow aS_1b|\lambda.$$

12. (a) If S derives L, then $S_1 \rightarrow SS$ derives L^2.

15. It is normally not possible to use a grammar for L directly to get a grammar for $\overline{L}$, so we need another, hopefully recursive description for

$\overline{L}$. This is a little hard to see here. One obvious subset of $\overline{L}$ contains the strings of odd length, but this is not all.

Suppose we have an even length string that is not of the form ww^R. Working from the center to the left and to the right simultaneously, compare corresponding symbols. While some part around the center can be of the form ww^R, at some point we get an a on the left and a b in the corresponding place on the right, or vice versa. The string must therefore be of the form $uaww^Rbv$ or $ubww^Rav$ with $|u| = |v|$. Once we see this, we can then construct grammars for these types of strings. One solution is

$$S \to ASA|B$$
$$A \to a|b$$
$$B \to bCa|aCb$$
$$C \to aCa\,|bCb|\,\lambda.$$

The first two productions generate the u and v, the third the two disagreeing symbols, and the last the innermost palindrome.

19. The only possible derivations start with

$$S \Rightarrow aaB \Rightarrow aaAa \Rightarrow aabBba \Rightarrow aabAaba.$$

But this sentential form has the suffix aba so it cannot possibly lead to the sentence $aabbabba$.

22. $E \to E + E\,|E.E|\,E^*\,|(E)|\,\lambda|\varnothing.$

Section 5.2

2. A solution is

$$S \to aA, A \to aAB|b, B \to b.$$

Note that the more obvious grammar

$$S \to aS_1B$$
$$S_1 \to aS_1B|\lambda$$
$$B \to b$$

is not an s-grammar.

6. There are two leftmost derivations for $w = aab$.

$$S \Rightarrow aaB \Rightarrow aab$$
$$S \Rightarrow AB \Rightarrow AaB \Rightarrow aaB \Rightarrow aab.$$

9. From the dfa for a regular language we can get a regular grammar by the method of Theorem 3.4. The grammar is an s-grammar except for $q_f \rightarrow \lambda.$ But this rule does not create any ambiguity. Since the dfa never has a choice, there is never any choice in the production that can be applied.

14. Ambiguity of the grammar is obvious from the derivations

$$S \Rightarrow aSb \Rightarrow ab$$
$$S \Rightarrow SS \Rightarrow abS \Rightarrow ab.$$

An equivalent unambiguous grammar is

$$S \rightarrow A|\lambda$$
$$A \rightarrow aAb\,|ab|\,AA.$$

It is not easy to see that this grammar is unambiguous. To make it plausible, consider the two typical situations, $w = aabb$, which can only be derived by starting with $A \rightarrow aAb$, and $w = abab$, which can only be derived starting with $A \rightarrow AA$. More complicated strings are built from these two situations, so they can be parsed only in one way.

20. Solution:

$$S \rightarrow aA|aAA$$
$$A \rightarrow bAb|bb.$$

Chapter 6

Section 6.1

3. Use the rule in Theorem 6.1 to substitute for B in the first grammar. Then B becomes useless and the associated productions can be removed. By Theorems 6.1 and 6.2 the two grammars are equivalent.

8. The only nullable variable is A, so removing λ-productions gives

$$S \rightarrow aA\,|a|\,aBB$$
$$A \rightarrow aaA|aa$$
$$B \rightarrow bC|bbC$$
$$C \rightarrow B.$$

$C \rightarrow B$ is the only unit-production and removing it results in

$$S \rightarrow aA\,|a|\,aBB$$
$$A \rightarrow aaA|aa$$
$$B \rightarrow bC|bbC$$
$$C \rightarrow bC|bbC.$$

Finally, B and C are useless, so we get

$$S \rightarrow aA|a$$
$$A \rightarrow aaA|aa.$$

The language generated by this grammar is $L\left((aa)^* a\right)$.

14. An example is

$$S \rightarrow aA$$
$$A \rightarrow BB$$
$$B \rightarrow aBb|\lambda.$$

When we remove λ-productions we get

$$S \rightarrow aA|a$$
$$A \rightarrow BB|B$$
$$B \rightarrow aBb|ab.$$

16. This is obvious since the removal of useless productions never adds anything to the grammar.

21. The grammar $S \rightarrow aA$; $A \rightarrow a$ does not have any useless productions, any unit productions, or any λ-productions. But it is not minimal since $S \rightarrow aa$ is an equivalent grammar.

Section 6.2

5. First we must eliminate λ-productions. This gives

$$S \rightarrow AB\,|B|\,aB$$
$$A \rightarrow aab$$
$$B \rightarrow bbA|bb.$$

This has introduced a unit-production, which is not acceptable in the construction of Theorem 6.6. Removal of this unit-production is easy.

$$S \rightarrow AB\,|bbA|\,aB|bb$$
$$A \rightarrow aab$$
$$B \rightarrow bbA|bb.$$

We can now apply the construction and get

$$S \rightarrow AB\,|V_bV_bA|\,V_aB|V_bV_b$$
$$A \rightarrow V_aV_bV_b$$
$$B \rightarrow V_bV_bA|V_bV_b$$

and

$$S \rightarrow AB \,|V_c A|\, V_a B|V_b V_b$$
$$A \rightarrow V_d V_b$$
$$B \rightarrow V_c A|V_b V_b$$
$$V_c \rightarrow V_b V_b$$
$$V_d \rightarrow V_a V_b$$
$$V_a \rightarrow a$$
$$V_b \rightarrow b.$$

8. Consider the general form for a production in a linear grammar

$$A \rightarrow a_1 a_2...a_n B b_1 b_2...b_m.$$

Introduce a new variable V_1 with the productions

$$V_1 \rightarrow a_2...a_n B b_1 b_2...b_m$$

and

$$A \rightarrow a_1 V_1.$$

Continue this process, introducing V_2 and

$$V_2 \rightarrow a_3...a_n B b_1 b_2...b_m$$

and so on, until no terminals remain on the left. Then use a similar process to remove terminals on the right.

9. This normal form can be reached easily from CNF. Productions of the form $A \rightarrow BC$ are permitted since $a = \lambda$ is possible. For $A \rightarrow a$, create new variables V_1, V_2 and productions $A \rightarrow aV_1 V_2$, $V_1 \rightarrow \lambda$, $V_2 \rightarrow \lambda$.

12. Solutions: $S \rightarrow aV_b \,|aS|\, aV_a S$, $V_a \rightarrow a$, $V_b \rightarrow b$.

15. Only $A \rightarrow bABC$ is not in the required form, so we introduce $A \rightarrow bAV$ and $V \rightarrow BC$. The latter is not in correct form, but after substituting for B, we have

$$S \rightarrow aSA$$
$$A \rightarrow bAV$$
$$V \rightarrow bC$$
$$C \rightarrow aBC.$$

Section 6.3

2. Since aab is a prefix of the string in Example 6.11, we can use the V_{ij} computed there. Since $S \in V_{13}$, the string aab is in the language generated by the grammar and can therefore be parsed.

For parsing, we determine the productions that were used in justifying $S \in V_{13}$:

$S \in V_{13}$ because $S \to AB$, with $A \in V_{11}$ and $B \in V_{23}$

$A \in V_{11}$ because $A \to a$

$B \in V_{23}$ because $B \to AB$, with $A \in V_{22}, B \in V_{33}$

$A \in V_{22}$ because $A \to a$

$B \in V_{33}$ because $B \to b$.

This shows all the productions needed to justify membership; these can then be used in the parsing

$$S \Rightarrow AB \Rightarrow aB \Rightarrow aAB \Rightarrow aaB \Rightarrow aab.$$

Chapter 7

Section 7.1

2. The key to the argument is the switch from q_0 to q_1, which is done nondeterministically and need not happen in the middle of the string. However, if a switch is made at some other point or if the input is not of the form ww^R, an accepting configuration cannot be reached. Suppose the content of the stack at the time of the switch is $x_1x_2...x_kz$. To accept a string we must get to the configuration (q_1, λ, z). By examining the transition function, we see that we can get to this configuration only if at this point the unread part of the input is $x_1x_2...x_k$, that is, if the original input is of the form ww^R and the switch was made exactly in the middle of the input string.

4. (a) The solution is obtained by letting each a put two markers on the stack, while each b consumes one. Solution:

$$\delta(q_0, \lambda, z) = \{(q_f, z)\}$$
$$\delta(q_0, a, z) = \{(q_1, 11z)\}$$
$$\delta(q_0, a, 1) = \{(q_1, 111)\}$$
$$\delta(q_1, b, 1) = \{(q_1, \lambda)\}$$
$$\delta(q_1, \lambda, z) = \{(q_f, z)\}.$$

(f) Here we use nondeterminism to generate one, two, or three tokens by

$$\delta(q_0, a, z) = \{(q_1, 1z), (q_1, 11z), (q_1, 111z)\}$$

and

$$\delta(q_0, a, z) = \{(q_1, 11), (q_{10}, 111), (q_1, 1111)\}.$$

The rest of the solution is then essentially the same as 4(a).

9. This is a pda that makes no use of the stack, so that is, in effect, a finite accepter. The state transitions can then be taken directly from the pda, to give

$$\delta (q_0, a) = q_1$$
$$\delta (q_0, b) = q_0$$
$$\delta (q_1, a) = q_1$$
$$\delta (q_1, b) = q_0$$

11. Trace through the process, taking one path at a time. The transition from q_0 to q_2 can be made with a single a. The alternative path requires one a, followed by one or more b's, terminated by an a. These are the only choices. The pda therefore accepts the language

$$L = \{a\} \cup L (abb^*a).$$

14. Here we are not allowed enough states to track the switch from a's to b's and back. To overcome this, we put a symbol in the stack that remembers where in the sequence we are. For example, a solution is

$$\delta (q_0, a, z) = \{(q_0, 1)\},$$
$$\delta (q_0, a, 1) = \{(q_0, 1)\},$$
$$\delta (q_0, b, 1) = \{(q_0, 2)\},$$
$$\delta (q_0, a, 2) = \{(q_0, 2)\},$$
$$\delta (q_0, \lambda, 2) = \{(q_f, 2)\}.$$

We have only two states, the initial state q_0 and the accepting state q_f. What would normally be tracked by different states is now tracked by the symbol in the stack.

16. Here we use internal states to remember symbols to be put on the stack. For example,

$$\delta (q_i, a, b) = \{(q_j, cde)\}$$

is replaced by

$$\delta (q_i, a, b) = \{(q_{jc}, de)\}$$
$$\delta (q_{jc}, \lambda, d) = \{(q_j, cd)\}.$$

Since δ can have only a finite number of elements and each can only add a finite amount of information to the stack, this construction can be carried out for any pda.

Section 7.2

3. You can follow the construction of Theorem 7.1 or you can notice that the language is $\{a^{n+2}b^{2n+1} : n \geq 0\}$. With the latter observation we get a solution

$$\delta\left(q_0, a, z\right) = \{(q_1, z)\}$$
$$\delta\left(q_1, a, z\right) = \{(q_2, z)\}$$
$$\delta\left(q_2, a, z\right) = \{(q_2, 11z)\}$$
$$\delta\left(q_2, a, 1\right) = \{(q_2, 111)\}$$
$$\delta\left(q_2, b, 1\right) = \{(q_3, 1)\}$$
$$\delta\left(q_3, b, 1\right) = \{(q_3, \lambda)\}$$
$$\delta\left(q_3, \lambda, z\right) = \{(q_f, z)\}$$

where q_0 is the initial state and q_f is the final state.

4. First convert the grammar into Griebach normal form, giving $S \rightarrow aSSS$; $S \rightarrow aB$; $B \rightarrow b$. Then follow the construction of Theorem 7.1.

$$\delta\left(q_0, \lambda, z\right) = \{(q_1, Sz)\}$$
$$\delta\left(q_1, a, S\right) = \{(q_1, SSS), (q_1, B)\}$$
$$\delta\left(q_1, b, B\right) = \{(q_1, \lambda)\}$$
$$\delta\left(q_1, \lambda, z\right) = \{(q_f, z)\}.$$

7. From Theorem 7.2, given any npda, we can construct an equivalent context-free grammar. From that grammar we can then construct an equivalent three-state npda, using Theorem 7.1. Because of the transitivity of equivalence, the original and the final npda's are also equivalent.

9. We first obtain a grammar in Greibach normal form for L, for example $S \rightarrow aSB|b, B \rightarrow b$. Next, we apply the construction in Theorem 7.1 to get an npda with three states, q_0, q_1, q_f. The state q_1 can be eliminated if we use a special stack symbol z_1 to mark it. A complete solution is

$$\delta\left(q_0, \lambda, z\right) = \{(q_0, Sz_1)\}$$
$$\delta\left(q_0, a, S\right) = \{(q_0, SB)\}$$
$$\delta\left(q_0, b, S\right) = \{(q_0, \lambda)\}$$
$$\delta\left(q_0, b, B\right) = \{(q_0, \lambda)\}$$
$$\delta\left(q_0, \lambda, z_1\right) = \{(q_f, \lambda)\}.$$

11. There must be at least one a to get started. After that, $\delta\left(q_0, a, A\right) = \{(q_0, A)\}$ simply reads a's without changing the stack. Finally, when

the first b is encountered, the pda goes into state q_1, from which it can only make a λ-transition to the final state. Therefore, a string will be accepted if and only if it consists of one or more a's, followed by a single b.

Section 7.3

4. At first glance, this may seem to be a nondeterministic language, since the prefix a calls for two different types of suffixes. Nevertheless, the language is deterministic, as we can construct a dpda. This dpda, goes into a final state when the first input symbol is an a. If more symbols follow, it goes out of this state and then accepts $a^n b^n$. Complete solution:

$$\delta(q_0, a, z) = \{(q_3, 1z)\}$$
$$\delta(q_3, a, 1) = \{(q_1, 11)\}$$
$$\delta(q_1, a, 1) = \{(q_1, 11)\}$$
$$\delta(q_1, b, 1) = \{(q_1, \lambda)\}$$
$$\delta(q_1, \lambda, z) = \{(q_2, z)\}$$

where $F = \{q_2, q_3\}$.

9. The solution is straightforward. Put a's and b's on the stack. The c signals the switch from saving to matching, so everything can be done deterministically.

11. There are two states, the initial, non-accepting state q_0 and the final state q_1. The pda will be in state q_1 unless a z is on top of the stack. When this happens, the pda will switch states to q_0. The rest is essentially the same as Example 7.3. Thus we have $\delta(q_0, a, z) = \{(q_1, 0z)\}, \delta(q_1, a, 0) = \{(q_1, 00)\}$, etc. with $\delta(q_1, \lambda, z) = \{(q_0, z)\}$. When you write this all out, you will see that the pda is deterministic.

15. This is obvious since every regular language can be accepted by a dfa and such a dfa is a dpda with an unused stack.

16. The basic idea here is to combine a dpda with a dfa along the lines of the construction in Theorem 4.1, with the stack handled as it is for L_1. It should not be too hard to see that the result is a dpda.

Section 7.4

2. Consider the strings $aabb$ and $aabbbbaa$. In the first case, the derivation must start with $S \Rightarrow aSB$, while in the second $S \Rightarrow SS$ is the necessary first step. But if we see only the first four symbols, we cannot decide which case applies. The grammar is therefore not in $LL(4)$. Since

similar examples can be made for arbitrarily long strings, the grammar is not $LL(k)$ for any k.

4. Look at the first three symbols. If they are aaa, aab, or aba, then the string can only be in $L(a^*ba)$. If the first three symbols are abb, then any parsable string must be in $L(abbb^*)$. For each case, we can find an LL grammar and the two can be combined in an obvious fashion. A solution is

$$S \rightarrow S_1|S_2$$
$$S_1 \rightarrow aS_1|ba$$
$$S_2 \rightarrow abbB$$
$$B \rightarrow bB|\lambda.$$

Looking at the first three symbols tells us if $S \Rightarrow S_1$ or $S \Rightarrow S_2$ is necessary. The grammar is therefore $LL(3)$.

7. For a deterministic CFL there exists a dpda. When this dpda is converted into a grammar, the grammar is unambiguous.

9. (a)

$$S \rightarrow aSc|S_1|\lambda$$
$$S_1 \rightarrow bS_1c|\lambda.$$

This is almost an s-grammar. As long as the currently scanned symbol is a, we must apply $S \rightarrow aSc$, if it is b, we must use $S \rightarrow S_1$, if it is c, we can only use $S \rightarrow \lambda$. The grammar is $LL(1)$.

Chapter 8

Section 8.1

3. Take $w = a^m b^m b^m a^m a^m b^m$. The adversary now has several choices that have to be considered. If, for example, $v = a^k$ and $y = a^l$, with v and y located in the prefix a^m, then

$$w_0 = a^{m-k-l}b^m b^m a^m a^m b^m,$$

which is not in L. There are a number of other possible choices, but in all cases the string can be pumped out of the language.

7. (a) Use the pumping lemma. Given m, pick $w = a^{m^2}b^m$. The only choice of v and y that needs any serious examination is $v = a^k$ and

$y - b^l$, with k and l non-zero. Suppose that $l = 1$. Then choose $i = 2$, so that w_2 has $m^2 + k$ a's and $m + 1$ b's. But

$$(m+1)^2 = m^2 + 2m + 1$$
$$> m^2 + k.$$

Since w_2 is not in the language, the language cannot be context-free. Similar arguments hold a fortiori for $l > 1$.

(f) Given m, choose $w = a^m b^{m+1} c^{m+2}$, which is easily pumped out of the language.

8. (b) The language is not context-free. Use the pumping lemma with $w = a^m b^m a^m b^m$ and examine various choices of v and y.

10. Perhaps surprisingly, this language is context-free. Construct an npda that counts to some value k (by putting k tokens on the stack) and remembers the k-th symbol. It then examines the k-th symbol in w_2. If this does not match the remembered symbol, the string is accepted. If $w \in L$ there must be some k for which this happens. The npda chooses the k nondeterministically.

12. Use the pumping lemma for linear languages. With a given m, choose $w = a^m b^{2m} a^m$. Now v and y are entirely made of a's, so w is easily pumped out of the language.

15. The language is not linear. With the pumping lemma, use

$$w = (\dots (a) \dots) + (\dots (a) \dots)$$

where $(\dots($ and $)\dots)$ stand for m left or right parentheses, respectively. If $|u| \geq 1$, we can easily pump so that for some prefix v, $n_((v) < n_) (v)$ which results in an improper expression. Similar arguments hold for other decompositions.

20. Use $w = a^{pq}$, where p and q are primes such that $p > m$ and $q > m$. If $|vy| = k$, then

$$|w_{i+1}| = pq + ik.$$

If we choose $i = pq$, then

$$w_{i+1} = a^{pq(1+k)},$$

which is not in the language.

Section 8.2

1. The complement is context-free. The complement involves two cases: $n_a(w) \neq n_b(w)$ and $n_a(w) \neq n_c(w)$. These in turn can be broken into $n_a(w) > n_b(w)$, $n_a(w) > n_c(w)$, $n_a(w) < n_b(w)$, and $n_a(w) < n_c(w)$. Each of these is context-free as can be shown by construction of a CFG. The full language is then the union of these four cases and by closure under union is context-free.

5. Given a context-free grammar G, construct a context-free grammar $\widehat{G}$ by replacing every production $A \to x$ by $A \to x^R$. We can then show by an induction on the number of steps in a derivation that if w is a sentential form for G then w^R is a sentential form for $\widehat{G}$.

9. Given two linear grammars $G_1 = (V_1, T, S_1, P_1)$ and $G_2 = (V_2, T, S_2, P_2)$ with $V_1 \cap V_2 = \varnothing$, form the combined grammar $\widehat{G} = (V_1 \cup V_2, T, S, P_1 \cup P_2 \cup S \to S_1 | S_2)$. Then $\widehat{G}$ is linear and $L\left(\widehat{G}\right) = L(G_1) \cup L(G_2)$.

   To show that linear languages are not closed under concatenation, take the linear language $L = \{a^n b^n : n \geq 1\}$. The language L^2 is not linear as can be shown by an application of the pumping lemma.

13. Let $G_1 = (V_1, T, S_1, P_1)$ be a linear grammar for L_1 and let $G_2 = (V_2, T, S_2, P_2)$ be a left-linear grammar for L_2. Construct a grammar $\widehat{G}_2$ from G_2 by replacing every production of the form $V \to x, x \in T^*$ with $V \to S_1 x$. Combine grammars G_1 and $\widehat{G}_2$, choosing S_2 as a start symbol. It is then easily shown that in this grammar

$$S_2 \Rightarrow S_1 w \Rightarrow uw$$

   if and only if $u \in L_1$ and $w \in L_2$.

15. The languages $L_1 = \{a^n b^n c^m\}$ and $L_2 = \{a^n b^m c^m\}$ are both unambiguous. But their intersection is not even context-free.

21. $\lambda \in L(G)$ if and only if S is nullable.

Chapter 9

Section 9.1

2. A three-state solution that scans the entire input is

$$\delta(q_0, a) = (q_1, a, R)$$
$$\delta(q_1, a) = \delta(q_1, b) = (q_1, a, R)$$
$$\delta(q_1, \square) = (q_2, \square, R)$$

   with $F = \{q_2\}$.

It is also possible to get a two-state solution by just examining the first symbol and ignoring the rest of the input, for example,

$$\delta(q_0, a) = (q_2, a, R).$$

7. (a)

$$\delta(q_0, a) = (q_1, a, R)$$
$$\delta(q_1, b) = (q_2, b, R)$$
$$\delta(q_2, a) = (q_2, a, R)$$
$$\delta(q_2, b) = (q_3, b, R)$$

with $F = \{q_3\}$.

(b)

$$\delta(q_0, a) = \delta(q_0, b) = (q_1, \square, R)$$
$$\delta(q_0, \square) = (q_2, \square, R)$$
$$\delta(q_1, a) = \delta(q_1, b) = (q_0, \square, R)$$

with $F = \{q_2\}$.

10. The solution is conceptually simple, but tedious to write out in detail. The general scheme looks something like this:

(i) Place a marker symbol c at each end of the string.

(ii) Replace the two-symbol combination ca on the left by ac and the two-symbol combination ac on the right by ca. Repeat until the two c's meet in the middle of the string.

(iii) Remove one of the c's and move the rest of the string to fill the gap.

Obviously this is a long job, but it is typical of the cumbersome ways in which Turing machines often do simple things.

12. We cannot just search in one direction since we don't know when to stop. We must proceed in a back-and-forth fashion, placing markers at the right and left boundaries of the searched region and moving the markers outward.

19. If the final state set F contains more than one element, introduce a new final state q_f and the transitions

$$\delta(q, a) = (q_f, a, R)$$

for all $q \in F$ and $a \in \Gamma$.

Section 9.2

3. (a) We can think of the machine as constituted of two main parts, an *add-one* machine that just adds one to the input, and a multiplier that multiplies two numbers. Schematically they are combined in a simple fashion.

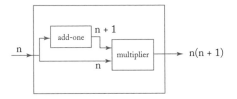

5. (c) First, split the input into two equal parts. This can be done as suggested in Exercise 10, Section 9.1. Then compare the two parts, symbol by corresponding symbol until a mismatch is found.

8. A solution:

$$\delta\left(q_0, a\right) = \left(q_i, a, R\right),$$
$$\delta\left(q_0, c\right) = \left(q_0, c, R\right) \text{ for all } c \in \Sigma - \{a\},$$
$$\delta\left(q_0, \square\right) = \left(q_j, \square, R\right).$$

The state q_0 is any state in which the *searchright* instruction may be applied.

Section 9.3

2. We have ignored the fact that a Turing machine, as defined so far, is deterministic, while a pda can be non-deterministic. Therefore, we cannot yet claim that Turing machines are more powerful than a pushdown automata.

Chapter 10

Section 10.1

4. (a) The machine has a transition function

$$\delta : Q \times \Gamma \to Q \times \Gamma \times \{L, R, S\}$$

with the restriction that for all transitions $\delta\left(q_i, a\right) = \left(q_j, b, L \text{ or } R\right)$, the condition $a = b$ must hold.

(b) To simulate $\delta\left(q_i, a\right) = \left(q_j, b, L\right)$ with $a \neq b$ of the standard machine, we introduce new transitions $\delta\left(q_i, a\right) = \left(q_{jL}, b, S\right)$ and $\delta\left(q_{jL}, b\right) = \left(q_j, b, L\right)$ for all $c \in \Gamma$, and so on.

6. We introduce a pseudo-blank B. Whenever the original machine wants to write $\square$, the new machine writes B. Then, for each $\delta(q_i, \square) = (q_j, b, L)$ we add $\delta(q_i, B) - (q_j, b, L)$, and so on. Of course, the original transition $\delta(q_i, \square) = (q_j, b, L)$ must be retained to handle blanks that are originally on the tape.

9. This does not limit the power of the machine. For each symbol $a \in \Gamma$, we introduce a pseudo-symbol, say A. Whenever we need to preserve this a, we first write A, then return to the cell in question to replace A by a.

11. We replace

$$\delta(q_i, \{a, b\}) - (q_j, c, R)$$

by

$$\delta(q_i, d) = (q_j, c, R)$$

for all $d \in \Gamma - \{a, b\}$.

Section 10.2

1. For the formal definition use $\Gamma_T = \Gamma \times \Gamma \times ... \times \Gamma$ and $\delta : Q \times \Gamma_T \to Q \times \Gamma_T \times \{L, R\}^m$, where m is the number of read-write heads. One issue to consider is what happens when two read-write heads are on the same cell. The formal definition must provide for the resolution of possible conflicts.

To simulate the original machine (OM) by a standard Turing machine (SM), we let SM have $m + 1$ tracks. On one track we will keep the tape contents of the OM, while the other m tracks are used to show the position of OM's tape heads.

		a	b	c	d		tape content of OM
	$\square$					$\square$	
	$\square$		x			$\square$	position of tape head # 1
	$\square$				x	$\square$	position of tape head # 2

SM will simulate each move of OM by scanning and updating its active area.

4. This exercise shows that a queue machine is equivalent to a standard Turing machine and that therefore a queue is a more powerful storage device than a stack. To simulate a standard TM by a queue machine, we can, for example, keep the right side of the OM in the front of the queue, the left side in the back.

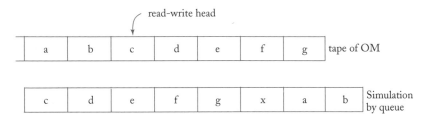

A right move is easy as we just remove the front symbol in the queue and place something in the back. A left move, however, goes against the grain, so the queue contents have to be circulated several times to get everything in the right place. It helps to use additional markers Y and Z to denote boundaries. For example, to simulate

$$\delta\left(q_i, c\right) = \left(q_j, z, L\right)$$

we carry out the following steps.

(i) Remove c from the front and add zY to the back.

(ii) Circulate contents to get $bzYdefgXa$.

(iii) Add Z to the back, then circulate, discarding Y and Z as they come to the front.

8. We need just two tapes, one that mirrors the tape of the OM, the second that stores the state of the OM.

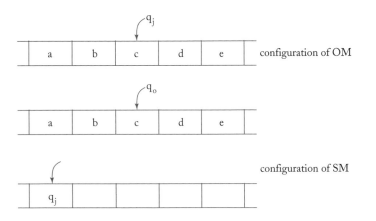

SM needs only two states: an accepting and a non-accepting state.

Section 10.3

3. (i) Start at the left of the input. Remember the symbol by putting the machine in the appropriate state. Then replace it with X.

(ii) Move the read-write head to the right, stopping (nondeterministically) at the center of the input.

(iii) Compare the symbol there with the remembered one. If they match, write Y in the cell. If they don't match, reject input.

(iv) With the center of the input marked with Y, we can now proceed deterministically, alternatively moving left and right, comparing symbols.

For a completely deterministic solution, we first find the center of the input (e.g. by putting markers at each end, and moving them inwards until they meet).

6. Nondeterministically choose a value for n. Determine if the length of the input is a multiple of n. If it is, accept. If $a^n \in L$, then there is some n for which this works.

Section 10.4

3. An algorithm, in outline, is as follows.

(i) Start with a copy of the preceding string.

(ii) Find the rightmost 0. Change it to a 1. Then change all the 1's to the right of this to 0's.

(iii) If there are no 0's, change all 1's to 0's and add a 1 on the left.

(iv) Repeat from step (i).

8. Let $S_1 = \{s_1, s_2, ...\}$ and $S_2 = \{t_1, t_2, ...\}$ Then their union can be enumerated by

$$S_1 \cup S_2 = \{s_1, t_1, s_2, t_2, ...\}.$$

If some $s_i = t_j$, we list it only once. The union of the two sets is therefore countable. For $S_1 \times S_2$, use the ordering in Figure 10.17.

Section 10.5

2. First, divide the input by two and move result to one part of tape. This free space initially occupied by the input. This space can then be used to store successive divisors.

4. (e) Use a three-track machine as shown below. On the third track, we keep the current trial value for $|w|$. On the second track, we place dividers every $|w|$ cells. We then compare the cell contents between the markers.

a	b	c	d	b	c	d		input
		x				x		dividers
1	1	1						trial value of lwl

6. Use Exercise 16, Section 6.2 to find a grammar in two-standard form. Then use the construction in Theorem 7.1. The pda we get from this consumes one input symbol on every move and never increases the stack contents by more than one symbol each time.

7. Example:

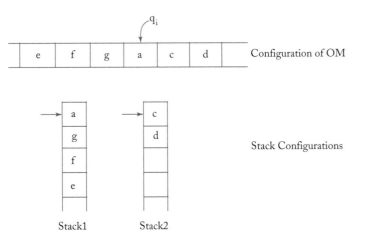

Configuration of OM

Stack Configurations

Stack1   Stack2

Stack1 contains the symbol under the read-write head of the OM and everything on the left. *Stack2* contains all the information to the right of the read-write head. Left and right moves of the OM are easily simulated. For example, $\delta(q_i, a) = (q_j, b, L)$ can be simulated by popping the a off *Stack1* and putting a b on *Stack2*.

Chapter 11

Section 11.1

2. We know that the union of two countable sets is countable and that the set of all recursively enumerable languages is countable. If the set of

all languages that are not recursively enumerable were also countable, then the set of all languages would be countable. But this is not the case, as we know.

6. Let L_1 and L_2 be two recursively enumerable languages and M_1 and M_2 be the respective Turing machines that accept these two languages. When represented with an input w, we nondeterministically choose M_1 or M_2 to process w. The result is a Turing machine that accepts $L_1 \cup L_2$.

11. A context-free language is recursive, so by Theorem 11.4 its complement is also recursive. Note, however, that the complement is not necessarily context-free.

14. For any given $w \in L^+$, consider all splits $w = w_1 w_2 ... w_m$. For each split, determine whether or not $w_i \in L$. Since for each w there are only a finite number of splits, we can decide whether or not $w \in L^+$.

18. The argument attempting to show by diagonalization that 2^S is not countable for finite S fails because the table in Figure 11.2 is not square, having $\left|2^S\right|$ rows and $|S|$ columns.

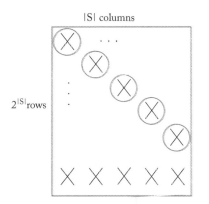

When we diagonalize, the result on the diagonal could be in one of the rows below.

Section 11.2

1. Look at a typical derivation:

$$S \overset{*}{\Rightarrow} aS_1 bB \Rightarrow aaS_1 bbB \overset{*}{\Rightarrow} a^n S_1 b^n B \Rightarrow a^{n+1} b^{n-1} B \Rightarrow a^{n+1} b^{n+1} B \Rightarrow ...$$

From this it is not hard to conjecture that the grammar derives

$$L = \left\{ a^{n+1} b^{n+k}, n \geq 1, k = -1, 1, 3, ... \right\}.$$

3. Formally, the grammar can be described by $G = (V, S, T, P)$, with $S \subseteq (V \cup T)^+$ and

$$L(G) = \{x \in T^* : s \Rightarrow_G x \text{ for any } s \in S\}.$$

The unrestricted grammars in Definition 11.3 are equivalent to this extension because to any given unrestricted grammar we can always add starting rules $S_0 \rightarrow s_i$ for all $s_i \in S$.

7. To get this form for unrestricted grammars, insert dummy variables on the right whenever $|u| > |v|$. For example,

$$AB \rightarrow C$$

can be replaced by

$$AB \rightarrow CD$$
$$D \rightarrow \lambda.$$

The equivalence argument is straightforward.

Section 11.3

1. (c) Working with context-sensitive grammars is not always easy. The idea of a messenger, introduced in Example 11.2, is often useful.

In this problem, the first step is to create the sentential form $a^n B c^n D$. The variables B and D will act as markers and messengers to assure that the correct number of b's and d's are created in the right places. The first part is achieved easily with the productions

$$S \rightarrow aAcD | aBcD$$
$$A \rightarrow aAc | aBc.$$

In the next step, the B travels to the right to meet the D, by

$$Bc \rightarrow cB$$
$$Bb \rightarrow bB.$$

When that happens, we can create one d and a return messenger that will put the b in the right place and stop.

$$BD \rightarrow Ed$$
$$cE \rightarrow Ec$$
$$bE \rightarrow Eb$$
$$aE \rightarrow ab.$$

Alternatively, we create a d plus a marker D, with a different messenger that creates a b, but keeps the process going:

$$BD \rightarrow FDd$$
$$cF \rightarrow Fc$$
$$bF \rightarrow Fb$$
$$aF \rightarrow abB.$$

4. The easiest argument is from an lba. Suppose that a language is context-sensitive. Then there exists an lba M that accepts it. Given w, we first rewrite it as w^R, then apply M to it. Because $L^R = \{w : w^R \in L\}$, M accepts w^R if and only if $w \in L^R$. The machine that reverses a string and applies M is an lba. Therefore L^R is context-sensitive.

6. We can argue from an lba. Clearly, there is an lba that can recognize any string of the form wuw. Just start at opposite ends and compare symbols until you get a match. Since there is an lba, the language is context-sensitive and a context-sensitive grammar must exist.

Chapter 12

Section 12.1

3. Given M and w, modify M to get $\widehat{M}$, which halts if and only if a special symbol, say an introduced symbol #, is written. We can do this by changing the halting configurations of M so that every one writes #, then stops. Thus, M halts implies the $\widehat{M}$ writes #, and $\widehat{M}$ writes # implies that M halts. Thus, if we have an algorithm that tells us whether or not a specified symbol a is ever written, we apply it to $\widehat{M}$ with $a = \#$. This would solve the halting problem.

7. Given (M, w) modify M to $\widehat{M}$ so that (M, w) halts if and only if $\widehat{M}$ accepts some simple language, say $\{a\}$. This can be done by M first checking the input and remembering whether the input was a. Then M carries out its normal computations. When it halts, check if the input was a. Accept if so, reject otherwise. Therefore $\widehat{M}$ accepts $\{a\}$ if and only if M halts. Now construct a simple Turing machine, say M_1, that accepts a. If we had an algorithm that checks for the equality of two languages, we could use it to see if $L\left(\widehat{M}\right) = L(M_1)$. If $L\left(\widehat{M}\right) = L(M_1)$ then (M, w) halts. If $L\left(\widehat{M}\right) \neq L(M_1)$ then (M, w) does not halt and we have a solution to the halting problem.

10. Given (M, w) we modify M so that it always halts in the configuration $q_f w$. If the given problem was decidable, we could apply the supposed algorithm to the modified machine, with configurations $q_0 w$ and $q_f w$. This would give us a solution of the halting problem.

13. Take a universal Turing machine and let it simulate computations on an empty tape. Whenever the simulated computations halt, accept the Turing machine being simulated. The universal Turing machine is therefore an accepter for all Turing machines that halt when applied to a blank tape. The set is therefore recursively enumerable.

Suppose now the set were recursive. There would then exist an algorithm A that lists all Turing machines that halt on a blank tape input in some order of increasing lengths of the program. See if the original Turing machine is amongst the Turing machines generated by A. Since the length of the original program is fixed, the comparison will stop when this length is exceeded. Thus, we have a solution to the blank tape halting problem.

16. If the specific instances of the problem are $p_1, p_2, ..., p_n$, we construct a Turing machine that behaves as follows:

$$\text{if problem } = p_1 \text{ then return false}$$
$$\text{if problem } = p_2 \text{ then return true}$$
$$\vdots$$
$$\text{if problem } = p_n \text{ then return true}$$

Whatever the truth values of the various instances are, there is always some Turing machine that gives the right answer. Remember that it is not necessary to know what the Turing machine actually is, only to guarantee that it exists.

Section 12.2

3. Suppose we had an algorithm to decide whether or not $L(M_1) \subseteq L(M_2)$. We could then construct a machine M_2 such that $L(M_2) = \varnothing$ and apply the algorithm. Then $L(M_1) \subseteq L(M_2)$ if and only if $L(M_1) = \varnothing$. But this contradicts Theorem 12.3, since we can construct M_1 from any given grammar G.

6. If we take $L(G_2) = \Sigma^*$, the problem becomes the question of Theorem 12.3 and is therefore undecidable.

8. Since there are some grammars for which $L(G) = L(G)^*$ and some for which this is not so, the undecidability follows from Rice's theorem. To do this from first principles is a little harder. Take the halting problem (M, w) and modify it (along the lines of Theorem 12.4), so that if (M, w) halts, $\widehat{M}$ will accept $\{a\}^*$ and if (M, w) does not halt, $\widehat{M}$ accepts $\varnothing$. From $\widehat{M}$ get the grammar $\widehat{G}$ by the construction leading to Theorem 11.7. If $L\left(\widehat{M}\right) = \{a\}^*$, then $L\left(\widehat{G}\right) = L\left(\widehat{G}\right)^* = \{a\}^*$. But

if $L\left(\widehat{M}\right) = \varnothing$, then $L\left(\widehat{G}\right) = \varnothing$ and $L\left(\widehat{G}\right)^* = \{\lambda\}$. Therefore, if this problem were decidable, we could get a solution of the halting problem.

Section 12.3

1. A PC-solution is $w_3 w_4 w_1 = v_3 v_4 v_1$. There is no MPC-solution because one string would have a prefix 001, the other 01.

3. For a one-letter alphabet, there is a PC-solution if and only if there is some subset J of $\{1, 2, ..., n\}$ such that

$$\sum_{j \in J} |w_j| = \sum_{j \in J} |v_j|.$$

Since there are only a finite number of subsets, they can all be checked and therefore the problem is decidable.

5. (a) The problem is undecidable. If it were decidable, we would have an algorithm for deciding the original MPC-problem. Given $w_1, w_2...,$ w_n, we form $w_1^R, w_2^R..., w_n^R$ and use the assumed algorithm. Since $w_1 w_i ... w_k = \left(w_k^R ... w_i^R w_1^R\right)^R$, the original MPC-problem has a solution if and only if the new MPC-problem has a solution.

Chapter 13

Section 13.1

2. Using the function $subtr$ in Example 13.3, we get the solution

$$greater\,(x, y) = subtr\,(1, subtr\,(1, subtr\,(x, y))).$$

7.

$$g\,(x, y) = mult\,(x, g\,(x, y - 1)),$$
$$g\,(x, 0) = 1.$$

9. (a)

$$
\begin{aligned}
A\,(1, y) &= A\,(0, A\,(1, y - 1)) \\
&= A\,(1, y - 1) + 1 \\
&= A\,(1, y - 2) + 2 \\
&\;\;\vdots \\
&= A\,(1, 0) + y \\
&= y + 2.
\end{aligned}
$$

(b) With the results of part (a) we can use induction to prove the next identity. Assume that for $y = 1, 2, ..., n - 1$, we have $A(2, y) = 2y + 3$. Then

$$\begin{aligned} A(2, n) &= A(1, A(2, n-1)) \\ &= A(1, 2n+1) \\ &= 2n + 3, \text{ from part (a).} \end{aligned}$$

Since

$$\begin{aligned} A(2, 0) &= A(1, 1) \\ &= 3, \end{aligned}$$

we have a basis and the equation is true for all y.

15. If $2^x + y - 3 = 0$, then $y = 3 - 2^x$. The only values of x that give a positive y are 0 and 1, so the domain of μ is $\{0, 1\}$, giving a minimum value of $y = 1$. Therefore

$$\mu y (2^x + y - 3) = 1.$$

Section 13.2

1. (b) Use $C_T = \{a, b, c\}$, $C_N = \{x\}$ and $A = \{x\}$. The non-terminal x is used as a boundary between the left and right side of the target string and the two w's are built simultaneously by

$$V_1 x V_2 \rightarrow V_1 a x V_2 a \,|V_1 b x V_2 b|\, V_1 c x V_2 c.$$

At the end, the x is removed by

$$V_1 x V_2 \rightarrow V_1 V_2.$$

3. At every step, the only possible identification of V_1 is with the entire derived string. This results in a doubling of the string and

$$L = \left\{ a^{2^n} : n \geq 1 \right\}.$$

5. A solution is

$$\begin{aligned} V_1 * V_2 &= V_3 \rightarrow V_1 1 * V_2 = V_3 V_2 \\ V_1 * V_2 &= V_3 \rightarrow V_1 * V_2 1 = V_3 V_1. \end{aligned}$$

For example

$$1 * 1 = 1 \Rightarrow 11 * 1 = 11 \Rightarrow 11 * 11 = 1111,$$

and so on.

Section 13.3

1.

$$P_1 : S \to S_1 S_2$$
$$P_2 : S_1 \to a S_1, S_2 \to a S_2$$
$$P_3 : S_1 \to b S_1, S_2 \to b S_2$$
$$P_4 : S_1 \to \lambda, S_2 \to \lambda.$$

5. The solution here is reminiscent of the use of messengers with context-sensitive grammars.

$$ab \to x$$
$$xb \to bx$$
$$xc \to \lambda.$$

8. Although this is not so easy to see, this is one way to solve Exercise 7. Take any string, say a^{255}. This can be derived from a^{127} by applying $a \to aaa$ once and $a \to aa$ 126 times. Then a^{127} can be derived from a^{63} in a similar way, and so on. Thus every string in $L(aa^*)$ can be derived.

References

for Further Reading

A. V. Aho and J. D. Ullman. 1972. *The Theory of Parsing, Translation, and Compiling.* Vol. 1, Englewood Cliffs, N.J.: Prentice Hall.

P. J. Denning, J. B. Dennis, and J. E. Qualitz. 1978. *Machines, Languages, and Computation.* Englewood Cliffs, N.J.: Prentice Hall.

M. A. Harrison. 1978. *Introduction to Formal Language Theory.* Reading, Mass.: Addison-Wesley.

J. E. Hopcroft and J. D. Ullman. 1979. *Introduction to Automata Theory, Languages and Computation.* Reading, Mass.: Addison-Wesley.

R. Hunter. 1981. *The Design and Construction of Compilers.* Chichester, New York: John Wiley.

R. Johnsonbaugh. 1996. *Discrete Mathematics.* Fourth Ed. New York: Macmillan.

Z. Kovahi. 1978. *Switching and Finite Automata Theory.* Second Edition. New York: McGraw-Hill.

A. Salomaa. 1973. *Formal Languages.* New York: Academic Press.

A. Salomaa. 1985. "Computations and Automata," in *Encyclopedia of Mathematics and Its Applications.* Cambridge: Cambridge University Press.

Index